INTERCOMMUNION

INTER-COMMUNION

*

THE REPORT OF THE THEOLOGICAL
COMMISSION APPOINTED BY THE
CONTINUATION COMMITTEE OF THE
WORLD CONFERENCE ON FAITH AND
ORDER TOGETHER WITH A SELECTION
FROM THE MATERIAL PRESENTED TO
THE COMMISSION

Edited by
DONALD BAILLIE (*Chairman*)
(*Church of Scotland*)

JOHN MARSH (*Secretary*)
(*Congregational Union of England and Wales*)

SCM PRESS LTD
56 BLOOMSBURY STREET
LONDON

First published 1952

Made and printed in England by
STAPLES PRINTERS LIMITED
at their Rochester, Kent, establishment

GENERAL PREFACE

*

The second World Conference on Faith and Order was held at Edinburgh in 1937. Reflection on its Report led to the conclusion that many, if not most, of the issues on which Christians are divided have their roots in different conceptions of the nature of the Church. A passage in the Report suggested that, besides a direct examination of this doctrinal question, a study of the ways of worship characteristic of different churches might be a profitable undertaking, and this led some members of the Continuation Committee to press for a discussion of the theological principles underlying what in his Conference sermon Archbishop William Temple had called 'the greatest of all scandals in the face of the world', the maintenance of barriers against completeness of union at the Table of the Lord.

Hence in 1938 and 1939 three international theological commissions were appointed, to study (i) the Church, (ii) Ways of Worship, and (iii) Intercommunion. In spite of difficulties and delays they have carried on their work. Papers were written and circulated. Meetings to discuss them were held when and where possible. In the summer of 1950 each had an extended meeting at which its report was put into its final form, and approved.

These reports, together with a selection of the papers contributed in the course of the enquiries, are now published. It should be clearly understood that their purpose is to provide material for discussion by the delegates of the Churches when they meet for the third World Conference at Lund in Sweden in 1952. Invitations to that Conference have now been issued, and Churches are in process of appointing their delegates. These volumes will best fulfil their function if their readers will remember their purpose, and use them to ensure among the members of the various Churches a widespread understanding of the questions which their representatives will be going to Lund to discuss.

LEONARD HODGSON

Christ Church,
  Oxford
June 1951

CONTENTS

★

EDITORIAL PREFACE

*

This composite volume is published by authority of the Theological Commission on Intercommunion under the Commission on Faith and Order of the World Council of Churches, and it falls to us, as Chairman and Secretary, to present it to the public. It is hardly necessary in our Preface to describe the plan of the book, as that is made sufficiently clear by the Table of Contents and the statement on page 17, but a few words of explanation may not be out of place.

Part I gives the text of the Report of the Commission. It will be seen that the membership of the Commission was gathered from a wide variety of Churches; and thus it was inevitable, in view of the controversial nature of the subject, that only a Report which frankly acknowledged disagreements as well as agreements could be signed by all the members. The summary of disagreements will be found in the closing pages of the Report. It is perhaps a hopeful sign that in our discussions it was sometimes more difficult to agree upon the definition of our differences than to agree upon the definition of our agreements. But it is a matter for thankfulness that along these lines it has been possible to produce a Report which all the members could sign, though with certain minor reservations given in footnotes; even if the Report has finally to record a feeling of disappointment.

Part II consists of purely historical surveys by a number of scholars invited by the Commission to this task.

Part III, which occupies the greater part of the volume, is a collection of independent essays contributed by selected scholars and theologians (only a small number of whom were actually members of the Commission). These were naturally selected from as wide a variety of Churches as possible, but they were not asked to speak authoritatively for their Churches, or to describe the positions taken by their Churches in the matter of Intercommunion; nor do their contributions in any way represent the findings of the Commission itself. Their papers are to be regarded rather as original theological essays, whose aim is to throw light, from a variety of standpoints, upon the fundamental problems involved. In particular, it seems necessary to state that in inviting and including in the volume as an appendix the paper by the Rev. G. I. F. Thomson (see

9

pages 388–396) the Commission does not commit itself to any judgment upon the value or justification of the experiment there described, but simply to the view that the record of such an experiment is relevant and valuable in our present situation.

Appendix A is included as a useful work of reference. It was undertaken by Mr. Hickinbotham at the request of the Commission, which is greatly indebted to him for the skill with which he has discharged the task.

This Preface must conclude with a hearty expression of thanks to all the members of the Commission on Intercommunion, to the World's Student Christian Federation for permission to print the essays Nos. IX and XVII which have been slightly adapted from the Student World, and to all the others who have helped the work by contributing to this volume; and an expression of hope that the volume may be of some service to the Churches in preparing for the Third World Conference on Faith and Order and in helping them towards a deeper understanding of the problems of intercommunion.

D. M. BAILLIE
JOHN MARSH

MEMBERSHIP OF THE COMMISSION

*

NOTES

★ No communication was received from these members of the Commission about the signing of the Report. Professor Askmark and Professor Kovalevsky were present at the drafting session of the Commission.

Page 6, line 19: After the sentence ending 'church life', Mr. Brandreth would like to add: 'This is true also for the bulk of Anglo-Catholics'.

Page 7, lines 29ff.: Professor Clavier would prefer to read: 'is *seldom used* as a specific designation . . . but generally in the wider sense'.

Page 9, line 34: Professor Clavier would prefer the text to read: 'and as belonging to the main teachings in the New Testament'.

Page 16, lines 38 and 39: Professor Clavier would prefer: 'to teach that the *Presence of Christ is truly and really given in the sacrament to the faith of the receiver.*'

Page 29, *Agreement* (1): Mr. Brandreth would have preferred: 'as in greater or lesser degree possessing *vestigia ecclesiae*'.

Page 30, *Differences*: Professor Clavier would have preferred to have as the first Difference: '(1) We are not all agreed as to the kind and degree of unity which is in the purpose of God for the Church of Christ on earth'.

† Mr. Brandreth and Professor Clavier sign the report only with the above notes recorded.

Part One

THE REPORT OF THE COMMISSION

THE REPORT OF THE COMMISSION

*

I. *Introduction*

In August 1939 the Continuation Committee of the Second
World Conference on Faith and Order adopted the following
resolutions:

(i) That a Commission be appointed to study the subject of
Intercommunion;

(ii) That the terms of reference of this Commission be as follows:

   (*a*) To set forth the existing situation as regards the rules and
customs regulating intercommunion and open communion
in the different Christian bodies;

   (*b*) To set forth the grounds on which intercommunion or
open communion are allowed or disallowed;

   (*c*) To consider the principles which should govern the practice
of the ecumenical movement in regard to intercom-
munion and open communion;

   (*d*) To present to the Committee at its meeting in 1941 a
Report embodying the results of the Commission's work.

The outbreak of war in Europe almost immediately after this
resolution was taken made it impossible to carry it out as originally
planned. In the summer of 1940 Dr. Hodgson, as Secretary of the
Continuation Committee, suggested to the Executive Sub-com-
mittee by correspondence that in the altered circumstances the
Commission on Intercommunion should be organised in two
sections, one with its headquarters in the United States, the other
with its headquarters in Europe, and this plan was approved.
In October of the same year the American section was organised,
with the late Dr. Hugh Thomson Kerr, of Pittsburgh, as Chairman, and Dr. Charles W. Lowry as Secretary. In 1942 they
presented a Report dealing with the matters numbered (*a*), (*b*)
and (*c*) above, so far as concerned the churches in U.S.A. and
Canada; and this was published by the Faith and Order Secretariat as No. 98 of their booklet publications. The circumstances

of war made it impossible for the European section of the Commission to be organised at all. But the Secretary, Dr. Leonard Hodgson, collected from a large number of churches, mainly in Britain and the Dominions, information about their practice in this matter, and the result was the booklet published in 1944 by the Secretariat (No. 99), *Rules and Customs of Churches concerning Intercommunion and Open Communion*.

The next step was taken when the Faith and Order Executive met again at Geneva in February 1946. The American section of the Commission on Intercommunion had performed its task and made its Report, but no European section had come into existence. It was now resolved to ask Professor D. M. Baillie, of the University of St. Andrews, to be Chairman of the Commission in Europe, and Professor Hamilcar S. Alivisatos, of the University of Athens, to be Vice-Chairman. A Commission was duly formed, and Dr. George Johnston (then of St. Andrews, now of Hartford, Conn.) agreed to act as Secretary, but had to resign in the following year on his removal to America. The Commission held its first meeting at Clarens, Switzerland, in the autumn of 1947, when Professor John Marsh (then of Mansfield College, Oxford, now of Nottingham University) was appointed Secretary. Subsequent meetings were held at Baarn in Holland in September 1948; at Chichester, in July 1949; and at Bièvres, near Paris, in September 1950. From the start the endeavour was made to include some representatives of Churches beyond Europe, particularly of the 'younger Churches', though circumstances have made it difficult to secure the participation of members from distant lands. The membership of the Commission has been enlarged from time to time; and since it became clear that the American section had concluded its immediate task and had ceased to function, a certain number of American members were added at a late stage to the Commission formed in Europe. In 1948, when the Continuation Committee became transformed into the Faith and Order Commission of the World Council of Churches, with three Theological Commissions under it for special tasks, our Commission, without any reference to American and European sections, became simply the Theological Commission on Intercommunion.

It soon became clear to the Commission that its main task now was to go beyond the collection and systematisation of the rules and customs actually prevalent in the various Churches. That task had already been performed in the booklets Nos. 98 and 99 mentioned above. There remained the still more difficult task of penetrating beneath the rules and customs to the fundamental theological issues that are involved, in the hope that through a deeper theological understanding of their own and each other's basic principles in the matter of intercommunion, the Churches might be brought closer together and led towards a solution of the painful problems involved. Papers on those theological issues were read at the meetings of the Commission by scholars from various Churches, and the issues were freely discussed. The Commission set before itself as its main task, in preparation for the next World Conference on Faith and Order, the production of a composite volume consisting of the following parts:

I. The Commission's Report (as here) on the problem of intercommunion, designed to form the material for discussion at the next World Conference on Faith and Order.

II. A short history of the problem of intercommunion, written in four chapters by different scholars.

III. A collection of theological essays on the fundamental principles underlying the problem of intercommunion. The idea has been to select the writers from as wide a variety of Churches as possible, but to ask them not so much to represent the views of their Churches, as to make original theological contributions, from their various points of view, in thinking out the underlying issues.

IV. A summary and classification of the actual rules and practices now in force in the various Churches in the matter of intercommunion, partly based on the material collected in booklets Nos. 98 and 99.

II. *The Terminology*

The original terms of reference in the appointment of the Commission spoke of both 'intercommunion' and 'open communion', and in the course of discussion it became clear that these could not be adequately treated without some treatment of 'intercelebration'. But also it soon became apparent that a good deal of confusion and variety of usage attaches to these three terms themselves. It may well be, as Dr. Hodgson pointed out in a valuable statement to the Commission, that this is unavoidable in the present divided condition of Christendom. 'Our problems concerning intercommunion arise in a Christendom divided into a number of "Churches" which are not simply the local congregations of the one Church, but denominations related to one another somewhat after the manner of sovereign independent states, themselves sometimes divided geographically into fellow-members of an Anglican, Lutheran, Methodist, Presbyterian or other family. Were this not so, were we really one Church, there would be no need of the prefix *inter-*. We should simply all be in communion with one another. The word *inter*-communion pre-supposes different Churches, which may or may not be in communion with one another'.

Here the Orthodox Eastern Church is in a different position from the other Churches adhering to the World Council. It does not regard itself as one Church among others, but as alone confessing that fullness of Christian truth which makes the Church fully to be the Church. An Orthodox cannot conceive of sacramental fellowship in distinction from the full fellowship of church life. Hence, as we shall see, neither in the Slavonic languages nor in Greek is there any word which accurately translates 'intercommunion'.

It is fairly easy to define the terms under consideration in a way that would be sufficiently clear at least from the point of view of the Anglican Communion (which holds one of the key positions in this whole matter) and of the English language. Thus, to quote Dr. Hodgson again, 'intercommunion should be used to mean the result of an agreement between Churches of different denominations whereby the communicant members of each may freely communicate at the altars of either' (e.g. the 1931 agreement between the Church of England and the Old Catholic Churches, or that between the American Episcopal Church and the Polish National Catholic Church in the United States). But 'there are also the cases in which, without any such agreement between Churches, a church may by unilateral action welcome members of other churches to share as guests in its Communion Services. This may conveniently be called open communion. If two churches welcome each other's members, and the members of both are allowed to accept the invitation, the open communion is mutual;

if the invitation is only given or accepted in one direction, it is one-sided'. As regards intercelebration: 'Intercommunion and open communion both imply the existence of separately organised denominational churches, in each of which the Sacrament is administered by its own ministers. If members of other churches are welcomed by either inter- or open communion, but ministers are not allowed to act as celebrants except in the services of their own Churches, there is not so close a degree of inter-Church unity as where an interchange of ministers would also be permitted. For this freedom of ministers to officiate sacramentally in either church, the term "intercelebration" is convenient'. Where full freedom of intercelebration is combined with full freedom of mutual participation in the Holy Communion, this may be described as 'full communion'. (See the report of the Lambeth Conference 1930). Even from the Anglican point of view it is necessary to complicate these distinctions further by the use of the terms 'limited intercommunion' and 'limited intercelebration' with reference, e.g., to the relation between the Church of England and the Church of South India.

But from the points of view of other Churches, the relevance of the above definitions is not so clear. An Eastern Orthodox, for example, would find it difficult to separate unity of fellowship in the Eucharist from unity of fellowship in *all* the sacraments and indeed in the whole life of the Church. Professor Zander has remarked that 'in speaking of intercommunion as partaking together of the Lord's Supper we greatly narrow the idea of it and artificially give it an exclusively sacramental ecclesiological sense. . . . But such a narrow use of the term is quite illegitimate'. Even as a matter of language, it has been pointed out that in the East the Greek word *koinonia* is not used at all as a specific designation of what in the West is called the Sacrament of Holy Communion, but only in the wider sense which covers the whole of church fellowship.[1] There appears, moreover, to be no word in Greek or in any of the Slavonic languages which corresponds to the word 'intercommunion': the idea could be expressed only in a periphrasis. Again, the Lutheran Church in Germany has no name for the sacrament corresponding to the term 'Communion', but speaks simply of the *Abendmahl*, and the

[1] For the wider connotation of the term 'Communion', cf. Yves M-J. Congar and Dr. P. W. Evans, pp. 141ff. and 191ff.

only word corresponding at all to 'intercommunion' is *Abendmahlsgemeinschaft*.

Some would maintain that full communion between Churches demands unity of order, while intercommunion may exist between Churches that have unity of doctrine without unity of order; but others would object to this distinction on the ground that doctrine and order cannot thus be separated, questions of order being themselves fundamentally questions of doctrine. The matter becomes further complicated when we remember that, e.g., Presbyterians and Congregationalists regularly and on principle and by long tradition invite communicant members of *all* branches of the Christian Church to partake with them at the Lord's Table. This is not a question of agreements with specific Churches, but has become a universal principle of these Churches. And yet a Congregationalist minister could not, e.g., become a minister of the Church of Scotland (which is Presbyterian) without petition to its General Assembly; and moreover, if his petition were granted, he would normally be re-ordained, so that this is not merely a matter of church government, but of church order. Should the relation between these two Churches, then, be described as full communion, or intercommunion, or mutual open communion? It seems clear that none of the terms as above defined is precisely applicable.

Thus it seems impossible in the present ecclesiastical situation to find any clear definition of the meanings of the terms and their relations to each other which will make sense equally from the points of view of all the Churches that are concerned. We must simply try to use the terms as clearly as possible, making sure at each point that we are penetrating beneath terminology and are talking of real things.

III. *The Nature of the Problem*

The whole problem arises from the fact that Christendom is divided into a number of 'Churches', which are separated more or less widely from each other in faith and order, doctrine and practice, history and tradition, but which nevertheless (though there are exceptions) recognise each other as 'Churches', i.e. as truly parts of the Church of Christ. That must be true at least in some sense of all the Churches which adhere to the World Council of

Churches: whatever claims any one Church may make for itself, it does nevertheless, by adherence to the World Council of Churches, acknowledge that something of the theological reality of the Church is present in other Christian communions. If there were no denominational divisions there could be no problem of intercommunion.[1] It is evident that for Churches which do not recognise each other as Churches, there can be no problem of intercommunion; and any one Church which stands upon completely exclusive claims cannot recognise a problem of intercommunion at all. The problem exists only for those who recognise that within the one Church of Christ there are *Churches*, not in a merely local or regional sense (as in the New Testament) but in the sense of denominations which make conflicting claims, and therefore in certain situations find themselves in actual competition with each other.

Now there is agreement on all hands that this is an absurd and indeed a tragic and sinful situation, quite at variance with the New Testament pattern. In the New Testament the word 'church' is used in only two ways: in the singular, as meaning the one Church of Christ, which is His Body, with 'one Lord, one faith, one baptism', with one *koinonia*, a unity that transcends all distinctions; and in the plural, as meaning the local congregations of that one Church, the church in Corinth, or the church in Philippi, or the church in Jerusalem. The idea of *Churches* as denominations at variance with each other is not only absent, but utterly remote, from the New Testament. But it has now for many centuries been a familiar fact, almost all over the Christian world, making the problem of intercommunion inevitable. Thus the problem has a long history, the significance of which must not be overlooked as constituting the chief factor in later developments. A sketch of the history will be found in a later part of this volume.

But within the last generation the problem has assumed a much more acute and urgent form. This is due mainly to the growth of the Ecumenical Movement itself. There has been a widespread rediscovery of the doctrine of the Church as the Body of Christ and as belonging to the very essence of the Gospel. This has led to a new and profound sense of the tragedy and sinfulness of our

[1] On this, see the document issued by the World Council of Churches Central Committee at Toronto, 1950, on *The Church, the Churches and the World Council of Churches*.

divided state, since if we really believe in one Holy Catholic Church we ought not to be separated from each other. And yet the experience of the Ecumenical Movement has itself taught us not to seek easy and shallow ways of reunion through a flabby grasp of doctrine and a glossing over of our differences of belief. The Ecumenical Movement, by deepening the sense of the Church, and bringing members of widely different Churches together in Christian fellowship, has driven many Christians to seek a deeper understanding of the distinctive positions of their own Churches. Thus paradoxically the growth of the ecumenical consciousness has led to a widespread revival of 'confessional' or denominational consciousness, and a great many Christians (especially of the younger generation) have at the same time become much more ecumenically-minded and developed a new and lively interest in the question: Why am I an Anglican? or Why am I a Lutheran, or an Orthodox, or a Presbyterian, or a Baptist? The very coming together of the Churches shows them how different they are from each other (as well as how close they are in their fundamental Christian faith). Thus at the very same time there has emerged a new desire for intercommunion and a new realisation of its difficulties; and so the problem has become acute.

All this has come to a head in a quite special way in the ecumenical gatherings that have been such a notable feature of Christendom in our age. At such gatherings there is frequently a very deep and rich experience of Christian fellowship in faith and worship, study and discussion, but the fellowship has to be rudely broken at the point where it ought to be deepest, in the Sacrament of Holy Communion, in which it is impossible for members of all the Churches to unite in receiving the Body and Blood of Christ. At a later stage of this Report we shall have something to say about the various ways of facing that practical problem. At the present stage we are concerned simply to point out to the Churches that the problem has become quite acute. The pain and scandal of the situation seem to be felt most keenly of all among the younger generation of Christians within the Ecumenical Movement, and this has found very strong expression in the World's Student Christian Federation. However difficult it may be to find any satisfactory solution, we are all agreed that it is highly salutary to be reminded over and over again of the urgency of the problem, and we regard it as our duty to say this with the utmost earnestness to the Churches that we represent.

Many nationals of the younger Churches of Africa and the East also feel keenly the scandal of Christian disunity. They see the divisions of Christendom as mainly of western origin imposed upon them by foreign missionaries, and they regard the imported restrictions upon intercommunion as shackles needing to be cast off in order that the indigenous churches may find their true fellowship one with another. Here is a ferment of life which faces the whole Ecumenical Movement with crucial decisions.

IV. *Can Intercommunion precede Reunion?*

We are all agreed that the question of intercommunion between Churches cannot be separated from the question of the outward and visible unity of the Church. The whole Ecumenical Movement not only stands for a realisation of our hidden unity in Christ, but also seeks for a greater outward and visible unity, though it is not yet clear what kind and degree of corporate unity of organisation or organism is the ultimate desideratum for the Church of Christ on earth. However far off the visible consummation of our unity may be, we believe that we can never settle down to be content with anything short of it, or the Ecumenical Movement would lose its soul. It is this greater outward and visible unity and not any particular conception of it that we mean by the term 'reunion' and it is in this context that we must discuss intercommunion. So far we are all agreed.

But when we proceed further to discuss the relation between intercommunion and reunion, we find a very definite cleavage of opinion and conviction. This is largely conditioned by our various inherited doctrines of the nature of the Church and its unity, even while we are seeking to think together ecumenically. Whatever view we hold, we all find it difficult to determine the exact degree of corporate or dogmatic unity which would be required to justify intercommunion.

(*a*) On the one hand, and especially in Anglo-Catholic, Orthodox and some Lutheran circles (not to speak of the Roman Catholic Church, which is not represented on the Commission on Faith and Order) it is held that any extensive practice of intercommunion between separated Churches which differ in order or doctrine would, however well-intentioned, imply a disrespect for truth and indeed for the sacrament itself, and would even be a betrayal of the ultimate hope of reunion which ought to dominate our thinking and our practice. Those who take this point of view would remind us that ecclesiastical division is always a painful and shameful wound in the Body of Christ, and that to heal it lightly by covering it with an easy intercommunion is a disservice to the true life of the Church. The real tragedy and shame and sin is not merely that we cannot come together to the Lord's Table, but that we are separated from each other in our whole church life, living in schism from each other when we ought to be One Body. So long as that situation remains, we ought to feel the pain and shame of it acutely and constantly, and we should be merely accepting a false anodyne if we anticipated the healing of the breach by a regular and comfortable custom of intercommunion. Further, it is sometimes urged from the same point of view that since Holy Communion is not an individual act, but an act of the Church, as One Body, it cannot properly be celebrated as a joint act of bodies which in their church life are separated from each other.

It should, however, be remembered that it is always difficult to determine what degree of actual corporate union is required to justify intercommunion. The various Churches that make up the Anglican Communion in different regions of the world are entirely autonomous, without any unity of government or jurisdiction, and yet they are in full communion with each other. The same is true of the various Orthodox Churches, which together make up what we sometimes call the Orthodox Church. In these cases the distinction is, of course, not one of doctrine or order, but merely of geographical location and territory. And yet even within that framework there are anomalies, such as the fact that in New York City there are five Orthodox Archbishops for the same territory and yet all of these jurisdictions are, of course, in full communion with each other across their divisions. But further, the 'Catholic' point of view does recognise the possibility of regular intercommunion between Churches that are denominationally distinct as, e.g., in the cases of the agreement between the Church of England and the Old Catholic Churches or the agreement between the Protestant Episcopal Church in the U.S.A. and the Polish National Catholic Church in the U.S.A. These are anticipations or, rather, partial realisations, of actual organic union by an agreed practice of intercommunion. And a small measure of such anticipation is seen in all the provisions that some episcopal Churches make for open communion in emergency or, in some cases, at gatherings devoted to the cause of Christian unity. Thus, even those who maintain that general intercommunion should not be adopted as a means to help forward reunion, do not regard that as the last word on the subject. If they did, indeed, they would not take part in ecumenical discussions on intercommunion at all. Nevertheless, they have at this point a fairly clear general principle to which full justice must be done if any progress is to be made in further discussion of the problem.

(b) On the other hand there is the view, especially characteristic of 'Reformed' Churches (including Presbyterians, Congregationalists and most Baptists), but also held by many Methodists and by Lutherans and Anglican Evangelicals, that intercommunion, understood as open communion, need not and should not wait for reunion, but is a step towards it, and a preparation for it. There are, indeed, many in various Churches who would maintain that if *complete* intercommunion and intercelebration could be achieved between the several Churches, this is all the reunion that is required. Thus there would remain a variety of autonomous Churches in different countries, and possibly even in the same country, varying from each other with a healthy diversity, and without any actual centralised unity of organisation or government, but with a fundamental unity of faith expressed in Word and Sacraments, and therefore intercommunion and intercelebration. But many others who look forward to ultimate reunion of a more organic kind, and who regard our present divisions with sorrow, shame and penitence, hold that in the meantime the tragic situation is *less* tragic if we can have intercommunion with each other across denominational boundaries. Also there are some, especially among Lutherans, who believe that the Lord's Supper is supremely a means of the forgiveness of sins. Thus they believe that the inherently sinful situation of our division will never be overcome without the grace of common forgiveness which the sharing together in the Lord's Supper would bring. In this sense, unity as love is the fruit of the Holy Communion.

In many Presbyterian and Congregationalist churches (and in some other churches, too,) it is a normal part of the communion service to invite all communicant members of any branch of the Church of Christ to come to the Lord's Table and partake. This is not a recent fruit of the Ecumenical Movement, but an established tradition. Thus it is difficult for those who have grown up in a tradition of open communion to understand the position of those who maintain that intercommunion must not precede actual organic reunion. To a Presbyterian, for example, it has become quite unthinkable that communicant members of Anglican or Methodist or Congregationalist or Baptist churches, who wish to partake in the Communion Service in a Presbyterian church, should be refused permission, or even that they should not be freely invited. This they would claim, is not because of any supposed 'individualism' of Calvinistic theology, any failure to realise the corporate nature of the act of communion as an act of the Body of Christ, any lack of a sense of the visible Church; for traditional Calvinistic theology has laid immense stress upon the corporate nature of the sacrament and upon the visible Church. Nor is it due to any slackness concerning conditions of admission to the Lord's Table, for Presbyterian and Congregationalist churches have laid immense and distinctive stress on 'the fencing of the Table' with a view to excluding unworthy communicants who would profane the sacrament and 'eat and drink judgment to themselves'. Rather is the practice of open communion based on the conviction that not only one's own Church but also other Churches are true Churches, parts of the Church of Christ; and that in spite of the tragic and sinful divisions there is a fundamental unity sufficient to justify common participation at the Lord's Table; and that, while it is the duty of a church to exercise supervision and discipline over its own members, it is not called to do this for the members of other churches individually. Indeed, it could not do so, but it accepts them as being communicant members of those other churches; at the same time there remains, in the last resort, the responsibility which lies on each man's own conscience. Those who occupy this standpoint may look forward earnestly to an actual reunion of the Churches, recognising at the same time that this cannot be forced or hurried, because a premature and vaguely-grounded union, however well-intentioned, would mean a sacrifice of truth at those points where the separate Churches are making their distinctive witness, and there would be loss instead of gain, the impoverishment which comes of compromise rather than enrichment. But, they would maintain, the practice of intercommunion would involve no such risk, as no Church would be thereby surrendering its witness, but all would be recognising that they have a fundamental unity of faith which justifies their coming together at the Lord's Table. There are, indeed, some who hold that intercommunion of this kind is in principle involved in our recognising each other as we do in the World Council of Churches.

What, then, are the limits of such intercommunion? For it seems plain that there must be some limits. There must be a certain amount of agreement between the teaching of separate Churches if they are to have intercommunion with each other. Intercommunion becomes a practical problem only between Churches in substantial doctrinal agreement on the essentials of the faith. Some Churches would be satisfied with this measure of agreement; others would demand full agreement on all points of doctrine. For many who are against any wide policy of intercommunion the real difficulty seems to be not the mere fact of separation, but the fact of divergence in sacramental doctrine and order. Thus it is necessary for us now to make a brief examination of these issues.

V. *Divergence of Sacramental Doctrine as a Barrier to Intercommunion*

There are many to whom the whole idea of intercommunion between widely separated Churches seems highly artificial, insincere and even irreverent, on the ground that the different Churches mean quite different things by the Sacrament of Holy Communion, so that common participation would not be a real *koinonia* but a shallow pretence. There can be no doubt that this is felt very strongly in some quarters, and even in quarters where there is also a deep concern about the problem and a warm Christian charity. Thus even the 'open' communion services which have been held in recent years at certain ecumenical gatherings (especially conferences of Christian youth), while deeply inspiring to some people, have made a very different impression on others, because they seemed to present the distressing spectacle of a diverse crowd, from very varied Churches and traditions, gathering together at the Lord's Table without any sufficient unity of belief about what they were doing there. This kind of difficulty is felt mainly from the standpoints of certain Lutherans, Eastern Orthodox and

Anglo-Catholics, all of whom would say that what they believe about the meaning of Holy Communion is so different from what Presbyterians and Baptists and Congregationalists believe, that intercommunion, except in special circumstances of emergency, would be an artificial and dishonest compromise. And even on the 'Protestant' side there are circumstances in which this difficulty might be felt. Many a Presbyterian might feel that he could not fitly receive communion at an Anglican Eucharist of a really 'high' Anglo-Catholic type (even if in a certain ecumenical situation he were invited to do so): he would hesitate, not through any uncharitable judgment of disapproval, but simply because the celebration was either unintelligible to him (so that he could not receive communion with understanding and faith), or because it seemed to be based on doctrine which he did not believe, so that it meant something different from what Holy Communion meant to him.

An important instance of the kind of divergence in eucharistic doctrine which exists within the Ecumenical Movement is the difference in doctrine between Lutheran and Reformed Churches on the Continent. Lutherans in general lay much more stress on doctrine than on order. No one particular view of church order is essential to Lutheranism. A Lutheran Church may have bishops or may not have them, may claim an unbroken apostolic succession for its ministry through the laying on of hands, or may not claim it. But Lutherans in general lay great stress on *doctrine*, as the basis of the unity of the Church, and upon agreement in doctrine as the true basis of intercommunion. And, in particular, they are greatly concerned for the Lutheran doctrine of the Lord's Supper in its distinction from the Reformed or Calvinist doctrine. To a Lutheran it is vital to believe that, in the Sacrament of the Lord's Supper, the Body and Blood of Christ are really present 'in, with and under' the elements of bread and wine. Lutherans, however, do not all lay the same amount of stress upon the doctrinal difference at this point, and therefore there are considerable differences of practice in the Lutheran Churches in the matter of intercommunion with other Protestant Churches. The Reformed or Calvinist Churches tend to make much less of this difference in eucharistic doctrine because, while they do not teach that the Presence is 'in, with and under' the elements, it is of the essence of their tradition to teach that the Body and Blood of

Christ are truly and really present in the Sacrament to the faith of the receiver.

Another important instance of the kind of doctrinal difference which many would regard as a sufficient obstacle to intercommunion is the difference between those who find in the Eucharist a sacrifice of the Body and Blood of Christ and those who do not. Thus some Anglo-Catholics and Orthodox would say that while the Sacrament of the Lord's Supper is to Protestants a potent means of grace, worthy of the greatest reverence, it means something quite different from the eucharistic sacrifice in which they themselves believe. The latter is not merely a means of grace in which Christ is truly present to the faith of the Church, but is an offering made by the Church to God upon the altar in union with the sacrifice of Christ, and thus a sacramental representation of the once-for-all sacrifice on Calvary and of the perpetual sacrifice that is being offered by our great High Priest 'beyond the veil' on the heavenly altar. To those who take this view of the Sacrament it seems dishonest and futile to practise intercommunion with the Churches which reject this view, because in the celebrations of the other Churches they would not find what to themselves is the essence of the Sacrament, and in their own celebrations those who belonged to the other Churches would find at the centre something which they could not accept or believe.

It would be foolish to dismiss this difference too lightly, but it is possible also to exaggerate it. It must be remembered that, for example, both the Orthodox and the Anglo-Catholic doctrines of the Eucharist are very different from that implied in the late medieval practice of 'sacrifices of masses' against which the Reformation reacted so strongly (as may be illustrated by the Anglican Article XXXI). It must also be remembered that the central Protestant tradition has never reduced the Sacrament of the Lord's Supper to a mere symbolic memorial feast. On the one hand the Church of England liturgy itself does regard the Eucharist as, among other things, a *memorial* of the sacrifice of Christ, as a 'perpetual memory of that His precious death until His coming again'. And, on the other hand, the Churches of the Reformation tradition, while objecting to the 'sacrifice of the Mass', do emphasise the Godward as well as the manward aspect of the Sacrament. It is 'an oblation of all possible praise to God' (Westminster Confession) and may also include as in the Book of Common Order of the Church of Scotland (1940), a prayer of self-offering: 'our souls and bodies to be a reasonable, holy and living sacrifice unto Thee'. The Prayer Book Order of Holy Communion is very widely used among Methodists with only small modifications and a very large number of Reformed and Presbyterian worshippers could use it and find in it little that would be doctrinally repugnant or alien to themselves. And, indeed, a very large number of Methodists and Reformed churchmen (including Presbyterians, Baptists, Congregationalists) agree that in the Sacrament Christ, being actually present, unites us by faith with His eternal sacrifice that we may plead and share in its benefits. Plainly, then, there is a possibility of theological, liturgical and devotional understanding between Christians separated in various traditions.

It is fatal to true ecumenical understanding to pretend that differences are less real than they are. There is a deep and real difference of *ethos* and doctrine in eucharistic worship as practised among our Churches, which must not be minimised. A frank acknowledgment of the differences, together with penitence for our frequent failure in love and mutual understanding, is an indispensable prerequisite for any movement towards intercommunion.

It must not be forgotten that within the Anglican Communion itself, and within any one of the Churches that belong to it, there is probably as wide a doctrinal divergence upon the meaning of Holy Communion as anywhere else, and precisely along those lines of 'Catholic' and 'Protestant'. It became quite clear in the discussions of the nature of the Church at the Amsterdam Assembly of the World Council of Churches that this distinction of 'Catholic' and 'Protestant' cuts right across the denominations; and that is nowhere more true than in the interpretation of Holy Communion. Thus there are many Anglicans who take a less 'high' view of the Sacrament than many Presbyterians. And yet all Anglicans, with their very divergent interpretations (which are a frequent subject of controversy among themselves) are members of one communion. The doctrinal divergence in interpretation does not hinder their unity of communion.

All this suggests that in this matter of intercommunion between separated Churches there is a greater difficulty than that of divergent eucharistic doctrine. In some quarters at least, the fundamental obstacle is not difference of doctrine, but difference of order.

VI. *Difference of Order as an Obstacle to Intercommunion*

It has already been remarked that when Lutherans are intransigent on the question of intercommunion and open communion, it is difference of doctrine rather than difference of order that is regarded as the obstacle. For example, the Lutheran Church of Sweden, while claiming and maintaining unbroken apostolic succession through episcopal ordination, is in communion with all Lutheran churches in other countries, whether or not they claim such succession, or have episcopal orders at all. The main obstacle for Lutherans is divergence of sacramental *doctrine*. But in face of this position Eastern Orthodox, Old Catholics and many Anglicans are accustomed to protest that they cannot allow such a distinction between *doctrine* and *order*, because to them order is quite essentially a matter of doctrine. They cannot allow that the question of episcopal or presbyterian or congregational order is merely a matter of church government and organisation. To them episcopacy is not merely of the *bene esse* of the Church of Christ, but of its *esse*, and the episcopate in the apostolic succession is an essential part of that whole sacramental order within which alone the sacraments, in the full and regular sense, can exist.

From this point of view, only those who have been ordained in a Church of that character are qualified to celebrate Holy Communion, and only those who have been duly confirmed in such a Church are normally qualified to receive it. Thus a decisive question between any two Churches as regards intercommunion and intercelebration is the question whether each regards the other's orders as valid, and the recognition of validity requires not only substantial dogmatic agreement but also unbroken apostolic succession through episcopal ordination.[1]

This may be illustrated from the negotiations that have taken place between certain of the Orthodox Churches and the Church of England, and from the relation that has come to exist between the Church of England and the Old Catholic Churches with which it has full intercommunion. The point may be even more clearly illustrated by the questions that have arisen in recent years between the Church of England and certain other Churches with which it is not in communion. Since the formation in 1947 of the

---

[1] For Orthodox and many Anglo-Catholics this dogmatic agreement must include agreement on the doctrine of orders.

Church of South India (through a union between certain dioceses of the Church of India, Burma and Ceylon, the Methodist Church and the South India United Church, which had not episcopal orders) the Church of England has decided that it is not in full communion with that newly-formed Church, and can have only what may be called 'limited intercommunion' with it. The ground of this decision is not a dissatisfaction with the credal orthodoxy of the Church of South India, but primarily the fact that that Church includes many ministers who have not been episcopally ordained and many communicants who have not been episcopally confirmed. A further illustration may be found in the proposals put forward by the Archbishop of Canterbury in a sermon preached before the University of Cambridge on the 3rd November 1946, with a view to a measure of intercommunion between the Church of England on the one hand and the English Free Churches and the Church of Scotland on the other. What the Archbishop suggested as a means of growing 'towards full communion' was 'a giving and receiving of episcopacy' in an arrangement by which 'each communion, episcopal and non-episcopal, should contribute the whole of its separate ministry to so many of the ministers of the other as were willing to receive it.' These proposals make it clear that the lack of episcopal ordination in those other Churches as at present constituted is regarded as a fundamental obstacle to intercommunion.

It may well seem that here we have reached the most difficult point in the whole problem of intercommunion, and indeed that the difficulty is insuperable. For there is an interpretation of the unbroken apostolic succession through episcopal ordination as being of the very *esse* of the Church of Christ which cannot afford to compromise. On this interpretation it may seem to be an inevitable conclusion that a Church which does not possess the apostolic succession in that sense is not really a Church at all; it is not part of the supernatural institution through which sacramental grace flows, for its orders are not valid, and the sacramental system is entirely dependent on valid orders. Thus the non-episcopal Churches might be regarded as truly Christian fellowships and their services regarded with the utmost respect as efficacious means of grace to those who take part in them, but the sacraments administered in those churches would not be sacraments in the true sense at all.

If that position is taken and maintained with complete logical rigidity, the very possibility of intercommunion between the Churches maintaining it and the non-episcopal Churches is excluded at the outset, and that would seem to be an end of the matter.

It must be remembered, however, that there is also an Orthodox and Anglo-Catholic interpretation which would not allow the question of 'valid orders', any more than that of eucharistic doctrine, to be isolated in this way. There is, underlying it, a whole complex of belief about the visible Church, comprehending the problems of forms of liturgy, and of liturgical practice, and the conception of the meaning of common worship. Thus apostolic succession is not regarded as the decisive point which constitutes a 'Church', but as one indispensable element among a variety of others, which together make up the essential pattern of 'the Church'; and non-episcopal Churches are regarded as defective in not exhibiting the full outline of the pattern, and not, by Anglicans at least, as 'no-Churches'. The belief in 'valid orders' is not, then, a 'position' demanding to be maintained with 'logical rigidity', nor is it primarily a matter of church law; it is intimately bound up with the whole complex fact of the Church's life of faith and worship.

While non-episcopal Churches often feel that insistence upon a particular form of this 'essential pattern' is itself a distortion of the New Testament view of the Church, they do not regard this as a barrier to intercommunion. But it is on this whole question of the pattern of the Church and not on the isolated factor of valid orders that agreement must be reached if intercommunion is to be possible.

There are, moreover, other signs that the situation is not hopeless. It is worth remembering that even these Churches which make the most exclusive claims for episcopal order do nevertheless allow for certain exceptions in the administration of the sacraments in cases of emergency, on the truly Catholic ground that God is not bound by His own appointed means of grace, and this in itself constitutes a qualification of the extreme position in the matter of validity. But it is still more important to remember that, as has already been remarked, all the Churches which adhere to the World Council of Churches do thereby acknowledge in each other something of the true reality of the Church of Christ, and that in itself is a fact of immense significance. Further, it is a very notable fact that Orthodox and Anglo-Catholic churchmen, who might be expected to dismiss the whole idea of intercommunion as unpractical, are very far from taking that attitude; indeed some of them show a quite special concern about the problem and pursue it with special eagerness. Again, it is important to remember that the Anglican Communion, which holds such a key position in these matters, is very far from being united in an exclusive and intransigent claim for episcopal orders as being of the *esse* of the Church. This claim, indeed, is not only qualified by many Anglicans as indicated above, but is also rejected by many others who hold that it is inconsistent with Anglican formularies and doctrine, and irreconcilable with much Anglican history and practice. Ever since the Reformation many members of the Church of England have fully recognised the Reformed Churches outside England as true branches of the Church of Christ and have valued and exercised the liberty, allowed to members of the Church of England, of welcoming members of such Churches to occasional communion as visitors and of themselves communicating with those Churches in similar circumstances. This recognition is still accorded and the custom of spiritual hospitality based upon it is still observed and valued by many in the Anglican Communion, and in modern times this is often given a wider interpretation so as to include the English Free Churches and the Churches overseaswhich have sprung from them.

A further hopeful sign is that the principle of 'comity', whereby the missionary societies, and the Churches which have come into being by their activity, refrain from competing with each other in a given area, has been recognised for many years by most of the Anglican and Protestant Churches. This constitutes a new factor in the relations between those Churches. Even if, as may generally have been the case, this policy was accepted because the areas to be evangelised could not otherwise have been covered by missionary activity, the result has inevitably been a recognition in some measure by both Anglican and non-episcopal Churches that the denomination evangelising an area does, in fact, represent the universal Church in that area. A further result of the policy of comity is that members of one denomination moving to an area in which another is operating are deprived of regular reception of the sacraments unless some arrangement of intercommunion between the two denominations is made to meet the situation. For this reason such arrangements are in many of these areas the normal practice.

When all is said, however, it remains true that the difference of order between the Churches which claim the episcopal succession and other Churches appears to be at the present time the most formidable obstacle in the way of intercommunion.

VII. *The Problem of Communion Services at Ecumenical Gatherings*

Mention has already been made in this Report of the problem of services of Holy Communion in the setting of ecumenical gatherings. This is a very special phase of the problem of intercommunion. It is not an entirely new phase. It has existed for at least a whole generation. But the growing strength of the Ecumenical Movement, in the formation of the World Council of Churches, and in the work of the World's Student Christian Federation, has sharpened the problem in recent years, and at the same time has given rise in various quarters to a feeling that the working solutions which have hitherto been accepted are not wholly satisfactory, and may even be dangerous. When under the auspices of an organisation like the World Council or the W.S.C.F., Christians from many different Churches are gathered together for a week, or two or three weeks in conference, sharing daily in common worship, conducted by varieties of churchmen in turn, what should they do in the matter of Holy Communion? Those individuals who are accustomed to weekly or daily celebrations may, of course, attend celebrations and take Communion in neighbouring churches. But is anything further possible in the way of corporate Communion within the framework of the ecumenical gathering?

There appears to be general agreement on the principle that a body like the World Council of Churches or the World's Student Christian Federation must not, as such, hold its own Communion Services, because such a body is not a Church. And yet the life of such a body, met in conference for a period, cannot be complete without Holy Communion. Thus it is natural that there should be a desire for something more than the mere opportunity for individuals to take Communion in neighbouring churches. And thus at ecumenical gatherings it has frequently been arranged, within the framework of the programme, that representatives of various Churches should hold Communion Services according to the order of their Churches for their own members and the members of other Churches with which they have (complete or limited) inter-communion. In some cases it is possible that a very large number of the members of an ecumenical gathering – a number including members of many different communions – can unite at the Lord's Table. And yet such a service can never be called *the corporate Communion of the conference*, so long as there remains even the smallest group of members who cannot conscientiously partake. Thus it is plain that the tragic and painful disunity of the Church presents itself in a particularly acute form at ecumenical gatherings, and that there is no perfect solution of the problems of policy which arise in that situation.

There are three possible ways, which have been seriously suggested, of dealing with this question of policy for ecumenical gatherings.

(1) There is the method of quite separate and simultaneous Communion Services for different denominational groups. This might mean that every denomination represented arranges its own service. This is so obviously undesirable that it is seldom tried. But it is frequently arranged that in the course of an ecumenical gathering there should take place simultaneously such and only such separate services of Holy Communion as will give every member, whatever his Church may be, the opportunity of making his Communion at one or other service. This deliberate going apart for Holy Communion is indeed a terrible step. But it is felt by some that this is no more terrible than our actual separation as Churches, and that so long as the latter continues, it is right and salutary that we should be sharply reminded of it in our ecumenical gatherings, instead of glossing it over. Yet it must be admitted that this method of going our several ways apart in simultaneous Communion Services has one great drawback: it deprives us of the opportunity, which an ecumenical gathering ought to make possible, of entering somewhat into one another's traditions by being present at each other's Communion Services. So a second method has come to be commonly employed in ecumenical gatherings.

(2) The second method is that of non-simultaneous Com-

munion Services according to the different traditions, with non-communicating attendance for those who cannot actually receive Communion. In some cases the celebrant (e.g. if he is a Presbyterian minister) will invite members of all branches of the Church of Christ to receive Communion, and many who are of different Churches from his own will accept the invitation. But there are many who, according to the discipline of their own Churches, cannot accept the invitation. And in many cases the celebrant (e.g. if he is an Orthodox priest) cannot, according to the discipline of his own Church, issue the general invitation. In all cases, however, it is possible for those who cannot communicate to be invited to attend the service and share spiritually in the worship. This practice has been widely followed for a good many years in the Ecumenical Movement, and has been valued highly by those who have had experience of it. It gives Christians of different traditions an opportunity of uniting in common worship at this quite central service of Holy Communion, even if they cannot all receive Communion together, and this in itself may have the effect of quickening the longing to overcome our tragic divisions and reach a more visible unity. Moreover, there is probably no better way of reaching a deeper understanding of the spiritual life of another Church than by being present as a worshipper at its Communion Service; this is confirmed by the experience of many who have practised it.

Yet in recent years certain difficulties have been expressed in respect of this method.

Some have suggested that it is a profanation of the Sacrament to use it with a pedagogical intention, for mutual instruction in our variant traditions. Yet the Sacrament *is*, in one of its aspects, a 'showing forth' of Christian truths and realities, and there is no profanation if celebrant and worshippers have a real intention of worship. (It is true, of course, that this may sometimes be difficult for a worshipper at a Communion Service which is very different from that with which he is familiar.)

Others maintain, from the point of view of certain Churches, that non-communicating attendance is contrary to the very nature of the Sacrament, of which the partaking of the elements is an essential part. This may at first sight seem a natural objection for those Churches which have no such practice as eucharistic worship apart from actual communicating. Yet even those Churches often strongly encourage their young folk who have not yet reached communicant status to be present as worshippers at Communion Services.

But the most radical objection to this practice comes from those who maintain that it is the Lord Himself who gives the invitation to His own Table, and that when this invitation comes to them through the mouth of the minister of Christ, they cannot refrain from partaking without incurring the guilt of refusing Christ's own most gracious invitation. They would therefore feel bound to absent themselves from any service at which they were forbidden by church regulations to partake of the elements. Though it might be answered that the same refusal is involved in absenting themselves from the service, it remains true that non-communicating attendance is profoundly unsatisfactory to those who hold this view. Another answer to the objection comes from those who would say that the voice of the Lord is to be heard in the regulation of the Church which prohibits them from communicating as much as in the invitation given in the service they are attending.

But, further, it is maintained in various quarters, that the use of this method is a betrayal of the ecumenical task in so far as it almost inevitably involves an acquiescence in the confessional *status quo*. And it would be generally agreed that the practice would be highly dangerous if it came to be complacently accepted as a satisfactory *modus vivendi* and thereby kept us from feeling the pain of our divisions.

(3) The third method of dealing with the problem is what has been somewhat extravagantly described as 'sacramental fasting'. This does not mean simply that an ecumenical gathering meets the situation by neglecting to make any provision for Communion Services, but something more positive. It means that, in view of the sinfully divided state of the Church, the members of the gathering are expressly invited to abstain from Holy Communion for the period of the gathering and to join instead in a common service of contrition, repentance and prayer for reunion. This method certainly avoids the danger of making any improper use of the Sacrament, and it is realistic in its recognition of the disunity of the Church. Moreover, it seems to some to be a sound way of leading Christians in conference to bear personally, by a renunciation, a share of the burden and pain of the present disunity at the same time as they pray for unity; and it is in such a

spirit that this way has been suggested. Yet there are some obvious objections to it. It would bear very differently upon different people. To those who are not accustomed to very frequent Communion there would be no 'sacramental fasting' involved in doing without it for a week or more. To others it would indeed make a great difference, but they would feel that such an abstention cannot be regarded as a worthy self-denial, but would be rather a withholding from God of an offering which He desires us to make. Some, indeed, would go further and say that we have no right in any circumstances to neglect the duty which is incumbent on the Church of offering the Eucharistic Sacrifice to God every Sunday and holy day or even every day. For these various reasons it seems impossible to recommend the method of so-called 'sacramental fasting', and on this conclusion there is fairly general agreement.

It is clear, from this outline of three possible solutions to the problem posed for ecumenical gatherings by our separation from one another in the Holy Communion, that no perfect solution of the problem is at present possible. Each of the proposed solutions has its advantages; each has its disadvantages. In the case of the third ('sacramental fasting') the disadvantages are so serious that, on such evidence as we have, it has never been tried at any representative ecumenical gathering, and we cannot, as we have said, recommend it in any circumstances which we can envisage. But we would suggest that ecumenical gatherings differ so widely in their character and purpose that the right course must be decided in the light of the circumstances of each occasion. In some circumstances the first course would be preferable, in others the second, in yet others (should time allow) a combination of both might be most fruitful.

In order to decide, it is necessary to be clear about certain principles which should govern the decision. We urge the following considerations upon *all those responsible for ecumenical gatherings*:

(1) Nothing must be done to obscure the truth that it is *Churches* and not ecumenical committees or conferences that have the right to celebrate the Lord's Supper. In practice, this distinction is easily obscured because it is often the same people, acting as ministers of their Churches rather than as members of a committee, who will actually conduct the Communion Services; but

their difference of capacity should be kept clear. Nevertheless, a certain responsibility falls upon the committee as such, e.g., in deciding which services are to be held at times when delegates can fairly be expected to attend if they so wish and without conflicting with engagements that are part of the conference programme.

(2) Because our divisions are radically sinful as well as tragic in character, the conference authorities should not make provision for separate Communion Services without at the same time making provision for a corporate expression of penitence for our divided state. This is generally best provided through a carefully prepared *joint* service of preparation at some point in the conference programme.

(3) To call ecumenical conferences is, at any time, a serious responsibility before God, and not the least serious aspect of them is this acknowledgment of our sacramental division. Consequently, a heavy *pastoral* obligation rests upon those who involve others in such experiences, and this is especially, though not exclusively, true of conferences for young people or for any not habituated to the tensions of an ecumenical meeting. Preparation for worship, and especially for the eucharistic worship, should therefore be taken fully as seriously by the promoters of a conference as the preparation of any other aspect of the programme. This may involve not only carefully written preparatory literature and forms of service for use at the conference, but also provision for dealing pastorally, theologically and personally with the perplexities caused by the worship during the conference itself.

(4) Ecumenical conferences have many forms, purposes and constituencies, and often the way of dealing with the question of Communion Services must be decided in the light of these factors. Absorption in the issues of Communion and intercommunion may divert the attention of the conference from its main purpose. But in a conference of any duration these issues are bound to be present or even prominent. The World's Student Christian Federation has wrestled strenuously with the problem for many years and continues to stimulate the thinking of the Churches. Ecumenical leaders of long experience are in grave danger of forgetting the pain and bewilderment of those who come freshly to these problems or the indifference of those who have never thought about them. We urge the World Council (in all its

agencies, though Faith and Order must feel a special responsibility) to make continuous provision for study, education and prayer on these issues. It is largely through a right handling of them in ecumenical meetings that they will become living issues throughout the whole life of our churches. Only as they are faced, with all the struggle and suffering which they imply, in prayerful obedience to the guidance of the Holy Spirit, who has led us thus far in recognition of each other, will He lead us into further unity.

VIII. *Summary of Conclusions*

While it is not the function of this Commission to propose to the various Churches any practical steps to be taken or lines of policy to be followed, it is our duty to sum up as concretely as possible the conclusions that emerge from the studies and discussions conducted by the Commission. These may be formulated under the heads of agreements and differences.

(a) *Agreements*

(1) We are agreed in recognising all the Churches embraced in the World Council of Churches as in some sense participating in the reality of the Church of Christ.

(2) We are agreed that this One Holy Catholic and Apostolic Church ought to have visible unity in the world, and therefore disunity is in itself a sinful state.

(3) We are agreed that it is through the corruption of sin that our common loyalty to truth has often brought us tragically into division. Even beyond this we all agree that every Christian body has in its history specific sins against other Christians to repent of and confess.

(4) We are agreed that the existing disunity of the Church reaches its most painful point at the Lord's Table, when members of different Churches cannot meet together to celebrate and receive Holy Communion.

(5) We are agreed that, while there are wide differences in the theological interpretation of this sacrament, even within individual Churches and cutting across their boundaries, yet there is a certain fundamental unity of conception. Such a unity exists inasmuch as this dominical sacrament is everywhere con-

trolled by the words of the institution, and is everywhere a memorial of Christ's death and a Sacrament of His Body and Blood in which He is truly present to give Himself to us, uniting us to Himself and to His eternal sacrifice, through use of His appointed elements of bread and wine.

(6) We are agreed that even in the present divided state of the Church we ought to be deeply concerned about the possibility of a wider practice of intercommunion and intercelebration, and to continue to explore every way by which this may be attained without any sacrifice of principle.

(7) We are agreed that it is especially painful and the scandal more apparent when Christians from various Churches who come together in ecumenical gatherings cannot all unite in the Sacrament of Holy Communion in the course of their meetings; and we are agreed that none of the already tried ways of meeting this problem is wholly satisfying or unobjectionable. Thus we are agreed that this particular problem should be quite especially laid upon the conscience of the Churches and the leaders of the Ecumenical Movement.

(b) Differences

(1) We are not all agreed as regards the measure of intercommunion which may precede and anticipate fuller union of the Churches. While all are agreed that Churches which are not actually united in government and jurisdiction may be in full communion with each other, and that even Churches which are not in full communion with each other may practise a measure of intercommunion and intercelebration, some are prepared to go much further than others in this direction. Some hold that it is right for a church to invite to the Lord's Table those who are members of any branch of the Church of Christ, and that such a measure of intercommunion rightly precedes reunion. Others maintain that there cannot be a real unity at the altar unless there is a unity of the whole life of the Church, and therefore intercommunion cannot, as a general rule, be allowed, to precede or anticipate actual union.

(2) We are not agreed as to the requisite basis of intercommunion, and therefore we are not agreed as to what may justifiably be regarded as an obstacle in principle to intercom-

munion. Even among those who feel constrained to emphasise the obstacles, there is not general agreement as to their nature. Some regard the lack of unity in doctrine as the main obstacle; others in addition are concerned about the lack of unity of order and regard the problem of valid orders and apostolic succession as the main difficulty. This latter difficulty is in fact the greatest obstacle that has to be overcome in the movement towards intercommunion.

In presenting our Report we desire to say:

(1) We are deeply thankful for the opportunity given to us of meeting together during these years in intimate fellowship and discussing the problem of intercommunion in a more ecumenical setting than has ever before been possible.

(2) We have learned much from each other in our discussion which has illuminated both the possibilities and the complexities of the subject. The essays now published will contribute to an increased mutual understanding. Nevertheless many hopes which may have been aroused by the expectation of our Report will be disappointed. We share that keen disappointment, and we feel that neither we nor the Churches from which we come have yet gone deeply enough into the penitence from which healing may arise.

(3) With all possible earnestness we commend the cause of intercommunion to the Churches. The subject demands a heightened awareness of the critical issues at stake and a greater mutual sensitiveness. The underlying theological problems require far more searching and systematic study, with a full measure of Christian faith, hope and charity, penitence and prayer.

Finally, we would all bear witness to our unspeakable gratitude to the Lord of the Church for His gift of this precious Sacrament. It is because we are united in gratitude to Him for His gift that we feel so keenly our inability to receive it in full fellowship.

Part Two

SOME HISTORICAL STUDIES OF THE PROBLEM

I

TERMS OF COMMUNION IN THE UNDIVIDED CHURCH

*

Georges Florovsky

Orthodox Oecumenical Patriarchate (Exarchate for the Russians in the West)

(United States of America)

'The Undivided Church': the term may be vague and a bit ambiguous, and yet it has been successfully used in certain ecumenical quarters to denote the state of the Church Militant before the canonical split between the East and the West, finally consummated in the eleventh century. In a sense it was a modern substitute for an earlier slogan, coined already in the age of Reformation: *consensus quinquesaecularis*. To be sure, there were manifold splits, and conflicts, and tensions, in the early Church as well. Communion between the East and the West had been many times broken before the Churches were ultimately separated. Some big provinces of the Church in the East broke away from the Catholic unity, based on the decisions of the Ecumenical Councils at Ephesus and Chalcedon. The Iconoclastic controversy was another violent cut across the body of the Church. The whole history of the first ten centuries of Christianity has been precisely a history of schisms and their healing, and the healing was never complete. Nevertheless there was a sense in which the Church at this epoch could still be described as undivided. There was still a very considerable and traditional 'consensus' in essentials. It is so obvious when we compare the scope of dissensions then with 'the unhappy divisions' of modern times. Ecumenical Councils were possible at this epoch, even in the periods of the most bitter strife. Representatives of the most divergent convictions could confer together on the points of divergence, and the split would be consummated only after all hopes of reconciliation had been frustrated. The controversy itself was possible at all because

47

there was some common ground. In no case had the Apostolic Succession been broken, at least before the formal split, and this Succession was unanimously regarded as a token and a guarantee of unity. One could always appeal to certain uncontroverted standards. The terms of unity were under discussion throughout the whole period, and the terms of unity were the terms of communion.

We have to keep in mind that the early Church had not yet been fully unified in its administration. Gradually the local churches were brought together into some larger units, under the presidency of Provincial Metropolitans, and then of the Patriarchs —and yet a very large autonomy had been preserved in these local churches. The true unit of the Church was (and is still, at least in theory) precisely a local church, under a bishop. The growth of Papal claims for a universal authority and jurisdiction ultimately wrecked the unity of the Church. The highest authority in the Church was a Council, i.e. a representative gathering of all ruling bishops, and each of them had a right to speak not only for his particular church (a diocese, or a local community), but precisely for the Church Universal. And what was sought was not just a majority vote, but rather a unanimity, or consensus. The history of the Trinitarian controversies in the fourth century supplies abundant material on this matter. Only with great difficulty can one find his way through the labyrinth of creeds, composed by various groups and synods at that epoch. But ultimately we discover a red thread going across many divisions. What was important in this search for the Catholic faith was precisely a belief in consensus. There was no compromise in the final reconciliation of the 'Old Nicene' group with the new 'Homoiousian' (cf. the Council of Alexandria under St. Athanasius in 363). It was rather a re-discovery of the consensus that was obscured by the use of discordant phraseologies. And no such consensus could be established between the 'Nicenes' of all descriptions and the Arians. For several decades, between 325 and 381, there was no commonly accepted presentation of the Catholic belief. But there was an intensive search for such a presentation. It is difficult to see to what extent a factual unity of the Church had been kept at that time, i.e. communion between the local churches. No generalisation is permissible. In many cases communion was actually broken, including the famous 'Schism of

Antioch', which, however, had not only doctrinal reasons. Yet we should not forget that many champions of Orthodoxy were, at least for some periods of time, still in communion with bishops and churches of a very doubtful orthodoxy of belief, including St. Basil or St. Cyril of Jerusalem, to quote but the most conspicuous instance. Two main conclusions can be drawn from an impartial study of this tumultuous epoch. First, consensus was regarded as a prerequisite of communion, and therefore communion could be kept or practised as long as there was a justifiable hope of an ultimate consensus; on the other hand, every reasonable suspicion of a real dissension in essentials would justify, in the then situation, an (at least provisional) break of communion (as it were, by precaution). As a matter of fact this was the normal procedure in an age when there was no unified administration of the Church Universal. A member of any local church would be, as a rule and in principle, entitled to be admitted to any other local church in any other place, where he might happen to reside, provided he could prove not only his own good standing but also the orthodoxy of his original church. Sometimes difficulties would arise. The best known instance in the early period is the Paschal controversy between Asia Minor and the West (in the second century). In a period of debate the scrutiny would obviously be very rigorous and strict. Secondly, the main prerequisite of communion would be the validity of orders, i.e. ultimately an unbroken Apostolic Succession. It was the main guarantee of the good standing of a particular local church itself. One has, in addition, not to forget that at this period the Apostolic Succession was never regarded *in abstracto*, i.e. there was a question not only of a continuity in consecration, but above all of a continuity within the limits of every particular or local church. 'Abstract' consecrations were prohibited and disavowed, and no titular or nominal bishops were allowed to function as such. In the best case, and by the use of 'economy', they would be given bishop's honours, but no bishop's rights or privileges. And finally both conditions were closely correlated: strictly speaking, no valid continuity could be recognised or admitted outside of a Catholic consensus. The ultimate reason for that was deeply grounded in an organic conception of the Church. Unanimity (in essentials) was just the formative factor of the Church (as far as its human aspect was concerned). Were this unanimity broken, the unity itself was broken, and no room for communion left. The limits or the scope of this unanimity could be variously circumscribed, and in some cases a narrow description had to be overruled by an authoritative statement of a wider and more competent instance, on a wider basis of charity and understanding. This was, for example, the case of the 'Neo-Nicene' group. In some other cases, on the contrary, there was an obvious danger of compromising the adequacy of the dogmatic standing. To this category belong all the unsuccessful attempts to restore communion of the Chalcedonian Orthodox with the Monophysites. Consensus needed to be real and spiritual, and not just nominal, or achieved by evading the controversial issues.

In brief, there was no problem of intercommunion (in the modern sense of the term) in the undivided Church. It was so precisely because the Church was undivided, at least in aspiration. There was simply the question of 'full communion', i.e. of membership in the Church. And there were identical terms of this membership for all, or at least identifiable or equivalent terms, if we consider the variety of actual language used in the Church. On some occasions it was of primary importance to assure the identity of meaning of the terms used for the same conception in Greek, or Latin, or Syriac. And there was some room for misinterpretation, in a literal sense. Possibly some of these misinterpretations considerably handicapped the agreement between Byzantium and the East, especially Armenia. Yet, as a rule, there was some liberal room for variety, which is not to be mistaken for compromise. The reconciliation of St. Cyril of Alexandria with the Orient was by no means a compromise, but rather a re-discovery of a wider consensus. In any case there was but one desire—to establish the complete identity of a universal Orthodox Faith, which in itself was the main term of communion. It was, however, not to exclude a legitimate use of theological freedom. The Alexandrinian and the Antiochene trends of theology happily survived along with each other in a perfect communion, if not without some occasional tensions, yet within the same and undivided Church. The only intercommunion practised in the undivided Church was the communion between the various local churches, within an objective consensus and a recognised 'unity of the undivided (Catholic) episcopate', to use an admirable phrase of St. Cyprian. But this unity was, in the last resort, not so much a unity of administration, as a unity of Faith (or *Orthodoxia*).

Now there was still a very urgent problem with which the Church had persistently to deal time and again, precisely because she was engaged in the healing of schisms and the realisation of a true unity. It was the problem of schism itself. On the whole, all schisms were utterly abhorred as such, as a flagrant violation of the essential unity of the Church: 'the Church is one', she simply cannot be divided. We may leave this wider problem aside in the present context.[1] We have to confine ourselves now to its implications. And this was precisely the problem with which the Church actually dealt in the age of the Councils. Or, rather, there was a series or a complex of problems arising from time to time and always 'situation-conditioned', and accordingly solved every time with an eye on the concrete situation. These decisions were never codified, at least with authority, and do not easily admit of a generalisation. All these decisions were casual, and probably this was their strength. There was no concern with a rigid theory, but rather a preoccupation with an immediate harm already done, with a sickness to be cured. The problem can be put (as it has been actually put) in this form. People involved in an actual break of communion (including clergy and bishops) are now admitted to a full membership in the Church. Their personal or individual guilt or sin is adequately covered by their repentance. There is no longer any question of their moral integrity, or of the integrity of their belief. Yet what is their status? As a matter of fact there was no special question if the Church were dealing with 'dissenters' in a narrow sense, i.e. with those who had lapsed for a time, after having been in full communion with the Church. Their unhappy secession could be forgiven and their occasional sickness cured by an appropriate discipline, more or less rigorous or charitable. In any case there was an exercise of charity and forgiveness, i.e. of a discipline of penance. However, it took some time before some measure of unanimity was achieved even on this matter (we would have to recall the rigorism of St. Cyprian and the whole problem of Donatism, and all kindred trends through the ages). There were some doubts about the limits of

[1] Cf. two articles of mine on this subject: 'The Limits of the Church', in *C.Q.R.*, October 1933, and 'The Doctrine of the Church and the Ecumenical Problem', in *E.R.*, 1950, II.

the Church's authority in the dispensation of spiritual charity and forgiveness, in so far as some issues of order and administration were inevitably involved in the problem. And these issues were spectacularly burning in a more complicated case, which was unfortunately the most usual, viz. in the case of a perpetuated and inveterate schism. The first question of this sort the Church had to consider was the whole problem of an heretical baptism —and we know that from the very beginning the emphasis was not only on the actual heresy but no less on the schismatic character of every heresy, i.e. on the fact of the separation (or a temporal separatedness) itself. Next came the problem of heretical (and deliberately schismatic, i.e. administered with a definite aiming at separation or rivalry) orders (ordination and consecration). Of course there was no question of intercommunion with heretics and schismatics. Heresy had to be abrogated first, and schism cured. So there was a new question about what to do with those ex-heretics and ex-schismatics who had never been before within the fold of the Church, i.e. strictly speaking, with a specific and peculiar type of neophytes, for these were now for the first time to be admitted to full membership in the Catholic Church. The question was especially difficult in the case of those who had a reason to claim clerical status. The real point was precisely this: would not a recognition of a Christian status of the reconciled schismatics and heretics, be it their baptism or their orders, imply a tacit intercommunion with those schismatic and heretical bodies, in which that status had been acquired? To recognise a schismatic baptism would amount to an intercommunion in baptism. To receive a priest ordained by heretics would amount to a recognition that these heretical bishops did somehow belong to the unity of an undivided episcopate. In other words it would mean that a particular schism (or heresy), in some enigmatic sense, had still been a part of the Church Universal, i.e. that unity had never been actually broken, but only rather disguised. Or again, it would mean that communion had never been really broken. It is well known that such was, in fact, the mind of St. Augustine: that does not mean, of course, that he underestimated the disruptive and sinful character of any schism. And the Western Church has been officially committed ever since to this interpretation of the schismatic sacraments. It is more difficult to identify the mind of the Eastern Church. St. Augustine's conception was never formally repudiated in the period under discussion. On the other hand, those conciliar decisions by which the Church in the East had been bound for centuries were 'ecumenical' decisions, as the Ecumenical Councils were synods of the Church Universal, and not just Eastern synods. We are not concerned, in the present context, with the problem of application of the ancient canons to the modern situation, which obviously could not have been anticipated at that time. Nor have we to discuss to what extent such an application (or 'extrapolation') can be canonically justified. We have to deal with a plain historical question: was there any definite *theological* conception behind those *canonical* regulations, which were from time to time promulgated and enforced by the lawful authorities of the Church, in the period of Ecumenical Councils and later, up to the separation between the East and the West in the eleventh century? It has been sometimes suggested that all these canonical measures were simply practical measures, which it would be a mistake to condense in any theory. Possibly there was no theory at all. It was rather a practice of charity, which it really was, to be sure. Yet, on the other hand, it is difficult to see how charity in the Church can be totally detached from the rule of Faith. In any case the theological question must be asked. An exhaustive survey of all the historical evidence is of course quite beyond the scope of the present inquiry. We have to confine ourselves to some typical instances. The most comprehensive regulation on the whole problem is offered in the 95th canon of the Council in Trullo (692), which at the same time did codify and authenticate all the previous synodical decisions. The Council openly rules that Nestorians and Monophysites should be received into the Church by a renunciation of their errors, Arians and Apollinarians by the sacrament of the Holy Chrism. In neither case was there any question of a new baptism. But this was by no means a new practice: it was, on the contrary, the authorisation of current practice. The canon does not mention the clergy in particular. Yet there is no doubt that Nestorian and Monophysite clergy were usually admitted to communion in their orders. This practice was quoted as a precedent at the VIIth Ecumenical Council (787), and accordingly the Iconoclast bishops and clergy were restored to the Church in their orders, which were illegally acquired in the heresy. It is true that at this point some serious objections were raised, not so much of a theological as of an historical nature: what was the custom and the rule of the early Church? Obviously there was no rigid uniformity in practice. Yet the final decision seems to imply that some illegal (or 'illicit') sacraments could be still regarded and recognised as valid (i.e. 'real'), or, in other words, there was no impelling duty to administer those sacraments again in the Catholic Church, which had already been conferred in the schism or heresy. The distinction made between various categories of schismatics or dissenters seems to suggest that there was some objective difference in their Christian status. It is true that no coherent synthesis had ever been offered on the matter. No doubt there were some real variations in practice, and this is the main objection which is usually raised by those who hesitate to make any doctrinal inference from the canons. Yet obviously the main doctrinal issue had been openly raised already by St. Basil. He felt himself compelled to do so in the face of a confused canonical situation. His advice or opinion, first given in a letter to Amphilochius, the Bishop of Iconium (ep. CLXXXVIII, a. 374), was incorporated as a canon into the Canonical Codex of the Church, authorised and authenticated by the Council in Trullo. First, some variety in the existing practice is plainly admitted (with regard to schismatic baptism) and it is suggested 'that we should follow the custom existing in each region, embarrassing as it may be. Secondly, St. Basil introduces a distinction between different types of schism, already made by the ancients'. He distinguishes three cases: heresy, schism, and illegal congregation (*parasynagoge*). The first is completely broken off and alienated in faith. A schism is at variance (with the Church) on questions that admit of a remedy. A conventicle is rooted simply in insubordination. This classification is not, however, so simple to apply as might be expected. This becomes obvious when St. Basil comes to the case of an 'inveterate' schism (he had in view particularly the Cathari, i.e. the Novatians). At this point he refers to St. Cyprian and obviously accepts his point of view, that sacramental life expires 'because of the severance of continuity', i.e. by the fact of separation itself. An alienation in faith separates from the Catholic body—there is no communion where there is no consensus. But an alienation in what taken by itself may admit of remedy, seems to have ultimately the same consequences. 'For those who separated first had ordination from the fathers, and through the imposition of their hands possessed the spiritual gift; but those who had been cut off, becoming laymen, possessed the power neither of baptising nor of ordaining, being able no longer to impart to others the grace of the Holy Spirit from which they themselves had fallen away.' One may pretend that St. Basil was simply quoting St. Cyprian and giving his arguments without making them his own. The context, however, does not allow so easy an escape. St. Basil acquiesces in a milder practice, it is true, but only 'for the sake of discipline', which was the true basis of such a mild practice. He would abstain from the severity which may endanger reconciliation. And he was prepared to apply this dispensation even in the case of an illegal episcopal consecration. In fact, St. Basil does not speak of discipline but of a 'Catholic economy'. On the other hand he hesitated to disavow the mild practice in order to avoid a worse confusion (as it is clear from his later letter to the same Amphilochius, ep. CXCIX, a. 375). On the whole, St. Basil was quite aware of the theological issue involved in the discharge of discipline. Yet he did not press it. The stress he laid on the moment of separation can be easily understood against the concrete situation he had to face. Of course St. Basil was seriously concerned with the restoration of a doctrinal unity which had been so grievously endangered in his time, and he was prepared to use charity and wisdom in order to heal the dissensions. At that time there was dire controversy between local churches, precisely on theological issues. For St. Basil, to be sure, an alienation in faith meant also an estrangement from the Catholic Church. Yet, under present circumstances, a canonical communion between the orthodox and the heterodox bishops had not yet been broken. It led to those intricate cases with which the later synods had to deal, namely that the consecration of some leading 'Orthodox' bishops appeared to be compromised by an irregular status of their consecrators (such was the case of St. Meletios of Antioch and of St. Cyril of Jerusalem). In such a situation it would have been unwise, nay detrimental to 'catholic economy', to lay primary stress on a factual heresy as long as communion had not been formally and openly broken. On the other hand, in an inveterate schism the spiritual estrangement was consummated and all links with the Catholic body deliberately broken. St. Basil was first concerned with the reality of communion. Before an authoritative condemnation of errors and a formal enforcement of a definite doctrinal standard there was still some hope of curing the internal disease. This hope would be lost every time an actual break took place. And for that reason an agreement in matters of faith would not, by itself, restore the broken unity. It accounts for a certain ambiguity in the argument of St. Basil. He hesitated to admit that a separated minister, openly outside of the communion with the Catholic Church, could act, as it were, *on behalf of* the Church in which he had no status whatever and whose communion he had deliberately avoided. But such was, strictly speaking, Augustine's solution. For St. Augustine, indeed, schismatic bishops and ministers were acting, even against their own intention, on behalf and in the interest of the Church Catholic. Was then the unity of love of secondary importance? What makes St. Augustine's conception difficult is precisely his emphasis on the elements of unity, which seems to imply that distortion of an actual unity does not vitiate the integrity of these constituent elements. But the unity under discussion is not so much a canonical order, as the ultimate catholicity of the spirit. Is not this catholicity openly frustrated by the spirit of sectarianism? We are not surprised, therefore, to discover that, in spite of a comparatively mild discipline enforced by the Councils, theological doubts were not completely removed and that a great Byzantine canonist of the twelfth century, Theodore Balsamon, the titular Patriarch of Antioch, hesitated to recognise any orders conferred outside the catholic communion of the Orthodox Church. On the other hand, even at a later date, no immediate conclusion can be drawn from the fact of the separation of the Churches, i.e. the schism between the East and the West, inaugurated by the mutual excommunications in 1054. There are many instances of a continued intercommunion between the Churches after the schism had been officially promulgated.[2]

Let us summarise. In the light of the doctrine and practice of the 'Undivided Church' the following guiding principles can be formulated:

1. The Church is one. This unity is both based on and expresses two things. On the one hand it is rooted in a dogmatic consensus, however wide or narrow it may be. The Church of that time

[2] The whole question needs a careful re-examination; some valuable material can be found in the recent study, *The Byzantine Patriarchate*, by Br. George Every, S.S.M. London, S.P.C.K., 1947.

was just building its theological system, which had to be an adequate scheme of the 'faith that was once delivered unto the saints', and therefore admitted of no innovation. A Catholic communion (and no other could be allowed) was visualised only on the basis of an integral unity in faith. On the other hand, the actual communion (or communication) was of vital importance, for the very reason that Christianity is not just a doctrine but the Body. For that reason any isolationism would not only inhibit the normal life but endanger the reality of any spiritual life at all.

2. Accordingly no intercommunion would be allowed, if the term be given its modern connotation, which was indeed quite unknown in the early Church and alien to its spirit. Any intercommunion between the local churches would presuppose, at that time, an actual unity, both visible and invisible, on the basis of a common confession of faith and of an unbroken continuity of sacramental structure (and above all, of the 'Apostolic Succession'). No exception could be allowed from this general rule.

3. The whole problem of the limits of the Church had been thoroughly discussed, and its practical implications were clearly seen. Divergent opinions on the matter were offered, but no final synthesis had been accomplished. Yet even when a distinction had been admitted between a strictly canonical boundary and an ultimate charismatic or sacramental limit, it was never regarded as permissible to transgress the canonical limit: whatever the real status of 'separated (Christian) bodies', no communion could go beyond the canonical limit, simply because this limit indicated the absence of unity. Communion and an integral unity were exact correlatives.

THE PROBLEM OF INTERCOMMUNION
IN THE REFORMATION

★

Ernst Bizer

Evangelical Church in Germany (Lutheran)

(Germany)

The division of the Evangelical Church when the Lord's Supper is celebrated is an heritage from the Reformation. Just when the Gospel was being newly discovered this division arose, a division which we would greatly like to overlook or forget but which we lack the power to overcome. The consequence is that wherever the results of the Reformation are taken to heart the self-same division breaks out again.

It is obviously an *exegetical* question whether this division is necessary or right. According to the Reformers themselves, the Eucharist has to be discussed on the basis of the New Testament only. It will not suffice to-day simply to repeat the exegesis of the sixteenth century. But it is both useful and fruitful to enquire into the interests and motives that led to division then; for if we do so, we are bound to see the depths and the ramifications of the problem. A study of the past can thus keep us from treating the subject superficially, and show us the issues which confront us to-day as the heirs of the Reformation.

Certain general considerations need to be kept in mind: The dispute about the Eucharist at that time was not just a theoretical matter, of interest only to professional theologians. The men who took over the Mass as the centre of the Church's life (where indeed it rightly belongs) could not think of the Eucharist as a mere appendage to ecclesiastical activity, but as the central and indeed (according to Luther's own utterances from time to time) the *only* Service of Worship in the Church. If no understanding could be reached on that point there could be no possibility of joining in common worship. Of necessity the Church had to divide. That much was agreed on all hands. Luther did not simply issue a warning about participating in the Mass, but also about sharing in the Reformed (Calvinist) celebration of the Lord's Supper. Similarly the Reformed (Calvinists) warned their members about going to a Lutheran celebration. Thus the city of Zurich forbade its students, during the negotiations for union, to take part in the Lord's Supper at Strassburg.[1] In 1555 the city of Bern did not permit any intercommunion with Calvin.[2] To share in a service of worship implies an agreement with the teaching that is given in it; so to share in the worship of another confession is clearly to make a false confession.

But in addition to this there was a general belief that what was at stake was not just one isolated point of doctrine, but the whole Gospel. The struggle was recognised as a *contentio de fide*. It was not just that there was a difference about the meaning of the words 'This is my body', but rather that an understanding of the *whole* Gospel revealed itself in the exegesis of these words. The presuppositions of the exegesis and conclusions arrived at else-where entered in as factors to determine the exposition. That is still true to-day and it is an encumbrance upon all our questions and our answers.

Lastly, there was at that time a generally shared conviction that while the division was a necessity, its occurrence constituted a challenge to overcome it so that it should not become permanent. The Evangelical cause has suffered much from the division, but it has always been more than a political manoeuvre when opponents have been brought together again and again. For the Church can only be *one*. Time and again Luther assures us that unity is his heartfelt concern,[3] and his activities in the years 1530-44 provide historical proof of that. Bucer and his friends put their whole strength for many years into the service of union and did their irksome tasks tirelessly. Melanchthon and Calvin also worked for the same cause. Even Calvin's writings against Westphal are to be understood in this way. It is a false historical perspective to see the Reformation as time of division and opposition, and to over-look these strivings for unity. That they did not attain their end

---

[1] CR 12, Nr. 1,039.   [2] CR 15, Nr. 2,308.
[3] E.g. WA Br 6, 24, 27; WA 38, 298 f.

detracts nothing from their impressiveness, though it faces us with the question why they failed.

I

It will be an aid to clarity about Luther's motives and interests if in the first place we consider how the possibility of Inter-communion with the *Catholic* church was destroyed for him.

Luther explicitly derives his understanding of the Mass from the concept of a 'Testament' (in his sermon on the New Covenant, i.e. on the Holy Mass, 1520,[4] and in 'The Babylonian Captivity of the Church'[5]). A testament is the last irrevocable will of a dying man 'so that he can leave his property behind him already assigned, and appoint whom he will to share it'.[6] Thus did the 'eternal divine person' Jesus Christ irrevocably dispose of His goods. The goods, the fortune, the inheritance that is thus divided is the forgiveness of sins, 'as if He should say: "Behold, O men, I promise you and bequeath to you with these words the Forgive-ness of all your sins, and Eternal Life . . ." '[7] At the same time Christ instituted the celebration of the Eucharist as a memorial feast, so that Faith, Hope and Love should be strengthened by it, or that 'we might be renewed at the very point where we had declined'. The elements 'Flesh and Blood under the bread and wine' are the seals of this promise. But a celebration of the Eucharist is more than a feast commemorating what happened long ago. It is the living present reality of that past. 'For every-thing in this Sacrament must be alive. That is why He has not composed it of a dead letter and seal, but of a living word and sign, which we can lay hold of afresh each day.' When the priest elevates the Host, he shows us the seal and sign of the Sacrament, 'by which Christ has bequeathed to us remission of all our sin and eternal life'. The hymn in Matthew 21. 9 is the witness to this 'that we thus receive gifts from God, and do not sacrifice or give to Him'. The celebration of the Eucharist is the place where Christ promises us His bequest, and at the same time divides it and gives it to us.

As a consequence of this the words of the will or testament are seen to have a decisive importance. They must be kept continually

[4] WA 6, 349 ff.   [5] WA 6, 489 ff.   [6] WA 6, 357.
[7] WA 6, 358.

in mind, and faith must be exercised on them. For without the words the Sacrament would become meaningless, and would lose its relation to us. It is here that the famous words occur: 'Here there is more emphasis on the Word than on the symbols, for the Sermon is nothing else than a proclamation of Christ's word which He spoke Himself and which the Mass repeats "This is my body, this is my blood", etc. What is the Gospel itself other than a proclamation of this testament? With these words Christ has condensed the whole Gospel in a short summary. For the Gospel is nothing else than a proclamation of divine grace and the forgiveness of all sins, given to us through the passion of our Saviour.'[8]

Thus the first charge against the Catholic celebration of the Mass is that it has turned Christ's promise into a 'secret' word of consecration. 'Has not the devil stolen the chief part of the Mass from us in his own masterly way, and left us with a silence?' 'But what demon has told them that this word, which ought to be the most universal and public of all amongst Christians—clergy and laity, men and women, young and old alike—should be shrouded in the greatest secrecy? For "this word is God's own vow and promise and testament". There is indeed "much more emphasis on the word than on the symbols". It is possible to have this sacrament without the symbols, but not without these words of promise "without which the Sacrament is a dead nothing". Where the words are suppressed less than half the Mass is retained.'[9]

These words are answered on the human side by faith, which receives them as God requires. Indeed there is no other way to receive the promise than in faith,[10] and it is given us for faith's sake. 'For the Mass counts most with him who has most faith; it is adapted to faith, and to nothing else at all.'[11] For the Sacrament 'does nothing of itself without faith. Indeed God Himself who governs everything, can do no good to a man unless he has firm faith. How much less then can the Sacrament achieve alone?'[12] Where the Sacrament is not related to faith it becomes idolatry, and because it has not been rightly understood it 'must of necessity follow' that confidence rests upon what is done, and the people think that they are doing God a service. But that simply turns the

---

[8] WA 6, 374.   [9] WA 6, 363.   [10] WA 6, 514.
[11] WA 6, 375.   [12] WA 6, 371.

Mass into its opposite, 'for a testament is no *beneficium acceptum, sed datum*'.[13] 'Where is the heir who, because he wants to do his father or his benefactor a favour, simply accepts the testamentary document instead of the inheritance that has been left him?'[14] Wherever the Mass is conceived of as a 'work', it cannot be understood as 'God's word or promise, and a sacred symbolism of bread and wine, under which Christ's flesh and blood truly are'.[15] But if the Mass is not a 'work', then it cannot be celebrated for others, and cannot benefit them, for faith is not transferable.[16] And a third error, perhaps the worst of all,[17] follows from this, the understanding of the Mass as a sacrifice. This is to lose the whole Gospel, Christ, comfort, and all God's grace, for it is 'to give something to God in the Sacrament so that He should in return give us everything'.[18] Certainly we should at all times bring ourselves as a sacrifice to God, but such a sacrifice does not belong 'essentially and necessarily to the Mass'.[19] Only in connection with the prayers which we lay on Christ, and which He in turn offers to the Father, can Luther find place for the notion of sacrifice here. At the same time it is clear in the 'Babylonian Captivity' how little Luther will attack the Mass from this point. He contents himself with suggesting a re-application of the sacrificial language to the unconsecrated elements or the prayers.[20] He has very little to say about the *Communio sub utraque*. 'For there is more emphasis on the Word than on the symbols.'[21] The withholding of the cup is an instance of Papal arbitrariness, which can be tolerated because the Word is more important than the symbols, though that does not mean we can neglect them.

It is clear that everything is made to depend on the idea of the Word as an effective promise. The secret reading of the words of institution and the neglect of preaching are signs of God's wrath, a signal showing how much hold on the Gospel has been lost. To prevent the understanding of the Sacrament as a divine promise and so to destroy the Church is the work of the devil. The suppression of the Word in the Mass shows 'without doubt that nowadays all priests and monks, including the bishops, and their spiritual superiors, are idolaters, living in the greatest danger through such ignorance, misuse, and derision of the Mass, or

[13] WA 6, 364.	[14] WA 6, 520.	[15] WA 6, 365.
[16] WA 6, 521.	[17] WA 6, 365.	[18] WA 6, 368.
[19] WA 6, 368.	[20] WA 6, 524.	[21] WA 6, 374.

Sacrament, or promise of God'.[22] *The reformed doctrine of the Word as God's means of communication and God's promise*, and the corresponding doctrine of faith as the one service man can render is the starting-point and the concern of the critique of the Mass.

This is manifest all through Luther's 'Babylonian captivity of the Church', especially in the third part of the section dealing with the Sacrament. And here Luther discusses transubstantiation and the *communio sub utraque*, and introduces the question of conformity to Scripture. *Communio sub utraque* is required because it conforms to Scripture. Nothing scriptural must be altered, because even with *one* alteration in what Christ instituted, all His commandments are reduced to nothing. 'For in holy Scripture above everything else the whole is bound up with each individual part.'[23] The issue here is about an express command of Christ Himself, which neither Church nor Pope has the authority to modify or change. They must not derogate Christ's words. So Luther concludes that it is 'godless and tyrannical' to withhold the cup from the laity; not even an angel dares do that—how much less should a Pope or an ecclesiastical council![24]

These same considerations govern the discussion of transubstantiation. Transubstantiation is confessedly a doctrine of Thomistic schoolmen; but it is no article of faith. To put it quite simply, it is superfluous. Its rejection rests upon the exegetical principle that neither men nor angels must distort the meaning of God's words; rather must they be left, *quantum fieri potest*, in their simplest meanings. So unless some special considerations prevent it, they should be understood in their natural and grammatical meaning, and so give no occasion to the opponents of the Gospel to scoff.[25] But here no such considerations apply. So it is far better to believe with the people that Christ's flesh and blood is truly comprised here. The disastrous thing is to make Aristotle a judge of such high matters. 'Why not dismiss such impertinent curiosity and simply abide by Christ's words, giving up all claim to know what happens at the Mass, content only that the true body is really there, in virtue of the words of consecration? Is it necessary for us fully to comprehend the ways and means by which God acts?'[26] It is indeed past mortal understanding how the bread is Christ's body; but the believer willingly yields his

[22] WA 6, 517.   [23] WA 6, 503.   [24] WA 6, 506.
[25] WA 6, 509.   [26] WA 6, 510.

intellect in obedience to Christ, and simply and firmly believes, not only that Christ's body is in the bread but that the bread is Christ's body, as the words of institution say. *Maior est spiritus sanctus quam Aristoteles*. Remember that reason itself can come no nearer to understanding Christ in His two natures!

II

We have so far made clear the two things which were decisive for Luther. The Sacrament is to be understood as the promise and gift of God by which the troubled believer receives faith and consolation and strength; and it must be understood in obedience to the given test of Scripture without recourse to the intellect. Luther's opponents seemed to him to fail on both these counts. Rejection of his conception of the Sacrament involved an inevitable and immediate contradiction of his conception of faith, i.e. it implied another doctrine of the Holy Spirit, of certainty and assurance and consolation in the Gospel. Moreover, this contradiction seemed to him so badly grounded exegetically that he could not treat his opponents seriously, and in their own right, but saw them as another form of the rationalistic aims which in the Roman Church had made use of Aristotle. So it was no small issue that was at stake for Luther. To attack his understanding of the Eucharist was to attack his understanding of salvation and of the Scriptures, and to give a place to the intellect which it did not merit. Verily for Luther this was a *contentio de fide*.

These three considerations dominate his controversy with *Karlstadt*. As to the first: Karlstadt 'wants to reach the spiritual prematurely', but he fails to show how the spirit reaches us. With impressive ardour Luther defends the proposition 'that the outward should and must precede the inward, and the inward come only after and through the outward; which means that God has decided to give the inward to no man save through the outward'.[27] He holds to the view that forgiveness of sins should be received in the Sacrament. And he sees his opponents as 'miserable, stupid, hopeless, melancholy souls, who fear the sound of a rustling leaf, and do not fear God—as is the way of the ungodly (Psalm 36. 2)—and in addition freely criticise His actions and His words'.[28] Behind Karlstadt's conception of the symbolic stands

[27] WA 18, 136.   [28] WA 18, 134.

the theology of 'experience', and the consequent presumptuous sense of security of the man who wants to live by the richness of his own experience, and so has no use for the Word. Karlstadt's reliance upon subtle reason is part of this presumption, for this is offered as above all things the reason for basing upon John 6. 63 the view that the flesh of Christ is of no benefit at all.[29] Naturally, then, the chief concern here is the exegesis of the words of institution and their protection against Karlstadt's sophistical and pedantic interpretation.

But Luther finds the same themes recurring in Zwingli, though in his case with better presentation and surer foundation. Thus in the writings against Zwingli there are many references to his earlier works. Hence, too, the occasional judgment that the Swiss reformer meant to fall back entirely on an inner word.[30] So here, too, there was a fight about the Word, and so in consequence about the distribution and the consolation of the Sacrament. For Luther it was the authority of Scripture both in principle and in fact that was at stake over against the claims of reason (Zwingli) or subjectivity (Schwenkfeld). Zwingli's rhetoric and Schwenkfeld's mysticism are alike in that they treat the Word lightly.[31] This point is made most clearly in the *Syngramma der Schwaben* which Luther twice published, and which is directed against Oekolampad's defence of the Zwinglian position.[32] Here Luther puts in the very centre of his thinking the conception of a miraculous creative Word which bestows as it promises; and so this work is one of the most noteworthy of the whole Reformation.

Luther repeats against Zwingli his distinction between the *meritum Christi* (on the cross) and the *distributio meriti* (in the Sacrament). In the Eucharist there is conveyed forgiveness 'not because of what is eaten', 'but because of the Word, by which He dispenses so costly a forgiveness amongst us, and says: This is my body, which is given for you'.[33] Against this position Zwingli held that *factum* and *usum* were one; they flow into each other 'like waters into the sea'. But Luther sees an immediate parallel: for even Romans 1.16 does not call the Gospel a power of God, but a sign of His power. So he rejects Zwingli's distinction

---

[29] WA 18, 182, 192.   [30] WA 26, 489.   [31] WA 26, 449.

[32] Printed in Ch. M. Pfaff, *Acta et Scriptura Ecclesiae*, *Wittenberg*. Tübingae, 1720.

[33] WA 26, 294.

C

between God's commandments and 'such discourses or speeches which simply inform us of what took place', by which distinction we are said to be able to repeat the latter without actually effecting anything.[34] Zwingli maintained, *quod verbum facti non efficiat factum, sed narret factum*;[35] Luther answered: What God says, He can also do.[36] It follows therefore for him that our Lord's command to repeat the sacramental actions implies that everything occurs as the words state. He says 'it is sophistry and puerility in handling God's Word' to think of the words simply as narrative. God 'has bound His promise and His action to our speech'.[37]

So now once more in this controversy the 'sign' has come to the fore and assumes a critical significance. But here too the issue is about the Word, in so far as the validity of these actual words is questioned, one letter of which is, for Luther, greater than the whole world; 'for whoever despises one single Word of God, of a certainty has nothing greater that he can despise'.[38] His opponents succeed in making the text uncertain! Or they mingle 'Reason' with it as they maintain: *Absurditas huius sensus repugnaret intellectui etiam fideli.*[39] That is to say, the issue here is the understanding of the whole Christian faith. 'If a line encircling a besieged town is broken, the town is no longer encircled, and the ring round it gradually breaks up.'[40] And further, the issue is about the proper exegesis of Scripture, which should not be distorted by reading into it the deliverances of Reason. The rationalism of such exegesis and Luther's opposition to it can be seen most clearly in the doctrine of Christ's ascension. 'They say it is a contradiction for Christ's body to be both in heaven and in the Eucharist. But they offer no proof. So we say in opposition that there is no contradiction whatever, since both are in fact attested by Scripture. And our "no" is just as strong as their "yes".'[41] 'I always hope that their handling of Scripture could match their handling of their own dreams.'[42] Perhaps the thing that agitated Luther most was that Zwingli did not at this point understand his questions and so dismissed his objections quite superficially. Luther sees here no seriousness, but plain wantonness, blasphemy against God.[43] And this showed itself not only in the results but in the exegetical

[34] WA 26, 282.   [35] WA 26, 285.   [36] WA 54, 157.
[37] WA 26, 284.   [38] WA 26, 450.   [39] WA 26, 286.
[40] WA 54, 158.   [41] WA 26, 314.   [42] WA 26, 288.
[43] WA 26, 305; 54, 154.

method itself. So far Luther's fight against Zwingli is in fact the same as that which he fought against Erasmus. What he had once found in the garb of humanist scepticism he finds anew in the hermeneutic devices of *tropus*, *heterosis*, and *alloiosis*—the devil's larvae, and Scripture's 'mistress'.[44] This exegesis is for him a dangerous folly, though one which can easily be seen through. Wantonly is the man lost who lets himself be led astray by it, 'because he will not do what is necessary for him to see how he is made a fool of'.[45] So it follows that the Church is robbed of Christ, as man and as God, by Reason; for how can anyone believe in the article about Christ becoming man if he has no belief in the Eucharist? Such an exegesis 'results in such a Christ as I would not want to imitate, that is to say, that henceforth Christ neither is nor does with His life and passion any more than any other poor saint'.[46] It appears a simple consequence of all this that the fight should continue in a controversy over Christology. In reference to this it is said that Luther held Zwingli and his teaching to be definitely un-Christian.[47] For him this fight is a struggle with the devil himself, and Zwingli and Oekolampad are the devil's ambassadors.[48]

Luther's own interpretation of the words of institution is well known. By the aid of a figure of speech (*synecdoche*) and the additional help of the doctrine of ubiquity he so interprets the 'is' as to maintain in the strongest language the presence of the body and blood of Christ. Even for the unworthy and the godless the presence is there, and of such a kind that the body of Christ is bitten with the teeth, but yet again of such a kind as to leave the presence completely incomprehensible and irrational, in so far as the 'inherence' is not in any way to be understood locally. The opposition to transubstantiation is quite clear but not essential. Whether bread and wine are left after consecration is not worth a moment's argument for Luther.[49] Yet it must be noted that even where he speaks of ubiquity he intends to introduce no new doctrine, but merely to show that in some measure the 'inherence' can be made apprehensible by reason, and how little the pietists reckon with the divine omnipotence. But this is not put forward as the indispensable and obligatory foundation of eucharistic

[44] WA 26, 319; 346.   [45] WA 26, 427.   [46] WA 26, 319.
[47] WA 26, 342.   [48] WA 26, 402; 437.   [49] WA 26, 462.

doctrine. 'Let them have the choice and themselves try to speak in simpler fashion.'[50]

It is understandable then that Luther never consciously gives an account of what the 'use' of this bodily presence is. Once indeed he can say that the body and blood are a nourishment unto eternal life. He can say that it is no small matter to touch the body of Christ, or be touched by it, as happened in some of the familiar gospel stories; or he can say that Christ's blood is not powerless as to be simply a sign of the new covenant. The presence of Christ hidden in the eucharistic elements is a 'sign' in the same sense as the earthly life of Jesus was a 'sign'.[51] But in all such sayings he does not argue from the use of the presence, but from the text of Scripture, for the understanding of which, to be sure, the *analogia fidei*, the *analogia* of *his* faith is normative.

III

The Marburg conversations produced at any rate some understanding, in that Luther saw that his opponents did not mean to say that there was only bread present, 'but the body and blood were there too, though not corporally but spiritually'.[52] But after that the inner disunity of Protestantism showed itself in the Parliament of Augsburg in 1530, when it proved necessary to submit not one but three confessions to the Emperor. Immediately after the Parliament, when it became clear that opposition from the Emperor was unavoidable, Bucer began his efforts at mediation which after lengthy negotiations led to the Concord of Wittenberg in 1536. Luther often emphasised how much the Concord meant to him.

Bucer himself had already come a good way. He had attached himself to Zwingli, and by his work on Lutheran writings had given his attention to the cause of the conflict. He now advocated the spiritual presence, which Zwingli had also conceded: *verum corpus vere dari*,[53] and indeed said that Christ was truly present in the Eucharist, i.e. 'He is present in the bread, in our own mouth and body.'[54] This seemed to Luther to assist the Concord, so long

---

[50] WA 26, 451.   [51] WA 26, 478.
[52] WA 54, 153. For the following, cp. E. Bizer, *Studien*, etc., 1939.
[53] Op. 11, Nr. 1,157.
[54] Lenz, Correspondence, etc., 1, 27.

as it was made clear that the body of Christ is in the *signs*. 'This article must be clearly expressed in the formula of concord.'[55] It is obvious why he was so emphatic on the point: for only so is the independence of the gift from our subjective experience guaranteed. As early as the first negotiations in Coburg, Luther had called attention to the two points of Bucer's position which failed to satisfy him. He objected to Bucer's idea that the body of Christ could be eaten in a spiritual manner only, and so could only be received by believers. This latter point, the *manducatio impiorum*, came increasingly to the fore. Luther states the grounds for his position explicitly: the gift we receive must remain undivided; it should and it must remain independent of the recipient's faith. But for Bucer and his associates the formula 'spiritually' or 'by the Spirit' remained characteristic. Luther, however, because of his insistence that the body is given even to the *godless*, was not willing to go further, and preferred 'the modest agreement with its modest truce' to an ambiguous unity.[56]

By 1531 Bucer seemed already to have reached in essentials the position which received sanction at Wittenberg. But he knew that the Swiss would not go so far with him. He had indeed persuaded the South German cities, but could not bring Zwingli to agreement. In 1532 the cities adopted the Augsburg Confession alongside their own, but in Frankfurt and Augsburg alike this partial unity begat only further confusion. This caused Luther to explain to the Frankfurters that in his view the claim that the body is given to the godless could not be met by the concession of a spiritual presence.[57] He sent an open challenge to Augsburg.[58] On his own premises Bucer could not admit that the godless partook of the body, though he went so far as to say: 'But yet those who have an historical faith eat the body of Christ together with the bread, though they eat it to judgment.'[59] Bucer could say this because, when all has been said, an historical faith is still the work of the Holy Spirit. Luther could find it acceptable, because it left the gift in the Eucharist independent of the inner experience of the recipient.

The next step was a meeting in December 1534 between Bucer and Melanchthon at Cassel, after both sides had shared in some admittedly difficult co-operation in Wurttemburg. The meeting

[55] WA Br 6, 29.   [56] WA Br 6, 24.   [57] WA 30, III, 543, 564.
[58] WA Br 6, 510.   [59] Bizer, p. 63.

convinced Melanchthon of Bucer's good will, but in addition
Luther himself could no longer find it possible to reject the results
of the conversations.[60] He simply wanted to wait until the
troubled waters on either side had settled. For Bucer had now
made his position clear in a negative manner: there was a rejection
of the *coniunctio physica*, of every kind of materialisation of the
body of Christ, of the *opus operatum*. But positively Bucer also
admitted the reception and participation of the body in terms of
Luther's own explanation by *synecdoche*. From the critical standpoint the question does not seem to have been the *manducatio
impiorum*. But Bucer was once again rejected by the Swiss. Bullinger would have nothing to do with the Lutheran understanding
of the 'exhibition' of Christ's body, i.e. the Lutheran idea of the
Word; neither the ministrant nor the Word bestow the eucharistic
gift. *Si quicquam post Deum exhibet corpus Christi verum, ipsa fides,
quae et ipsa donum Dei est, exhibet; sine hac minister nihil nisi signum
exhibet. Ubi vero fides est, fidei beneficio non verborum aut ministerii,
exhibetur corpus Christi.*[61] Here once more in actual fact the point
at issue was the nature and scope of faith's activity. The outcome
was only new misgiving, and new dissension. Bullinger had really
put his finger on the sore point. Bucer himself declared afterwards
in a public statement from the pulpit that he had so far learnt
nothing of the *administration* of the body and blood.[62]

Augsburg gave rise to the final step, for it had an urgent interest
in the public confirmation of the agreement. The preachers there
succeeded in overcoming Luther's suspicion of Bucer's fundamental position, and they tried to arrange a general assembly of
all South Germans with Luther. Bucer gave an explicit assurance
that the charge against him was false, viz. 'that we make the
presence of the body and blood of Christ in the sacrament depend
on our faith, as though Christ's body and blood would not be
present if no one believed'. Much rather, he affirmed, his position
should be put by saying 'that the body and blood of Christ is
truly present, not on account of our worthiness or unworthiness,
but only through and in virtue of the institution of Christ'.[63]

In the Wittenberg negotiations Luther once more called the
whole matter in question. He suspected some deception was being
practised, since he had got an impression from certain letters and

[60] CR II, 823, 827; WA 38, 300.   [61] *Studien*, p. 84.
[62] Germann, Forster, pp. 55, 57.   [63] WA Br 7, 272.

writings that the Swiss were definitely not in agreement with him, and the others not very much either. But it was no good covering the old errors up under a cloak of peace. For this reason his demands were sharp and clear: the retraction of the old teaching and an acknowledgment of the *manducatio oralis* and the *manducatio impiorum*.

Bucer agreed to the retraction inasmuch as he had not previously understood Luther's teaching aright. The *manducatio oralis*, however, he explained by saying that the (terrestrial) mouth could not really touch or contain the (celestial) body; yet that the body of Christ was so related to the bread as to enable it to be said that the body was taken in the hand, in the mouth, even in the stomach. That is, he conceived of the presence of Christ *cum pane*. The *manducatio impiorum* he rejected as far as it concerned the 'entirely godless, who had no belief in the words of the Sacrament'. The Eucharist was not instituted for them, i.e. the promises did not concern them, and so they received nothing. But anyone who partook 'without the faith that makes a man really godly' simply in the *fides historica*, 'he receives, with the godly, the body and blood of the Lord', though he receives it to judgment. To avoid the doctrine of the *opus operatum* he simply says that the body of the Lord is 'offered and administered' to the faithless in precisely the same way as to the believers, but that the faithless partake of it simply *sacramentaliter*, and do not eat *re vera*. In the same way the Gospel is preached to the believer and unbeliever alike, but is not really received by the latter.

But that is not enough for Luther! It fails to explain the presence of Christ 'by virtue of Christ or through His power', but rather explains it in terms of the power of faith and of our own thoughts, which 'create' the presence. For Luther the Word is not 'for the first time true when we believe it'. So the point at issue, the *contentio de fide*, is once more sharply defined. After that, however, agreement is reached by saying that the *unworthy* receive the body of the Lord. Here Bucer made his position quite clear, that the sacramental gift was only 'shown and offered' to the faithless, because the institution of Christ must not be made to depend upon faith; yet the faithless take and receive the signs only, not the substance. But if anyone believes the words of institution at all, he receives what the words say, to salvation or damnation. Later on Bucer so expounded this position as to say that *dead* faith truly receives the body and blood. Therewith Luther confessed himself content; he had 'no wish to quarrel' about the godless. 'Because matters are with you as with us, we are at one, and we recognise and receive you as our dear brothers in the Lord, so far as concerns this article.' 'And Capito and Bucer began to weep, and then on both sides we gave thanks to God, with clasped hands and reverent demeanour.' On the basis of the negotiations Melanchthon drew up the agreement, and once more pointed out expressly to Bugenhagen the remaining points of difference. The article itself states 'that even to the *unworthy* the body and blood of Christ are truly distributed and that the unworthy truly receive the same, thus fulfilling the institution and the command of the Lord Christ'. But such persons receive them to their judgment 'because they misuse them'.

After so much negotiation and enquiry, even after the Witten-berg Conference itself, there can be no doubt at all that Luther thoroughly understood Bucer's reservation. Bucer had but given expression to the view he had long since held. Moreover there can be no doubt that Bucer had parted from Zwinglianism and drawn nearer to Luther. He now recognised the external presence of the supernatural body and its distribution by the ministrant. But there remains the distinction that for him the bread *is* not the body, but that it is with or alongside the body, so that both are present together. The *synecdoche* is, as it were, a somewhat looser bond than with Luther. Christ is to be related to the bread much as the hand is related to the gift which it offers. But in this way he gains the advantage of being able to understand the presence as the presence of a *person*. He is always repeating the formula: 'The body and blood of Christ, that is to say, Christ Himself.' But his stubborn rejection of the *manducatio impiorum* is no isolated polemic, but part and parcel of his whole way of thinking about the body of Christ, which is something sublime, above the world of the mind, and to be apprehended by the believing soul alone. The unbeliever lacks the means to receive what is offered him. Consequently he receives nothing, not because nothing is offered him, but because he is unable to lay hold of what it is.

The fact that at this point, when Bucer's position lay before him in full and written detail, Luther yielded and never afterwards revoked the Concord shows to what conclusions it came. When Bucer had come so far to meet him, no one was in danger of not receiving what he believed himself to receive. So no one was betrayed. And no one could make the reality of the eucharistic gift dependent upon the recipient's faith. Bucer's admission that even dead faith receives the eucharistic gift implies that faith is the instrument of our knowledge, that it does not create the sacrament and is not itself the *Mysterium*. The dispute is thus no longer a *contentio de fide* and so could be forgotten. On a later occasion Luther once said to Bucer that he had never been concerned about the ways and means of the presence and its reception, but always about the presence and its reception themselves; and he added that he, Luther, could put up with more than could others of his like-minded brethren. That rightly describes his position: he saw the boundaries within which intercommunion was possible.[64]

By contrast in Switzerland no concordat was achieved. Differences were recognised. Wittenberg upheld an objective meeting with Christ, but the Swiss maintained that 'the fruit and use of the body is only truly shared, understood and received by faith'.[65] They stood by their previous statements and position: a separation between the sign and the reality, participation only by the believing soul and by true faith. Luther was prepared to give them time for consideration, too, for he saw the inadequacy of their position.[66] But the Swiss did not see their previous confessions as steps on the way to the truth which could now be left behind, but rather as the truth itself. The Swiss found the mediators from Strassburg, who for their part spoke with great candour, just tedious. They were honest enough to see that their position could not be reconciled with the Lutheran.[67] So in 1544 Luther himself opened up the cleavage afresh, so as to show the whole world once more that he wanted to have no dealings at all with the Zwinglians. He was content that in their written answer to him[68] they had clearly shown that he had rightly interpreted the situation. *Nam hoc petivi, hoc volui illo meo scripto, quo offensi sunt, ut testimonio publico suo testarentur, sese esse hostes meos.*[69]

---

[64] *Studien*, p. 198.   [65] *Studien*, p. 149 f.   [66] WA Br 8, 149.
[67] WA 54, 119.   [68] Extracts can be found in WA 54, 126 ff.
[69] WA Br 11, 264.

IV

This was the same position that Luther held over against Melanchthon.[70]

Melanchthon had the same concerns as Luther and gave away nothing that was of importance to him. There is no real room for doubt about that. Evidence is provided in Melanchthon's judgment on the Swiss: 'they maintain that the Sacrament is not a sign of God's good will towards us, but only a sign of our belief'; they acknowledge no presence of Christ, but a mere representation, as if in some tragedy; and their conception of Christ is rationalist and philosophical, for they think He is tied to some quarter of heaven, just as Homer imagined his Jupiter to be.[71] So it is clear that for Melanchthon the Sacrament is a sign of God's good will towards us, that something more than a mere dramatic representation takes place, namely an actual *actio* of God: Christ must remain free from spatial restrictions, and there is nothing here that is subject to the adjudication of reason.

Nevertheless his standpoint is clearly distinguished from the Lutheran. The difference is twofold. First, he is not concerned about the words of institution. It seems that he never dealt with these systematically. Rather does he clarify their meaning by theological reflection on the possibility of the presence of Christ. Thus in the 'Admonition', which he composed in 1534 for Philip of Hesse: if Jesus were a creature and not at the same time God, then He would rule the world, and for that reason could not be with us. But through His divinity He shares in God's omnipresence. 'Therefore I conclude that with the bread and wine there is not figuratively, but really, the body and blood of Christ, that is to say, Christ Himself. So we must keep hold of the words, which are our witness that Christ means to be with us, that He is essentially with us; and for a witness that He is with us, He says, He gives us His body, and in that way indicates that He is not just another creature exalted over and above us, but that He is essentially and actually present with us.'[72] But perhaps the more important difference is the second, that Melanchthon associates the presence of Christ with the eucharistic *action*, not with the

---

[70] For the following cp. H. Gollwitzer, *De coena Domini*, 1937, p. 65 ff. I certainly cannot accept all his conclusions.

[71] CR 21, 467; 1, 1,048, 974.   [72] CR 2, 800.

eucharistic elements. *Sacramentum* and *ceremonia* are for him identical in meaning. He can say: 'Christ is present in His Sacrament,
not because the priest effects some change, or because the words
that he utters possess a certain power to change the elements,
but because he purposely performs the rite which Christ has
instituted.'[73] Or again, 'Christ is present in the action which He
has instituted as an *agens liberum*; He does not choose to be
enclosed in the bread after the eucharistic action is over; that is,
He is not "tied" to the bread.'[74]

But in the celebration of the Eucharist there is achieved a real
meeting of the risen and regnant Christ with the person who
celebrates. This is a truly objective meeting, a true *actio Christi*
which is bound up with the elements, i.e. does not occur simply
in the devout soul. Melanchthon tried to convince Bucer that
Christ was present *cum signo*, just as God was not present in the
Holy of Holies simply to the souls of the saints, but also at the
Mercy Seat itself;[75] he taught that with the signs Christ was
present *efficax*.[76] The signs are thus not 'empty signs' but *signa
exhibitiva*, 'of which the taking and receiving should be done in
such a manner as to become at the same time the taking and
receiving of the body of Christ'—*quo posito aliud ponitur*.[77] For
Christ has bound Himself at this point by a *pactum*,[78] i.e. here, at
this point, the meeting of Christ and the worshipper is accomplished.

This connection of Christ's presence in the Eucharist with the
rite or ceremony meant that the 'event-character' of the meeting
between Christ and the worshipper was strongly emphasised. It
followed only on the *act* of eating and drinking. It was impossible
in any way to retain the presence in the elements. On these
premisses catholic abuses could be avoided. There is no transubstantiation or change; there is no adoration of the Sacrament,
and to carry it round in procession is idolatry. Such practices
denote a materialisation of the divine, a limitation of divine
freedom. But God is not a 'thing' at man's disposal, so that it can
be said (as Osiander did) that the bread is our God.

But it is now quite plain that Melanchthon was perfectly well
aware of his differences from Luther, in whose position he saw
the danger of the *inclusio Christi in pane*. He was, for example,

[73] CR 15, 1,109.   [74] CR 5, 208.   [75] CR 2, 470.
[76] CR 3, 514.   [77] CR 2, 808.   [78] CR 2, 224; 315.

greatly disturbed that Luther should have left transubstantiation as an option for the evangelicals of Venice.[79] For his part he contested this change-effecting power of the Word.[80] In particular he rejected Luther's doctrine of ubiquity as a new doctrine in conflict with tradition, because it nullified the reality of the body. A body which was really ubiquitous seemed no longer a body to Melanchthon. To this extent he is at one with the Reformed theologians. His special achievement, however, was his belief that he could give an adequate basis to the real presence of Christ without having recourse to this auxiliary aid. A real body confessedly requires a real place for itself; so the distance between Christ and ourselves must be overcome. So Melanchthon combined two affirmations which at that time seemed irreconcilable. At one and the same time he affirmed the spatial separation of Christ from us, *and* His real presence with us. But he did it in such a way as to avoid for the most part all speculation about it. He could also say that for Christ all places are alike present. Finally he understood the *communicatio idiomatum* in such a way that the human nature of Christ, though not His human body, partook of the divine omnipresence; so human nature and the human body are not for him identical in meaning.

This clearly raises the question anew—how far can he speak of a real presence. He does it himself repeatedly, as indeed seems to him to be required by the words of institution. On this point those words are for Melanchthon, as for others, an immutable norm, and in this respect he is a pure Lutheran. His answer goes something like this: Christ has Himself related His presence to the process of eating and drinking, and in that process He deals with men according to His human nature. Since it is *His* dealing that takes place, He is *wholly* there, i.e. present also with His *body*. There can of course be no question of an identity of the bread and wine with the body and blood of Christ; but Christ makes use of these elements to hide Himself beneath them.

Somehow it always happened that Melanchthon kept silent about the *manducatio oralis*. But we can easily infer what that silence meant, from his general position. All things considered, it seems right to say that had the matter been of importance for him he would have given it some emphasis. But the fact seems to be that the *manducatio oralis* cannot be given a place in his

[79] CR 5, 208.   [80] CR 15, 1,109.

system. In some form or other it presupposes a change in the
elements. And yet it is not possible on that account to say that
the godless and the unworthy receive nothing in the Eucharist,
for Christ really comes to them, though their unbelief neither
sees nor recognises Him. In so far as this blindness is an offence,
it is an offence against Christ. But the meeting with Christ rests
upon His institution, and His will, not upon our faith. So the
godless in fact savour nothing, though the position is avoided
where the doubter can only reach assurance about the eucharistic
gift by gaining assurance about his own faith. This does not alter
the admittedly unusual way in which Melanchthon says that the
forgiveness of sins is not received in the Eucharist, 'but I seek the
forgiveness of sins in the Word, i.e. through faith *per verbum
commonefactus in filium Dei*'. His contemporaries understood by
that 'that he meant to say that we are only reminded of the forgiveness of sins in the Eucharist, but do not actually receive it
there'.[81] Sometimes the proclamatory nature of the Word is
watered down to a mere *commonefactio*, so that the Sacrament in
turn threatens to become a mere memorial. This is the critical
point in Melanchthon's whole theology, not only in his doctrine
of the Eucharist. All that he says is that here faith is nourished and
strengthened, and yet again, not so that this faith must have its
own certainty in itself. The essential thing remains that Christ
waits on the elements. The outer and the inner effects are not
divided into two actions. From its meeting with Christ faith
creates a new assurance.

So far then, and these considerations seem to me decisive,
Melanchthon's doctrine of the Eucharist is strongly Lutheran in
character. Yet in other directions it is as un-Lutheran as it could
possibly be. But if ever it fell to Luther to bring peace to a
troubled conscience, he had no need to turn to Melanchthon!

There can hardly be any doubt at all that Luther was quite well
aware of the differences. It would have been a singular coming
together of the two great theologians in the little town if Luther
had not failed to note them, or if Melanchthon had been obliged
to conceal his opinions for upwards of ten years. Indeed we know
that Melanchthon was sometimes apprehensive that Luther's
attack would be directed against himself,[82] for example, on the

[81] CR 10, 812; 8, 937.
[82] WA 54, 123; CR 5, 476, 462, 473 f., 499. Enders, 16, 59.

occasion of Luther's final missive against the Swiss. It was then that he no longer dared to pass on a letter of Bucer's to Luther, and wanted to leave Wittenberg. His fears were groundless, if Luther knew nothing of the differences between them. And yet Luther did not turn against him; on the contrary, on 12th November 1544, six weeks after the completion of the Shorter Catechism, he wrote to the Italians that if they should ever hear that Luther or Melanchthon had consented to the *furor* of the sacramentarians, they should, for the Lord's sake, not believe it. Unless one is willing to ascribe complete blindness to Luther and a wholly unworthy dissimulation to Melanchthon there remains but one possible conclusion, that Luther really saw the differences, and in spite of them found no occasion to proceed against Melanchthon, i.e. that here too he maintained intercommunion in spite of another conception of the circumstances and nature of the presence of Christ in the Eucharist.

V

Bucer himself never came to his full fruition as a theologian. After the Schmalkaldic war he did not venture to go to Switzerland,[83] but sought exile in England, where he died. In Strassburg itself the Lutherans entered upon his inheritance. Melanchthon recorded their agreement in the *Confessio Augustana variata*, and himself appealed to it from time to time.[84] It was in fact very well adapted to his own outlook. But he, too, was disposed of by the strict Lutherans. Calvin then became Bucer's disciple and heir. The question arises whether in his sacramental doctrine he keeps to the lines laid down in the Concord, whether, that is, his teaching really maintains a middle position between Luther and Zwingli, or whether, as his Lutheran opponents claimed, he was not the real pacemaker of Zwinglianism, the *princeps omnium superiorum et posteriorum Sacramentariorum*, whose distinction it was to defend the Zwinglian error better than anyone else.[85]

At any rate Calvin himself was quite clear about his deviation from Luther. In the 1536 edition of the Institutes he very distinctly rejected Consubstantiation, the presence of the glorified

[83] CR 13, Nr. 1,240.
[84] Wolters, *Konrad von Heresbach*, 1867, p. 272.
[85] Westphal, Correspondence 1, 263.

body, and the identification of the elements with the body and blood of Christ. In 1538 he says that Luther outstrips Marcion in his teaching about the body of Christ.[86] But his rejection of Zwingli (and of the Service which was held in Zurich) is even sharper. He had shared in a number of sessions with the Swiss, when they were discussing the Concord, though without himself actually taking part in them; and in the end he acknowledged the Concord during his stay in Strassburg (1538-41). Otherwise he would hardly have been accepted in Strassburg; and yet he pronounced publicly upon it,[87] and was known in Wittenberg as Bucer's companion and on occasion was the subject of friendly reference by Luther. He conducted a friendly correspondence with Melanchthon, but also with Brenz and Andreae. The Lutherans could not think of him as one of themselves, but he must have appeared to them as a man who stood for the ideas of the Concord.

Luther had formulated his requirements: subordination to the text of Scripture, so that exegesis should not be complicated by rationalistic deductions, and recognition of the objective and therefore oral reception of the eucharistic gift, even by the unworthy. But no one criticised the Zwinglian use of Scripture more sharply than Calvin: 'If we admit your conclusions, we can no longer prove anything from Scripture,' he said to Bullinger![88] On the other hand he adopted the Reformed conception of the ascension, and at this point he did not overcome the rationalism of his predecessors, and the Lutherans saw in it a deposit of Zwinglianism: Christ was being treated like some eighth planet![89] But, like Melanchthon, he also argued for the *personal* presence of Christ, who is present *essentialiter*, that is, personally with us, and that presence takes place in the Eucharist. The Sacrament is not just a picture, but an *administratio*, a *dispensatio*, of grace, in which God uses the elements as His instruments. There are no 'empty signs', but what they represent is offered to the elect.[90] Faith and the Spirit come from the Word and Sacrament. So the Eucharist helps faith to grow.

Of course there can be no question of anything but a *spiritual* participation. Christ is personally present, that is, He is there in Spirit, and He is received in the Spirit. But it ought to be made

[86] CR 10, 2, Nr. 87.   [87] CR 9, 841.   [88] CR 12, 880.
[89] Westphal, Correspondence 1, 252.   [90] E.g. CR 12, Nr. 1,039.

quite clear at once, that what is presupposed by 'Spirit' is in no
sense to be identified with subjective assurance. 'In coming to the
Eucharist, I bring nothing of my own, but Christ offers me what
He has for my food.'[91] He adopts Bucer's position quite clearly
when he says: *Absit ut sentiam in coena tantum fideles Christo com-
municare.*[92]

Nevertheless, it is not in this manner that the 'spiritualisation'
of the Sacrament is overcome. That is shown in the following
quotation: 'while we look at the bread and wine here on earth,
we must raise our souls to heaven to partake of Christ. And *when*
we thus seek Him above the elements of this world, *then* He is
present to us'.[93] Grace is received in the Sacrament 'in so far as
everybody brings the vessel of faith with him, so as to receive
what is there represented'.[94] No one should imagine 'that we can
be united with Christ in any other way than by our rising, in our
souls, into heaven'.[95]

Such propositions provide the starting-point for Calvin's agreement with Bullinger, in which he went step by step with
Bullinger, and which was formulated in the *Consensus Tigurinus*
of 1551. But that seemed to the Lutherans to show that Calvin
also was a *tectus sacramentarius*.[96] It is understandable that the
Lutherans were provoked by this confession.[97] It is enough to
refer to what was said about the words of institution: *qui in
solemnibus coenae verbis . . . praecise litteralem sensum . . . urgent, eos
tanquam praeposteros interpretes repudiamus. Nam extra controversiam
ponimus, figurate accipienda esse, ut esse panis et vinum dicantur id quod
significant.*[98] Yet here quite obviously the lines which Luther laid
down are not followed. To be sure, the Sacrament has its reality
ex Dei parte, independent of our faith; but this reality consists in
this: *ut per ea nobis suam gratiam testetur Deus, repraesentet atque
obsignet;*[99] the elements put pictures before our eyes, *quasi in rem
ducendo*, they remind us of God's benefits, they establish and confirm His promises,[100] and yet the Spirit alone is the sole seal.[101]
The *manducatio impiorum* is expressly rejected, since not all are
capable of receiving Christ and His gifts, and everyone receives

[91] CR 12, Nr. 880.   [92] CR 7, 705.   [93] CR 12, 1,039.
[94] CR 7, 701.   [95] CR 7, 705.
[96] Westphal, Correspondence 1, 127.
[97] CR 35, 689.   [98] Chap. 22.   [99] Chap. 18.
[100] Chap. 7.   [101] Chap. 15.

the gifts *pro fidei suae mensura*.[102] The unbeliever receives no more than if he had not come,[103] and the believer gains no more than he has before he comes, for faith is required before he comes to the Sacrament. In any case this is no longer what Luther required in the Wittenberg formula; much more is it, as Bucer rightly remarked, a repetition of what had been stated in the Basle Confession[104] which at the time Luther had found inadequate for the Concordat. Indeed this statement inevitably raises the doubt whether I can receive anything directly from the Sacrament, which doubt can only be overcome if I can get an assurance that I do not doubt, but believe! The distinction becomes clear in the imagery which Calvin himself uses: just as the sun would shine in vain if God gave us no eyes to behold it, so would God enlighten us in vain through the signs if He gave us no 'eyes of the Spirit' to see them.[105] But in actual fact these two acts *must* be distinguished, the first (the shining of the sun, the illumination in the signs) is intelligible enough in itself; but as for the second (my seeing of the sun or the signs) I have to look over and beyond it for that certainty which enables me to receive the consolation of the Sacrament. In the Lutheran view the position is that God gives His gift and His Spirit in one and the same act. Is it necessary or desirable thus to reach the Spiritual prematurely? Calvin indeed maintains that grace is offered to the unworthy; but it is a conditional offer; they receive no more than an offer, and only receive the eucharistic gift itself when on their side they possess something more by the power of the Spirit.

Calvin does not confuse the nature and use of the Sacrament as his opponents accuse him of doing. But the *magna distantia* between heaven and earth brings it about that he must place the gift of the Spirit in heaven in order to have a valid Sacrament. He can indeed say that he would gladly agree with his opponents if they were of the opinion that the same gift is given to both.[106] The grounds for that are trinitarian, for Christ cannot be separated from His Spirit; that would be sacrilege. But the opponents maintain that Christ is received by the godless, about whom they themselves say that they possess not even a drop of His Spirit. So the *manducatio impiorum* is a having *Christi sine Christo, avoir Jésus Christ sans l'avoir*. But that can only be interpreted to mean that

---

[102] Chap. 18.   [103] Chap. 19.   [104] CR 13, Nr. 1,240.
[105] CR 37, 25.   [106] CR 37, 27.

in actual fact both believer and unbeliever alike receive the same thing, in so far as what *both* receive is a pointer to Christ, which only turns into the gift of His presence when we truly have Him in the Spirit!

Connected with this is the view that the character of Christ's promise or testament is no longer visible. The Confession certainly points from the signs to the *promissio*.[107] When Calvin goes into the matter in more detail[108] he only emphasises that it is through the Word that papal superstition is avoided and the Sacrament kept from becoming an ancient mystery cult. But the promise also 'leads' us to Christ. The Lutherans would say: Christ comes to us in the promise! For Calvin the promises are *scalae*, ladders, *per quae ad coelos conscendere liceat*, because Christ must not be sought elsewhere, and because we can find peace nowhere save in Him; they are *adjumenta ad se (Christum) quaerendum*. Just at the moment when it is affirmed that the Sacraments mean nothing more than the Word itself indicates, the Word is made a mere 'signpost'; it no longer does what it says. It is the Spirit who joins us to Christ and makes His gifts effective in us: and the preaching of the Gospel is no longer a 'testament' in the Lutheran sense, but only a '*testimonium*' of His work. This was given very clear expression on the Lutheran side at the time, and moreover attention was drawn to its connection with the doctrine of election.[109] If it is the case that the reception of God's gift presupposes election, must one then first be assured of election before one is sure of having the gift? But the question was asked only because even then an anti-predestinarian twist could be given to such thoughts, and that was certainly not Lutheran.[110]

So once more at this point the struggle had to become a *contentio de fide*. It is clear from his correspondence that Calvin would gladly have said more.[111] Bucer assured him that if he had not let the reins go loose he would have been unable to tighten them later. It was indeed no small matter for Calvin that he had achieved so much in Zurich. But it was at the price of the Lutherans turning against him and refusing to acknowledge his appeal to Bucer.[112] If this were Calvin's standpoint, then the

[107] Chap. 10.   [108] CR 37, 21.
[109] Westphal, Correspondence I, 247.
[110] Westphal, Correspondence I, 1,132.
[111] CR 13, 1,240.   [112] CR 37, 11.

spread of Calvinism must have seemed dangerous to them. But Calvin felt their attack to be quite unwarranted. He believed he could rightly appeal to Luther[113] and Bucer, and that he had satisfied their demands. He (rightly) defended himself against the charge that the Eucharist was for him a *nudum et inane signum*.[114] What he said was in his view a consequence of the ideas of spiritual participation and of maintaining the true corporality of Christ. But the supremacy of faith that resulted, since only faith reached to these realities, was no longer tolerable to the Lutherans. For them it was not a question of words or syllables, but of the truth of Christ's testament and of the *certitudo* of conscience, *quae ubi extra Dei vocem certo acquiescerent, non invenientur*.[115]

Melanchthon kept silence in spite of attempts to bring him out of his reserve. But here, too, Westphal saw aright, when he said that Melanchthon and Bucer alike declared *nunquam secessurus se a formula consensionis communis facta cum pluribus ex Germania superiori, anno ni fallor 36, cum Luthero*.[116] Or when he reported: *D. Philippus saepe eos revocat ad consensionem illam factam Wittembergae . . . et ea formula praecidi occasiones multorum dissidiorum et contentionum in S. Coena posse affirmat*.[117]

[113] CR 37, 18. [114] CR 37, 7.
[115] Westphal, Correspondence 1, 296.
[116] Westphal, Correspondence 1, 217.
[117] Westphal, Correspondence 1, 119.

ABBREVIATIONS

The following abbreviations were used in the foot-notes to this chapter:

CR   *Corpus Reformatorum*
WA   Works of Luther (*Weimarer Ausgabe*)
WA Br Letters of Luther (*Weimarer Ausgabe. Briefwechsel*)

III

INTERCOMMUNION FROM THE SEVENTEENTH TO THE NINETEENTH CENTURIES

*

Ernest A. Payne

Baptist Union of Great Britain and Ireland

(Great Britain)

In the period from the seventeenth to the nineteenth century the question of 'intercommunion', or—better—'mutual open communion', appears rarely to have been directly examined and discussed on doctrinal grounds by the non-Roman Churches. Where it presented itself it was as a practical issue, which arose suddenly and unexpectedly. Different Churches have taken various attitudes. In some cases, even within one communion, practice has changed, or there has been division of opinion. Outward circumstances have altered and many cross-currents of motive and belief are discernible.

The main problem only arises where there is some measure of mutual recognition of churchmanship. Where two communions have both been national Churches, the cases that have provoked discussion and action have concerned individuals who, as visitors or exiles in a foreign land, desired access to the Sacrament. Where Churches have overlapped geographically, the question has only presented itself if there has obviously been a considerable measure of common belief and practice, or if each has been strong enough to compel some kind of recognition from the other. Clearly, three different types of situation are provided by the relationships between the Protestant Churches of the Continent and the Church of England, between the Church of England and the English Free Churches, and of the Free Churches to one another. But the diverse issues involved in these three types of relationship have not always been separable from one another. Moreover, questions of discipline and the exclusion from the Sacrament of the morally unworthy have often become entangled with questions of recognition.

Even a cursory survey of the varied attitudes taken by the main Reformed traditions shows important changes of opinion and practice, and often continuing tension within individual communions. What follows makes no pretence to completeness, but the facts recorded may well be illuminating for the discussion of contemporary issues.[1]

The Lutheran Churches

In the Lutheran tradition there has been a constant emphasis on the need for doctrinal unity as the basis of church fellowship and, therefore, also of fellowship at the Eucharist (*Abendmahlsgemeinschaft*). The deadlock at Marburg in 1529 came because Luther believed that the Swiss theologians were doctrinally unsound. On his way home he put together the Schwabach Articles and declared that 'the Church is nothing else than believers in Christ who hold, believe and teach the above enumerated articles'. Later the Augsburg Confession became the accepted doctrinal standard. Though insisting that every child in the community should be baptised, Luther sought to confine the Lord's Supper to genuine Christians. In this matter of discipline he even expressed a wish for an examination prior to the Lord's Supper and suggested that participants should have special seats where they could be seen by the congregation as a whole. This is one of the points at which the German reformer approached the idea of a confessional or voluntary Church.[2] In later Lutheran practice the power of excluding manifest sinners from the Lord's Table till they gave proof of amendment rested with the ecclesiastical authorities, but the State enforced Baptism.

On a number of occasions there have been attempts at union with other Reformed Churches. The Wittenberg Concord (1536), in the negotiations for which Martin Bucer shared, was of only

---

[1] It is to be noted that the pamphlet, *Rules and Customs of Churches Concerning Intercommunion and Open Communion* (World Conference on Faith and Order, No. 99), records present practice and contains practically no historical material.

[2] Cf. Karl Holl, *Gesammelte Aufsätze*, I, p. 359: '*Volkskirche und Freiwilligkeitskirche, beides hat Luther gewollt.*'

limited range and brief duration. Of more importance for our present purpose was the *Consensus of Sendomir* (1570), which united the Lutherans, Calvinists and Bohemian Brethren of Poland and neighbouring Slavic lands. The agreement involved an exchange of preachers, the sending of delegates to one another's general synods and mutual open Communion. Though the Consensus survived effectively for only a few decades, 'the spirit of union which produced it passed into the three Brandenburg Confessions of the seventeenth century and revived in the Evangelical Union of Prussia'.[3] In central and western Germany, from the middle of the sixteenth century, there was growing division among the main Reformation traditions, in spite of several colloquies of theologians and the strenuous efforts of individuals. The Lutherans of Germany refused to recognise the union between the Lutherans of France and the Huguenots which was achieved at the Synod of Charenton (1631) and, thereafter, the Lutheran Churches of Germany and Scandinavia went their own way. The question of communion fellowship with those of other Christian traditions rarely, if ever, arose. Under the leadership of King Frederick William IV, the United Church of Prussia was established in 1817 out of Lutheran and Reformed Churches. The union was conceived as accomplished by the use of a common order for the Communion service, but the whole project caused considerable opposition and was of waning effect.

Writing of more recent practice from the standpoint of a Scandinavian Lutheran, Dr. Einar Molland says:

'As to *intercommunion*, it is impossible to provide evidence from our confessional documents. Nor have the conditions for intercommunion, as far as I know, been discussed in the leading Lutheran teaching. But I think the Lutheran attitude is clear. The Scandinavian churches practise intercommunion *inter se* and with other Lutheran churches without any regard to the existing differences of church order in the Lutheran Communion. Most members of the Scandinavian churches will feel

---

[3] P. Schaff, *History of the Creeds of Christendom*, III, pp. 386 f. Cf. G. Slosser, *Christian Unity*, pp. 36-37. For an account of an interesting but abortive early eighteenth-century attempt at union, led by a Moravian bishop and involving the Anglican Church, see Norman Sykes, *Daniel Ernst Jablonski and the Church of England*, 1950.

no obstacle against communicating, e.g. in the Anglican Church when they are permitted to do so, as they generally will have little or no hesitation respecting communicating in Reformed churches. . . . As regards the Holy Communion celebrated in our churches, we see no obstacle against admitting to it all baptised Christians who earnestly desire to receive the body and blood of Christ in our Church.'[4]

But individual cases of this kind have been relatively few till recent times. Dr. Einar Molland draws particular attention to the overwhelming confessional unity of the Scandinavian countries.[5] In the reply sent by the bishops of the Church of Sweden to the resolutions of the Lambeth Conference of 1920, it was stated that:

> 'To individual members of foreign communions who have desired more occasionally to take part in Holy Communion in our Church for the strengthening of their inner life, this right has been conceded as a duty of charity. A refusal of this right in such cases, *in casu necessitatis*, will hardly have occurred in our Church.'[6]

It was pointed out, however, that 'a concession of this right *in genere* to the members of a certain communion' would presuppose an essential doctrinal unity. There is no difficulty in the case of churches accepting the Augsburg Confession. Only in the United States do there seem to have been cases where direct acceptance of it has not been insisted on.[7]

The Zwinglian Tradition

Though there have never been 'Zwinglian Churches' in the strict sense, the attitude of Zwingli came to have considerable influence in a number of directions. Certain of Zwingli's early views on the sacraments helped to shape the attitude of the Swiss Brethren (one of the original Anabaptist groups), though on other matters the Anabaptists were sharply opposed to him. The Zurich reformer believed that it was the duty of the Christian magistracy

---

[4] *Union of Christendom* (ed. by Kenneth Mackenzie), pp. 442–443.

[5] *Ibid.*, p. 429.

[6] G. K. A. Bell, *Documents on Christian Unity*, I, p. 186. Cf. *Union of Christendom*, pp. 319–320.

[7] *Ibid.*

rather than the congregation to exercise the discipline of the Church *totius ecclesiae nomine*. In Zurich in 1532 compulsory Baptism and compulsory attendance at the Eucharist were instituted, though public sinners under judgment from the magistrates for civil offences were excluded from the Table. Parallel with this, perhaps as its consequence, went much less emphasis on any 'fencing' of the Table than was customary in Lutheran and Calvinist circles. Zwingli's doctrine *est ergo eucharistia gratiarum actio, animi exultatio, confessio* influenced many later theologians and Churches and, when any idea of compulsory attendance had been abandoned, encouraged the practice of freedom of access and an open invitation. Zwingli gave prominence to the significance of the Supper for the Church rather than for the individual. He was most anxious to distinguish the presence of Christ in the Sacrament from His full presence at the *Parousia*. These emphases, also, led to a less rigid attitude regarding those who might come to the Table.

It is to be noted that Thomas Erastus (1524-83), the professor of medicine at Heidelberg, who gave his name to 'Erastianism', a doctrine widely influential in seventeenth-century Anglicanism, was the vigorous exponent of Zwinglian teaching regarding the Lord's Supper. His theory was

> 'that the pastoral office is only persuasive, like that of a professor over his students, without any direct power; that Baptism, the Lord's Supper, and all other gospel ordinances, were free and open to all; and that the minister might state and explain what were the proper qualifications, and might dissuade the vicious and unqualified from the Communion, but had no power to refuse it, or to inflict any kind of censure. The punishment of all offences, whether of a civil or a religious nature, belonged, according to this theory, exclusively to the civil magistrate.'[8]

It has been usual to father on to Erastus theories which make the Church a mere 'creature of the State'. It should be recognised that the open invitation to the Lord's Supper favoured by many Free Churches appears to be of the same parentage.

---

[8] W. M. Hetherington, *History of the Westminster Assembly of Divines* (4th edition, ed. by R. Williamson), 1878, p. 134.

Reformed (Presbyterian) Churches

In Geneva and other Swiss cities, in large parts of Holland and in Scotland, churches of the Calvinist tradition were, or proceeded as if they were, the only churches of the area. The elders and pastors formed a consistory for purposes of discipline, fined those who failed to attend church and handed over more serious offenders to the civil power for punishment. It became customary to issue certificates or tokens (*méreaux*) to those whose religious knowledge and character were considered after examination to be satisfactory, and these admitted to the Lord's Supper. In the Reformed Church of France in the seventeenth century former adherents of the Roman Church were not received at Communion until they had been instructed in the Reformed faith and had made a public renunciation of the errors of the Mass. At the Synod of Charenton (1631)—to which allusion has already been made—it was agreed that those who accepted the Augsburg Confession should be admitted to the Lord's Table.

It is significant that at the famous Synod of Dordrecht (1618-19), attended by many members of the Dutch and other Reformed Churches, and even by some representatives of the Church of England, the Lord's Supper was not celebrated, although the proceedings lasted for some months. There is, however, considerable evidence that in the seventeenth century individual Anglicans and French Reformed churchmen had access to one another's Communion services. Pierre Du Moulin (1568-1658), who was for twenty years pastor at Charenton, visited London in 1615 and was bidden by James I to work for a union of all the Reformed Churches. He wrote:

'We assemble with the Englishmen in their churches, we participate together in the Holy Supper of our Lord, the doctrine of their Confessions is most agreeable unto ours.'[9]

Similarly, John Cosin (later Bishop of Durham), while chaplain to the Anglican royalists in Paris, regularly communicated in the Reformed Church at Charenton.

Like older continental documents, the Westminster Confession (1647) was drawn up with national unity of belief and practice in mind. It aimed at defining 'the true religion' in Calvinist terms,

[9] Quoted by G. Slosser, op. cit., p. 86.

and proceeded on the assumption that the Sacrament must be offered to all who profess the faith thus set out, but could be withheld as a matter of discipline. The Westminster Assembly, which drew up the Confession, consisted of some defenders of episcopacy, a small group of Independents, a large majority of Puritan divines and certain lay assessors. There were revealing debates on the question of the exclusion of 'scandalous and ignorant persons' from Communion and a request was made to Parliament for authority to exclude. When this was conferred in 1645, it was with the proviso that a person so excluded must have the right of appeal, and ultimately appeal to Parliament itself. This was unacceptable to the Presbyterian divines as it in effect subordinated the proposed national Church to the civil magistrates. Appeal to a board of Central Commissioners—a scheme suggested in 1646—was an attempt at a compromise between Erastians and Calvinists. It proved impossible, however, to establish Presbyterianism in England, not only because of the opposition of those loyal to episcopacy but also because of the growing strength of the Independents, Baptists, Quakers and other radical groups.

Richard Baxter (1610-91) was one of the most interesting figures of his age. His ideal was 'comprehension', but by this he meant a single, national Church, not mutual recognition or reciprocity by diverse groups. Baxter strongly disapproved of the promiscuous giving of the Lord's Supper. The rules of the Worcestershire Association (1653) laid down that only those who consented to discipline should participate in Communion.[10] Baxter, however, desired a system of church discipline which would be acceptable to moderate episcopalians, Presbyterians and Independents. The Lord's Supper could then have been administered in the parishes as a symbol of the unity of the Church.

When the Act of Uniformity of 1662 drove the English Presbyterians into Nonconformity a new situation arose. The resulting Presbyterian churches had to determine their relationship to Independent churches. In the 'Heads of Agreement' of 1690 there

[10] Cp. R. Baxter, *Certain Disputations of the Right to Sacraments*, 1657, and his correspondence and controversy with John Humfrey (1620-1719), one-time Vicar of Frome, whose first publication was *A Humble Vindication of a Free Admission unto the Lord's Supper*, 1651. Humfrey was ejected in 1662 and became minister of a Congregational church in London.

was readiness to go some way towards 'mutual open Communion' between Presbyterians and Independents. In the middle of the eighteenth century William Whiston, who had joined the General Baptists in 1747, tried to include the latter in a wider union based on the 'Heads of Agreement'. But the Agreement was never very widely operative and there are not a few instances where, even if Presbyterians and Independents worshipped together and shared a pastor, they separated for the observance of the Lord's Supper. In the course of the eighteenth century many of the older Presbyterian churches either died out or passed gradually into Unitarianism.

In Scotland it was hardly necessary to face the question of 'intercommunion' until the nineteenth century. By then there was unwillingness to attempt any definition of 'the true religion' which might exclude Christians of other traditions from occasional attendance, at least, at the Lord's Supper, though the Presbyterian practice of 'fencing the Table' imposed some barriers of a doctrinal as well as a moral kind. It was in Scotland that the sacramental token was most generally used.[11] On his visit to Scotland in 1764 John Wesley took Communion in the Presbyterian Church, though it appears that some of the early Methodists were repelled from the Lord's Table by Presbyterian ministers. Wesley's ordinations for Scotland were eleven only, and all between the years 1785 and 1788, when he was an old man. There seems some evidence that he sanctioned for his societies an Order of Communion Service similar to that of the Church of Scotland.[12] Charles Simeon, the Anglican evangelical, took Communion in the Presbyterian Church in 1796,[13] and this was not an isolated instance. In the nineteenth century there is traceable a fairly general tradition of mutual reception by the Church of England and the Church of Scotland, though no formal agreement was ever made. Both are established Churches and the Sovereign enjoys the peculiar position of membership in each. There were Scottish churches in London and a few other centres at

---

[11] Cp. G. F. Hill, 'Token', *E.R.E.*, XII, and A. A. Milne, *Communion Tokens of the Presbyterian Churches in Ireland*, 1920. A number of the English Free Churches maintain the custom of the presentation of 'cards' or 'tickets' by members of the church.

[12] Cp. Wesley F. Swift, *Methodism in Scotland*, 1947, pp. 54, 61.

[13] Cp. Charles Smyth, *Simeon and Church Order*, p. 137.

the end of the eighteenth century, but it became general for Scots in England to communicate in Anglican churches, where no English Presbyterian church is available.

In the course of the nineteenth century the Reformed Churches on the Continent showed a growing tendency towards a Communion opened to faithful members of any Protestant and non-Roman Church. Invitations to a Reformed Communion service, which have been given at several ecumenical gatherings in the last few decades, and notably at the First Assembly of the World Council of Churches in Amsterdam in 1948, are in line with this tendency. They are not regarded by the Reformed Churches as an innovation. Many in the Reformed tradition regard the invitation to the Lord's Supper as given in the name of Christ and the Church Universal, not in the name of a denomination.

The Church of England

Throughout the Elizabethan and Stuart periods the Church of England proceeded on the assumption that it was in England the only true Church, and that the whole population should be regular in attendance at the Eucharist. Absence from church services was an indictable offence,[14] and prosecutions, particularly after 1660, were frequent. The resources of the civil magistrates were employed to enforce conformity in ritual and doctrine. Discipline for church offences was exercised by the civil authority. Under the Test Act of 1673, which remained in force until 1828, all persons appointed to public office were required to 'receive the Sacrament of the Lord's Supper, according to the usage of the Church of England'.[15]

The Anglican Church was, however, compelled to face the question of its relationship to the Reformed Churches of the Continent. The question was an urgent practical issue for Anglicans when abroad and for foreign churchmen, often exiles, in England. It was specially provided in the Act of Uniformity of 1662 that its penalties should not extend 'to the foreigners or aliens of the foreign Reformed Churches allowed or to be allowed by the King's majesty, his heirs and successors in England', and this confirmed privileges which had existed for more than a century.

---

[14] Cf. 1 Elizabeth, cap. 2 (1559), 35 Elizabeth, cap. 1 (1593).
[15] Cf. 25 Chas. II, cap. 2.

The weight of opinion in the Anglican tradition from the days of Archbishop Whitgift (1530(?)-1604) to those of Archbishop Wake (1657-1737) appears to have been in favour of a recognition of the foreign Protestant Churches which even went as far as occasional mutual open Communion, at least for individuals.[16] The case of John Cosin has already been cited. Archbishop Ussher of Armagh (1581-1656) went so far as to declare:

> 'For the testifying my Communion with these Churches (which I do love and honour as true members of the Church Universal), I do profess that with like affection I should receive the blessed Sacrament at the hands of Dutch ministers if I were in Holland, as I should at the hands of the French ministers if I were in Charentome.'[17]

Professor Norman Sykes has drawn attention to Archbishop Wake's official and formal authorisation of intercommunion between members of the Church of England and members of the Reformed Church of Zurich in 1717.[18] There has been considerable discussion as to the importance which should be attached to the words and actions of individual theologians and bishops. It is undeniable, however, that the question of the recognition of foreign Reformed Churches has again and again forced itself upon the Church of England since the sixteenth century, and that in general the ancient rubric requiring confirmation before Communion has been interpreted as a disciplinary regulation for members of the Church, not applicable to visitors from the Reformed Churches of Scotland and Europe.

At least until the middle of the nineteenth century, Anglicans travelling abroad do not seem often to have hesitated to take Communion in Lutheran and Reformed Churches. The practice of Reginald Heber, later bishop of Calcutta, may be cited. When on the Continent in 1806 he communicated with the Lutherans and, writing from Calcutta in 1825, stated:

[16] Cf. the evidence given in H. A. Wilson, *Episcopacy and Unity*, 1912; A. J. Mason, *The Church of England and Episcopacy*, 1914; N. S. Sykes, *The Church of England and Non-Episcopal Churches in the 16th and 17th Centuries*, 1948; G. K. A. Bell, *Christian Unity*, 1948.

[17] Quoted by G. J. Slosser, *op. cit.*, p. 87.

[18] *Theology*, May 1948, pp. 176 f. Cf. Wake's letter to William Beauvoir quoted by G. J. Slosser, *op. cit.*, pp. 75-76.

'Were I to return to Germany, I would again, as before, humbly and thankfully avail myself of the preaching and sacramental ordinances of the Lutheran Evangelical Church, not doubting that they are a true Church of Christ, and that the Spirit of God is with them, as I trust He is with us also. . . . I have no right or desire to judge devout and learned divines of another national Church. If they come to sojourn among us, satisfied with the commission which they have received, or if they desire our help in their efforts to convert the heathen, I gladly meet them as Christians and fellow labourers . . . I gladly admit them (as I should desire myself to be admitted in Germany or Holland) to the Communion of our Church.'[19]

After the Toleration Act of 1689 the further question presented itself of the relationship of the Anglican Church to the now legally recognised Dissenting bodies. The desire of individuals for a more comprehensive national Church inspired a number of tentative schemes of reunion or mutual recognition in both the eighteenth and nineteenth centuries, but these never came within sight of success. The practice of 'Occasional Conformity' (which meant taking Communion at the parish church though a member of a Nonconformist church) was fairly general in the early years of the eighteenth century, particularly among Presbyterians and Independents. It had a good as well as a bad side. Whilst there were some who took Communion merely to qualify for civil or municipal office, there were others who did so from more spiritual motives. Many of the older Methodists never regarded themselves as having surrendered their membership in the Anglican Church. As late as 1818, Dr. Olinthus Gregory and Robert Hall, the noted Baptist preacher, corresponded about 'occasional conformity' as practised by Baxter and Howe and showed their approval of it.[20] The close fellowship between those Anglicans and Dissenters who were influenced by the Evangelical Revival led certain of the former to take communion on occasion with the latter. Instances are recorded in the cases of William Wilberforce,[21] Hannah More and Claudius Buchanan, though their action was sharply challenged. This practice never became widespread, and 'occasional

---

[19] George Smith, *Bishop Heber*, 1895, pp. 295-297.
[20] Robert Hall, *Works*, I, pp. 98, 119.
[21] *Life of Wilberforce*, IV, p. 318; *Correspondence of Wilberforce*, II, pp. 366-367.

Communion' from either side seems almost entirely to have died out by the middle of the nineteenth century, when controversy between Anglicans and Nonconformists again became sharper.

In 1870 a notable incident took place, which F. J. A. Hort, who was present, regarded as 'the beginning of a new period in church history'.[22] Those engaged in the preparation of the Revised Version of the New Testament were invited by Dean Stanley to a Communion Service in Henry VII's Chapel at Westminster Abbey. The company consisted of ten Anglican divines, including the Archbishop of Dublin (R. C. Trench), three Presbyterians from Scotland, a Baptist, a Congregationalist, a Methodist and a Unitarian. The original suggestion came from B. F. Westcott (then Canon of Peterborough, later Bishop of Durham). The holding of the service—and in particular the presence at it of Dr. Vance Smith, the Unitarian—resulted in considerable public controversy at the time. A resolution condemning the presence of a Unitarian among the Revisers was passed in the Upper House of the Convocation of Canterbury. A similar resolution was rejected by the Lower House, which, however, passed an expression of regret at the offence caused by the fact that a Unitarian received the Holy Communion at Westminster Abbey. The presence of the other Nonconformists does not seem to have been seriously challenged. Throughout the controversy Dean Stanley and Dr. Westcott, supported by J. B. Lightfoot, Hort and others, defended the action that had been taken.[23]

It is worthy of note that on New Year's Day, 1857, A. C. Tait, then Bishop of London, and later Archbishop of Canterbury, had, during an international Y.M.C.A. conference in London, administered Communion to all the delegates in spite of public criticism in advance. Later in the same year the Evangelical Alliance held a conference in Berlin in the course of which an unofficial Communion Service was held for the English-speaking delegates. The regular words of administration were used, but no other form of liturgy. Henry Alford, who had recently been

[22] A. F. Hort, *Life and Letters of F. J. A. Hort*, 1896, Vol. II, p. 135.
[23] R. E. Prothero, *Life and Correspondence of A. P. Stanley*, 1893, pp. 216 f., gives the terms of the open invitation that was issued and an account of the subsequent controversy. Cp. Arthur Westcott, *Life and Letters of B. F. Westcott*, 1903, Vol. I, p. 391, and A. F. Hort, *Life and Letters of F. J. A. Hort*, 1896, Vol. II, pp. 135 f.

appointed Dean of Canterbury, took part in the service and administered the elements. His action was severely criticised in England, but he was defended by C. T. Longley, then Bishop of Durham and later Archbishop of Canterbury. 'How much I have resented the bigotry and uncharitableness which the Communion has excited,' wrote Longley to Alford. 'It is very right that at home we should keep out of *canon* shot, but widely as the range has been extended of late years, I never before heard that it could be stretched across the Channel.'[24]

At a number of other international conferences of the Evangelical Alliance—for example, in New York (1873) and in London (1896)—united Communion Services were arranged and Anglican leaders took part in them. But those who were associated with the Evangelical Alliance were only from one school of thought in the Church of England.

English Nonconformity

From the beginning of their history as separated bodies all the main groups of English Dissenters (with the exception of the Quakers) emphasised the centrality of the Lord's Supper in their faith and practice. There was a general insistence on the necessity of 'filling up one's place' at the Lord's Table, and those guilty of lapses in this matter were subject to discipline. There was, however, and remains, considerable divergence of opinion and practice about the 'terms of Communion', that is, as to who may rightly be admitted to the Table of a local church.

1. *The Elizabethan Separatists.* The earliest Separatists, or Brownists, are said to have renounced Communion with 'all Reformed churches except such as should be of their model.[25] Only those who were members of one of their local "gathered churches" were permitted to sit down with them at the Lord's Table.' Unless a group had been properly formed into a 'church state' and had a duly appointed pastor, the Lord's Supper was not observed. Internal dissension on matters of doctrine and practice often led to the withdrawal of Table-fellowship. It is to be noted that one of the points on which Robert Browne criticised the followers of Henry Barrowe was the latter's refusal to hold

[24] I owe this reference to Miss Ruth Rouse.
[25] D. Neal, *History of the Puritans*, I, p. 247.

Communion with any who were not members of other churches. A more liberal tradition among Separatists found representatives in the seventeenth century in John Bunyan and in men like Walter Cradock, Vavasour Powell and Morgan Llwyd, who stood in Wales for what was called 'mixed Communion'.

2. *The Independents.* Certain of the early leaders of the seventeenth-century Independents were not strictly 'separatists', i.e. they had not surrendered the hope of a national Church organised according to their own principles or allowing them adequate freedom within its borders. A number of Independents, or Congregationalists as they came to be called, accepted parish livings under the Commonwealth. Like the Presbyterians, they refused the Lord's Supper to those of whose faith they were not assured and Baptism to the children of those who were not active church members. 'The refusal was sometimes resented, and in some cases the parishioners tried to enforce what they believed to be their rights by an appeal to the law.'[26] Two aspects of the matter are specifically dealt with in the 'Savoy Declaration' drawn up in 1658 by Thomas Goodwin, John Owen and others on behalf of the representatives of 120 Congregational churches.

'XIV. . . . They who are engaged in the work of publique Preaching, and enjoy the Publique Maintenance upon that account, are not thereby obliged to dispense the Seals to any other than such as (being Saints by Calling, and gathered according to the order of the Gospel) they stand related to, as Pastors and Teachers. . . .

'XXX. Churches gathered and walking according to the mind of Christ, judging other Churches (though less pure) to be true Churches, may receive, unto occasional communion with them, such Members of those Churches as are credibly testified to be godly, and to live without offence.'

The difficulties facing Nonconformists after 1662 led to a number of local fellowships which included Independents and Presbyterians, or Independents and Baptists, occasionally all three groups, though, as already mentioned, these sometimes separated for the observance of the Lord's Supper. It seems that throughout

---

[26] R. W. Dale, *History of Congregationalism*, p. 378.

D

the eighteenth and the early nineteenth century churches usually classed as Independent were prepared to admit to their membership and to occasional Communion those belonging to any of the Nonconformist traditions. But strangers, even if coming from other Independent Churches, were expected to present letters of recommendation before sharing in the Communion Service. In the account of the customs of the London Church of which Dr. Isaac Watts (1674-1748) was pastor 'in the Celebration of Worship and Exercise of Discipline as they are practised among us at present, 1723', it is stated:

> 'When any person who is a member of another church, among the three denominations of Dissenters, viz. Presbyterians, Independent or Baptist, desires occasional Communion with us, for one or two months or more, for special and justifiable reasons . . . we then only give notice of it to the church, just before the first time of their Communion with us; provided always that we know the person, or that he be recommended to us by his own pastor, or by some persons whose testimony we can entirely rely upon. . . .
>
> 'Now, if persons continue more than a twelvemonth in occasional Communion with us, we think it proper to give them notice, that they should either return and communicate with their own pastor and people, or that they should be dismissed entirely to us, in order to become members of the society with which they constantly communicate.'[27]

As the eighteenth century progressed, Zwinglian teaching became more influential in Independent and Congregationalist churches. This and the changed conditions of the nineteenth century led to the practice which is now general of an open invitation to the Lord's Table.[28]

3. *The Baptists.* Baptist practice has varied considerably. The General (i.e. Arminian) Baptists were in origin an offshoot from older Separatist groups. They were at first strict in matters of communion, having Table fellowship only with their own

[27] John Rippon, *The Baptist Annual Register for* 1801 *and* 1802, pp. 600-601.
[28] Cf. *Rules and Customs*, etc., p. 30, and John Marsh, Paper read to the Commission on Faith and Order at Baarn, September 1948, Minutes, pp. 58 f.

members.[29] But in the seventeenth and eighteenth centuries they were subject to Anabaptist (Mennonite), Quaker and Socinian influences. What is called 'Free Communion' (i.e. Communion open even to the unbaptised) is said to have arisen in Poland at the end of the sixteenth century under the leadership of Faustus Socinus.[30] Mosheim, writing in 1755, says that the General Baptists 'do not reject from their Communion any who profess themselves Christians'. Though many of the General Baptist churches declined in strength in the eighteenth century, or became Unitarian, it seems likely that their practice (not unrelated to the Zwinglian tradition) had influence in the nineteenth century when 'open Communion' became more general in the Free Churches.[31]

The Particular (i.e. Calvinistic) Baptists, whose history began in 1633, were subject to early and recurrent controversy as to the 'terms of Communion'. In the seventeenth century John Bunyan was the outstanding representative of a 'mixed Communion' tradition, favouring church and Table fellowship between Baptists and Paedobaptists. His opponents would admit only baptised believers to the Lord's Table and sometimes only the members of the particular local church (a practice still followed by a few Strict Baptist churches in England and by some Baptist churches in the United States). A General Assembly of 'Pastors, Messengers and ministering Brethren', held in London in 1689, agreed that each church must have liberty in this matter;[32] but controversy was vigorous at the end of the eighteenth century and again early in the nineteenth century. The opposition to 'mixed communion' was on the ground that it involved Communion with those whom most Baptists regarded as 'unbaptised', and that this would be irregular and contrary to Scripture. During the nineteenth century, however, most Baptist churches adopted 'open Communion', in common with the other Free Churches. As early as

[29] John Smyth in his *Paralleles, Censures, Observations*, 1609, expressly repudiates occasional conformity or Communion with the established Church. Cf. *Works* (ed. by W. T. Whitley), II, p. 371.

[30] Cf. Robert Robinson, *History of Baptism*, 1790, pp. 464-465; T. Crosby, *History of the English Baptists*, 1738, III, App. I.

[31] But note that even a General Baptist church like Horsham, where Matthew Caffyn (1628-1715) had been minister, did not adopt 'Free Communion' till 1829. See Emily Kensett, *The History of the Free Christian Church, Horsham*, 1921, pp. 106 f.

[32] J. Ivimey, *History of the English Baptists*, 1811, I, p. 409.

1844 it was stated that half the Baptist churches in England practised 'open Communion' and that a considerable number had 'open membership'. The example of C. H. Spurgeon (1834–92) was important, and influential beyond his own denomination. 'Mr. Spurgeon's position was Calvinistic, accompanied by open Communion. . . . The Tabernacle . . . admitted people to the Lord's Table who were not baptised (i.e. as believers), and refused them membership unless baptised.'[33] This remains the practice of most Baptist churches in and around London, in the north of England, in Wales. In the southern states of America and on the continent of Europe there is usually a closed Table as well as closed membership. But a considerable number of Baptist churches in England and in the northern states of America have opened their membership as well as their Table to other Christians besides those baptised as believers, on the ground that the mediating position is an unsatisfactory compromise. In every case acceptance into membership of the local fellowship depends upon the decision of the church meeting.[34] In certain churches, both in England and America, a form of 'associate membership' has been introduced. Those who have not been baptised as believers may share in the church meeting and vote on a number of issues, but are not eligible for the diaconate or the pastorate.

4. *The Methodists.* John Wesley wished to remain a member of the Church of England, and both administered and communicated as often as he could in the parish churches of the land. He practised and enjoined frequent Communion. He regarded the Lord's Supper as a 'converting ordinance' and led hundreds of those who heard him preach directly to the Lord's Table. Methodists flocked in such crowds to the celebrations in some of the parish churches that there was not accommodation for them. Moreover, the parish clergy were often hostile to the revival movement and

[33] W. Y. Fullerton, *C. H. Spurgeon*, p. 291. The so-called Strict Baptists are a group of churches which rejected the moderate Calvinism of Andrew Fuller (1754–1815) and were reinforced by certain groups which broke away, some from the Anglican Church, during the nineteenth century controversies over baptismal regeneration. They are not in fellowship with the Baptist Union of Great Britain and Ireland. They have usually a 'closed' Table as well as membership.

[34] On the historical material see E. A. Payne, *The Fellowship of Believers*, 1944. For a modern statement of the present varieties of practice see *A Report on the Question of Union between Baptists, Congregationalists and Presbyterians*, 1937.

were unwilling to administer the Sacrament to Methodist converts. From 1753 onwards pressure was put on Wesley to allow
celebrations in Methodist preaching-houses that people might not
be deprived of this means of grace. The Supper was at first
administered by ordained clergymen of the Church of England
who had attached themselves to Wesley and his movement. Not
till some years later was there any general authorisation to his
preachers to administer the sacraments. His first ordinations were
in 1784 for America, 1785 for Scotland and 1788 for England.
Wesley never authorised any unordained person to administer the
Lord's Supper and insisted that Methodist sacramental services
should be at a different time from those of the parish church, so
as to avoid the appearance of a rival altar. The Methodist Conference of 1786 laid down that permission for services at the same
time as those in the parish church should only be given if the
parish minister was notoriously wicked or heretical, if there were
not enough churches in the town to hold half the people, or if
there was no church at all within two or three miles. Even then,
at least part of the service from the Anglican Prayer Book should
be read. Evening Communion Services gradually became customary among Methodists and probably passed from them to the
older Dissenting bodies, who had formerly favoured services in
the afternoon of the first Sunday in the month. The Conference
of 1795 adopted a 'Plan of Pacification', which remained in its
essentials in force among Wesleyans until Methodist Union in
1932. 'The Lord's Supper', it was declared, 'shall be administered
by those only who are authorised by the Conference.' The
authorisation, in special circumstances, of lay-preachers came in
only gradually, probably to meet the needs of the growing
population and under the influence of the more radical Methodist
groups. It seems to have passed from Methodism to the older
Dissenting bodies in the nineteenth century, for many of the same
reasons and as a reaction against the claims made for the priesthood by the Tractarian Movement. The form of service used by
Wesleyans continued to be based on the Anglican Prayer Book.
It was agreed in 1795—and reaffirmed on various occasions, and
as recently as 1920—that

'No person shall be suffered, on any pretence, to partake of
the Lord's Supper among us unless he be a Member of Society,

or receive a Note of Admission from the Superintendent (or from the Preacher administering), which Note must be renewed quarterly.'[35]

The following resolution was adopted in 1889:

'It is most important that a united and earnest attempt should be made to secure the presence of all our Members, and the showing of Tickets, at the Lord's Supper. As regards strangers occasionally attending our services, who desire to participate with us, they may reasonably be expected to assure the Minister of their fitness, by explaining to him that they are Members of another Church, or for what reason, not being Members of any church, they desire to be Communicants; and such occasional cases can be met by the issue of a special Note of Admission by the Minister. That the Table of the Lord should be open to all comers is surely a great discredit and a serious peril to any Church.'

By the end of the nineteenth century, however, the practice of presenting tickets was falling into disuse. Of recent decades it has become customary in Methodist, as in most other English Free Churches, to issue an open invitation.

The more democratic Methodist groups which separated from the parent Conference during the nineteenth century—the Primitive Methodists, for example, and the United Methodists (formed of a union of the Wesleyan Association and the Wesleyan Reformers)—always made more use of laymen than did the Wesleyans and were in their attitude and procedure more like the Free Churches of the congregational type.

*   *   *

A number of the general factors which operated in the Free Churches during the nineteenth century have already been mentioned. The increase and movement of population were of great importance and also experiences which came with the growth of the modern missionary movement and united Christian organisations like the Bible Societies, the World's Evangelical Alliance

[35] For this and other details in this paragraph see *A Summary of Methodist Law and Discipline*, 5th revised edition, 1923.

and the Keswick Convention. The beginnings of the Ecumenical movement also played a part. By the end of the century the main Free Church traditions (with the exception of certain Baptist churches and the Churches of Christ) may be said to have reached the stage of 'mutual open Communion'. In 1892 a National Free Church Council was established and at its annual gatherings large joint Communion Services were held. This development no doubt encouraged the growth of the practice of issuing an 'open invitation'.

The Puritan Tradition in America

One or two special developments in North America deserve notice. In 1631 the legislature of Massachusetts limited the franchise to full members of the Puritan church and admission to Communion was strictly controlled. Though generally sympathetic with the Puritan outlook, however, and under 'strong social and political temptation', a large percentage of the population refused to ally themselves with the New England churches.[36] In 1647 non-communicants were allowed the right of citizenship in the towns of Massachusetts. Throughout the seventeenth century young people had to make public confession of their religious experience before being admitted to Communion. By the second quarter of the eighteenth century, to meet the decline in the number of communicants, a 'Half-Way Covenant' was accepted. Baptised parents, who were not communicants and could give no public evidence of regeneration, were allowed to have their children baptised, if the grandparents had been communicants.

During the nineteenth century the American churches were subject to many of the same influences that were at work in Europe. The Disciples of Christ, under the leadership of Alexander Campbell (1788-1866), who had had both Presbyterian and Baptist connections, instituted a weekly Eucharist, but it was open only to full members who had been immersed as believers. The Baptist churches of the southern States remained conservative in belief and practice. Those of the north shared with the other churches in a movement which led gradually to the establishment of 'mutual open Communion' and an 'open invitation'.

[36] Cf. A. L. Drummond, *Story of American Protestantism*, 1949, pp. 56-57, quoting J. Truslow Adams.

A new phenomenon was the appearance in America, as in certain other lands, of churches of the same denomination separated from one another not by theological differences but by race and colour, and often in practice out of communion with one another.

*   *   *

What has been said indicates something of the complexity of the influences, theological and practical, which have been at work shaping the situation of the twentieth century. Certain Churches which were at first ready to employ compulsion that everyone in their territories receive the sacraments are now insistent upon tests and conditions before their access. On the other hand, a number of Churches which began with a very strictly guarded Table now stand for open access and desire general open Communion. There have been cross-currents at work in most of the Churches. Questions of 'terms of Communion' and the right and duty of discipline have become entangled with those relating to the recognition of other Christian bodies as Churches. Theological ignorance and indifference have sometimes been as powerful as theological intransigence. The demands of a new situation have often brought changes with which an older theology has had to come to terms. The difficulties the Churches face to-day will not, however, be satisfactorily overcome without a patient uncovering of the forces which have been at work in the past and which have led to the present situation.

IV

INTERCOMMUNION IN THE ECUMENICAL MOVEMENT

★

O. S. Tomkins[1]
Church of England
(Great Britain)

Since intercommunion is a problem of relationship between Churches, it acquires a particular acuteness in the Ecumenical Movement as the *locus* at which the Churches meet each other. The problems which the Churches bring to the World Council become its problems. Because there is a problem between certain Churches of their relationship to one another in the fellowship of the Lord's Supper, the problem is made acute when representatives of those Churches meet with each other in close Christian fellowship and so bring into sharp focus an estrangement which is more easily ignored or forgotten when the same representatives return to their various lands and Churches and become reimmersed in the interests and demands of their separated lives. The Ecumenical Movement did not create the problem of intercommunion: it simply gives it a setting in which it cannot be ignored.

This historical survey will deal first with a movement which, more than any other, pioneered in the ecumenical field and grappled with many ecumenical problems before the Churches as such became aware of them. For over fifty years the World's Student Christian Federation has been bringing together Christian men and women from the colleges and universities of the world into fellowship in Christ. There they have not only achieved a united witness in evangelism, study and action, but they have also

[1] For Section I the author is greatly indebted to a memorandum by Mr. W. Nicholls, a secretary of the W.S.C.F., revising an article written for the *Student World* in 1939 by the Rev. F. H. House.

raised questions for the Churches from which those students came. A succession of men and women has learned in the Federation the essentials of ecumenical life and has provided many of the leaders who later, as responsible churchmen, have had to face, on behalf of their Churches, the questions which the Federation first posed to them. As will be seen, the Federation continues to pioneer and to put to the Churches fresh questions and new insights on old problems, including that of intercommunion. We might have drawn illustrations from others of the international Christian youth movements, but we have thought it a better use of our space to deal in some detail with the W.S.C.F. as affording the most articulate and thorough-going example.

Secondly, we sketch the actual practice with regard to intercommunion at some of those great international Christian conferences which are the landmarks of that whole varied development known as the Ecumenical Movement. The International Missionary Council, the Universal Christian Council for Life and Work and the Faith and Order Movement have all had to face the problem sooner or later. It will be clear from this section that a bewildering variety of answers has been given, so the second section goes on to deal with the situation as it stands at present in the World Council of Churches, the most recent and the most formal expression of the Ecumenical Movement. Since one of the tasks of the World Council is to enable its member Churches to challenge one another in the depth of Christian love and truth, we shall seek to formulate in concluding this section some of the questions which the Churches must seek to answer as they face each other through their representatives in ecumenical gatherings.

I. *Communion and Intercommunion in the World's Student Christian Federation*

Early discussions. The Federation was originally a product of the Protestant 'Evangelical Movement'. Its strength lay in the strong personal faith and self-discipline of the members and in their missionary zeal. There was little thought about the Church or the Churches, and worship was conducted on traditional evangelical lines. In Germany and the Scandinavian countries, where practically all the members of each National Movement belonged to a single confession, it was easy for all to attend occasional services of Holy Communion at conferences and on similar occasions. In

England the Movement's first conferences were held in connection with the Keswick Convention, and it was usual for the evangelical vicar of the parish church of St. John to invite all the students, whether they were Anglicans or not, to receive the Holy Communion on Sundays. In the United States likewise no questions were raised, and for the same reasons. All the members shared a common theological outlook and none was concerned to raise difficult questions of ecclesiastical loyalty. But in principle, if not in practice, the Federation aimed at including all Christian students in its membership.

The Federation as a whole took a decisive step forward from an 'undenominational' to a more fully *inter-confessional* status, when the General Committee at Prinkipo in 1911 declared its opinion 'that it is desirable that no student, to whatever branch of the Christian Church he may belong, should be excluded from full membership in any National Movement within the Federation'.[2] But it was many years before the consequences of this decision were worked out with regard to worship. Individual Orthodox and Roman Catholic students became members, but at Federation conferences the majority were always Protestant and the common worship was still in the old forms of a non-liturgical and undenominational Protestant tradition. The problem of intercommunion was avoided by the Federation officers simply abstaining from asking any church authorities to arrange Communion Services at meetings of the General Committee or the annual student conferences.

On the whole the policy of the National Movements followed similar lines. The guiding principle was the avoidance of 'ecclesiastical controversy'. Movements of which the overwhelming majority of the members belonged to one Church or to Churches between which intercommunion existed commonly arranged for united Communion Services to be held. Thus the German, Swedish and French Movements frequently arranged for an evening celebration of the Holy Communion as the final act of a conference. Similarly the camps and conferences of the Russian Orthodox Movement in France, Bulgaria and Esthonia usually included a celebration of the Holy Liturgy with Communion on the Sunday mornings, and the Bulgarian Orthodox Movement

[2] Minutes of General Committee, Prinkipo, 1911.

arranged for the celebration of the Holy Liturgy in the student chapel three or four times a year.

On the other hand, the National Movements which included in their membership many who were members of Churches not 'in full communion' with one another, adapted their policies in accordance with differences of denominational 'church consciousness'. Roughly speaking, members of the 'younger Churches' were relatively more conscious of the essential unity of all professing Christians and relatively less conscious of the claims of denominational loyalty and discipline. Thus in China and India it was the custom of the Movements to ask the clergy present at a conference to arrange a single Communion and to expect all to take part.

A compromise solution. But, where denominational 'church consciousness' was strong, the Movements again sought the safest course. No united Communion services were arranged. Usually facilities were given to the ministers of different Churches to announce the times and places of the different Communion Services and other activities were not arranged by the conference authorities at these times. Often these announcements contained as a matter of principle an invitation to 'members of any branch of the Christian Church' or to 'all who love the Lord Jesus' to attend and to receive the Sacrament. But it was made quite clear that these invitations were given by the representatives of the Churches and not by the leaders of the Movements.

In a preface to the first edition of the Federation prayer book, entitled *Venite Adoremus*, the General Committee of the Federation stated very clearly its conviction: 'The Sacrament of Holy Communion is in a special sense the province of the Churches as such. . . . Matters of Communion and intercommunion are questions of church discipline outside the province of the World's Student Christian Federation. It is hoped that members of the Federation will enter deeply into the life of their own confession and so find their sacramental life nourished in their own Churches.'[3] The 'statement of the interdenominational position of the British S.C.M.' said simply: 'The service of Holy Communion . . . is a Sacrament of the Christian Church. The Student Christian Movement is not a branch of the Church. . . . It there-

---

[3] Minutes of General Committee, Chamcoria, 1935.

fore follows that it is not permissible for the Movement to hold services of Holy Communion.'[4] It does not follow, on the other hand, that the leaders of the Movements were unaware of the supreme importance of the sacramental worship of the Churches or that many members did not desire to have services of inter-communion at conferences. But it did simply imply a redirection of the activities of those who desired immediate intercommunion. As an exceptionally important article by Tissington Tatlow put it: 'The end (intercommunion at the summer conferences) is to be achieved, not by asking the General Committee of the Student Movement to take action outside its province, but by seeking to move the Churches.'[5]

Non-communicating attendance: Chamcoria, 1935. A new stage of Federation policy arose from an experiment which owed much to leaders of the Russian Student Christian Movement. Since 1927 the Russian and the British Movements have organised a series of Anglo-Orthodox student conferences which have given birth to the Fellowship of St. Alban and St. Sergius. A statement of the aims of the Fellowship describes most clearly the central inspiration of the student conferences as well: 'The centre of the work of the Fellowship is liturgical worship and it has been by entering into this, as represented in the two Churches concerned, that both the individual life of members has been enriched and a spiritual unity has been discovered, which is deeper than the points of difference.'[6] In practice this means that the whole life of the conferences has been centred in daily celebrations of either the Anglican Eucharist or the Orthodox Liturgy. All members of the conference attend these celebrations. As intercommunion has not been approved between the Churches concerned, it is not possible for all to receive the Sacrament together; but *acts of spiritual communion* are encouraged by the publication of special forms of prayer and by careful explanations of the services.

In 1935 the Federation itself considered the whole question at its General Committee at Chamcoria (Bulgaria) and issued a state-

[4] Statement of the interdenominational position of the British S.C.M., 1932 and 1935.

[5] *The Student Movement*, Vol. XXIII, p. 139. See *The Story of the Student Christian Movement*, p. 777.

[6] Statement of policy of the Fellowship of St. Alban and St. Sergius; see the quarterly *Sobornost*.

ment of policy. This statement concludes with the following paragraph: 'The Committee would suggest, in this regard, that the most practicable step at this moment is that members of different traditions should take opportunity of attending each other's services of Holy Communion, seeking to enter as far as possible into the worship of their fellow Christians, without communicating when doing so if it is against the discipline of their Church. Such action has been tried in specific instances and has led to a deeper appreciation of each other when it has been taken sincerely in an honest effort to understand the other tradition. It may seem strange to some to suggest attendance at a service without partaking of the elements: it would seem, however, to be the only way both of recognising realistically the fact of our divisions and of expressing a positive desire for understanding and fellowship.'[7]

Spiritual intercommunion. As a result of this recommendation special arrangements for Communion Services and for 'non-communicating attendance' at them were made at international meetings planned by the Federation staff. The first significant attempt at the Federation level to put the new policy into practice was made in the programmes of the General Committee of 1938 and of the European Theological Students' Conference of the New Year 1939. At these meetings the arrangements for the week-end services were as follows: on the Saturday night there was a united preparation for Communion at which the plan for the services was given by a minister of a Reformed Church, and a service of preparation containing much traditional material[8] was led by an Anglican priest. Early on the Sunday morning all the members of the Conference were invited to *attend* the celebration of the Anglican Eucharist, and those who were members of the Anglican Church or of Churches in communion with the Anglican Church were invited to *receive* the Sacrament. Later on all the members of the Conference were invited to attend a Reformed (Presbyterian) service followed by Communion. In accordance with the convictions of the Churches concerned it was announced that 'members of any branch of the Church of Christ would be welcomed at the Table of the Lord'. On the other hand, as at the

[7] Minutes of General Committee, Chamcoria, 1935; *Venite Adoremus I,* Preface, p. 8.
[8] See *Venite Adoremus II,* pp. 91-95.

Anglican service, arrangements were made for the convenience of those who attended the service but who were not able to receive the Sacrament. Finally, on the Monday morning, there was a celebration of the Holy Orthodox Liturgy attended by nearly all the members of the Conference, but at which only one or two of the Orthodox received.

These 'ecumenical adventures' as they were called were considerably criticised. There was a long discussion of them at the Federation Executive in August 1938. On the one hand it was said that for many students, especially those from the 'younger Churches', it was both painful and bewildering to be asked to attend two or three different Communion Services at none of which all could receive the Sacrament together. It was better to have one service at which all could receive or, if that were really impossible, then to have no Communion Service at all. On the other hand, the leaders of the neo-Calvinist revival said that 'acts of spiritual communion' could easily become a substitute for the actual reception of the Sacrament, that they were the expression of a human and sentimental rather than a truly spiritual fellowship, and that to encourage students to attend the services of which the doctrinal implications were explicitly or implicitly condemned by the teaching of their own Churches was to encourage disloyalty and to betray true 'ecumenism'.

In favour of the new move it was said that it was the only kind of plan for ecumenical worship which truthfully reflected the actual relation of the different Churches. Those who took part spoke of the spiritual reality of the experience with its mingled pain at our continued divisions and joy in the revelation of the spiritual treasures of another Church. The Orthodox contended strongly that the Orthodox Church could only be understood through the Liturgy, and, on the other hand, that only when they saw the Communion Service of the Protestant Church were they really forced to recognise Protestants as Christian brothers. Others spoke of what they had learnt spiritually by attendance at the Orthodox Liturgy. The objections of the neo-Calvinists were answered by the argument that careful explanation and preparation would meet most of the suggested dangers. The result of the discussion was that the statement of policy made by the General Committee of 1935 was allowed to stand for the time being.

After the Second World War. The policy adopted by the Federation at Chamcoria in 1935 was the general rule during the war period and the few years after the war, in the few large meetings possible in the war period, and at the General Committee of 1946, and in the large meetings of the years that followed. Thus it may be said to have been given a fair trial and it bore undoubted spiritual fruit. It provided for many students and, indeed, leaders, an ecumenical education which could perhaps have been obtained in no other way. Through its use members of the Federation learned to understand the inner life of other Churches; sometimes indeed they came away from such services more deeply divided than before from the communion in question, in other cases with a deep sense of spiritual fellowship with it and of the tragic and sinful nature of our divisions. But in either case it was because they had seen this communion in its existential reality and not as a set of people professing a number of intellectual theological statements which were relatively meaningless to others.

Nevertheless the dissatisfaction with the policy of Chamcoria, 1935, seems to have grown during the post-war period. It seems that during this time the Federation made a definite step forward in its understanding of itself in relation to the Church and the Churches. The discussions of the post-war period are marked by a new readiness to emphasise the reality of the Federation as part of the life of the Church and of its fellowship as a *koinonia* in the Holy Spirit. The battle for loyalty to a particular Church had been won, and because there was no danger of the Federation being thought of as *a Church*, it was possible to be much bolder in affirming the presence in it of certain real *marks* of the One Holy Catholic Church.

This new consciousness of the Federation as part of the life of the Church inevitably had its effect on the attitude of its members towards questions of Communion and intercommunion. Thus in the area of the younger Churches impatience with confessional divisions became stronger and more articulate, stimulated by the organic unions achieved in some of their areas and under active discussion in others. In the area of the older Churches where, as has been said, consciousness of confessional divisions had always been much stronger, there came to be a much deeper sense of the scandal and sinfulness of division at the Holy Communion, which was felt as much by those who were opposed to intercommunion as by those who were in favour of it. By 1948 the Federation was beginning to feel that the time had come for a re-examination of policy and a search for some more creative practice at conferences and meetings. It was asked whether the Chamcoria decision still accurately reflected the relationships of the Churches to one another, especially in view of the formation of the World Council of Churches, and whether, even if this was not so, non-communicating attendance was in fact the best practice which the Federation should officially approve.

The strongest challenge to Chamcoria came at the Asian Leaders' Conference held at Kandy, Ceylon, in January 1949. At that conference a Federation consultation was held, in the course of which a discussion of Communion Services and the question of intercommunion took place. Among points vigorously made were these:

(a) In its conferences or meetings the Federation should not put on the programme any Communion Service except open Communion Services, namely, services in which all Christians are invited to take part.

(b) If such a policy should prove unpracticable the Federation should cease holding any Communion Services during its conferences and meetings . . .

(c) These two general rules should not exclude the possibility for each particular confessional group to organise Communion Services of their own . . .

(d) Intercommunion between members of different Churches is meaningless and even hypocritical if it is not founded on a real spiritual unity. In this way the question of Communion Services is closely tied with that of thought, prayer and action for the reunion of the Church, and when there is no such deep concern for this reunion there is no room for intercommunion of any kind.

The Asian delegates to the General Committee at Whitby, 1949, came to the meeting eager to urge a policy of this nature on the Federation as a whole. There they met with representatives of the European and American Movements who came from a background of strong confessional loyalty, and an extremely creative discussion took place within the small group charged with this question. This group made a fresh examination of all

the practices known to be observed within the National Movements and the Federation itself on the question of Communion
Services at its conferences and meetings. It endeavoured to understand as deeply as possible the real spiritual reasons why such
sharply conflicting attitudes on intercommunion were held by
members of the Federation. It found no basis for agreement in the
policy urged by the Asian delegates, but it was far from rejecting
their contentions out of hand. It found that the attitude of the
Calvinist members of the Federation had significantly changed
during the period since 1938 and that their objections to the policy
of non-communicating attendance had altered in character. They
were now to be found amongst the strongest supporters of the
Kandy suggestions of one common service or none, and they
emphasised now much more the idea that the essence of the
Sacrament lies, according to our Lord's institution, in the partaking of the elements, and that it is the Lord Himself who issues
the invitation to His own table, and that one who hears this
invitation given through the mouth of the minister of Christ at
the Lord's Supper cannot refuse it without incurring the guilt of
rejecting Christ's own gracious invitation. They were no longer
so concerned, on the other hand, with the doctrinal differences
about the Holy Communion which in 1938 had seemed to them
to constitute a serious barrier to intercommunion. This at least is
true of their attitude to Churches within the ecumenical fellowship. It is extremely doubtful whether their objection to taking
part in a Roman Catholic service would have decreased in any way.

It is also true to say that the delegates coming from the 'Catholic' tradition, while retaining their principle that intercommunion
is the goal of reunion and not a means to it, felt strongly the same
call to the fullest fellowship possible within the life of the Federation. They found themselves compelled to assert what for them
was a peculiarly paradoxical view, that while the visible Church
is to be found in those societies which through their apostolic
faith and episcopal succession have historical continuity with the
Church founded by Jesus Christ, yet they were forced to recognise
in the Federation the same *koinonia* of the Holy Spirit that belongs
to the Holy Catholic Church. Thus for them all the question of
intercommunion was not a wholly closed question and in spite
of the relative naturalness for them of non-communicating
attendance, they were ready to listen to new suggestions.

Finally, the General Committee, while rejecting as its own official policy the Kandy suggestions, and while no longer giving its exclusive blessing to the practice of non-communicating attendance, took the radical step of saying that this question could never be answered until we had the reunited Church for which we prayed. They refrained from adopting as their official policy any of the traditional practices in the Federation and its Movements and said, rather, that each conference constituted a new situation which must be thoughtfully and prayerfully approached in the light of certain basic principles already found valid in the life of the Movements. They suggested that when the application of those principles demanded the holding of more than one celebration of different confessions on the same day, they should be held at the same hour and preceded by a common service of preparation.

Thus, while the suggestions of Kandy did not become a Federation policy, it is not true to say that the Federation at Whitby rejected intercommunion as a means to reunion on the ground that our inability to have Communion together was simply a sign of our actual divisions. The Federation did not and could not have endorsed in this manner the view of its 'Catholic' members any more than it could have accepted at this stage the views of the younger Churches which, it is fair to remark, are not universally held even by all members of those Churches. To adopt either of these courses at the present stage of the Ecumenical Movement would have been to split the fellowship of the Federation and to make it something narrower than it is. The Federation's present policy seeks to do justice to the deepest conscientious and theological convictions of all its members and it calls upon them all continually to rethink their positions in the light of those held by others and of their experience of ecumenical fellowship within the Federation. It believes that if we are open to the leading of the Holy Spirit, God will show us the way forward, but it does not pretend to say what that way will be. It does, on the other hand, point to the organic reunion of the Churches as the only fully satisfactory solution.

II. *Practice and Principle in the Ecumenical Conferences*

We must now cast back to examine the various practices which were in fact adopted in the various big ecumenical conferences since 1910. The thought and practice of the World's Student

Christian Federation has affected the wider conferences, but they do not exhibit the same coherent development, nor the same continuous attention to the problem of Communion and inter-communion at ecumenical gatherings. We are not here concerned with the *non-sacramental* worship at any of these conferences. It must be remembered that the Communion Services here recorded took place in a context of daily corporate worship, carefully prepared and of very great variety of traditions, which was often the most moving and best remembered element in the conferences. But the whole matter of worship in general at ecumenical gather-ings is another, and even longer, story. We only note here in passing both the anomaly of being united in prayer but not in sacrament and the promise that lies in the fact that our separation in worship has never been absolute.

The World Missionary Conference, Edinburgh, 1910. The question of a joint Communion Service appears simply not to have been raised. The Report contains this note:

> 'On Sunday, 19th June . . . in the morning at 9 a.m. there was a Communion Service in St. Giles' Cathedral to which delegates and other visitors were invited by the minister and kirk-session. The invitation was largely responded to by mem-bers of many denominations and different nationalities, and the hour was felt to be one of hallowed fellowship. In this con-nection, it may also be mentioned that there was a daily Cele-bration for members of the Anglican communion at 8 a.m. in the Church of St. John the Evangelist.'[9]

Delegates received the Sacrament in the various churches in Edinburgh as each would have done had he been there on a private visit.

Jerusalem, 1928. Since there is a certain inner coherence in each of the three ecumenical strands, it is simpler to follow right through the practice of the three great missionary conferences. The Minutes of the Jerusalem Conference contain no reference to a Communion service, but a service was held which made a deep impression on those who were present. Arrangements for it were not an official *act* of the I.M.C. committee but were in the hands of various leading members of the conference who felt, in

[9] *Report of Edinburgh, 1910*, Vol. IX, p. 31.

the words of one of them, that 'we were on the high tide after more than a week of intimate and heartening fellowship', and that Christians met in the Holy City on Easter Day could do no other than seek the widest fellowship in the Lord's Supper which it was possible to achieve. Finally it was arranged that the service should be led by an American Methodist, Dr. F. J. McConnell, Bishop of Pittsburg, and an Anglican, Canon Charles Raven; the form of service was principally that of the American Methodist Church and so practically identical with that familiar to Anglicans. However, the communion of the people followed the practice familiar to the Reformed, in that the consecrated bread and wine were brought to the congregation in their places by four 'Deacons' representing different races and confessions. These assisting ministers were Dr. Cheng Ching Yi (Peking, Church of Christ in China), Dr. S. K. Datta (of Lahore), William Paton (English Presbyterian) and C. E. Wilson (Baptist Missionary Society, Britain). It happened that the two Anglican bishops present, Dr. Donaldson of Salisbury and Dr. Temple of Manchester, had commitments entered into months earlier to be preaching at churches elsewhere in Jerusalem. Practically the whole conference was present and almost all received the Sacrament except a few members of the Society of Friends who attended in 'silent fellowship'.

Tambaram, 1938. This conference saw two 'open' Communion Services. On 18th December a service was conducted by Dr. C. Y. Cheng and Monsieur Anet 'after the manner of Reformed and Free Churches' to which the members of all Churches were invited as communicants and those who acted as servers were of many different nationalities. A week later (Christmas Day) the service was according to the Anglican rite and, again, all members of the conference were invited by those responsible for the service to come and to receive the Sacrament. The celebrant on this occasion was Bishop Azariah of Dornakal and he was assisted by other Anglican bishops from Nigeria, China, Japan, the United States and England. Again these services were not a responsibility of the conference committee as such, but were arranged by members of the conference who believed themselves called to do so, without thereby implicating any who thought their action wrong or unwise; since no Orthodox were present, those with such hesitations would have been a small group.

When the Edinburgh Conference of 1910 was called, it was on
the clear understanding that its purpose was co-operation and that
contentious questions of the Churches' faith and discipline would
not be raised. This understanding has underlain the tradition in
the International Missionary Council that such subjects as intercommunion are not proper material for discussion or resolution
at their conferences. Where some kind of action has been necessary it appears to have been agreed by informal consultation
between responsible leaders present for any given occasion, so that
any consistent policy was neither expected nor achieved.

Stockholm, 1925. To turn now to the 'Life and Work' tradition,
the official report of the Stockholm Conference[10] contains scant
references. The Holy Communion was celebrated according to
the English rite at 8 a.m. each day, both in the Jacobs Kyrka and
in the English church.[11] There were two Sundays during the
conference. On the first, 23rd August, there was a joint Service
of Preparation for Holy Communion, conducted at 9 a.m. in the
Engelbrekt church by Bishop Max von Bonsdorf, and at 11 a.m.
a Communion Service at which the Bishops of Växjö and Lund
with six other Lutheran pastors were the officiating clergy. Dr.
A. J. Brown, the American Joint President of the Conference,
was the preacher. The service has priority of mention in the
Report and the sermon is there reported in full, but clearly it was
not meant to be 'the Conference service', since the Report lists
eight other services held at the same hour in other churches,
including the English, French and Russian churches in Stockholm,
at which members of the conference were the preachers. It is not
clear how many of these other eight (apart from the Russian
Orthodox Liturgy) were also Communion Services.[12] Although
the Report does not say so, the invitation at the Engelbrekt
church service was to all baptised and communicant members of
any Christian Church to be present and to receive the Sacrament.

A significant insight into the mind of Archbishop Söderblom
on these questions is given in a description he gives of this service.
Father Max Pribilla, S.J., had suggested that Söderblom had hoped
to unite the members of all the Churches represented at Stockholm

[10] Ed. G. K. A. Bell, Oxford University Press, 1926.
[11] *Op. cit.*, p. 14.
[12] *Op. cit.*, pp. 345-358.

in a common celebration of the Eucharist.[13] Söderblom replied that he had never had any such intention, but gives his own description of the service.

'For a variety of reasons we were quite unanimous in our judgment, that although the idea was fine and uplifting and worthy of the occasion, it could not possibly take place. In the first place because of the time left at our disposal. An entirely open Communion would have taken at least an hour and a half; or rather should we say that, since many of the four thousand or so who were present but were not actually members of the Conference would certainly have wanted to participate and would not, on our principles, have been able to be refused, the service would have taken three hours or even longer, compared with the otherwise regularly allotted time of one-and-a-quarter to one-and-a-half hours for the main services of the Conference. There were other reasons, too. In the present situation, for example, our Eastern brethren would have been unable to participate. In a service where all the members of the Conference were, so to speak, officially present, this division would very likely have caused offence. So it was a demand of both necessity and of love that the Eucharist be omitted from the closing service in the year of grace 1925. But the services of the Stockholm Conference were not arranged by the Conference Committee but by the local churches, which to my mind should always be the case, and which will always be the demand of Swedish custom. So absolutely no discussion took place about the celebration of the Communion during the High Mass in the Engelbrekts church. This service was verily the high point of the whole Conference. The extraordinary thing happened there that does not yet exist in the contemporary life of the Church, but which can from time to time happen by the Grace and Power of God, as something deeply rooted in Christian faith, in the nature of the Eucharist, and as prophetic of the future. We sat together. The eucharistic liturgy was sung. The superhuman mystical moment drew near. The words of institu-

[13] Max Pribilla, S.J., *Um Kirchliche Einheit*, Lausanne-Rome. Herder, Freiburg im Breisgau, 1929, XXI, p. 332. Söderblom's reply is entitled *Pater Max Pribilla und die Oekumenische Erweckung. Einige Randbemerkungen von Nathan Söderblom, Upsala*, 1931, Almquist und Wiksells Boktryckeri.

tion were quietly read, the Lord's Prayer solemnly recited, and the Sanctus rose powerfully from the lips of priests and choir and congregation. One of the clergy said the Pax Vobiscum, and while the Agnus Dei was being sung by the congregation the Saviour's guests went to the altar in silent prayer. They all lifted up their hearts unto the Lord, and so they were united with the saints and with their fellow-Christians in heaven and on earth. They knelt and knew the real presence of the Saviour as they received the elements at the priests' hands. Then the whole body of them went back to their places together, as is the custom with us. Then more came forward. How long would the Eucharist last? Who would come? Lutherans of all shades came, those who can only be compared for exclusiveness to Romans and a few Anglo-Catholics, and others more ecumenically minded. Presbyterians came and Congregationalists, Methodists, Anglicans (among them the leading personalities of the Anglo-Catholics), Baptists, members of the Czechoslovak National Church and members of Eastern, but not Orthodox Communions, Disciples of Christ, Waldensians, Quakers. No conclusions can be drawn from that Pentecostal miracle. The participants did not belie their convictions, nor the principles of their churchmanship or of their movement. They felt that the Spirit of God was there, and that they were commanded by Him to let down the barriers for once and to experience the unity that is *in Christo* at His table.'

On the second Sunday, which fell outside the conference programme as such, the delegates were all taken by special train from Stockholm to Upsala, where a closing service was held in the Cathedral at which Archbishop Söderblom preached. The service was the Swedish *Högmässa*, without Communion.[14]

Oxford, 1937. This conference followed a similar pattern on the second of the Sundays which it contained, 25th July, in that it was the Established Church of the country of meeting which held a Communion Service to which all were invited. The Archbishop of Canterbury was the celebrant in St. Mary's (the University Church) at such a service for the delegates, whilst the Bishop of Chichester was celebrant in a parallel service in St. Aldate's for

[14] The text of the sermon and of the service are given in the *Report*, pp. 73-9 745 and 770-791.

the associate and youth delegates for whom there was not space in St. Mary's. There was a celebration of the Orthodox Liturgy in Hertford College Chapel at 8.30 a.m., the Anglican Services being at 8 a.m. The previous evening Canon F. A. Cockin (then Vicar of St. Mary's) had led a service of preparation for Holy Communion to which all the Conference had been invited.

But on the previous Sunday, 18th July, there had been three Communion Services at different hours: Anglican at 7.15 and 8 a.m. in St. Mary's; Orthodox at 7.30 a.m. in Hertford College Chapel and 'after the manner of Churches of the Reformed tradition' in Mansfield College Chapel. Although this arrangement made possible a certain amount of that non-communicating attendance at Communion Services of other traditions which we have noted as part of the W.S.C.F. tradition at this period, there is no indication in the conference literature that this practice was suggested to the delegates.[15]

Subsequent comment on the Oxford Conference has included two notes: first, that the 'open Communion Service' (often referred to as a 'united Communion Service') was for many delegates the spiritual climax of the whole conference; secondly, the Orthodox felt that here the Church of England, through the Archbishop of Canterbury, acted in a purely 'Protestant' way without giving expression to its tradition of 'Catholic order' such as they expect of it.[16]

Lausanne, 1927. To turn to the 'Faith and Order' tradition, we may properly consider not only the practice but some of the statements of that part of the Ecumenical Movement specifically concerned with such subjects as this.

The Lausanne Conference *Report*[17] contains no reference whatever to any arrangements for Communion Services. These were held to be strictly a matter for the representatives of the several Churches present at the conference to make suitable provision for themselves. The machinery of conference notices and so on was available to notify delegates as to what those arrangements were, but they were not, on principle, recorded by the editor of the

---

[15] Refs.: *Oxford Conference Report*, pp. 18-21, 285 and 288.

[16] The grounds for the Archbishop's action are, of course, no part of the subject of this essay but are fully set out in this volume under 'the rules and practice . . . of the Church of England'. See Appendix, pp. 362-367.

[17] Ed. by H. N. Bate, 1928.

Report as being in any sense part of the conference proceedings. Neither do the recorded proceedings of the three Saturdays (7th, 14th and 21st August) contain any reference to a corporate act of preparation for Holy Communion. However, on the middle Sunday there was held at 8.30 a.m. a 'Service of Penitence and Intercession', drawn up by Canon E. S. Woods (later Bishop of Lichfield) and led by Bishop Brent, Pastor Merle d'Aubigné and Pastor Sandegren. The service was inspired by the sorrow which lack of sacramental unity engendered.

The Eglise Vaudoise arranged on 14th August, the second Sunday, a service of Holy Communion in the Cathedral to which it extended an invitation to all members of the conference, an invitation which was conveyed to the conference by its President, Bishop Brent. (See German Report of the Conference, p. 341.) Over a thousand persons received communion, kneeling at two great tables which had been spread, from the hands of the four officiating ministers.[18]

The proposal that there should be a Communion Service as the closing act of the whole conference as such was warmly pressed by Dr. Peter Ainslie (Disciples in America) and Bishop Hognestad of Bergen, but the suggestion was not accepted (see German Report, pp. 404 and 420).

Section VI of the Lausanne Conference was concerned with 'the Sacraments'. When the report of the section was debated in plenary session there were naturally references to the division of Christians from one another at the Lord's Table, but it was brought to a crisis by a resolution moved by Dr. William Adams Brown to add certain considerations to the material before the drafting committee of this section. The three main points were:

'(1) The possibility, pending the solution of the larger and more important difficulties above referred to, of some provision at future conferences for united or simultaneous celebration of the Sacrament, in a form consistent with the present law of the several Churches, which could express to the world the spiritual unity to which we have already attained.

[18] They were Bishop H. Ostenfeld (Danish Lutheran), Dr. August Lang (German Reformed), Dr. Henri Monnier (French Reformed), Dr. William Adams Brown (American Presbyterian), assisted by two ministers of the Cathedral. The service is described by William Adams Brown in *Towards a United Church*, pp. 109-110.

'(2) The possibility, without prejudice to the doctrinal position of each Church, of providing in communities where no other possibility of partaking of the Sacrament exists for the admission to Communion, under proper safeguard, of members of other Christian bodies resident in or visiting those communities.

'(3) The possibility, under similar safeguards, of making early provision for some form of intercommunion or, if that be not immediately possible, joint or simultaneous celebration in the new Churches in non-Christian lands.'

Various delegates, notably Bishop Charles Gore, protested that this was to introduce too contentious material too late in the conference. Dr. A. E. Garvie, who was presiding, concurred with that view and Dr. Brown, accepting it as sound, withdrew his resolution.[19] The Report of Section VI finally said no more on the subject than this closing sentence: 'We close this statement with the prayer that the differences which prevent full communion at the present time may be removed.'

Edinburgh, 1937. The conference records[20] contain a note that 'no meetings or services were arranged for by the conference during the daytime on Sundays, so that members should be left free to worship in Edinburgh churches, many of which provided special services on these two Sundays'. Among such services was a Communion Service in St. Giles' Cathedral, conducted after the tradition of the Church of Scotland, to which, it was announced by the Cathedral authorities, all members of the Conference would be welcomed as communicants. On the same morning there was a service of Holy Communion in the Scottish Episcopal Cathedral of St. Mary, and the Holy Liturgy of the Eastern Orthodox Church was celebrated in Holy Trinity Church, Dean Bridge. It appears that the Church of Scotland and the Episcopalian services were fixed for the same hour by independent decisions long before the conference, though the effect may have been to embarrass some Anglicans who regretted the coincidence of the two.

[19] For Dr. W. A. Brown's own account of the discussion, see *Towards a United Church*, pp. 105-106.
[20] See *Edinburgh*, 1937, ed. L. Hodgson, p. 77.

The conference itself had considerable discussion on the subject of intercommunion.[21] In the final revision of Chapter VI of the Report on 'The Church's Unity in Life and Worship' there was some vigorous debate. Both those who advocated and those who opposed intercommunion feared that their convictions were inadequately expressed in the draft. The Report first defines the term:

'A second aspect of church unity is commonly indicated by the term "intercommunion". This is the fullest expression of a mutual recognition between two or more Churches. Such recognition is also manifested in the exchange of membership and ministrations.

'We regard sacramental intercommunion as a necessary part of any satisfactory church unity. Such intercommunion, as between two or more Churches, implies that all concerned are true Churches, or true branches of the one Church.

'We think that it should be pointed out that the word "intercommunion" has at present several different connotations. In the fullest sense it means a relation between two or more Churches in which the Communion of each is open to all members of the other at all times. This is to be distinguished from relations in which the Communion of one Church is "open" to members of other Churches without complete reciprocal recognition, and still more from the occasional welcoming of members of other Churches by a Church whose normal rule would exclude them. We believe that "regularity" and "mutuality" belong to the full meaning of intercommunion. When this term "intercommunion" is used in discussion of church unity its meaning should be clearly defined.

'We must note also the occasions on which at a gathering of Christian people united in a common enterprise, a Church has invited all who have full status in their own Churches to receive the Holy Communion according to the rite of the inviting Church. This has occurred both at Oxford and at Edinburgh during the conferences held this year. It is to be distinguished both from "intercommunion" and "open communion" as usually understood, and from such "joint celebration" as took place at Jerusalem in 1928.'

[2] *Op. cit.*, pp. 183-184, 251-252, 265-266, 359, 366.

Then, when it comes to list seventeen items under: 'What can we do to move towards the unity we seek?' the twelfth item is headed 'Increase of intercourse'. The first two paragraphs read:

'We draw attention to the multiplying examples of exchange of membership, of interchange of pulpits and of intercommunion on the part of the different Churches in all parts of the world, and, subject to proper understanding and regulation, believe that these practices should be encouraged.

'Where occasional Communion is admitted in the practice of a Church but is not formally recognised by its law, it is desirable that, where principles permit, this apparent incongruity should be removed as soon as possible in order to avoid misunderstanding, both on the part of the recipient and of members of the communion extending the invitation. Where hesitancy still remains because of this ambiguity or for any reason, the communicants of one Church, whether ministers or laymen, should be encouraged to be present, even if they do not participate, at the sacraments of other Churches. And such presence should be regarded as an act of common worship expressing the measure of spiritual unity already attained.'

The third paragraph was finally agreed in a form suggested by the chairman, Archbishop William Temple, to run:

'We feel moved to say in this connection that neither those who press for intercommunion nor those who feel obliged to oppose it should condemn the others, but should in all ways respect one another's consciences; but all Christians should be saddened by every hindrance to the fellowship of full communion with all sincere disciples of our Lord.'

Amsterdam and Oslo Youth Conferences, 1939 *and* 1947. Before looking at the Amsterdam Assembly and the present situation, we must briefly consider two important world conferences of Christian Youth which did something to bring the thought and practice of the W.S.C.F. before a wider constituency and influenced subsequent practice. The Amsterdam and Oslo conferences were organised by co-operation between the W.S.C.F., the World's Y.M.C.A., the World's Y.W.C.A. and the Youth Commission of the World Alliance for International Friendship through the Churches and the World Council of Churches

Provisional Committee (the latter two being fused later into the Youth Department of the World Council of Churches). So a very varied constituency of Christian youth could be anticipated. Considerable pains were taken, in the preparatory years, to present the worship intelligibly to the young delegates. A long and searching discussion at the preparatory committee of 1937 issued in the decision to try what was the then policy of the W.S.C.F. over Communion Services at a wider gathering. A specially written brochure, in the hands of all delegates, introduced them to the conference worship in general and said this about the Communion Services in particular:

'When the members of the conference go to the Communion Services on the Sunday and Monday they will experience the fact that Christendom is divided. They will see that it has been considered impossible to arrange one Communion Service for all members of the conference—a service at which we might all receive the Sacrament together and manifest our unity in Christ. There will be altogether four Communion Services: one according to the Dutch Reformed rite for members of the Reformed and "Free" Churches which is open to all baptised members of other Churches who wish to partake of the Sacrament; one according to the Lutheran rite for Lutherans and others who are entitled to and wish to receive the Sacrament in the Lutheran Church; a third according to the Anglican rite for Anglicans and members of Churches in communion with the Anglican Church; and a fourth (on Monday morning) for the members of the Orthodox Churches. But though we cannot all receive the Sacrament together, it should be noted that all members of the conference are invited to *attend* all these services.

'None the less this manifestation of the disunion of Christendom will certainly be a most distressing experience. To most of us it will be more distressing than all differences in doctrine and opinions. It is therefore useful that we should know beforehand that there will be no possibility of receiving the Holy Communion together and that there are serious reasons for this fact which we must try to understand. We must remember that we are not only Christian individuals who can act as if the present disunion of Christendom did not exist, but we are members of different Churches and have to be loyal to our Churches. The fact of the four Communion Services is an outcome of the serious differences in sacramental doctrine represented by our Churches and of the different attitudes to intercommunion adopted by our Churches in accordance with the character of their eucharistic doctrines.

'In the following paragraphs members of the Churches concerned explain the positive eucharistic teaching of those Churches and the meaning which they attach to the different parts of the service. Thus it is hoped that members of other Churches will attend and be able to enter deeply into worship even when the forms are strange to them, and also that they will be able to understand the attitudes of the different Churches on the question of intercommunion.'

Then, after fourteen pages introducing the teaching and tradition of the several Communion Services to be held, it concludes:

'It is clear from what precedes that at some of the Communion Services all the members of the conference will be invited to receive the Sacrament, but that some will not feel free to accept the invitation; while at other services the invitation will be limited to certain sections of the conference. None the less it is hoped that all members of the conference will not only receive the Sacrament at one of the services to which they are specially invited, but will also consider attending other services. Attendance at the Communion Service of another Church, even without communicating, has been found by many to be a very profound ecumenical experience.

'There will be a Service of Preparation for all members of the conference on the Saturday night. This will not be primarily concerned with our divisions, but with our unity in Christ. We shall prepare together for the solemn act of receiving communion, and for the opportunity and responsibility of entering into worship which is unfamiliar to us. It is no small matter to take part in this joint preparation, for it will remind us that, however deep may be the tragic divisions in the Church, we serve one Master, and come to His table as His guests.'

There was a carefully prepared common service of preparation and penitence on the Saturday night, at which Dr. Robert Mackie (then General Secretary of the W.S.C.F.) gave an address which helped greatly to see the situation in true focus.

The conference *Report*[23] justly summed up the matter thus:

> 'The worship at the Amsterdam Conference was planned in the belief that ecumenism in worship means both seeking the greatest depth of unity in worship and sharing to the full the richness of the various Christian traditions. The divisions of the Churches and the lack of spiritual depth and experience of individual Christians make the achievement of this double purpose very difficult. But none can doubt that the Spirit of Unity and Life was at work at Amsterdam. Nearly all the delegates entered together into the worship expressed in most, if not all, of the different forms. Few failed to find their understanding of worship enriched by a heightened consciousness of the treasures both of their own communion and of other Churches and traditions. And through all the worship came a grander vision of the unity already given to those who worship the God and Father of our Lord Jesus Christ, and a more urgent longing for the completer manifestation of that unity in this world.'

The procedure at Oslo was practically the same as at Amsterdam, except that the most attended service, that of the 'host Church', was the Lutheran instead of the Reformed. In both cases the invitation to be communicants had been addressed to all baptised and communicant members of any Church, and in both cases the great majority of the conference had felt able to accept the invitation. However, at the Anglican service at Amsterdam the paragraph about attendance ran:

> 'All the members of the conference are invited to attend the service although it is not an "open Communion" at which delegates not in full communion with the Church of England can be invited to receive the Sacrament. It is the general rule of the Anglican Churches that their members should receive the Holy Communion only from priests of their own Church or of Churches in full communion with it. Greatly desiring to see the visible unity of the Church restored, the Anglican Churches nevertheless disallow indiscriminate intercommunion

---

[23] *Christus Victor: The Report of the World Conference of Christian Youth, Amsterdam,* 1939, p. 34.

or any such intercommunion as seems to approve the con-
tinuance of separately organised Churches.'

A similar attitude was finally adopted at Oslo, but only after
it had been widely announced that the service would be an 'open
Communion'. When the decision of the Anglican authorities was
made known shortly before the conference, the Conference Committee felt that it would cause unnecessary confusion amongst the
youthful delegates to give a prominent place to the Anglican
Communion Service, so the conference literature refers only to
the Lutheran and Orthodox services. The time and place of the
Anglican service were simply announced in the daily bulletin.

In the case of both these youth conferences the Anglican
authorities had considered that a conference of relatively uninstructed young people did not constitute a gathering for the
furthering of reunion in the sense envisaged by the Convocation
of Canterbury resolution.[24] Of course, this interpretation could
only be an advice, particularly weighty for Anglicans from the
Church of England, since based upon the opinion of the Bishop
of Fulham,[25] given after consultation with the Bishop of London
and the two Archbishops. Anglicans from other provinces did
not feel bound by it to the same degree, and some, particularly
Americans, had been specifically counselled by their bishops to
receive communion at the Reformed or Lutheran services. As
always, the Orthodox Liturgy was open to be *attended* by all,
though only Orthodox could be communicants.

In both conferences, intercommunion became a subject of lively
discussion and great heart-searching. The Anglican intransigence
(though resented by some Anglicans) brought the matter into
sharper focus, since most Protestants found the Orthodox minority
so utterly strange in any case that their 'closed Communion' was
just one more incomprehensible eccentricity. It was never clearer
that Anglicans provide a catalyst in this question when they do
not hold an 'open Communion'. Owing to the inevitable small-
ness of Orthodox delegations, under present conditions, and to
the absence of Roman Catholics, it is only when Anglicans join
the Orthodox in refusing intercommunion that the problem
reaches the numerical dimensions that compel attention. Whether

[24] See Appendix, p. 366.
[25] The suffragan bishop in charge of English churches in Northern Europe.

E

Anglicans wish to be a catalyst is a question that is argued elsewhere in this volume, but the effect on the minds of the younger
generation caused by the Anglican attitude at Amsterdam, 1939,
and Oslo, 1947, was undoubtedly a factor in the change of temper
in the W.S.C.F. by 1949 which has already been described.

Amsterdam Assembly, 1948. For a year before the Assembly met,
a small group had been appointed to think about its worship.
When the delegates received their Official Handbook they found[26]
this explanation which had been prepared by the group:

'The worship at the Assembly falls into two main types:

A. Worship arranged as part of the Assembly itself;

B. Worship arranged by the authorities of the Churches
represented at the conference.

'A. In the first category fall the *Opening and Closing Services*,
the service of preparation for the Holy Communion and the
daily worship at the beginning and the end of each day's work.
The form of all these services will be distributed to all present
in as full a version as possible, and in all three of the conference
languages.

'The half-hour of worship in the Koepelkerk from 9 to 9.30
a.m. each day will, incidentally, illustrate so far as possible the
diversity of church traditions, since the leader has been invited
to conduct the worship in the tradition to which he himself
belongs.

'The brief closing act of worship each day will be held
wherever the delegates may be (either in plenary session or in
committees or sub-committees) at the end of the day's work.
The experience of previous conferences has suggested that when
minds are tired there is great refreshment to be found in adhering to the same simple form each day. It is with this in mind
that this form of prayer is offered. The order for these services
may be found in English, French and German at the back of
the Handbook, pp. 109.

'B. *Services of Holy Communion*. Among services arranged by
the churches themselves are principally the services of Holy
Communion. These have been arranged on the following
principles:

[26] *Loc. cit.*, p. 25.

'(1) The Assembly as such does not hold services of Holy Communion, since it is a gathering of Christians representing diverse traditions and disciplines.

'(2) The Committee on Arrangements for the Assembly wishes to make facilities for services of Holy Communion on these two principles:

'(i) that each member of the Assembly should have the opportunity to participate *as a communicant* in a service of the Holy Communion;

'(ii) that each member of the Assembly should have the opportunity to attend, in the fellowship of prayer, the eucharistic worship of other traditions, even though, whether by reason of his own conscience or by reason of the tradition of the Church of which he is a member or which is holding the service, he cannot participate as a communicant.

'(3) The Committee desires, in accordance with these principles, that facilities for Holy Communion Services be arranged by the representatives at the Assembly of the following church traditions:

'(i) *Netherlands Reformed Church.* A service of Celebration of the Lord's Supper will be held in the *Nieuwe Kerk* (New Church, Dam) at 10.00 hours on Sunday, 29th August. The authorities of the New Church wish it to be announced that all members of the Assembly who are baptised, communicant members of their own Churches are invited to partake as communicants, and that ministers of other communions will assist in the celebration.

'(ii) A service of Holy Communion according to the rite of the *Church of England* will be held in the Lutheran Church (Spui) at 8.00 hours on Monday, 30th August. It is expected that only members of Anglican Churches, or of Churches on terms of mutual admission to communion with them, will receive Communion at this service. The presence of other members of the conference will be warmly welcomed.

'(iii) *The Holy Liturgy of the Eastern Orthodox Church* will be celebrated in the Lutheran Church (Spui) at 8.00 hours on Tuesday, 31st August. Although only those who are members of the Holy Orthodox Churches receive the Sacrament, members of all other Christian communions are cordially invited to be present and to participate in the fellowship of prayer.

'(iv) A service of Holy Communion according to the *Lutheran* rite will be held in the Lutheran Church (Spui) at 8.00 hours on Wednesday, 1st September. All Christians who are baptised and communicant members of Churches and who wish to receive the Body and Blood of our Lord Jesus Christ at this service are welcome.'

The four statements in section 3 had been drafted each by the leader of the tradition concerned who, in the judgment of the Worship Committee, had the best right to speak for his fellow members. There followed a series of more detailed arrangements for services including Communion Services in various churches in the city, catering for various traditions, which did not interfere in their hours with the official conference programme.

It will be observed that the general pattern is that of the Amsterdam and Oslo Youth conferences, including a similar interpretation (by the Archbishop of Canterbury) of the requirements for being a communicant at the Anglican service. Since it is of the nature of the Anglican conception of authority in the Church that such an interpretation could not be considered binding (especially upon those from other than the two English provinces) there were naturally Anglicans, ordained and lay, who felt bound in conscience to accept the invitation of the Dutch Reformed Church if their own Communion Service was not an 'open' one.

It also appears on this evidence that there are greater difficulties for Lutherans to attend a Reformed service than vice versa, since at Amsterdam in 1939 and 1948, when the host Church, being Reformed, issued an open invitation, there was a Lutheran service; at Oslo, when the national Lutheran Church held an 'open Communion', there was no Reformed service.

At the Amsterdam Assembly also, as at the two youth conferences, there was a service of common preparation. The *Report*[27] thus describes the service of preparation and the Communion Services which followed:

[27] See *Amsterdam Report*, pp. 40-42.

'There were services of Holy Communion according to the church usage of the Anglicans, the Eastern Orthodox and the Lutherans. The largest service was that in which our host Church, the Reformed Church of Holland, invited all baptised and communicant members of other Churches to participate. These services were preceded by the Service of Preparation on Saturday evening in the Nieuwe Kerk. The latter, a service simple and deeply moving, should be mentioned particularly. The liturgy expressed the sorrows and the hopes of this gathering which so earnestly desired unity but could not at this deepest level achieve its aspirations. The sermon, preached without manuscript and with deep feeling by Dr. Hendrik Kraemer, moved the congregation to real penitence while at the same time indicating that the unity so intensely desired was here in a measure foreshadowed. During this service those who must still be divided at the Lord's Table united in preparation to receive, though according to diverse forms, the Body and Blood of the One Lord in whom lies the only hope of unity.

'At the Communion Service on the following day some twelve hundred of the Assembly members took part. Ten ministers from different countries and different confessions sat in turn at the Communion Table and spoke the words of institution as each group of communicants came forward. It was an impressive service, expressing the fellowship of the Church at its deepest level.

'For two-and-a-half hours the representatives of the Churches and nations moved in groups of one hundred to find their places at the Lord's Table. There were men and women from all corners of the world, of all races. There were archbishops and laymen, youth delegates and aged church leaders. They came and at the Table each passed the bread and then the chalice to his neighbour.

'To the Anglican, Lutheran and Eastern Orthodox Communion Services the whole Assembly was invited, even though all could not partake of the elements: and this experience was deeply fruitful for all those who attended. Here was the possibility for many Christians to share in the central act of worship of Communions other than their own. The simple dignity of the Anglican service, the confessional strength of the Lutheran service, during which many non-Lutherans also received Communion, and the dramatic fullness of the Eastern Orthodox service—all contributed in no small measure to the worship of the Assembly.

'In addition to these provisions for all delegates, in the sense that all these acts of worship took place at times and places when all could be present if they wished, there were opportunities on many other occasions for private and corporate prayer and sacramental worship according to the traditions of the various Christians who were present. But these were not so much activities of the Assembly at worship as opportunities for the individuals who composed the Assembly to practise the life of devotion to which they were accustomed.

'The Assembly had much business to transact. It was a time of rush and strain. But the times of worship brought real refreshment when those who were met together on God's business together sought Him who had called them.'

Some Conclusions

Is it possible to discern, from this brief account of varied practices, any principles which govern the handling, at ecumenical conferences, of the problems of Communion and intercommunion? Gradually certain principles have emerged from the ecumenical conferences which preceded its formation to be accepted by the World Council committees as they plan ecumenical gatherings:[28]

(i) The World Council must be scrupulous to avoid appearing 'to hold Communion Services'. It is not the Church; it is not even a Church. At most it can provide facilities for the representatives of Churches present at its meetings themselves to provide their members with the eucharistic worship to which they are accustomed and, if it so decide, avoid arranging corporate, conference activities which conflict in time with such provisions.

(ii) It must be equally scrupulous to avoid suggesting that any one service, thus arranged, has the right to be called 'the corporate communion *of the conference*' so long as any minority, however small, is for conscience sake not communicant at it.

(iii) The regulations governing attendance (communicant or

[28] Cf. *The Report of the Committee on Worship* received by the Central Committee meeting at Chichester in 1949, of which see *Minutes*, pp. 48-50.

non-communicant) at such services is wholly the concern of the Churches as such or of individual consciences within them, and in no sense a prerogative of the Council in general or of any particular conferences or Assembly of it.

But other questions are not so easily settled.

(i) The location of responsibility among 'the representatives of the Churches' at a meeting is not easily decided. The same individuals are simultaneously representatives of their Churches and also presidents, chairmen, members and so on of the Council and of its various committees when they attend ecumenical gatherings. It is not always easy to distinguish in practice between decisions taken in these two different capacities by the same person or persons. Furthermore, in the Churches which make up the Council many different theories are held as to the authority which a particular church leader may have to take decisions binding upon fellow members of his own Church, let alone upon members of other Churches in the same 'denominational' or 'confessional' group. Yet administrative decisions arise at such meetings—for example, whether facilities for a Communion Service are to be sought from the 'conference authorities' and the conditions under which it shall be celebrated. Somebody has to make those decisions and to answer for the consequences.

(ii) Practical considerations may make it impossible literally to fulfil the desired principles; for example, the principle of the Amsterdam Assembly that 'each member of the Assembly should have the opportunity to participate as a communicant' was in fact violated because members of the Separated Eastern Churches could not be communicants at any of the four main Communion Services. Yet they were such a small minority that their Liturgy could hardly be made a fifth main service, especially since from the point of view of the vast majority it would seem liturgically indistinguishable from the Orthodox Liturgy.[29] There may have been other groups who in fact found themselves deprived of the Sacrament by the way in which this principle was worked out. Such difficulties are of course in direct ratio to the size and complexity of the gathering in question.

[29] In fact, Syrian Jacobite and Mar Thoma celebrations of Q'barna were arranged at early hours on weekdays, but it remained a breach of the enunciated principle governing the selection of only *four* main services.

(iii) Great varieties of conviction are to be found *within* Churches and confessions as the preceding *Report* of this Commission has made clear.[30] The Council and its officers can but appeal to responsible leaders in the Churches (subject to the complications just mentioned in (i)) to make arrangements in accordance with the practice of their several Churches. But when experience has already shown that apparently contradictory decisions will be taken by the same Church at different times, does it lay upon the conference authorities a responsibility to explain, or to give the Churches time and space to explain, in the conference programme the reasons for their action? The Anglican Churches (by virtue of their Catholic-Protestant tensions and the high degree of discretion allowed to individual bishops) are naturally a source of considerable bewilderment to others if not to themselves. Yet it must not be supposed that there are not considerable differences of opinion within the Protestant denominations. Some, for example, would have grave objection to open Communion if not based at least upon the *baptism* of all would-be communicants. Even among the Orthodox different opinions are to be found as to the grounds upon which non-Orthodox might conceivably be given sacraments in Orthodox churches. So long as Churches vary so much in their principles and practice, ecumenical gatherings will seem to reflect a variety of situations hard to distinguish from sheer chaos.

(iv) Ecumenical gatherings vary a great deal in character. Duration and the primary purpose of a gathering, the number and the age and experience of the participants—these and other considerations may properly influence those responsible for an ecumenical gathering in the decisions they take about providing facilities for church representatives to hold Communion Services. Many delicate questions can arise over the times and places where such services are held, the greater or less prominence which their announcement is given and the pains taken to ensure that all delegates know what is happening and why it is happening in the way it is. In any event, a heavy *pastoral* responsibility lies, in regard to this question as well as in regard to many others, upon those who are responsible for the administration of ecumenical conferences. The section of the *Report* of this Commission dealing with this aspect may do much to build up a commonly accepted

[30] See pp. 15-43.

standard wherever ecumenical gatherings are being organised.

The Ecumenical Movement reflects the Churches which compose it. Part of that reflection shows a perceptible increase in concern with the question of intercommunion. In Faith and Order, as we have seen, it has naturally received the most conscious attention, though it has been felt as a problem, sometimes acutely, in every part of the movement because felt increasingly in the Churches which compose it. The Edinburgh Conference Continuation Committee in 1939 recognised that the problem of intercommunion stood out as a problem for corporate consideration, stood out so prominently that it could not be one subject among others for the Liturgical Commission which Edinburgh had requested should be set up. It was accordingly made the sole subject of the Commission which, more than ten years later, produces this volume to show that the subject is indeed complex and urgent. Perhaps the main reason why the problem is now so widely recognised as important is that ever-increasing numbers have attended ecumenical gatherings of different kinds and have there found the problem unavoidable. Gradually, various methods of dealing with it have been evolved. There may be a danger that the Ecumenical Movement, prone to seek smooth running as all organisations tend to do, may try to find a formula which puts 'intercommunion' into its place, as one of the snags which are likely to occur and must be quickly and smoothly dealt with. But fortunately the problem is too alive for such easy resolution —or rather, the people who feel it are too alive to be so easily tamed. It has become 'a thorn in the flesh' for the Ecumenical Movement. Once again, it may be found the weakness in which strength is made perfect, the occasion to seek God's all-sufficient grace. When it is fully removed it will be because, by God's grace alone, the 'Ecumenical Movement' has ceased to be, and we have been given not 'intercommunion' but *communion* in an undivided Church.

Part Three

CONTRIBUTIONS TO THE PRESENT
DISCUSSIONS ON INTERCOMMUNION

V

AMICA CONTESTATIO

*

Yves M. J. Congar
Roman Catholic Church

(France)

These few remarks have no other pretension than that of possibly helping other Christians to a better approach to the problem of intercommunion. They would like to be friendly and brief. But it is impossible to say something useful on this subject without bringing into question an entire ecclesiology. Hence I have been able neither to be as brief as I would have wished, nor to avoid contradicting men for whom I feel a very sincere and even affectionate esteem.

The question of intercommunion is generally put, in the Faith and Order movement, from the sacramental point of view. It constitutes one of the most decisive elements in 'unity by mutual recognition'. It comprises two aspects: the admission to Communion of members of another Church, and the co-celebration of ministers belonging to different confessions (*communautés*). In both these cases the question is most often considered as one of sacramental discipline. This is certainly so, but it should not be forgotten that the sacramental (*sacramentaire*) problem involves an ecclesiological problem. Father Hebert has already most usefully drawn attention to this (*Intercommunion*, S.P.C.K., 1932). I believe that questions of vocabulary are of great importance, and that the study of words, of their use, and of their relations, often throws considerable light. It is certainly not by chance nor in vain that the same word 'Communion' designates, on the one hand, a sacramental act which is accomplished in the celebration of the Eucharist and, on the other hand, the church community, the very unity of the Church.[1] These two things have a very profound

---

[1] I think that from the semantic point of view one may see things in this way: the first usage of the word refers to the Eucharist. Excommunication was

connection with one another; it is nevertheless good to consider intercommunion successively from the ecclesiological and from the sacramental point of view. (*Distinguer pour unir. . . .*)

The Ecclesiological Question

Everything depends here on the relationship which one sees between the notion of 'Church' and that of 'Communion'. Two principal positions seem to me to confront one another: one is that of Roman Catholic theology, which is that held by the author of these lines; the other seems to me to be typically Anglican.

(a) *The Roman Catholic position.* The Church is an institution and a Communion. There are here two aspects which the Germans, both Catholic and Protestant, describe as *Heilsanstalt* and *Heilsgemeinschaft*, and consideration of them is often very illuminating. It can be said that what Jesus Christ founded is essentially the institution: for the 'people of God' had existed ever since the time of Abraham, and the Church is only the people of God under the New and final Dispensation (*Diathèkè*). The institution will, then, be constituted by the fact that Jesus Christ has been pleased to create, together with men, a people of God under the final régime of the benefits of the Covenant or gifts of God. The Church-as-community will be the people thus assembled and living by these gifts: *Societas fidelium*, according to the formula which is so frequent in the whole tradition that it has been possible to give it as the very definition of the Church (see the compendium of Launois).

When one studies what Jesus did to constitute the New and final Dispensation of the people of God, that is to say, in other

to begin with exclusion from sacramental Communion. The ecclesiological usage, which came later, itself comprised, and still comprises, two moments: *communio*, which is in the first place participation in a reality, the act or the situation of him who participates in a common good or is the member of a society, of a body. We say in this sense: to be in communion with. . . . It is, secondly, the body itself, the society, the Church, with which one is in communion. We say in this sense: the Orthodox Communion, the Anglican Communion.

These few pages question a great number of biblical, patristic, historical and theological notions which it is clearly not possible to justify here by references. I am obliged to keep my justifications in my files.

words, the constitutive elements of the Church-as-institution, one finds three things (which correspond, moreover, to the three functions of Christ the prophet, the priest and the king: truth, life and way): the deposit of the faith, and principally of the trinitarian faith; the deposit of the sacraments of the faith, in the first place of Baptism and of the Eucharist, but also of the other sacraments which we see the Apostles using, and above all the imposition of hands for the ministry; the deposit of the apostolic powers instituting a ministry of teaching, worship and government of communities. Such are the three means of salvation constitutive of the Church-as-*Heilsanstalt* and, moreover, representing the content of the 'tradition' of the Church. (*Id quod traditum est ei, id quod traditur.*)

As *Heilsgemeinschaft*, the Church is the society or the Communion (in the second sense of the word, see note 1) of those who have Communion (in the first sense of the word, see note 1) and hence participation in these means of salvation: that is, who profess the faith and observe the sacraments of the apostolic 'tradition', and recognise the authority of the ministers instituted in the succession of the Apostles. It will be noticed at once that there is a perfect correspondence between the different aspects of the ecclesiastical Communion and the constitutive elements of the Church-as-institution, and that what is said here agrees with the most classic expositions on the ecclesiastical Communion.[2] But may not these classic expositions themselves claim the most authentic tradition, and be illustrated by the example of the apostolic Church itself: 'They continued stedfastly in the apostles' doctrine and fellowship, and in breaking of bread, and in prayers' (Acts 2. 42)?

Catholic theology has become progressively more aware of what was implied by this unity of the Church-as-Communion corresponding to its unity-as-institution. It has realised more clearly that it was not only a question, for individuals or for local communities, of a conformity of faith, worship and constitution,

---

[2] These expositions, as we know, distinguish three elements in the ecclesiastical Communion. The whole matter could be put in the following table:

Communion	in faith	deposit of the faith	Christ truth
	in sacraments	deposit of the sacraments	„ life
	in submission to the authority of pastors	apostolic powers	„ way

at least in all which was part of the apostolic tradition, but that the Church was called to form a single people, a single Communion. To keep Communion is not only to participate faithfully in the means of salvation of the church-institution; it is to form a community and to act, not as an autonomous subject, but as a member of a single people or body. The sin of schism betrays a separatist attitude which destroys this reference of a part to its whole.

In this perspective, as Canon Lacey has already shown (*Unity and Schism*, p. 56 *et seq.*), there cannot properly be 'inter-communion'. There is or there is not Communion, but Communion is of its nature universal and indivisible, like the Church herself of which it is an aspect. Either one has or one has not Communion in the Church, with the Church; if one has it, one has it wherever the Church is to be found, allowance having been made for local particularities, sometimes considerable but always respectful of the apostolic deposit, of which one could say, adapting a saying of St. Cyprian repeated by St. Augustine: *Licet, salvo jure communionis, diversum sentire.* That is why a member of the Church, if he is not 'excommunicated', may communicate sacramentally wherever he finds the Church, and relive the blessed experience of Abercius of Hierapolis: 'Everywhere I have had brothers. . . . Faith led me everywhere. Everywhere it supplied me with a fresh-water fish, large, pure, that had been caught by a pure virgin.' Inversely, the general custom was,—although history presents some exceptions—and the Councils demanded, that any one of the faithful who had broken off Communion with his bishop or who had been excommunicated should be nowhere received at Communion. This was a disciplinary rule which can be understood if one keeps in mind the homogeneous and indissoluble unity of the Church, whose 'Sacrament', as St. Cyprian says, resides in the unity of the episcopate, whose members hold the charge *in solidum.* It should only be added — and this St. Cyprian misunderstood—that the local churches were not alone in having received from the Lord and the Apostles their unified structure. The Church is constructed, as far as the apostolic powers which are transmitted by succession are concerned, not solely on the plane of the local churches, but on the plane of her ecumenical, universal reality. History has done much for the Roman primacy, more than Catholic apologists for the most part recognise, but the institution does not derive from history; it is not only a fact of the *life* of the Church, but of her apostolic *structure*. That is why it involves the very rule of Communion. The role of the apostolic See *par excellence* is to act as a guardian and a criterion, at the same time as being a centre of Communion at the heart of the one Church, extending to the very ends of the earth.

(b) *The Anglican position*. The ecclesiology which is typically Anglican has been capable of variation in its exterior presentation. Many, now, who say they reject the 'branch theory', repudiate, in reality, much more the name and its application to the three classic branches than the fundamental principle. This principle is the one which is seen to be formulated from the moment when Anglicanism defined itself theologically, and which can be followed in this or that good collection of relevant passages.[3] If I have understood it aright, it amounts to establishing a certain disjunction between the one Church and the society, the body or the Communion to which the faithful concretely belong. There is only one universal Church, but its unity is not necessarily that of a single society or communion. It is realised in the order of those elements which we have seen to constitute the Church-as-institution, that is to say, besides grace and spiritual gifts, faith, sacraments and the powers of the apostolic ministry. That this unity should, further, be social, that of a single people or of a single communion, is certainly desirable, but it is not strictly necessary. At the present time, the one Church exists in a plurality of particular societies or 'Churches', or, as James I (=Casaubon) said, particular 'Communions': the Anglican, the Orthodox, the Roman, the Old Catholic, etc. Each of these Communions has its own traditions in regard to doctrines, worship and ecclesiastical constitution. That is legitimate and normal so long as the fundamental points are adhered to in the triple domain of belief, sacraments and ministry. According to whether one is more or less exacting with regard to these fundamental points, one will accord to fewer or to more Christian Communions the privilege of composing the Church and the right to claim the title 'catholic'

---

[3] For example, the anthology of H. Maynard Smith, published by A. C. Headlam, at the end of *The Church of England*, London, 1924, p. 240 *et seq.*; or the texts quoted in T. A. Lacey, *The Unity of the Church as treated by English Theologians*, London, 1898. Lacey goes as far as Pusey; it would be quite easy to continue the work.

which qualifies, not one communion, but a certain quality of fidelity to the heritage of the Apostles. In particular it is a question of knowing whether the episcopate, with the apostolic succession, belongs to the *esse* of the Church, to the fundamental points, or only to the *bene esse* of the Church, which it is not strictly necessary to realize in order to be part of the latter.[4]

The ecumenical work of the Faith and Order movement, whose true inspiration is Anglican, and the problem of inter-communion, are better understood in this perspective. Faith and Order does in fact seek to establish, by gradual approaches, a form of visible unity between the bodies or communions which are equally 'catholic', but at present divided; indeed, between all the Christian Communions at present separated. What should be this form of visible unity? It is known how Commission IV of the Edinburgh Conference distinguished three forms or three degrees of unity—mutual recognition, co-operation, organic unity—and how intercommunion appears in this framework, after the exchange of members and the exchange of ministers or of ministries, as taking furthest the expression of the unity of mutual recognition.

In the perspective of the work of Faith and Order, the matter is easy to understand. It can be asked, however, whether the question, put in this way, does not imply, in the ecclesiological domain, the problem peculiar to Anglicanism with its distinction between the unity of the Church and particular communions, that of the *esse* and of the *bene esse*, distinctions themselves founded on the notion of fundamental articles or marks. The Orthodox Church, which has not exactly the same position as that of the Roman Catholic Church with regard to the *concrete* requirements of the unity of the Church as a single society or people, takes nevertheless a similar position, in its *ecclesiological doctrine*, with

[4] This point is still discussed. One knows the texts invoked by Dom Gregory Dix in favour of the episcopal function being a part of the *esse* of the Church. It seems to me difficult, however, from the passages contributed by A. J. Mason, Norman Sykes, Bishop Bell, etc., to maintain that the Anglican tradition considers the episcopate as of the *esse* of the Church. A broad interpretation of the Preface of the Ordinal seems to win acceptance (Bp. Hunkin, Canon Hodgson, etc.), according to which, on any hypothesis, the requirement of the episcopate applies only to the Church of England; this latter will recognise, on certain conditions, the ministers of other Communions which, within their own framework, do not recognise the episcopate.

regard to the nature of the unity of the Church as unity of communion. I, for my part, am convinced that, except for the question of the Roman primacy (which is not always put in an adequate light), the ecclesiology of the Orthodox East and that of the Catholic West are basically the same on the dogmatic plane; they differ in the manner of conceiving *the canonical life* of the Church, that is to say the way in which it is organised as a society, and thus the concrete forms of its 'administration'. But both the one and the other hold that the Church is a single Communion. The differences which are characterised, in Orthodoxy, by the fact of autocephalous or autonomous Churches, and on occasion by the rites, are not absolutely comparable with those which Anglicanism admits in all the elements which do not concern the fundamental points: a domain whose frontier, we have seen, is not rigidly defined and embraces things, such as the episcopate, which the Orthodox Church would never admit could be called into question. That is why the Orthodox Churches, which have admitted, in limited conditions, that Anglicans might occasionally receive the eucharistic Communion in their Church, cannot admit total sacramental intercommunion. This would presuppose that they should concede intercommunion on the ecclesiological plane, that is to say the ecclesiological theory of particular Communions realising, each in its way, the Church, and reconstituting, through sacramental intercommunion, its visible and social unity.

The Sacramental[5] Question

The canonical or disciplinary position of the Roman Catholic Church is well known. Except in certain cases, it strictly forbids *communicatio in sacris*, i.e. participation in the truly liturgical celebration of non-Catholics or the instituting of a common liturgical celebration: cf. *Codex Juris can.*, c. 1258 and 731 §2, and *Monitum* of the Holy Office of 5th June 1948 (*Acta Sedis Apost.*, 1948, p. 257).

Except in certain cases, we have said. Certain of these cases are provided for by the law, but they are always connected with the

[5] In the original French, Fr. Congar employs both *sacramental* and *sacramentaire*, but the shade of difference cannot be captured in English, where both have been translated by 'sacramental'.

danger of death, before which barriers seem to give way. Thus any Catholic in danger of death may, if there is no other means of receiving his sacraments, provided the danger of scandal and apostasy is avoided, receive the sacrament of penance and, according to a current interpretation, the Eucharist and the unction of the sick, from a non-Catholic priest. Cf. Holy Office, 30th June to 7th July 1864 (Gasparri, *Fontes*, IV, n. 978; cf. Cappello, *De sacramentis*, n. 92). On the other side, a Catholic priest may give absolution and unction of the sick to dying non-Catholics, if he has reason to believe that they are in good faith, that they recognise and desire these sacraments, and that all danger of scandal is avoided: cf. Holy Office, *Rescript* of 17th May 1916 and *Reply* of 20th July 1898. Reliable authors interpret these dispositions in a relatively broad manner;[6] certain of them would even admit that in certain cases the Viaticum (Eucharist) might be given to Orthodox in danger of death. But in normal circumstances a Catholic may not receive the sacraments of non-Catholics, even in order to fulfil his Easter duty, nor give the sacraments to non-Catholics, even such as are of good faith and ask for them. On any hypothesis, co-celebration of consecrated ministers or active participation in the public worship of non-Catholic communions is forbidden.

Such are the dispositions of the law. History, that is to say life, has presented many circumstances which, without creating another law, have brought about and justified different derogations. The list of these would be long. I have noted a certain number of them: it is a file which I would willingly produce one day, were not others better placed to produce a far more complete one. These facts must be taken into account, since they exist, and without a consideration of them one would not have an exact view of the real position of the Catholic Church. But it must equally be affirmed that exceptional facts do not prescribe against the law, and that one cannot formulate a theory of the normal with the product of particular circumstances. Canon Lacey, in connection with this very question,[7] remarks on several occasions that one cannot take exceptional cases as the basis of a law. Certain

[6] For example, Vermeersch-Greusen, *Epitome Juris can.*, t. II, no. 16; Aertnys-Damen, *Theologia moralis*, t. II, n. 337; J. King, *The Administration of the Sacraments to Dying non-Catholics*, Washington, 1924.

[7] *Intercommunion*, in *Essays in Positive Theology*, p. 31 *et seq.*

people, impregnated with a nominalist, pragmatic and experimentalist spirit, have a tendency not to distinguish law from circumstances, the substance of a thing from its concrete mode of realisation, and not to see the truth except under the form of a more or less generalised statement of facts. Nothing is more contrary to the tradition of the Church, for which the words of canon, dogma, discipline, on the one hand, and on the other hand, of heresy, abuse, invalidity, have a meaning. Moreover, the prohibition of *communicatio in sacris* rests upon profound reasons, originating in the nature or the structure of things. The most important of these reasons seems to me to be the connection which exists between the sacraments and faith, on the one hand, and the sacraments and the Church, on the other hand.

It is an unshakable tenet of the whole of tradition to call Baptism 'the sacrament of faith', and it is a tenet at least of the western theological tradition to speak repeatedly of the 'sacraments of faith', *sacramenta fidei*. Not only Baptism, which has a special title to the name, but all the sacraments are sacraments of faith. This affirmation is of a richness which defies analysis. It implies that faith and sacrament are intimately mingled, springing each in turn one from the other. It is true to say that the sacrament presupposes faith and expresses it, but also that it nourishes and guards it, and that professed faith is only the expression of the sacramental celebration. Faith and sacrament are indissolubly associated in the economy of the means of salvation which constitute the Church (*Ecclesia constituitur, fabricatur, instituitur fide et fidei sacramentis*, say repeatedly the great scholastics). Invariably associated, they are, each and together, that which binds us to the Christ of Calvary, who is the unique source of salvation. It is faith, at the same time as the institution, which makes of certain signs used in worship true sacraments, and which confers on them a saving efficacity. That is why there can be no union in the celebration of the sacraments without union in faith. But, when both the one and the other exist, all that is needful is there in order that there should be Communion in the ecclesiological sense of the word; only a schism can prevent it. There is not even 'intercommunion'; there is just Communion, there is church unity. Such is in effect the relation between faith and the sacraments, on the one hand, and the Church on the other hand: they are constitutive of the Church. We have seen above that, together with the powers of the apostolic ministry, they are the creative elements of the Church-as-institution and, put into play by her, the generating elements of the Church-as-Communion. There is here, we said also, a profound reason for the identity of name between the eucharistic Communion and the church Communion. When one studies the texts of the theological tradition prior to the twelfth century, that is to say of a tradition imbued with the 'mystical' and sacramental (*sacramentaire*) sense (at that period, they were one and the same thing), one can see that (1) the historical humanity of Christ, (2) His operation in the sacraments, and (3) church unity were considered as situated on the same *trajectoire*, as principle, means and end.[8] The body born of the Virgin became the *corps communionel* of Christ (what present-day theology and since the twelfth century calls His mystical body), thanks to His sacramental and *mystérique* body. Such is the traditional view of things. It shows us how the sacramental celebration is so united to the mystery of the unity of the Church that it is only possible to be united in the former by being united in the latter.

Precisely, some will perhaps say: since the Sacrament engenders the Church, let us communicate in the Sacrament, and we shall thus come better to communicate in the Church; let us celebrate and pray together, we shall soon form a single ecclesiastical body. . . . This reasoning would perhaps be valuable if the Sacrament were a means *outside the Church,* which one could use in order to enter or to build her, as one takes a key to enter a house, and stones to build one. But not one of the constitutive elements of the Church is exterior to her: not faith, nor the Bible, nor tradition, nor the sacraments, nor the apostolic succession and powers. They can only be truly found and held in her. Faith is the faith *of the Church*, the sacraments are the sacraments of the Church. It is she, in reality, who celebrates, we have only the rank of ministers in her. Hence, in regard to reunion, intercommunion, as has been justly written[9] could be a fruit, an expression or an

---

[8] This view of things has been analysed in a masterly way by Père H. de Lubac, in his difficult but most illuminating book, *Corpus mysticum*, Paris, 1942 (2nd edition, 1949). We should also remember that certain authors, both ancient, for example, St. Albert the Great, and contemporary (A. E. J. Rawlinson, Bp. Palmer, L. S. Thornton, Chan. L. Cerfaux) think that the very designation of the Church as 'body of Christ' derives from its relation to the Eucharist, the body of Christ.

exercise of unity; it cannot be the principle of it if it does not exist. Besides, as we have already said, when unity is given, it is not of intercommunion that we should speak, but quite simply of Communion. At present we are, and very really, united *in Christ*—through grace and spiritual gifts, through certain sacraments, through the Holy Bible, etc. . . . that which unites us is already considerable !—but we are not united in one Church. The aim of the ecumenical movement is precisely to pass, if God wills it and grants to us to do it, from an invisible unity in Christ to a visible unity in the Church. Then, we would celebrate and communicate together.[10] Until then, intercommunion is, alas, impossible.

[9] Thus T. A. Lacey, *Intercommunion, loc. cit.: Unity and Schism,* lect. 6; L. Hodgson, *Essays in Christian Philosophy,* p. 159; A. M. Ramsey, *The Gospel and the Catholic Church,* p. 224.

[10] Gregory X had taken as the theme of his address to the council of union of Lyons in 1274 the text of Luke 22. 15: *Desiderio desideravi hoc pascha manducare vobiscum.*

VI

INTERCOMMUNION: A METHODIST
CONTRIBUTION

*

Rupert E. Davies
Methodist Church

(Great Britain)

The attitude of a faithful Methodist to the problem of inter-communion ought to follow logically and naturally from the Methodist doctrine of the nature of the Christian Church and its ministry. I hope that the attitude to be outlined in the next few pages fulfils that requirement, and, in order to show that it does, I must begin by sketching the doctrine in question. It is set out in the statement approved by the Methodist Conference of 1937, entitled *The Nature of the Christian Church according to the Teaching of the Methodists*.[1]

We believe that the Church is the whole congregation of Christ's faithful people in heaven and on earth, and that it includes all those of any communion who love the Lord Jesus Christ in sincerity and truth. It is actual and visible wherever the Word of God is preached, the sacraments of the Gospel administered and the Christian life lived. In virtue of the grace of God bestowed upon it and its members, it is the Israel of God and the Body of Christ; and within it the Holy Spirit sheds abroad the divine love and imparts the gifts which are needful to all those who minister to its members and to all those who share its life. It is the fellowship of the Holy Spirit and the divinely chosen instrument for the fulfilment of the divine purpose; it is set in the world to proclaim the Word of God by preaching and by sacrament, to practise and enjoy the fellowship of believers, to bring forth the fruit of the Spirit, to convert sinners to God and to multiply and

[1] Epworth Press, 1937.

perfect the children of God; and its ultimate purpose is the reconciliation of all things to Christ.

But, although the Church is the Bride of Christ and is indwelt
by His Spirit, it cannot yet claim to possess the wholeness of the
Gospel in the full and absolute sense. Its wholeness is eschatological; it both is, and is not, what God wills it to be. Only in
the world to come will the wholeness of the Gospel be fully
realised. For on this earth the sin and ignorance of man, even
redeemed man, renders such realisation unattainable. This applies
both to the primitive Church and to the Church of to-day, though
it may be true that the primitive Church, standing nearer in time
to the Incarnation of the Word, possesses more of the wholeness
than any communion can claim to-day. Yet despite its incompleteness, the Church, actual and visible to-day, does possess the
Word of God, which is Christ, the Catholic Faith, the Gospel
Sacraments, the Holy Scriptures, the Christian ministry.

Within this Church the supreme and essential ministry is that
of Christ Himself; it is in virtue of His presence in His Church
that we may call it the Body of Christ. The ministry of man or
men within the Church is derivative from and dependent on His
ministry. The Apostles, because of their unique personal relationship to Jesus Christ in the days of His flesh, and because of their
testimony to the resurrection which they shared with very few
others, had a special ministry in the early days; but their ministry
was, from the nature of the case, unrepeatable and incom-
municable. Their ministry was never the only ministry in the
Church. From the very beginning the whole Church possessed a
ministry derived from and bestowed by Christ Himself, and that
ministry the whole Church still possesses. There is no justification
in the words of Christ, in the whole of the New Testament, or
in any legitimate inference from the teaching of Christ of the
New Testament, for the view that the ministry of the Sacraments,
or of preaching, or of tending the flock of God, is limited to one
particular class of person within the Church. The whole Church
possesses this ministry by the gift of Christ Himself and in virtue
of being His Body and the fellowship of His Spirit. Naturally,
those within the Church who are endowed by the Spirit with
particular gifts and qualities are called by Christ in His Church
to the exercise of particular functions. But they exercise them on
behalf of the whole Church, and not in virtue of any commission

which belongs to them exclusively. For the proper ordering of the Church's life, it is desirable that those who have received a special training and are set aside by the Church for the performance of special functions should be charged by the Church with the administration of the Sacraments, and that it should not be open to any man to take it upon himself to teach or preach or celebrate the sacraments of the Lord's Supper or of Baptism. But this is a matter of Order and not of Faith, though Order is never to be neglected or despised.

The incompleteness and sinfulness of the Church on earth are shown by nothing more clearly than by the divisions which have appeared and still persist in the framework of the Church. The divisions which resulted in the cleavage of the Church of the East from the Church of the West, and in the formation of the great continuing Protestant communions, were the result of sin and blindness, but that sin and blindness was not, as a matter of history, limited to one side of the arguments which arose. It became necessary at the Reformation for those who saw the Gospel corrupted and contradicted to proclaim afresh the truths of the Gospel; but this is not to deny that they also were guilty from time to time of arrogance and falsification. Yet, in the conditions of the time in which they lived, the separations which occurred were inevitable. In England, in the eighteenth century, John Wesley was raised up by God to testify to neglected truth; and his witness made a further separation necessary, if the truth of the Gospel was still to be proclaimed. Yet we do not exculpate Wesley or his followers, any more than we exculpate the Church of England, from all sinfulness in the matter.

These schisms within the one Church of Christ intensify as well as display its incompleteness, and make it impossible to say that any one communion within that Church possesses anything approaching even that degree of wholeness which should belong to the Church on earth. 'Within the Christian Church—One, Holy, Catholic and Apostolic—the Methodist Church holds and cherishes a true place.'[2] But it makes no claim to be *the* Church; and it excludes no Church which confesses Jesus as Lord to the glory of God the Father. It acknowledges that its apprehension of Christian truth is incomplete, that its discipline of the Christian life is imperfect, that its ministry is limited to certain parts only

[2] *The Order of Service for the Public Reception of New Members.*

of the world (though it takes the world as its parish), and that its separation from other communions impoverishes its life and witness, and it humbly asserts the same of all other communions. But it affirms that the Churches 'are already one in Christ Jesus; they have not to create that unity; it is there; and it is the gift of God'. Therefore it acknowledges its duty 'to make common cause in the search for the perfect expression of that unity and holiness which in Christ already belong to the Churches'.[3]

Two parts of Methodist church life which are of immediate practical relevance to the present discussion can be seen to follow directly from the conception of the Church and ministry just expounded. In principle and theory we can deny to no member of our communion the right to celebrate Holy Communion; and in the days before Methodist Union in 1932 the lay administration of the sacraments, and not of Baptism only, was fairly common in the Primitive Methodist and United Methodist Churches. The united Methodist Church has laid it down, as a matter of Order and not of Faith, that the Administration of Holy Communion should be limited, in nearly every case, to ordained ministers; that it may be occasionally extended to ministers still 'on probation' who may be granted a special dispensation by the Methodist Conference; and that in highly exceptional cases, such as those in which many of our members would otherwise be denied, for long periods of time, the benefits of being present at the Lord's Table, specially selected laymen may be authorised by the Conference to administer Holy Communion. It is likely to make similar provisions in the near future for the administration of Baptism. Thus, although there is no bar in doctrine to the lay administration of the Sacraments, in practice we limit it most stringently, and there are many among us who would prohibit it absolutely. Probably there would be no final objection to its complete elimination, if this were required in the interests of reunion and if the other difficulties of reunion were satisfactorily overcome.

The other matter directly relates to intercommunion. We are in complete communion with all those Churches, acknowledging Jesus Christ as Lord, who are willing to be in communion with us. So much is this taken for granted as the necessary corollary of our doctrine of the Church that there is no written agreement to

[3] *The Nature of the Christian Church*, p. 39.

this effect with any Church whatsoever. A Methodist minister celebrating Holy Communion welcomes to the Table the members of any Christian communion who may be present—and may well extend the invitation to all who love the Lord in sincerity. A Methodist worshipping in a non-Anglican and non-Roman and non-Orthodox Church will quite unquestioningly regard himself as entitled to share in the Lord's Supper. This free intercommunion applies, of course, most obviously between Methodism and the other Free Churches of Britain and America; but it also operates between Methodism and the Lutheran and Reformed Churches of the Continent. Many Methodist ministers must have officiated at Lutheran Communions at camps for German prisoners-of-war; and English and American Methodists visiting Germany take Communion in a German Evangelical Church without asking or raising any questions.

As far as the relations of Methodism with Roman, Orthodox and Anglican Churches are concerned, it perhaps goes without saying that a Methodist minister welcomes to Communion any member of such a Church who is willing to come; and any Methodist would willingly take Communion from the priest of such a Church if he knew that the priest were willing that he should.

Such, then, is our doctrine, and such is our present practice. The Methodist Church is committed to the exploration of any method which may bring the separated Churches closer together, and to the use of any effective one. It is not, of course, committed as a whole to organic reunion as necessarily desirable; but it would certainly investigate any serious proposals to that end, as it will most seriously examine the suggestions contained in 'Church Relations in England'. On these points there is virtual unanimity among British Methodists, and probably among all Methodists. Even if there are some who would regard close co-operation between the Churches which stopped short of reunion as being the ultimate end of negotiations in England, there are very few who would echo the statement ascribed in 1951 to a notable Methodist: 'Behind all the talk of reunion lies . . . a deep, irreconcilable difference between the Catholic and Evangelical conception of what is really vital in religion. The first round of the battle has been lost already. In the union of the Churches in South India a vital principle has been conceded, the Anglicans insisting on having Bishops in the historic succession and that the act of ordination should be for the Bishops.'[4] To talk of a 'battle' is obsolete among us. We are none of us disposed to underestimate the difference between the Catholic and Protestant conceptions of the Church and its ministry. But we are much more disposed to seek possibilities of reconciliation than to estimate the prospects or results of a conflict.

There are, however, differences of opinion among us as to the right method of procedure in the near future. Some urge that we ought to negotiate and consummate some form of union with the other British Free Churches, and then turn our attention to the possibility of organic reunion with the Church of England. There are clear advantages in such a programme. We have already a very great deal in common with these Churches, especially in the matters of worship, theology, 'democracy' in church affairs, independence of the State, and loyalty to the principles of the Reformation. There are already in existence Free Church Councils in almost every district of Great Britain, as well as a Federal Free Church Council for the whole of the country. In very many places the people of the various Free Churches are in the habit of mingling freely with each other at all levels, secular as well as religious, and the ministers work together in all sorts of ways. Above all, the Churches are in full communion with each other. It is suggested, also, that it would be easier for the united Free Churches to hold fruitful discussions with the Church of England than for them to do so individually—easier from the point of view of the Anglicans to deal with one Church rather than with several, easier from the point of view of the Free Churches to present one front than several.

But there are also difficulties. There are differences between the Free Churches which are not always understood by Anglicans, even well-informed Anglicans, when they tend to lump the Free Churches together and treat them as one body. These are differences for the most part in church polity, roughly between the Presbyterian system, which the Methodists have adopted in a modified form, and the Independent system, which is common to Baptists and Congregationalists, and to other smaller groups. The difficulties for reunion which this involves have been brought out by the recent negotiations between English Congregation-

[4] *Methodist Recorder*, 19th April 1951.

alists and Presbyterians. But there is also the large doctrinal difference between the Baptists, and some smaller groups which take the same point of view, and the other Free Churches on the question of Infant and Believers' Baptism. This difference has been largely instrumental in preventing the Baptists from belonging to the Church of South India, and there is certainly no easy way of resolving it. Many Methodists would say that the difference between them and the Baptists on this point is as serious as the difference between them and the Catholics in the Church of England on other points. And Methodists, who are concerned that the ultimate aim of all conversations and negotiations should be the reunion of the Free Churches of Great Britain with the Church of England, are inclined to suggest that the union of Methodism with the other Free Churches might very well postpone the reunion of Methodism with the Mother Church. For Methodism, by uniting itself with Free Churches which have, on the whole, less concern with historical succession than Methodism has, would become part of a Church with which Catholics in the Anglican communion would be much less willing to enter into communion.

Because of these difficulties many Methodists lean to the view that we should seek to enter into communion, and perhaps into reunion, with the Church of England before thinking of union with the other Free Churches. After all, they say, Methodism came out of the Church of England, and has never lost its affinity with it. We use virtually the same Order of Holy Communion, and in many Methodist Churches it is the custom to use the Order of Morning Prayer from the Book of Common Prayer every Sunday morning. Our conception of the ministry is higher than that of the Baptists and Congregationalists, and in our church polity we have, in the Chairman of the District, a functionary much more readily comparable with a bishop than any in either of those two communions; in fact, American Methodism has bishops, though they make no claim to be in the Apostolic Succession in any Catholic sense.

In further pursuance of this view, there are some among us who wish the Methodists to revert to the status originally designed for them by John Wesley, that of members of a Society within the Church of England. But in this extreme form the view cannot be said to have much hold upon us. For, while it is true that

Methodism began as a Society, it has certainly become a Church, though preserving here and there faint traces of its origin as a Society, and we cannot undo this history even if we want to do so. But in its non-extreme form the policy of 'communion with Anglicanism first' is widely advocated, especially by those—and they are not few in the ranks of the ministry—who lay stress on the value of historical continuity without accepting that form of it which Catholicism appears to prescribe.

Yet it is doubtful whether this view is wholly realistic. Let us admit that the main tradition of Methodism is in some ways more akin to Anglicanism than it is to Nonconformity, and that many Methodist ministers feel somewhat happier in Anglican surroundings than they do among 'independents'. Let us admit that we can more easily 'take episcopacy into our system' than our Congregationalist and Baptist brethren. But the time that has passed since our separation from the Church of England has not left us liturgically or ecclesiologically where we were at the time of the separation. For good or ill, Methodism, by and large, has adopted the 'free' form of worship, except in the Order for Holy Communion (and even here many ministers, even of the main tradition, permit themselves abbreviations and modifications of the prescribed liturgy); and this adoption is not at all inconsistent with the emphasis on the 'ministry of the Word' which was always essential to Wesley and his followers, and has been partly effaced in Anglicanism by the Oxford Movement. The great majority of Methodists find themselves out of sympathy with Anglicans on this point more than on any other, and in such a way that they would find it unnatural to be in closer relations with them than with their fellow Free Churchmen. Moreover, the fusion of Primitive Methodists and United Methodists with Wesleyan Methodists in the union of 1932 has of course brought into the Methodist Church many Methodists who are as far away in theological and devotional outlook from Anglicanism, even 'central' Anglicanism, as the extremer Baptists and Congregationalists. It is probably true to say that these elements are becoming progressively more aware of the value of those parts in the 'Wesleyan' tradition from which they were at one time estranged, but there is a point of approximation to Anglicanism, in worship and procedure and in the doctrine of the Church, beyond which it will be exceedingly difficult to persuade them to go.

It seems, therefore, that Methodism will best serve the cause of reunion by giving neither form of rapprochement, to the Church of England or to the other Free Churches, priority over the other, and by working instead for the cause of 'all-round' reunion by all the ways, slow or moderately quick, which seem practicable. Thus, and thus only, can it preserve its position and influence as a 'bridge' Church—a title which is quite acceptable to us as long as it does not imply that we have no substantive existence as a Church in our own right! We are, or should be, able to understand the views and sentiments of the parties on either side of us in a way not open to any other outsiders; and it therefore becomes our duty to interpret the one to the other as fully, and for as long a time, as we can. If we become irrevocably linked to one party before we are linked to the other, we shall lose the power of mediation, and so, perhaps, definitely postpone and hinder the achievement of full reunion. Only if such full reunion is finally seen to be wholly impracticable shall we be entitled to choose either reunion with the Church of England, or union with the other Free Churches or another Free Church, as the case may be.

If this argument is sound, and it is the task of Methodism to work for 'all-round', not fragmentary, reunion, or such coming-together as we are able to achieve, for what kind of progress in the matter of intercommunion should Methodists press? In the past there have often been two schools of thought in all Churches on this subject. Some—including most Free Churchmen—have thought that free, or at least only moderately restricted, intercommunion should be allowed and encouraged as a necessary preliminary to conversations on unity. If we cannot have fellowship at the Lord's Table, they have said, what hope is there of resolving our differences? If we can have fellowship there, surely the Spirit will lead us on, in the strength thus provided, to a wider and more visible unity. There is strength in this contention. It is in the highest degree anomalous—and yet not uncommon—that Anglicans and Free Churchmen who are engaged in a common enterprise of evangelism and thereby enter into spiritual fellowship of a deep and lasting kind cannot take the Lord's Supper together or from each other's hands; it is still more anomalous that they cannot do so when actually engaged in conversations for the furtherance of Christian unity. Yet the objections, largely from the Anglican side, are also weighty. Intercommunion with little restriction seems to imply that the differences between the Churches are in the end of little importance, and easily solved by a few hours' patient sitting round a table (though that is not the lesson to be drawn from intercommunion between the Free Churches); and for many Anglicans it would mean not a reasonable compromise in the interests of reconciliation, but a surrender of their whole theological position.

It is therefore suggested, mainly by Anglicans, that the proper procedure is to work up to intercommunion as the climax of the whole movement towards reunion, and to eschew it until that climax is reached. This course can also be supported by strong argument. Since the Eucharist is the supreme act of worship of the whole Christian Church, it can properly be offered only by those who are in full unity with each other; and for Christians sundered by denominational walls to offer it together is to pretend to a unity which does not, in fact, yet exist. But it is by no means free from objection. To many Free Churchmen it seems to suggest that their sacraments are regarded as invalid and ineffectual until such time as their ministers are incorporated, or re-incorporated, into the Apostolic Succession, and to acquiesce in such a suggestion would be as much a betrayal of principle as unrestricted intercommunion would be for many Anglicans, for it would deny the grace of God which has been given to us times without number through our sacraments.

Therefore the expedient of partial, limited and occasional intercommunion has been adopted by many Free Churchmen and Anglicans, and seems to be the only way out of the difficulty which combines a reasonable degree of consistency with charity, and at the same time assists the cause of reunion. It grants the Free Churchman's claim to the validity and efficacy of his sacraments, and it safeguards the Anglican contention that full and complete intercommunion is possible only when those who offer it are completely in unity. Perhaps such acts of intercommunion should be performed only on high and solemn occasions, such as those which mark a step forward in church relations, either on the national or the local level, or those which inaugurate or conclude some occasion of united witness or evangelism. It might well be regarded, however, as a reasonable corollary to be drawn from the acceptance of the principle of occasional intercommunion, that members of non-episcopal Churches, who may

F

from time to time be denied the opportunity of taking Communion in their own place of worship or in other Churches in communion with their own, should be welcomed at such times to the Lord's Table in the Church of England, just as an Anglican communicant in similar circumstances would certainly be welcomed to full participation in a Free Church Communion Service.

Here, perhaps, a word of admonition may be delivered to Free Churchmen, and not least to Methodists. We are sometimes tempted to think and say that we are superior in Christian charity to our Anglican brethren because we both have free intercommunion among the Free Churches and are perfectly willing to admit to Communion in our Churches any Anglican—or, for that matter, any Orthodox or Roman—communicant who may wish to come; whereas the same does not apply the other way round. But, of course, it is not a matter of charity but of doctrine; there are many Anglican clergy who are deeply hurt by the knowledge that they are debarred for theological reasons which seem to them to be excellent from accepting Communion from a Free Church minister, and from giving it to such a minister or his people. But the theological reasons remain, and, when charity seems to conflict with doctrine, the Anglican, at least, tends to say that it must be the charity which is at fault; for charity is partly influenced by feeling, which is notoriously unreliable, whereas doctrine is solidly based on revelation and reason. A Free Churchman, and certainly a Methodist, tends to take the view that the mistake in such a case may well be in the doctrine, and that revelation has been imperfectly understood or applied. But this question belongs to another field of enquiry.

We may now come to the suggestions contained in *Church Relations in England*, and now in the field for discussion, for bringing the Churches in England closer together. It would be wholly inappropriate, both in view of the delicacy of the situation, and because the Archbishop of Canterbury has expressly asked for reserve to be exercised for the time being, to suggest the kind of decision that ought to be taken by the Methodist Church on the major issues involved. But it is perhaps allowable to offer some general consideration on some of the subjects discussed in the booklet which has appeared.

Firstly, there is little doubt that Methodists on the whole will receive with strong approval the statement of opinion that 'our divisions are to be regarded as implying schism *within* the Church'.[5] One of the most serious obstacles to closer relations between the Churches on the local and personal level, and to complete theological understanding, has always been the Anglican claim that the Free Churches are branches which have been broken off from the parent stem, doomed to gradual but certain death. It is this claim which has in the past gone far to account for, and even sometimes to excuse, the noisy beating of the Free Church drum which has from time to time disfigured Free Church Councils and assemblies. All the Free Churches have always asserted, on good historical grounds, that their departure from the Anglican fold, though regrettable, was necessary for reasons of pure theological and ethical principle—though they would not, of course, deny, at least in their considered statements, that the elements of contentiousness, spiritual pride and the schismatic temper entered the situation from both sides on many occasions. The recognition of the principle of 'internal schism' would remove a very formidable hindrance to the cause of unity; in fact, it might, when properly understood, entirely change the situation.

Next, it is fairly clear that the successful conduct of future discussions turns on three particular points. The first is this: how far is it possible for the Church of England to acknowledge the reality of the grace of Jesus Christ given to us through the ministries and sacraments of our own communions? There was a time when Free Churchmen virtually held that the absence of bishops in the Apostolic Succession was a necessary prerequisite for the grace of God to operate in the Church. But that time has now gone, and we see clearly that this opinion was the result of controversy and conflict rather than of sound reasoning from biblical principles. Free Churchmen have also held quite frequently that the form of church government to which they were addicted was the one and only New Testament polity, and that only those who accepted it were true members of the Church. But that view also has been long abandoned, as is clearly shown by the free intercommunion established between Free Churches with different polities. There is general agreement now among us

[5] *Church Relations in England*, p. 23.

all that any united Church in England would be episcopal in form. But we could clearly not accept such a form of government if such acceptance involved the acknowledgment that the grace mediated by our non-episcopal ministries and sacraments through many centuries in any sense lacked reality. Nor could we accept the suggestions that the mercies of God that have been granted to us have been 'uncovenanted'; we cannot abate our claim to be 'within the covenant' any more than we wish to deny to others a similar place. It may well be the case—it is to be hoped that it is the case—that the principle of 'internal schism' involves the recognition of that for which we are here contending. If it does, there will be great rejoicing in all responsible Free Church circles.

The second point is this: no Free Church, even after agreeing to 'admit episcopacy into its system', is likely to be willing to enter into reunion with the Church of England unless it is provided that it is at liberty to remain on terms of fellowship and intercommunion with those non-episcopal Churches with which it at present enjoys such relations. It is not easy to see how Anglicans can allow this condition of reunion, since for many of them it would be an acceptance of the view that non-episcopal Churches are true Churches, and thus a denial of some of their deepest convictions. This is in itself an argument for 'all-round' rather than piecemeal reunion, since the former would ensure that all the non-episcopal Churches with which the Free Churches desired to remain in communion were outside this country. But even then Methodists, at least, could scarcely be expected to sacrifice communion with the Methodist Church of America, nor any of the Free Churches with the Lutheran and Reformed Churches of the Continent. Some suggest that the only escape from this dilemma is a policy of 'masterly silence': if this were followed, the Free Churches would not ask for an explicit assurance from the Church of England that they were permitted to retain intercommunion with the Churches in question, but on the other hand the Church of England would not ask for an explicit assurance from them that such intercommunion would not be retained. It is urged in support of this suggestion that it is precisely by the policy of 'masterly silence' that the Church of England succeeds in holding within its unity men of vastly differing views on the ministry and the sacraments, and that in the difficult situation brought upon us by our 'unhappy divisions' it is right and proper that this awkward point should be decided in practice by the individual Free Churchman when he finds himself in a church not in communion with the Church of England.

Apart from the fact that this suggested solution savours somewhat of disingenuity, the trouble about it is that in practice it would be not so much 'masterly silence' as an 'open secret', since there is very little doubt in anyone's mind as to what course Free Churchmen would take in the situation just imagined, and the knowledge of it would cause grave and perpetual scandal in the minds of devout Anglicans to whom the whole of this question is of vital importance. But an easy alternative does not suggest itself. Perhaps it would be better to acknowledge openly that exact consistency in this matter is not attainable, because of the evil brought upon us by internal schism (for sin and blindness have caused not only the spiritual ills of separation, but logical difficulties about reunion); and to allow the Free Churches to retain the privilege of intercommunion with non-episcopal Churches without requiring any Anglican to acknowledge that the latter *are* true Churches.

Here is the third point: the Free Churches, if they 'took episcopacy into their system', would do so by the acceptance of an episcopate inaugurated through bishops of one or more of the historic episcopal Churches, and by adopting episcopal ordination as their rule in future. This would appear to create two orders of minister in each Free Church, the order of those who were born too soon to be episcopally ordained, and the order of those who were thus ordained at or after reunion—with the inevitable inference in many minds that the latter order was in some way superior to the former. It does not require much imagination to see that this situation would be, in fact, intolerable in any Christian community. This fact alone suggests that there is a clearly proved need for a service of wider commissioning which all clergy and ministers would be required to undergo. Is there any difficulty in asking all alike to acknowledge that their orders are defective—at least in respect of universality of exercise? A great number of Methodist ministers would acknowledge that their orders also lacked universality in the sense that they were not bestowed by the Universal Church, and many other Free Churchmen and many Anglicans would do the same. But there need be no argument as to *what* defects exactly were being supplied by the service of wider commissioning.

It sometimes seems, no doubt, to the Anglican that he is being asked to make more and larger concessions in the cause of unity than he can reasonably be expected to make. It certainly seems sometimes to the Methodist—and, no doubt, to the other types of Free Churchman—that excessive concessions are expected of him, too. But perhaps it would be better if none of us thought or spoke in terms of concessions, or certainly in terms of a bargain to be struck; and looked instead, in prayer together, without our usual presuppositions, for the best way in the actual circumstances of our time of preserving and handing on the treasure committed to all of us. History cannot be undone, and it is better not to try to rewrite it; but it can be used by the Holy Spirit, through us, to the fulfilment of His purposes.

VII

INTERCOMMUNION IN THE NON-CLERICAL TRADITION

*

A. T. DeGroot

International Convention of Disciples of Christ

(United States)

Fortunately for the Commission on Intercommunion its work is not defeated before it is undertaken. The open, exploratory condition of our search for intercommunion is assured in the fact that the nature of the Church itself (and consequently its fellowship acts) is undefined in the history of doctrine. Not until the late fifteenth century was any effort made to establish rigidly the confines and characteristics of the Church. *Die Kirche selbst hat sich bis heute noch nicht definiert,* as Robert Grosche stated (*Pilgernde Kirche,* 1938).

This can be called nothing less than a gift of the Holy Spirit, for it overreaches the plans of men, and leaves wide the doors of fellowship for future exploration and cultivation.

I. *Exploration*

For an exposition of some widely held positions concerning the Lord's Supper we may employ a series of propositions. They represent especially that church body known as Disciples of Christ (sometimes called Churches of Christ), which is thoroughly non-clerical, and where the Lord's Supper is an act of the total congregation, usually employing but not requiring an ordained minister for its observance.

In its sharpest point, non-clericalism divides from other church practice—although not necessarily from other church theory—by its insistence that the members of the church, the congregation, are its ministry. The ministry in all of its parts is looked upon as the function of the congregation. This position is in complete contrast to Roman Catholicism, wherein the ministry in its entirety is reserved to the clergy and the 'religious', and is in partial contrast to most of Protestantism wherein the preaching and liturgical ministries are reserved to a clerical group, although the laity may participate in the teaching, pastoral and social action ministries of the Church. Within the non-clerical point of view it is the Church through the members of its body which may raise up its ministry and ordain it to office without clerical control. This is a truly democratic process on the part of the membership. Even in the Methodist Church, which has a certain democratic impulse, while the congregation has a part in receiving and even in constituting the ordained ministry, it is the clergy that has the absolute, final control of admission by vote (the lay-members have no vote in this matter), and the congregation could not of its own power constitute a ministry to serve its spiritual needs. In Anglican doctrine and practice, of course, the bishops are the *sina qua non* in ordination. Such a position asserts that God is limited to the use of the clergy as the means of creating any further clergy, and is thus a self-perpetuating, clerical control; or, at least, it implies that man is limited by what God *did* do in establishing a clerical or episcopal system. In the latter claim, only history can provide the answer, and mere factual reporting declares that there is no agreement that such a class was established.

The historian of the Disciples of Christ in Australia relates the story of their beginnings of worship through small groups in that region as follows:

'While other Christians might have had the same urge to remember Jesus in such a Communion Service, still their understanding of the ministry of the Church hindered them from "administering the sacraments". There was, therefore, implied in the action of the Disciples of the Restoration Movement an understanding of the nature of the ministry of the New Testament Church. While some [not Disciples] believed that the ministry of the Church was confined to a special class of individuals, these reformers acknowledged that the ministry was not entrusted to a class but was found in the whole Church.'
(A. W. Stephenson, *Pioneering for Christian Unity*, p. 52.)

In the non-clerical concept the living congregation is competent to exercise the entire ministry of the Church, including the raising up and empowering of a ministry without a clergy interposing itself in the process. In practice, the existing ministry, through one or more representatives, usually joins with the remainder of the whole body in ordaining, but is not indispensable to the process.

Should it be thought, even feared, that such a concept of the leadership of the earthly body of Christ would cause the individual members and congregations to have a low regard for the ordinances, we may report that such has not been the case. Since about 1800, when the separate life of the Churches of Christ began, they have made the every Sunday observance of the Lord's Supper the chief characteristic, indeed the central purpose, of their worship. Their more than 8,000 churches around the world to-day try to follow the practice of the members of the primitive Church, who 'devoted themselves to the apostles' teaching and fellowship, to the breaking of bread and the prayers' (Acts 2. 42). Many of their smaller churches, unable by reason of some situation to maintain a local minister, have without fail continued to meet and observe the Lord's Supper under the guidance of the elected elders and deacons. Indeed, it can faithfully be said that the Lord's Supper has proved to be a life-giving ordinance for them. Many local churches enjoy a spiritual satisfaction in an unbroken succession of every Lord's-Day Communion Services across the years from the time they were 'set in order'. Upon the occasion of the centennial of the birth of the American phase of this fellowship, celebrated at Pittsburgh in 1909, 25,000 persons joined in the eucharistic feast held at Forbes Field. The Disciples of Christ provide what is probably the nearest approach to an annual Eucharistic Congress in Protestantism, at the time of their International Convention.

Our exposition may be stated in seven steps:

1. Communion must be within the Church (the body of Christ); i.e. the communicant should always be a church member. The Christian faith is always preserved in association with a community; it is a life we live with others.

2. Communion is primarily with Christ, the head of the body, not with members (the organs of the Church). Yet one could not be in communion with Christ and out of communion with the other members of the body. The corporate aspect of the Lord's

Supper is of its essence, as John Glas (1695-1773), a pioneer of the Disciples of Christ, noted.

3. Therefore, intercommunion concerns first a relation to God in Christ. At the same time it is a problem of relations of Christians with Christians.

4. The crux of the latter problem is whether we may say that the Eastern Orthodox, Presbyterian, Baptist and other believers are Christians—even if imperfect ones.

(a) If so, they may commune (with Christ) even as we—who are imperfect.

(b) If not, they, and we, whenever imperfect, may not commune.

(c) But this (b) is absurd, since none is perfect, save one, even Christ Himself.

[Note. The New Testament clearly realises (as in the Corinthian letter) the imperfection of the Church, as well as of its members (e.g. Peter; Gal. 2. 11).]

5. The only remaining problem is whether we, as imperfect Christians, care to have communion in association with other imperfect Christians. As Georges Florovsky, Eastern Orthodox, observes, 'the work of the Spirit in believers is precisely their incorporation into Christ, their baptism into one body'. To deny communion fellowship to these baptised into the one body is to claim to have command over the Holy Spirit, which is no less blasphemous than to claim to speak infallibly for God. Dr. J. A. F. Gregg, Archbishop of Armagh, speaking as an Anglican, is willing to 'recognise in one another the workings of the one Spirit' but unwilling to have communion in association with those whom he admits to have the ministry of that Spirit.

6. One answer is: we are so much more nearly perfect as Christians than other Christians are that we do not care to have them with us when both of us are endeavouring to commune with God in Christ.

On the ecclesiastical level this same spirit says: Our Church is so much more nearly perfect a Church than their sect that we do not (indeed, by our rules—or notions—*cannot*) care to have communion fellowship with them. We should remember Frederick

D. Maurice's dictum: 'The Church is a body united in the acknowledgment of a living *Person*; every sect is a body united in the acknowledgment of a certain *notion*.'[1]

7. Another answer is that imperfection and sin so beset us all, it is a high privilege for both to be joined in a common act of communion with God in Christ. 'Our faith is imperfect to the end.'[2]

II. *Interrogation*

If the authentic 'workings of the one Spirit' are not the qualification for Communion, what is?

1. Is it simply membership in a church? But most close communionists accept the Baptism of persons baptised, as Baptism into Christ and the Church, not as into a single denomination. Only Southern Baptists shut the gates to Heaven except through their denomination on this subject, and they are not absolutely unanimous in the matter.[3] If a Church can authentically baptise, can it not authentically commune?

2. Or, must the communicant believe alike about apostolic succession? Many members and ministers of episcopal Churches do not so believe; they merely accept episcopacy as a good working arrangement. What scriptural or historical ground is there for putting the communicant to such a test?

3. Or, must the communicant declare his belief in a Church's creed? For the first three centuries the Church had no formal creed. Was there no valid Communion during those centuries?

4. Or, must all who commune together agree as to what happens when the elements are blessed, whether Christ is spiritually, substantially, or consubstantially present? In Anglican churches there is no agreement on this point.

5. Or, is the issue not the qualification of the communicant but of the celebrant? Are the 'workings of the Holy Spirit' subject to a ministry in apostolic succession? Christian charity and honesty demand a frank answer.[4] There is little point in having a World

---

[1] *The Kingdom of Christ*, 1838, II, p. 338.
[2] *The Catholicity of Protestantism*, p. 77. London: Lutterworth Press, 1950.
[3] See Faith and Order Pamphlet No. 98, p. 9.
[4] The minutes of the 1939 meeting of the W.C.F.O. Continuation Committee, p. 14, require that we do this.

Council of Churches if Protestants by definition are not members of Churches. The official Report of the Second World Conference on Faith and Order, at Edinburgh, 1937,[5] said: 'In so far as Christians find themselves obliged by loyalty to Christ and to His Church to judge that the sacraments practised by other Christians are invalid, or doubtfully valid, they should, in the cause of Christian truth and charity, do all in their power to see that the precise meaning of their judgment, and the grounds on which they are obliged to make it, are clearly understood.'

A practical situation resulting from these problems is to be seen in the life of the Student Christian Movement to-day. These serious young people are told that their fellow students in the Movement are members of the body of Christ, but they are forbidden by their superiors in the closed Communion Churches to meet these acknowledged fellow members of the body of Christ as such at the Table of the Lord. When a persistent 'Why?' is reiterated, no clear and unevasive answer is given. The result is a feeling that there exists nothing less than a scandalous disregard for responsible and practical theology in life to-day.

III. *Exposition*

The Disciples of Christ would emphasise the continuity of our Lord with the apostolic Church. He came with a message and an invitation. These constituted a fellowship; they carried a constitutive element for all disciples. The apostolic witness embraced a secondary action (authorised, even initiated, by our Lord), the giving of symbolic expression to the original ideas (giving, in the Lord's Supper, 'parabolic action', to use Clarence T. Craig's phrase). The continuity is real; the parabolic action is secondary.

The tragedy of the Ordinance of Fellowship is the rise of a clerically operated set of barrier definitions, foreign to the intent of the original Lord's Supper, by which the clergy fence the Table. It is in effect a statement by the foot that the hand may not participate in the body. Instead of a clerical (partial) definition of the fellowship, what is needed is an utterance by the *body* declaring that all organs and elements of the body may share its ordinance, its act, of fellowship.

This is to return the Church to its structure and function of the

[5] Faith and Order Pamphlet No. 90, p. 10.

apostolic days when the clergy was raised up by a 'living congregation' (K. Barth) which was nourished by its feast of fellowship. At the point of the Lord's Supper, 'the body' must freely
breathe in fellowship, unhindered by its functional organs, the
clergy.

If the Church is a 'living congregation', and the Lord's Supper
is its corporate act of Communion, then a proper handling of
intercommunion among the Churches waits upon a conscious
acknowledgment by each Church of the Christian status of the
individuals in the Churches, who, through the promptings of the
Holy Spirit, seek Holy Communion, rather than waiting upon
legal approval of the denomination involved. The placing of the
privilege for Communion, and of responsibility for participating
in this essentially personal act, has been set by the Disciples of
Christ (as a Christian body) where they believe it belongs—in the
conscience of the Christian himself. The Disciples began and continue to-day with the proposition of Thomas Campbell in his
Declaration and Address of 1809:

> 'The Church of Christ on earth is essentially, intentionally,
> and constitutionally one; consisting of all those in every place
> that profess their faith in Christ and obedience to Him in all
> things according to the Scriptures, and that manifest the same
> by their tempers and conduct.'

The manner in which this acknowledgment of the full Communion status of all who claim it is administered by the Disciples
of Christ, is to place the responsibility for *spreading* the Lord's
Table upon the organised Church, but to place the responsibility
for *sharing* in the feast on the individual Christian. This is where
Paul placed it. 'Whoever, therefore, eats the bread or drinks the
cup of the Lord in an unworthy manner will be guilty of pro-
faning the body and blood of the Lord. Let a man *examine himself*,
and so eat of the bread and drink of the cup' (I Cor. 11. 27, 28).

The Church spreads the Table, but our Lord is the host. The
Church has no more reason to modify the guest list of those who
have been invited by the Lord to His table than I have to interfere
with the guest list of my earthly host.

This does not mean that the organised Church should never
deny the privilege of Communion. It does mean that such an act
would be unusual, particular (not general), and personally pur-

posive. That is, it means that such an action would normally arise from practical conduct and disposition rather than from variation in the minutiae of theological belief. Dean W. B. Blakemore has aptly stated this position in an interpretation of Thomas Campbell's Declaration:

> . . . 'those are Christians who have professed faith in Christ and who have professed obedience to Him. The profession is not of faith alone, but of faith and obedience. The "obedience" is a professed obedience. This does not mean that the profession of obedience is insincere; . . . it does mean that it is the one professing who judges whether or not, and in what sense he is obedient to Christ in all things according to the Scriptures. It is not those who hear the profession who make that judgment, though they obviously have the right to judge upon the sincerity of the profession by watching for its expression in terms of the professor's temper and conduct. In other words, the profession of obedience and later conduct must have integrity, but the content of both is to be decided by the professor in terms of what he believes obedience of Christ to mean.'[6]

Or, as Alexander Campbell said:

> 'But who is a Christian? I answer, every one that believes in his heart that Jesus of Nazareth is the Messiah, the Son of God; repents of his sins, and obeys him in all things *according to his measure of knowledge of his will.*'[7]

IV. *Invitation*

The tragedy of the Lord's Supper to-day is its unnecessary complexity. The beauty and power of the original feast of fellowship was its embrace of all who shared the touch and life of the Holy Spirit. Power will return when men's clerically constructed fences are consumed in the fires of common worship. 'The symbolism of the Sacrament is basically the oneness which we all experience in the mystical body of Christ, and it is for this reason that we dare not take it upon ourselves to shut out any one whom the Lord has accepted as His own.'[8]

[6] *The Scroll*, January 1950, pp. 147-148.

[7] 'The Lunenburg Letter', *Millennial Harbinger*, September 1837; italics added.

[8] F. D. Kershner, letter, 24th April 1950.

The experience of the Disciples of Christ leads them to believe that the Christian religion is most powerful in life when it avoids complexity and seeks simplicity of utterance. Samuel Johnson said: 'The rights of nations and of kings sink into questions of grammar, if grammarians discuss them.' When the Church was young, and vibrant, and conquering, all who had committed themselves to our Lord as their Saviour shared the feast of Communion. The Disciples endeavour to restore that condition.

The Lord's Supper represents the incarnation of the divine Agape in a human community. It is the appropriate symbol of that suffering Love which alone can heal the sins and sorrows of the world. There is something profoundly unifying and mystically harmonious about it which defies purely technical explication. Its awesome realities make two-way traffic on the bridge over which the 'workings of the Holy Spirit' have initiated the Communion of God with men.

The open Communion position of the Disciples of Christ is not a rational deduction projected as theory in advance of experience. It is a discovery through action on the part of workers for unity. The Disciples began as closed Communion Christians throughout their brotherhood, but have become at least ninety-nine per cent open Communion advocates. The slow shift from exclusion to inclusion in worship fellowship developed as they could not deny the effective presence of the spirit of Christ in the life of the membership of the various Churches. In the other elements of worship and work it was apprent that all hearts beat as one. Gradually it became clear to the Disciples that God alone is the judge of Communion fitness; and that while the Church may spread the Lord's Table, each communicant must 'examine himself' concerning intention and readiness for this remembrance.

The open Communion position that was adopted by the Disciples of Christ is in keeping with the larger framework of their non-credal programme on behalf of Christian unity. As in the case of historical efforts to define with precision the nature of the Godhead, they believe that the search for a uniform dogma of the Lord's Supper, on which closed Communion becomes open because all Christians agree fully on its theology and liturgy, is as futile as all other pursuits of unity through intellectual uniformity. The course of events does not encourage us to believe that there will ever be a new Nicaea issuing eucharistic dogma, for we lack the prospect of some new Constantine to demand the presence, dominate the decisions, and enforce, with the heavy hand of state police, the edicts of the assembled theologians. As the world moves toward freedom in politics and faith, the only ground giving promise of being occupied by all Christians is that of personal commitment and loyalty to Jesus Christ, apart from historically conditioned speculations as to the nature of things unseen. As one of the local church bulletins of the Disciples declares in its weekly announcement: 'This church is itself a community of good will where the differing points of view and convictions of its members are held in respect by all others, where brotherhood does not mean regimentation of thought but a common commitment to Christ as God's completest disclosure of Himself. We have no creed but Christ.'

It may faithfully be said that full intercommunion waits only upon act of will. The Churches can find the means of authorising officially whatever they sincerely and prayerfully desire to do. Can we say otherwise when we observe an archbishop in one nation preaching in our time in defence of a socialist state as a proper guardian of the nation's official Church, while a patriarch in another land likewise blesses a communist government as the consort of its ancient Church, and at the same time Free Churches in other regions warmly defend capitalism as the proper companion for their course in life? These utterances concerning official relations of state Churches with their worldly companions would scarcely have been dreamed of a century ago, even half a century ago—and, if dreamed of, the experience would indeed have been termed a nightmare! They are an act of will concerning new occasions that teach new duties.

In this matter of intercommunion and reunion there is no inherent impossibility of a change of mind and policy on the part of the Churches which at the present time seem more concerned to raise objections to intercommunion and to emphasise the differences of belief and practice among the denominations than to offer practical suggestion for a solution of the problem. A very close parallel to the situation with which we are dealing is afforded by the history of religious liberty. In the Middle Ages heretics were burned, a practice which was continued at the Reformation by both Catholics and Protestants. In many countries disabilities imposed on the adherents of Churches other than the established one continued into the nineteenth century. Yet to-day even those who accept a most rigid and exclusive orthodoxy would agree that religious liberty is right and would defend it as a specifically Christian heritage against the newly arisen 'religions' of nationalism and communism which have endangered it. Similarly the Churches' defence of slavery in the eighteenth and nineteenth centuries is now a thing entirely of the past. In all this it is sad to reflect that ecclesiastics have often shown less Christian charity than the man in the street. May it not similarly be the case that the common man's view that our denominational divisions and exclusiveness are non-Christian will eventually prevail? If so, this will be a further vindication of the 'non-clerical' character of the order which exists in the fellowship of the Disciples of Christ.

When we set over against such radical modifications of the Church's regulation of life the current barriers to communion fellowship one cannot but recall an injunction about straining out a gnat and swallowing a camel. The Churches are competent to regulate function on behalf of purpose. Failure in intercommunion is a failure in will and spirit, not an inescapable result of time-honoured canons. In the long run, those bodies and individuals that desire intercommunion have it; those that do not want it do not have it. It lies within the power of leaders in our time to mould the will of our brethren into the likeness of the will of Him who said, 'He that is not against us is for us' (Mark 9. 40).

VIII

A BAPTIST VIEW

*

(a) V. E. Devadutt
Baptist
(India)

In this brief chapter I will attempt, in the first place, to state the essential position of the Baptists with regard to the Lord's Supper and what their attitude generally might be in regard to inter-communion. I will then add a few constructive suggestions, but in making these I will claim no representative character.

The Baptist Practice

In talking about the Baptists, it is fair to recognise the existence of two broad groups among them, viz. the Strict Baptists and the Open Baptists. The Strict Baptists would be reluctant to recognise the Communion Service of any other Christian body but their own; they would be averse also normally to admit anyone to the Lord's Table who had not been baptised (immersed) *on the profession of Faith*. Among the younger Churches the Strict Baptists are few in number and on the whole within the Baptist Communion they are in a minority. The Open Baptists, on the contrary, would welcome gladly to the Lord's Table anyone who 'loves the Lord Jesus Christ', being willing that on each individual should rest the responsibility of communicating or refraining. They would also be ready to join with others at the Lord's Table, provided there is no insistence that in doing so they must subscribe to any specific interpretation of the Sacrament.

The divergence in the practice of the two types of Baptists shows, however, the regard in which they hold the Lord's Table respectively. The Strict Baptists, like some other branches of the Christian Church, desire obviously to safeguard the Sacred Feast against any danger of its being abused. The Open Baptists believe that the Table is of the Lord and that therefore access to it should be open to all who love Him and desire to serve Him.

The frequency with which the Lord's Supper is celebrated differs from country to country. In India it is usually held once a month. In some countries it is held twice a month, once in the morning service and once in the evening service. I believe that according to the tradition in Scotland it is not uncommon to have the Communion Service every Sunday, after one of the two main services.

As with the Reformed Tradition, so with the Baptists the most important part of Christian worship is the 'Preaching of the Word' and listening to it and accepting it in humble submission. There are, however, many Baptists who stress the intimate and vital connection between the 'Preaching of the Word' and the observance of the Lord's Supper.

Meaning and Interpretation

All Baptists would readily agree that the Lord's Supper is a memorial feast: 'Do this in remembrance of me'; many, however, would maintain that it is more than a mere formal memorial feast and that the Lord's Supper in a very real sense is a special means of grace. There would, however, be a variety of explanations of how this comes about. Few Baptists would be inclined to subscribe to the view that it is a re-presentation of the perfect Sacrifice once offered. Baptists generally would not find it easy to understand the meaning of the Real Presence of Christ in the elements on the Altar, in the sense in which that is understood by certain communions. They believe that the Real Presence is ever about us and that the Lord's Supper does not occasion the Real Presence in any manner different from the way in which that Real Presence is ever about us. The Lord's Supper is rather an occasion when a change might occur in the recipient's attitude and through such a changed attitude he may be brought into greater obedience to and intimacy with the ever-present Lord. Many Baptists would perhaps agree that in a moment like that the Communion in a very real sense does become a means of the grace of God to the communicant. On practically every occasion of the Lord's Supper the words of the Institution from one of the Gospels or I Corinthians are used. It is the normal practice for an ordained minister to conduct the service, but neither the use of the 'words of the Institution' nor the dispensing of the elements by an ordained minister would be treated by Baptists as indispensable for the administration of the Communion and much less for its validation. The validity of the Lord's Supper is in the Lord's own institution of it, and in so far as the individual recipient is concerned, in the faith in which he receives it. Most Baptists would probably find the explanation of why they recognise the Lord's Supper to be a special means of grace to be in the fact that, at the Service, the Fellowship of Believers in obedience to the command of Christ is present with one mind and heart to render thanks to God for His unspeakable gift to men in the Lord Jesus Christ and for His work of redemption in His cross, and to remember Christ, the Saviour, who continuously works among men, to worship Him, to re-offer its obedience unto Him, and to receive His life into the life of its members. It is on the union of the heart and mind of worshippers with one another, because of their common experience of the saving power of Christ, that Baptists would lay the greater stress rather than upon any ritual or ordained priest.

The Author's Comments

I presume the brief statement above represents fairly the essential position of Baptists with regard to the Lord's Supper. In theory, at any rate, intercommunion does not raise any serious problems to the majority of the Baptists and presumably a great part of the Baptist Communion would look with favour on any movement that works for the coming together of the various branches of the Church at the Lord's Table. While Baptists may not find any serious difficulties in joining in intercommunion, nevertheless they could do so only if they themselves are not asked to subscribe to any interpretation of the Lord's Supper which would take them far beyond their own position. They would not, I dare say, ask any other branch of the Church which might find itself ready to join in intercommunion to surrender any part of its own interpretation of the Lord's Supper. Perhaps intercommunion would be nearer realisation if there were a deeper appreciation of the differing interpretations that obtain in the various branches of the Church to-day concerning the Lord's Supper. There are certain values that each tradition is jealous to safeguard and we need sympathetic understanding of these values.

While it would be idle to ignore that what keeps the Churches separate even at the Lord's Table are certain stubborn doctrinal differences, nevertheless a sympathetic understanding of the values that the different branches of the Church cherish and are anxious to safeguard would be a help and might take us a step nearer the realisation of intercommunion.

To me, as a Baptist, the two values in my tradition that mean most are our insistence that the Table is the Lord's and that the 'faith' of the recipient of the Sacrament counts for a great deal. I am unwilling to think that these values are not recognised by others. In fact, they are recognised by almost all of the 'Protestant' tradition; I am sure those of the 'Catholic' tradition also recognise the importance of these two values. The difference would be one of emphasis and priority.

One of the points of departure between Baptist and certain other traditions would arise in regard to the 'objective' value of the Sacrament of the Lord's Supper. These traditions, while not discounting the value of the recipients' 'faith', would nevertheless perhaps make the 'objective' values of the Supper antecedent to the recipient's 'faith'. This seems a real point of departure. Nevertheless, the position need not be so disparate. Those who make the 'objectivity' antecedent to 'faith' do not belittle 'faith' or the spiritual condition of the recipient. The need for repentance that is insisted upon by all branches of the Church before one partakes of the Sacrament shows that they also emphasise the subjective conditions involved before the 'objective' becomes a means of grace. And again, conversely, 'faith' as a subjective attitude has an 'objective' reference. If 'faith' had no 'objective' reference it becomes merely a will to believe. The 'faith' that the Baptists insist on is anything but a mere will to believe. Its reference is to something that is totally 'objective', though the 'objective' may be beyond the reach of the senses and rational definition. 'Faith' has reference to the unspeakable gift of God in Christ and to His redemptive purposes in His life and death. Of course, the real difficulty of the Baptist is not in regard to the work of God in Christ. That is 'objective' enough for him; but the relation of that 'objective' fact to the Lord's Supper. In what sense can the indisputably objective fact of redemption through the sacrifice of Jesus Christ on the Cross be said to be reflected once again in the Eucharist, whenever it is celebrated? May not the Baptist pause here for a moment and think what implications there are in his belief that the Table is the Lord's and that the real Host at the Feast is the Lord Himself and not the administering individual? The Baptists would like to think of the risen and the living Christ —the Victor over death, whose presence is ever about us. But the resurrection was from the grave and before it was the suffering, pain and passion and death. The shame and suffering of the Cross preceded the glory of resurrection. And may there not be truth in the experience of many that one has to identify oneself with the passion of Christ before one can claim for oneself the merits of the passion and death that followed it? Now, if the Table is the Lord's and the real Host is the Lord Himself, the Lord that stands there is one who suffered pain and shame and who gave His life as a ransom for many. The Feast was instituted by the Lord that His followers may not forget the ransom offered by Him in His own death for sinners. If it was instituted with that urgent purpose, may there not be in the Feast something more than of a mere memorial significance? May it not be an occasion in a real sense for the participant in the Feast to enter into fellowship with the sufferings of Christ? There is something 'objective' here which cannot be defined—perhaps it is better not defined. Some of the hymns we sing seem to bring this out more clearly than our theological formulations.

On the other hand, Baptists rightly recoil from any suggestion that once the elements are consecrated they attain an autonomous efficacy. Those who emphasise the 'objective' value of the Sacrament should appreciate perhaps much more keenly than they are wont to do the meaning of the 'faith' of the believer. The subjective-objective import runs through the core of everything that is Christian. It is only at our peril that we can forget this. To those of us in India it will be suicidal to overlook its importance. The ancient sacrificial system of the Hindus at one period reached a point when it was believed that the sacrifice had such an autonomous efficacy that nothing more was needed than to perform it properly. Even the gods could not resist its influence once it was performed according to rule. That thought is not absent even to-day. 'Objectivity' can be carried to extremes in this way. The Indian mind may succumb to it easily. But apart from this, let us remember the significance of the work of Jesus on the Cross. The Cross is the opposite of coercion. God could coerce man if He so willed, but He uses love to constrain us. This means He respects the individual and his free response. 'Faith' evokes this free response and while in a sense 'faith' also is a gift of God, its birth in the individual does not annul the individual's responsibility and initiative. The significance of the subjective-objective reference lies here. God did something in Jesus Christ and continues to do it, and what God had done and continues to do is indeed never validated or invalidated by any thing man does or does not do. 'Faith's' reference is always to this indisputably objective fact. But what God had done in Jesus Christ and continues to do in Him is for *the individual*. *The objectively valid becomes efficacious for the individual when subjectively appropriated by 'faith'* aided, indeed, by the grace of God.

Personally I am prepared to believe that in the Lord's Supper there is something 'objective'; this follows from my belief that the Table is the Lord's and that He alone is the Host. But I cannot and dare not define too precisely what this 'objective' something connotes. I do not know if many of my fellow Baptists would go with me even so far. But I am also certain that they are right in insisting on the subjective condition of the recipient. If my fellow Baptists would appreciate something of the 'objective' signi- ficance of the Lord's Supper as that is understood by certain branches of the Church, and if these branches in turn would appreciate something of the great emphasis that the Baptists put on the subjective condition of the participants in the Supper, intercommunion in a real sense between Baptists and these others would be nearer realisation. I say intercommunion in *a real sense*, for as I have stated earlier, as far as the Baptists are concerned they would not, I presume, object to communicating with others even now, if conditions were not imposed on them.

Intercommunion to be real must be reciprocal. Without reci- procity there is no intercommunion. But certain branches of the Church will not be in a position to reciprocate in this matter the Baptist readiness to communicate with them, unless there is agree- ment on the nature of the Christian ministry and the ministry's relation to sacraments. Let it be frankly admitted that the Baptists will not be able to subscribe to the view that the Sacrament of the Lord's Supper cannot be validly administered unless it is cele- brated by a minister episcopally ordained. The question of what is a valid ministry is of much wider scope than the subject of this paper and we cannot enter into a discussion of it here. Nevertheless, the disagreement on it is not only one of the major causes of the divisions in the Church of Christ but one which is also preventive of intercommunion. But I presume that it is the desire of some at least that intercommunion should not wait agreement on all these problems that keep the Church of Christ divided to-day. If so, can we accept the position that is advocated by some of the leaders of the younger Churches in India to-day and start from that point? The position advocated by these leaders is that in a divided Church *ex hypothesi* and *a priori* no form of ministry can be accepted as being complete and fully adequate, and yet God has in His mercy used in His service and for His glory these ministries, incomplete and inadequate as they are. If we are humble enough to accept this view, it is not unlikely that we can reciprocate with perfectly good conscience every gesture that is made for intercommunion.

VIII

A BAPTIST VIEW

*

(b) P. W. Evans

Baptist Union of Great Britain and Ireland

(Great Britain)

In ancient liturgies, at a stage after the offering of prayers and the reading of the Scripture lessons, the command was given that 'none of the catechumens, none of the unbaptised, none of those who are unable to join with us in prayer', should remain: 'let the doors be shut'. In every community of Christian people even to this day something happens corresponding to that exclusiveness; there is no Church which does not in some sense practise 'Restricted Communion', though we no longer cite in connection therewith the text: 'Give not that which is holy to the dogs!' This familiar fact deserves further consideration for the light it may shed on modern practices of exclusion from the Table of the Lord. Within the New Testament we find at once the language of universal welcome and that of warning and prohibition. The Gospels contain 'Parables of Invitation' (Luke 14. 16-24; Matt. 22. 1-14) side by side with indications of exclusion that is self-exclusion. The seventy messengers were to invoke peace on every house into which they entered, but some because they were not worthy could not receive it. The Church must know when to open her doors and when to shut them; if the doors were never opened, the Church would be a prison; if her doors were never shut, she would resemble an hotel.

But the doors are shut to-day in a different fashion, and from the Lord's Table there are excluded those who cannot be described as catechumens or unbaptised or 'unable to join with us in our prayers'. Such restriction is reluctantly applied; it is not the result of bigotry or intolerance but of nobler motives. John Owen well said: 'Those who impose on pastors the promiscuous administration of these divine ordinances, or the application of the seals unto all without difference, do deprive them of one-half of their ministerial office and duty.'[1] Zeal for the safeguarding of the Sacrament is to be commended and respected by us all, but the problem before the Christian Church to-day is the exclusion of those who are not (in the language of the Prayer Book) 'open and notorious evil livers', but are 'religiously and devoutly disposed' to receive 'the most comfortable Sacrament of the Body and Blood of Christ'. No one questions the rightfulness of debarring from that Sacrament those who are openly unworthy, but in addition unconfirmed Christians, though baptised, are excluded. Though Baptism without Confirmation suffices for enrolment upon the Parochial Electoral Roll, it does not suffice for admission to Communion. In the Prayer Book the repulsion of anyone from the Table of the Lord is to be a matter of pastoral investigation and concern, and individual cases are envisaged so that pastoral admonition and ministry are required. But present-day limitations to Communion deal with whole classes of people *en bloc*.

The utmost credit must be given by Free Churchmen to the motives which underlie such restriction. Concern for the purity of the teaching of a particular Church, a sense of the importance of right doctrine to true Christian living, an estimate of the value of a disciplined and unified community—these we imagine to be among the motives which lead to the regretful exclusion of those who are accepted as fellow believers. Are the consequences of a wider, though still guarded, invitation to the Communion Service so harmful in practice as is feared? Free Church experience can offer guidance on the matter.

In an earlier page (*Intercommunion from the Seventeenth to the Nineteenth Centuries*, p. 103) there is an account of the development in the Free Churches of the practice of 'Open Communion', which has spread to such an extent that they have among themselves what may be described as 'mutual open Communion', and they gladly welcome to the Lord's Table Anglicans as well as Free Churchmen. The writer has known this practice as a church member for fifty years, and for a considerable time was minister of churches where the custom prevailed. Account ought to be taken of the consequences of such a remarkable degree of intercommunion. Its results can be assessed, though not precisely tabulated, and its influence upon the life and thought of the communions which

[1] *The True Nature of a Gospel Church*, ed. Huxtable, p. 69.

have given such free access to the Communion Table deserves consideration.

The practice, in the case of Baptists, goes back to the seventeenth century; in that age it was, as is well known, the subject of controversy between Bunyan and other Baptists. In 'A Reason for my practice in Worship', Bunyan spoke of the two 'figurative ordinances' ordained by Christ in His Church as 'of excellent use to the Church in this world. . . . But I count them not the fundamentals of our Christianity, nor grounds of rule to communion with saints; servants they are, and our mystical ministers, to teach and instruct us in the most weighty matters of the kingdom of God; I therefore here declare my reverent esteem of them; yet dare not remove them, as some do, from the place and end where by God they are set and appointed; nor ascribe unto them more than they were ordered to have in their first and primitive institution. It is possible to commit idolatry even with God's appointments.'[2] With a liberality of mind amazing in that age, Bunyan declared that the believer in Jesus Christ who is dead to sin and lives to God by Him 'hath the heart, power and doctrine of baptism. . . . The best of baptisms he hath: he is baptised by that one Spirit.' When St. Paul said (Rom. 15. 7) 'Receive one another, as Christ also received you, to the glory of God', the last phrase (said Bunyan) was 'put in on purpose, to show what dishonour they bring to God, who despise to have communion with them, who yet they know have communion with God'. If objectors to Open Communion said of those from whom they differed, 'we can pray and preach with them, and hold them Christians, saints and godly', Bunyan's name for that limited fellowship was 'piece-meal communion'. It must, however, be pointed out that Bunyan thought it a greater difficulty 'if a man want light in the Supper', i.e. if he should be mistaken or uninstructed about the Lord's Table. This being 'a part of that worship which Christ hath instituted for His Church, to be conversant in as a Church', and 'a duty incumbent on the Church as a Church, and on every member of that body as such' they are 'obliged in that case more closely to deal with the members'. Obviously the degree of want of 'light' about the Supper would have to be considered, but Bunyan's own arguments about those whose baptism lacked something essential from his own point of view are

[2] Works, II, 604.

capable of application to those whose beliefs concerning the Lord's Supper appear to others to be faulty. One of Bunyan's editors, George Offor, exclaimed triumphantly: 'Bunyan's principles have spread, are spreading and must soon become universal.' That was written a century ago, and the universal triumph still tarries. Baptists generally have not followed Bunyan fully, for he would have all privileges of church membership thrown open to 'visible saints' even if they differed from him about Baptism, but the majority of Baptists hesitate to go so far. 'Open Communion' is, however, widely practised, as is of course the case with other Free Churches in Great Britain.

What has resulted from a procedure of so long duration and such wide observance? The criticism is made by some Baptists that it has proved to be a denominational disadvantage, though different views are held among us on that point; Dr. John Clifford believed that it increased the number of people seeking Believers' Baptism, since that sacred rite could then be presented as a witness freely to be given and a privilege to be enjoyed, with no suggestion that it was a qualifying ceremony, and many Baptist ministers have found this to be the consequence. The question of denominational loss or gain is thus a disputed one, but in any case it is not the most important matter. No one has ever (to my knowledge) pointed to any doctrinal error or moral declension because of this wider fellowship at the Table of the Lord. Churches that adopt the wider terms of Communion do not revert to the narrower method, as they would surely do if spiritual loss ensued. Over all the areas of British Free Church life where Open Communion prevails, I know of no evidence at all that fellowship is thereby weakened, truth distorted, Christian conduct lowered or spirituality lessened. 'By their fruits ye shall know them'; admittedly the fruits do not always appear at once, and the results have to be assessed on a wide basis, but when they endure and are universal they cannot rightly be ignored. True, the objection has been made that we must not infer God's approbation from His blessing, for that would be to underrate and to presume on His goodness—an argument once expressed in the remarkable phrase: 'He mercifully overlooks what He cannot conceivably approve.' That plea can be urged from either side, however. The consequences of Open Communion which we have traced are not just merciful overlooking, but positive enrichment. Nor are they cases of exceptional treatment by divine grace, but normal and dependable blessing, lasting now through centuries and experienced in all kinds of communities by all sorts and conditions of men. They are not matters of ignorance which God has 'winked at', but instances of His approval, and they present to other Churches not sharing the practice a remarkable and significant example of widespread intercommunion in actual existence. Have the right deductions—or any—been drawn?

Anglicans used to be fond of quoting from Shorthouse's book, *John Inglesant*, the phrase: 'The English Church . . . offers the supernatural to all who choose to come.' That is not typical Free Church language, but we certainly believe the 'supernatural' is present where our Lord Himself has promised to be present, and we offer this 'to all who choose to come'. They must come within the conditions scripturally appointed for the service, however, so that in this sense the Communion is restricted and the invitation is not indiscriminate. It is usually given to 'all who love our Lord Jesus Christ in sincerity'. Furthermore, in most churches practising Open Communion this is regarded as something occasional rather than habitual; frequently the term 'guest Communion' is employed. C. H. Spurgeon held wide views on the admission of all believers to the Lord's Table, saying (in a letter dated 30th March 1886): 'I believe that we may commune with all who are truly in Christ. If Christ communes with them, we may. If they are in the Body of Christ, and we are in that Body too, it is clear that we do commune with them, and must do so, because of the one Life. Hence, because communion is there in fact and in reality, I would give the outward sign.' Yet he held that non-members of a church should not continuously and regularly communicate without regularising their position by seeking membership. That illustrates the strong instinct among those who practise Open Communion that it should not degenerate into a miscellaneous gathering of people who refuse to take seriously the obligations as well as the privileges of church membership.

In the light of this experience of Open Communion certain peculiarities in the attitude of Baptists towards problems of intercommunion can be better understood. They have thrown down the barriers on their side that hinder intercommunion, and are ready and wishful to join their fellow believers in any observance of the Lord's Supper to which they are invited; what more can they rightly do? The situation would be different if they were convinced that they had totally misunderstood the will of their Lord in the manner of their observance of the Sacrament, but honest and prolonged investigation and discussion have failed to achieve that result, and there is no immediate prospect of a debating triumph for either side.

Further, many question the assumption that Christian unity is only fully realised and expressed in intercommunion. The Fourth Gospel, in spite of its repeated references to the desire that Christians may be one, yet contains no explicit reference to the Lord's Supper. Certainly there might conceivably be intercommunion without real unity of heart and mind, though this would be near to profanity. Those who hold the view now stated would claim that sacramental unity is not prominent in the New Testament, though it has predominated in later history (and this, of course, raises the question whether such predominance is entirely apart from or opposed to divine guidance). Those who share this view point to other forms of manifesting Christian unity, such as united meetings for prayer, united evangelism, co-operation in witness and service, joint theological study and discussion and so forth, in which they enthusiastically participate. Archbishop Brilioth said at Amsterdam that mere co-operation is not unity; that is true, but neither is mere intercommunion. Neighbourhood during the Communion Service and mutual eligibility for each other's sacraments might exist side by side with little real brotherhood. Possibly the attitude described is in some cases due to a fear of overemphasis on sacraments, and Free Churchmen find justification for this in their own history, but it can also be traced to an esteem for the Sacrament so great that they would not have it separated from the genuine love of each for his fellow communicant which alone makes it the reality it ought to be. And when the Communion Service is styled 'the Lord's own service', it is not a mere quibble to claim that the name could also be given to preaching, which, like the Eucharist, was practised by our Lord Himself and enjoined upon His disciples. As far back as 1860, in a lawsuit of great importance to Baptists known as 'The St. Mary's, Norwich, Chapel case', a group of Tutors in our theological colleges said that they 'have always held, and still hold, that Baptism and the Lord's Supper are not sacraments but ordinances, *of the same nature as religious prayer and praise*, and the hearing of the preaching of the Gospel, and other acts of religious worship and service'. Nowadays it is unlikely that many Baptists would regard Baptism and the Lord's Supper as entirely 'of the same nature' as the other observances named, but probably all would agree in denying that the Communion Service has the exclusive importance in relation to Christian unity that many assign to it.

The reluctance just described to lay all the emphasis on the Lord's Supper has another cause. Among Baptists the term 'Communion' has never been restricted to the Sacrament, but has had a much wider connotation. Bunyan defined Communion as 'fellowship in the things of the kingdom of Christ'. John Owen in 1689 wrote of 'the Communion of the Church in all its sacred privileges'.[3] In the lawsuit just referred to it was stated in an affidavit:

> 'The word "Communion" was customarily applied by this church to the full communion of membership, including Communion in the Lord's Supper, and not to Communion in the Lord's Supper exclusively, but to it as one act or part of Church Communion—that is, of Communion in all privileges peculiar to the Church.'

Church fellowship is described in Baptist Confessions as meaning 'giving up themselves to the Lord and to one another'.

Celebrations of the Lord's Supper among us have a 'family' character, and this is not regarded as just a romantic atmosphere surrounding the Communion Service but an integral part of it. Usually, the occasion of the meeting of the Church around the Table of the Lord is employed for acquainting church members with joys or sorrows invading the lives of their fellow members; prayer and such aid as may be possible are solicited for them. New members are welcomed at the Communion Service, not because that service is the supreme privilege of church membership, but because that service is the place and time when they can best make the acquaintance of the rest of the membership, acquaintance which is expected to ripen into friendship. Almost invariably the offertory is devoted to the necessities of troubled people within the membership; this follows the administration of the Sacrament, and further symbolises the belief that the sharing

[3] *The True Nature of a Gospel Church*, ed. Huxtable, p. 25.

of the sacred rite is only part of the bond which unites church members. They share together in various forms of Christian service within the Church, and this also is felt to be a real Communion. He would be regarded as a faulty and mistaken communicant among us who concentrated only upon the Lord's Supper and neglected 'communion in all privileges peculiar to the church'.

This emphasis on a fuller meaning of the term Communion explains Baptist hesitation in dealing only with the Lord's Supper when greater unity among Christians is sought. It means also that we should be uninterested in, indeed dissatisfied with, any plan of intercommunion which was not fully reciprocal. There must not only be a gathering together for the reception of the Communion; there must be a growing together in every form of Christian fellowship. Is it envisaged that in the day of the hoped-for union united Communion Services will be held in the village chapel as well as, and as often as, in the parish church? If this were not so, what would have been achieved would only be an extension of hospitality on one side, not a real uniting of fellowships. Conscious as Free Churchmen are that in the fellowship of the Lord's Table they have known in truth the loftiest experiences which the New Testament associates with the Sacrament, they cannot but desire that others should share it. Further, they could not easily consent to a course of action which might seem to suggest that their own Communion Services were of a lower order. Some Anglicans would of course feel difficulty because of their doubts as to the minister's qualifications, and because of their knowledge—or opinion—that in the village chapel a doctrine of the Holy Communion prevailed which is not theirs. The former problem is at present under discussion between Anglicans and Free Churchmen, and can better be considered in the light of any conclusions they reach. As to the latter point: it has been repeatedly suggested that room for varieties of interpretation must be left in any conceivable union—as notably in relation to episcopacy. We are asked to receive the fact without thereby assenting to any theory. Cannot an analogous attitude be taken in regard to attendance at Communion Services other than our own? Cannot the earnest communicant be invited to come and take whatever he can sincerely find at the Holy Table? If others find more or other or less than he, need that prevent his own coming and receiving?

The doctrinal objections urged against intercommunion are often made in ignorance of the actual views of the Lord's Supper held by Free Churchmen. A Committee of the Church Union in a Report on 'Co-operation with Nonconformists' (Church Union, 1947) said: 'It is sometimes assumed that all Nonconformists regard the Sacrament merely as a memorial feast, but this Zwinglian view is as foreign to the official teaching of many Nonconformist bodies as it is to that of the Church of England.'[4] It has, of course, frequently been pointed out that Zwingli held a much fuller view than that popularly ascribed to him, saying, for example, in the Confession addressed to King Francis: 'We believe that Christ is truly present in the Lord's Supper; yea, that there is no communion without such presence. . . . We believe that the true body of Christ is eaten in the Communion, not in a gross and carnal manner, but in a spiritual and sacramental manner, by the religious believing and pious heart.' Dr. C. Anderson Scott was surely right when he urged that the deprecatory adjective 'merely' is unfair. 'This bread and wine are, to many Christians who may not go further, a figure of something very sacred, so sacred that it little beseems any other Christians to mock at their procedure or at the meaning they attach to it. There is no body of Christians whatever, observing the Lord's Supper, who mean by it *less* than a proclaiming of Christ's death till He come'. The view criticised therefore is not erroneous, though defective, and the question arises whether defective understanding of the full meaning of the Sacrament prevents its being a means of grace to the sincere communicant. The theology of the Christian Church has grown in fullness throughout the centuries, and the theory of the development of Christian doctrine implies that there were long ages in which doctrines were but faintly adumbrated. Yet no believer in such development holds that the means of grace were not effective in those unilluminated eras. Imperfect apprehension of the full implications of Christian doctrine was prevalent for long periods in relation to the redemptive work of our Lord as well as of His Person, but that inadequate understanding was not supposed to exclude the sincere but unenlightened disciple from fellowship with Christ or a share in 'the benefits of His Passion'. On what grounds is it held that defective sacramental theology has more adverse results?

[4] *Op. cit.*, p. 6.

G

Those who are unable to contemplate the admission of Free Churchmen to Holy Communion in episcopal churches do so because 'they feel that for Christians to receive the Holy Communion together implies that they are fellow members of one worshipping society ordered according to a known principle'.[5] Free Churchmen would answer that such agreement in Order is not discoverable by them in the New Testament, and would assent to the judgment expressed on the very next page of the document just quoted: 'There is no evidence that our Lord prescribed any one form of organisation for the Church.' Refusing to equate Order with Faith, they would also insist that Faith necessitates a living relationship to our Lord Jesus Christ, and that what common reception of the Holy Communion implies is that all the participants are in this sense one in Christ Jesus. Their inability to believe in the necessity of the one worshipping society being 'ordered according to a known principle' seems to gain pragmatic sanction from the fact that in all the differing companies into which the people of God are at present grouped the witness of likeness to our Lord is equally given. If there were some condition of Order which was ordained by Him or even nearer to His will than other forms, we should expect that fact to show its result in a finer discipleship than that exhibited where the supposedly preferable Order was absent—but who would claim that such spiritual superiority exists?

Everyone who believes that God has appointed that sacramental grace can only be mediated through episcopal ministries admits an exception in the case of Baptism. The immensity of that breach in theory seems to be too little considered. It is justified on the ground of necessity by those who accept the doctrine of Baptismal Regeneration; ought not the same plea to be allowed in the case of the Communion Service?

We are given to understand that, in episcopal communions, there are those who, left to decide for themselves, would have no difficulty in sharing with Free Churchmen in their sacraments and inviting them to participation in their own, but they refrain from action which their consciences would permit and their judgments approve because of regard for ecclesiastical authority and the wish to prevent division within their own ranks. These motives must

[5] *The Practice of Intercommunion and the Doctrine of the Church*, p. 6., S.C.M., 1938.

of course be respected, but the practical effect is that, whilst endeavouring to comprehend divergent schools of thought within one Church, a power of veto is given to one party. How is a beginning to be made in intercommunion? It appears unlikely that any procedure will at first be found possible which all members of every Church can accept, but some will be able conscientiously to avail themselves of the offered privileges; the hope would be that this number would increase until the practice became universal. There is no likelihood, though, that inter-communion will ever come about if those who are prepared for it allow themselves continually to be inhibited by the scruples of others.

We believe, therefore, that intercommunion can most effec-tively be forwarded to-day by growth in the practice of Open Communion among the Free Churches, and by the participation in it of those Christians who feel able to come. Thereby mutual knowledge would be increased, and it is likely that some misconceptions as to the solemnity and reality of the Sacrament among us would be removed. Not only should Free Churchmen invite all who love our Lord to share in the Communion Service, but they should continue to assert their own willingness to go to any Table of the Lord to which they are invited—not, however, as spectators but as partakers of the meal because members of the family. And if, as the result of this course of action, any of us should think that others were present who had no divine invita-tion and thus no right to be there, having made clear the meaning of the Sacrament and the conditions of rightful participation, can we not with a good conscience leave the intruder to be dealt with by the Host? What is meant by the Wedding Garment in Christ's parable (Matt. 22. 11)? Interpretations are abundant and diverse, but one fact stands out prominently—that the unqualified guest was dealt with, not by any fellow guest, but by the Lord Himself. Much of our concern for the safeguarding of the Table may be quite unnecessary. The cry should still be heard in our minds if not in our hearing: 'Let the doors be shut!' But they must not be shut on any whom Christ would have present, and it is better that we err in admission than in exclusion, for the man without the wedding garment will not receive the reality of the Sacrament. The Lord who founded the Sacrament is Himself the Guardian of it.

IX

CONFESSIONAL LOYALTY IN THE ECUMENICAL MOVEMENT

*

Georges Florovsky

Orthodox Oecumenical Patriarchate (Exarchate for the Russians in the West)

(United States)

It has been recently suggested that what we need most urgently in the Ecumenical Movement is a 'theology of the abnormal'. Christian theology, strictly speaking, is basically concerned with the abnormal, with the most radical deviation from the divine norm of existence, with fall and sin. Even in the redeemed world we are faced with an appalling impact of sin. Sin is indeed already forgiven and a new humanity has been inaugurated in and by the Second Man. The fatherly embrace of God is again charitably extended to the repentant. Yet repentance is still a task for man to perform, and it proves to be an exceedingly difficult one for frail man to accomplish. The prodigal son is still very slow in going back home. And therefore, in Christian theology, we find ourselves again and again in a paradoxical situation. Christian disruption, utter disunity in Christendom, is nothing but an antinomy and a paradox. The fold of Christ ought not to be disrupted. Theological intelligence fails completely to comprehend the predicament of disunity, created by human unfaithfulness and aberration.

The Ecumenical Movement, an endeavour to overcome and to heal the Christian schism, is inescapably a paradoxical venture. The final goal is, indeed, a reunited Christendom. Yet the nature and scope of this prospective unity and reunion is variously described and interpreted by Christians of different backgrounds and traditions. The method of *re*-union depends ultimately upon the conception one holds of the existing *dis*-union. And these conceptions utterly differ. Prescription always depends upon diagnosis. And, in our case, it is precisely the diagnosis that is uncertain and controversial. That is why it is so difficult to agree on the prescription. Several solutions have been suggested. Roughly speaking, one group of solutions can be described as a 'theory of a common denominator' and the other as 'the true Church and the secessions'. Let us examine them in turn.

A Common Denominator

The theory of 'a common denominator' amounts, in practice, to a recommendation to act *as if* there was no real schism, no true disruption, but rather only a sad misunderstanding, which could possibly be settled by some agreement. Christians are divided and mutually estranged indeed; nobody can deny this grim fact. Yet, in spite of all their unhappy divisions and separations, they are at one on many basic points. They are united in their common allegiance to the same Lord. One might have added, they are, above all, united in His redeeming will and love. He came precisely to recover the lost sheep and the scattered. In this perspective it seems but reasonable to disregard the existing dissensions and disagreements and to act accordingly, *as if* all Christians were really at one. Are not all these disagreements utterly human— human misconceptions—and unity a divine gift that has been already given free in Jesus Christ, the Lord of all flesh? It is precisely at this point that the problem of what is usually described as an 'open communion' arises and the predicament of the schism is felt most grievously and painfully. It seems to be a shameful scandal that those who proclaim their common allegiance to Jesus the Christ, the Son of the living God and the Saviour of the world, the only sure hope in ages past and to come, are still unable to join together at His Table. Much worse than that, a large part of them emphatically refuses to do so. The champions of an easy solution are utterly depressed by what seems to them to be obstinacy, lack of charity and brotherly understanding. It seems to them that the whole ecumenical endeavour is compromised by this obstinate resistance.

Now, from another point of view, it is not the ecumenical endeavour, but only a particular interpretation of it that is wrecked on the proposal of an 'open communion'. In fact, the whole theory of a common denominator comes into a blind alley, since it fails to carry a unanimous conviction. This fact in itself indicates that possibly the measure of existing unity or agreement has been somehow exaggerated and misunderstood. It suggests that the division probably goes much deeper than has been admitted by those who were ready to act together. It is indeed a dreadful thing that Christians cannot join together at one and the same altar. But it is exactly what should have been expected. For they are *really* divided. Several and separate Communion Services at an ecumenical gathering are but a spectacular projection of the very fact of the schism. And the schism cannot be overcome simply by agreements on our human level. One has to be courageous enough to bear the pain, and those who are compelled by their conscience to abstain from any 'open communion' suffer no less, but probably much more, than those who are prepared to go together.

The Marks of a Church

It is usually suggested that this obstinate refusal to join at the common Table is inspired by exaggerated 'confessional loyalty' and by a lack of true ecumenical comprehension. Now, the phrase 'confessional loyalty' is ambiguous and misleading. Surely, nobody would pledge his loyalty simply to a denomination, but only to the Church of Christ. The trouble is that this loyalty to the Church is variously conceived and interpreted. All 'confessions' identify themselves, in one sense or another, with the Church of Christ, 'Protestants' no less than 'Catholics'. In our present state of Christian confusion and chaos, one simply cannot escape some sort of discrimination between a 'true' and an 'untrue' Church. It is no good pretending that the whole guilt of intransigeancy is on one side. Moreover, it is no good bringing forward the charge of intransigeancy at all. For, in fact, the word is but another and depreciatory name for conviction. We have to recognise, boldly and humbly, that our deep convictions differ. Yet, in spite of that, we have to stay together. The whole burden of the ecumenical endeavour is tied precisely to this small phrase: 'in spite'.

Obviously, 'Protestants' would suggest that all empirical Churches should become Churches in very truth, and in order to accomplish this purpose should go through a certain kind of reform and purification, more or less identical with the European Reformation of the sixteenth and seventeenth centuries. They are committed, by the very logic of their belief, to an emphatic claim that the Churches of the Reformation are representative of a true kind of Church and that, consequently, no Church can ever be true unless it has gone through a process of reformation. Un-reformed means in this connection exactly un-true.

On the other hand, a 'Catholic' will never regard the Catholic Church as one particular denomination among many others. He will identify her with the Church of Christ. The claim may seem arrogant, it may easily be dismissed as a proof of spiritual pride or intransigeant hypocrisy. Yet, it is to be understood that a 'Catholic' is committed to this claim by the very logic of his belief and conviction. Again, it is to be understood that this claim does not unchurch those who do not belong to the Catholic Church of history. The most rigid 'Catholic' will regard all faith-ful Christians as related, in some sense to be defined, or even as belonging, to the Church of Christ. There is implied in the 'Catholic' claim no anticipation of the ultimate eschatological judgment. The claim is laid down on the level of history, i.e. on the level of Christian practice and action. The true composition of the Church is known to the Lord of the Church only—no 'Catholic' has ever doubted that, and St. Augustine has stated it most frankly and emphatically.

Perhaps the real point is this: was the Reformation a gain or a loss—a step forward or a step astray? Of course, this is only a rough way of putting it, and both the question and the answers must be carefully defined (which is, unfortunately, quite beyond the scope and the competence of the present paper). It may be very painful for a 'Protestant' to read this, it is very painful indeed for a 'Catholic' to write it. But it is not written to pain or offend anybody. Conviction is bound to be outspoken. And we have to share our respective pains, to bear each other's burdens, and to prove thereby our mutual confidence and our true brotherly affection. Both 'Protestants' and 'Catholics' are concerned with the marks of a true Church. The tragedy is that they identify these marks differently, or even in opposite senses.

Open Communion and Intercommunion

One may seriously doubt whether what is called an 'open communion' is open in the strict sense. The case seems to be rather obscure. There are two possible interpretations. Either it is presumed that all doctrinal convictions are at this point irrelevant, and that doctrinal conformity should not be regarded as a term of admission to Holy Communion; obviously, this assumption is itself a kind of doctrinal conviction, which is unacceptable for many Christians. Or, and this seems to be the case, an 'open communion' is open only to those who satisfy certain requirements, of an obviously doctrinal character, and such an 'open' table is still fenced. It is really irrelevant, whether a fencing formula is actually said or omitted: in any case it is implied.

In either case, the practice of an 'open' communion is justified by a certain particular conception of the Holy Communion, which is not acceptable to those who refuse to join. The opposition of an 'open' communion and a 'confessional' communion is wrong. Strictly speaking, an 'open' communion is also meant for a particular confession, i.e. for people of a particular persuasion, even if this persuasion is so wide as to ignore all doctrinal dissensions. An unbaptised member of the Salvation Army would usually be admitted, although he disbelieves the divine institution of the Sacrament. A member of the Society of Friends would also be admitted if he so wished, although it has been made clear that any Friend who finds himself in need of habitual participation is to be reminded that his place is probably not with the Society. The door seems to be ajar in the direction of vagueness and indifference.

But surely those who hold a 'Catholic' view of the Sacrament cannot conscientiously be admitted, since their belief in the sacrifice of the Mass is to be styled a 'corruption' and an 'erroneous doctrine' along with many of their other superstitions. A 'Catholic' therefore finds himself excluded from the 'open' communion by the implied terms of admission and by the conception of the rite therein implied. It is no good talking of his obstinate resistance. His participation would be a nonsensical betrayal on his side, and a concealed insincerity on the other. And, in the end, it would not promote the ecumenical fellowship at all. A sentimental gesture cannot solve the conflict of deep convictions. Unity of brotherly feeling is not yet unity of faith. Are we permitted in the Church to be satisfied with anything less than this unity of faith?

Briefly, there are three main objections which constitute a radical impediment to an all-inclusive and 'ecumenical' fellowship in the Holy Communion. *First*, utter divergence in the sacramental doctrine itself—possibly the conception of a sacramental sacrifice is the very point of demarcation. There can be no communion, because there is no *common* belief. *Secondly*, and this is but the wider context in which the first is to be seen, there are deep divergences in doctrine in general, although these divergences, in our own age at least, definitely cut across the historical confessions. And communion presupposes 'one mind', no less than 'one heart'. *Thirdly*—and this is probably the crucial point, at least in the practical field—there is utter disagreement on the doctrine of Christian ministry. A 'Catholic' cannot divorce order from faith, a very definite church order is for him an article of his integral Christian faith or dogma.

This fact has been partially recognised in recent times, in so far as many recent schemes of reunion included the restoration of an 'historical episcopate'. This restoration was, however, compromised and rendered meaningless (from the 'Catholic' point of view), since this order was emphatically excluded from faith or doctrine. For the 'Catholics', the point is not merely the restoration of an episcopal order, but the recognition of the sacramental character of the priesthood; but this still seems to many to be nothing but detestable 'sacerdotalism'. For a 'Catholic' an all-inclusive communion will be possible only after the integrity of the faith and the fullness of the sacramental fabric of the Church has been restored in the whole of Christendom. It will then be not simply a manifestation, by a human arrangement, of Christian charity and mutual recognition—and, in catholic conviction, the Sacrament of the Eucharist was not instituted or meant for that purpose—but a true revelation of the Holy Church of God, in all her power and glory.

The whole ecumenical situation is certainly complicated and obscured by the fact that those who claim for themselves the name of 'Catholics' (not merely in a vague and general, but in a concrete and specific historical sense) are also divided and are not in communion with each other. And at this point another serious and painful problem arises, that of intercommunion. The difficulty in this case is of a different, though similar, character. Again, what is required for intercommunion is obviously unity of faith and the integrity of the sacramental structure. Unless this is secured and avowed, no action should be taken. The practice of an occasional intercommunion (or even of an occasional open communion) adopted in certain episcopal Churches only confuses the issue. A true intercommunion can only be a corporate and Catholic action. In a case in which the sacramental integrity of two Churches which are not in communion with each other is mutually recognised, the unity of faith has still to be identified and emphasised by a corporate action of the Churches concerned, and not simply by a personal conviction of some advanced individuals. In the whole process there is no question of confessional loyalty, but solely of the Catholic truth.

A Fellowship in Search

The tragedy of Christendom is precisely that the truth of God is still divergently apprehended. What is a sacred treasury for some, is a deplorable superstition for others. What is an advance in the eyes of one part of Christendom is a step astray in the conviction of the other. Yet, *in spite* of all that, all Christians within the Ecumenical Movement and beyond its actual boundaries should pledge themselves to stay together and to profess their common allegiance to the same Lord and Master. It is a paradoxical situation, certainly. Yet it is exactly that paradox that makes the pledge so valuable and promising. They should stay together, exactly because they are divided. The pledge is valuable because it implies pain and tension. We are given the cross of patience to bear; let us glory in that cross. Our Christian pain is a token of recovery, a recovery which is to come from the Lord.

The Ecumenical Movement is primarily a fellowship in search. It is a venture or an adventure, not an achievement. It is a way, not the goal. And therefore an open communion would compromise the whole endeavour. It would be to pretend falsely that Christendom has already been reunited. We know only too well that it has not. Tension remains, compelling us to move on. For that reason we still have only an Ecumenical Movement and not a reunited Christendom. It is true, some unexpected agreements have been discovered and achieved recently, exactly in the process of a common search. Let them not be disavowed by any premature and unwarranted action, in which some of the partners in the discourse will never conscientiously participate. There is still a long and dangerous journey ahead.

It has been recently suggested that in the ecumenical conversation there has been a certain tendency to postpone agreements, even when they were possible; once an agreement on some particular point seemed to be at hand and rather imposing, the subject has been deliberately changed and another highly controversial topic brought into the discussion. Possibly this is an exaggeration. What is true, however, is that in the ecumenical discourse we do not trust our most compelling agreements. We behave once more in a most paradoxical manner. We mistrust ourselves because we have a deeper insight into the mystery under discussion, and we are aware of an ultimate disagreement which we are unable or perhaps too shy even to mention or to describe.

Possibly it is the reverse tendency that is more prevalent. There is a tendency to invite or even to compel one's opponents to think in categories unfamiliar or alien to them. A 'Protestant' theologian will write his books and make his statements in his particular idiom and primarily for his own edification and will expect the 'Catholics' to follow his argument. Usually he will be misunderstood, simply because his partner in conversation fails completely to follow his peculiar manner of speech. A 'Catholic' will habitually do just the same, and each will accuse the other of misconception and misunderstanding. The guilt obviously is on both sides. We have to learn each other's idioms or rather we have to create a true ecumenical and common language in theology and possibly to un-learn our party idioms. It is an enormous task; yet we can hardly escape it. We have to identify ourselves mentally with those partners in the discourse who do not share our own convictions, if we are going to arrive anywhere. Let us try to state the 'Catholic' conviction in the idiom of the 'Protestants' and let us invite them to talk to us in our own idiom. What is often taken to be confessional loyalty may prove to be inadequate phrasing of a commonly accepted truth.

The True Church

This paper is an attempt to write in a new and ecumenical language. Probably the attempt has not been successful. Probably some would detect in it a heavy confessional flavour, and others would complain of vagueness. And so it will not be out of place to summarise briefly my main contentions in a language familiar to myself. As a member and priest of the Orthodox Church I believe that the Church in which I was baptised and brought up *is* in very truth *the Church*, i.e. *the true* Church and the *only* true Church. I believe that for many reasons: by personal conviction and by the inner testimony of the Spirit which breathes in the sacraments of the Church and by all that I could learn from Scripture and from the universal tradition of the Church. I am compelled therefore to regard all other Christian Churches as deficient, and in many cases I can identify these deficiencies accurately enough. Therefore, for me, Christian reunion is just universal conversion to Orthodoxy. I have no confessional loyalty; my loyalty belongs solely to the *Una Sancta*.

I know well that my claim will be disavowed by many Christians. It will seem to be an arrogant and futile claim. I know well that many things I believe with full and uttermost conviction are disbelieved by others. Now, I do not see any reason whatever to doubt them or disbelieve them myself. All I can reasonably do is this, to proclaim my faith and to try to phrase it in such a way and in such a manner that my poor idiom may not obscure the truth. Because, I am sure, the truth of God carries conviction. It does not mean that everything in the past or present state of the Orthodox Church is to be equated with the truth of God. Many things are obviously changeable; indeed many things need improvement. The *true* Church is not yet the *perfect* Church.

The Church of Christ has to grow and be built up in history. Yet the whole and the full truth has been already given and entrusted to the Church. Revision and re-statement is always possible, sometimes imperative. The whole history of the Ecumenical Councils in the past is evidence of that. The holy Fathers of the Church were engaged in this task. Yet, on the whole, the deposit was faithfully kept and the testimony of faith was gaining accuracy and precision. Above all, the sacramental structure of the Body has been kept integral and intact. Here again, I know, this conviction of mine may be rejected as an illusion. For me it is a matter of evidence. If this is obstinacy, it is the obstinacy of evidence. I can only see what I actually do see. I cannot help it. But in no way am I going to 'un-church' anybody at all. The judgment has been given to the Son. Nobody is entitled to anticipate His judgment. Yet the Church has her own authority in history. It is, first of all, an authority to teach and to keep faithfully the word of truth. There is a certain rule of faith and order that is to be regarded as normal. What is beyond is just abnormal. But the abnormal should be cured, and not simply condemned. This is a justification for the participation of an Orthodox in the ecumenical discourse, in the hope that through his witness the Truth of God may win human hearts and minds.

X

INTERCOMMUNION IN THE YOUNGER CHURCHES

*

T. S. Garrett
Church of South India

(Great Britain)

The Situation To-day

Intercommunion from the standpoint of the 'younger Churches' must needs be considered in the setting of the advance of the Gospel during the past one hundred and fifty years in countries hitherto untouched by it, an advance which has been greater than that during any like period of Christian history. The Church's growth, even during the first three centuries of the Christian era, cannot compare with it, and Professor Latourette in his *History of the Expansion of Christianity* is amply justified in calling the nineteenth century 'the great century'. Whether the twentieth century will be viewed by future church historians as equally great in this respect cannot yet be foreseen. In one way, however, the evangelistic work of the nineteenth century has been crowned in the twentieth: in Africa and Asia younger Churches have emerged, in many cases largely self-supporting and, to an increasing extent, independent of their parent missions as regards internal administration and discipline and the development of their common life and worship.

All this is well known: the extent to which new problems have been thereby created in the relations between the different denominations has not been so generally realised. These new factors undoubtedly make the question of intercommunion, and so of ultimate union, more acute; but, at the same time, it is possible to conclude from an examination of them, that there is hope in the very heightened urgency of the situation that the Churches will be driven to find a solution.

In the first place, at the beginning of the nineteenth century, the divisions of the Church which had resulted from the Reformation still bore, for the most part, a national or racial character. They were each mainly confined to one country, or at most to one quarter of the continent of Europe, and could reasonably claim to be national Churches, giving an expression to Christian faith and life which was in accord with the spirit of the nation amongst which they were established. Before the period of missionary expansion, the principle, *cuius regio eius religio*, even discounting the mainly political motives which underlay adherence to it, carried a cogency which it is not easy at the present day to understand. For instance, the Church of England could claim to be the appropriate embodiment of English Christianity and could with a certain measure of justification (from the point of view of the time) display intolerance towards dissenting sects. To-day these same sects have become denominations with at least as good a claim to catholicity in the sense of 'world-wideness' as the Anglican communion, which has expanded in like manner itself. In territories within the British Empire the latter has retained a measure of the prestige and influence which has accrued to it through being 'established' in the mother country; but even within this area it is in many countries numerically inferior to more than one other denomination, a fact which Anglicans who have never moved outside the provinces of Canterbury and York find hard to realise. Similarly a lady, who had grown up amid the preponderance of Presbyterian church order in Scotland, is reputed to have been greatly shocked, on travelling East for the first time, to find that the Bible in India was not normally bound together with the Scottish Metrical Psalms!

Such far-reaching confessional groups with all the ecclesiastical organisation which they involve, each of which, even when it makes no exclusive claim to be the one true Church, nevertheless believes itself to have some distinctive Christian heritage which the others lack, are more formidable bodies and less easily moved in the matter of interdenominational relations than they would be if they had remained within the smaller dimensions of former years. At the same time, the very extension of a denomination has made real to its members in a new way the idea of the Church as a supra-national community and brought before them the scandal of division. This extension has also meant that the claim of a Church to be the true Church in a given country, on the grounds that it is the national Church, has had to be considerably modified, if not superseded. The assertion on the part of a denomination that it alone has catholicity, or that its faith and order are superior to and more catholic than others, may still be and, indeed, is made. But the vitality of other denominations, their power to enlarge their borders through the preaching of the Gospel, the indubitably Christian life and worship which their members display and, finally, their obviously church-like structure —all these, whatever the deficiencies and imperfections inherent in them, constitute a powerful counter-assertion to any claim by one denomination that it is the only Church. These same common marks of the *ecclesia* in the denominations have led to a widespread, though by no means universal, belief that no one denomination can rightly be regarded as having the sole title to be called the Catholic Church. The spread of this belief—in the younger Churches as much as anywhere else—is a hopeful sign to those who are convinced that in its acceptance alone lies the possibility of reuniting Christendom.

Secondly, the very enterprise of evangelism, and the conditions of the early life of a Church mainly composed of new converts and in process of growth to maturity, make the scandal and folly of our ecclesiastical divisions more apparent. Men and women are brought to the point of accepting Christ as their saviour and of renouncing, often in the face of opposition, the way of life which they have been leading in a non-Christian environment. What an anti-climax it is when they have to be told that Christians are not all united in that love which has been proclaimed to them as the specific mark of the Christian life! Any evangelist in a pagan land will also bear witness how puzzled simple believers in a newly formed congregation are by the regulations which forbid their being in full fellowship with their Christian brethren in a neighbouring congregation but belonging to a different denomination.

To be sure, there are manifold examples of the sorry spectacle of well-established congregations in the younger Churches exhibiting all the worst features of the sectarianism and complacency of their parent Churches, and priding themselves that they are Christians of a particular brand and not of another type which they regard as inferior. In this fruit of their work the missionary societies of our Churches come under the condemnation which

our Lord pronounced upon the Pharisees for making their prose-
lytes worse than themselves. But it is also true that many of those
well enough educated to understand the meaning of the doctrines
and practices peculiar to the different denominations are, nevertheless, increasingly impatient of them as belonging to an ancient
history of events which happened long before the Church came
to birth in their own land, as bearing little relevance to the tense
situation in which they find themselves in a pagan environment
and, finally, as demonstrating the deficiency of western Christianity, when compared with the Christianity of the New Testament. To their minds the only way to achieve a truly indigenous
expression of the essential faith of the Gospel is to break away
from the shackles which the foreign leaders of the Church have
imposed upon them by their own intolerance and narrow-
mindedness.[1] This challenging pressure of the evangelistic enterprise upon interdenominational relations is doubtless felt most
acutely in Churches newly established in non-Christian lands; but
the handicap thus created by our divisions is little less grave in the
countries of Europe and America, where the great bulk of the
population has drifted away from the Churches and needs to be

---

[1] In support of this contention two very moderate statements by Indian
clergy of high Anglican background may be quoted:
'This, then, is the crux of the problem. Is the Anglican Church prepared to
be in communion with an episcopally ordered Church like the C.S.I. which
is simultaneously in communion with non-episcopally ordered Churches and
which continues to have a Ministry which is not yet fully unified? How long
will the Anglican Church halt between two opinions? It must bestir itself and
make up its mind either to go forward now or presently, or be content for
ever to be relegated to a static position where she does not want—and is, therefore, isolated from—Reformed Christendom, and is equally not wanted by
Rome and the East.' The Rev. D. Chellappa in *The Madras Guardian*, 5th
October 1950.
'Indian Christians (especially those frequently under transfer in government
or other services), wherever they go, partake of Holy Communion in any
Protestant Church which welcomes them. This shows that the average Indian
Christian layman has no particular denominational loyalty. The late Bishop
Foss Westcott once said that the pain caused by lack of intercommunion is a
healthy pain, for it drives people to work vigorously for church union. This is
ingenious and seemingly sound; but in actual effect people who are denied
communion for denominational reasons drift apart more and more. Their
resentment against the Anglican Communion, in particular, increases, because
of what they consider to be a narrow spirit.' Canon Thomas Sitther. See also
additional note, p. 220f.

converted from a 'residual Christianity' to a living faith.

The third element in the position of the younger Churches—an element which will doubtless come to be regarded by future church historians as of paramount historical importance—is the recognition by the majority of Churches participating in the World Council of Churches of the principle of 'comity' in the evangelistic task. The missionary societies of the Churches accepting this policy, and the younger Churches which have come into being by their activity, refrain from competing with each other in a given area, with the consequence that almost every country or province in Africa and the East has been divided up into a number of areas. In each of these one denomination alone of those observing comity has responsibility for evangelistic work and the building up of the Church, though other denominations may possibly exercise pastoral care of their own people, if there are large enough groups of them to warrant their doing so.

This policy appears in most cases to have been accepted in the first place on grounds of expediency: i.e. because the areas to be evangelised could not otherwise have been covered by missionary activity. But its results have inevitably had ecclesiastical implications which are relevant to our subject. Firstly, for a denomination to refrain from competing with another in the latter's area of responsibility is tantamount to recognition in some measure of the position of the denomination evangelising that area as representing the universal Church there. It is a point of importance that the Anglican Communion has in its missionary strategy in general observed comity with non-episcopal Churches; although by no means all Anglicans would admit that this implies any judgment in favour of the latter's status as defined above.

This new situation has significance for the doctrine of the Church. It means that we have in the mission field recovered an element in the concept of Catholicity which has been lost wherever denominations have existed side by side in rivalry with one another and often catering for only one section or class of the community. This concept is basic to the idea of the Church in the New Testament, where the churches of Ephesus, Corinth and elsewhere are the *ecclesia* of God in their respective localities, the embodiment of the universal Church, the fellowship of the saints, in one particular community.[2] Those, who claim for their

[2] See J. E. L. Newbigin, *The Reunion of the Church*, p. 13.

doctrinal position the term 'Catholic' and who yet refuse to observe the principle of comity in evangelism overseas, need to be asked whether in this respect their Catholicity is not gravely deficient and whether they have not lost sight of an important aspect of the primitive form of the Catholic Church.

'Comity', however, like most half measures, creates as many problems as it solves. It means that, except where the denominational areas impinge upon each other, the different denominations live in isolation from one another with little chance of any exaggerations and distortions in their doctrine and common life being corrected by contact with heirs of a different heritage. The only opportunity for interdenominational relations for the rank and file of the laity is when members of one denomination move into an area in which another is operating.

This last point indicates a further consideration of consequence. It means that a convert to Christianity has to become a member of the denomination operating in the area in which he lives. Conviction that Anglicanism, for instance, is better than Methodism, or vice versa, cannot enter into his decision. The only consideration must be that of locality. Hence also those moving from one denominational area to another are, to all intents and purposes, unchurched and deprived of regular reception of the sacraments, unless some arrangement for accepting them as visitors at other churches than their own is made to meet their need. This, together with the requirements of evangelism described in an earlier paragraph, has been one of the main difficulties which have inspired a group of denominations established in the culturally and racially unified region of South India to take the adventurous step of uniting in a single Church. In many other areas it has necessitated arrangements for either full or limited intercommunion between Anglican and non-episcopal Churches. It is significant that the Churches which are the product of the past century's missionary expansion have been driven by the exigencies of their own development thus to move closer to each other in fellowship than have, in most cases, their parent Churches.

A Theological Approach

If this development of intercommunion and, still more, the plans, which are being made for reunion in other regions, as well as South India, are to be approved, it is necessary to attempt to justify them theologically.

The denominations and their expansion form part of the nexus both of ecclesiastical and secular history: it may therefore be fruitful to approach the consideration of their status as parts of the universal Church from the starting-point of divine revelation in history. The writer would accept the widely held view of biblical revelation, that it consists in a series of historical events and crises and human reaction to them, especially in the national life of Israel culminating, as it does, in the coming of the Christ. These together constitute a revelation of divine character and purpose in judgment and salvation. Our Lord's promise of the Holy Spirit to His Church should preclude us from regarding revelation in history as having ended with the closure of the Canon of the New Testament. The history of the Church must be regarded as a continuation of that same mode of revelation, provided that, as in our interpretation of Scripture, we bring all our understanding of God's working in the Church to the test of the supreme revelation of God in Christ.[3] Moreover, the uncompromisingly historical character of that focal point of Christian revelation is itself part of the mystery of the Incarnation and provides primary justification for treating the events and crises of the history of the Church, which is the Body of Christ, as continuing, in their measure, to reveal God's purpose for mankind.

It is customary in writing concerning the Ecumenical Movement to use the word 'denominations' in a bad sense. And rightly so; for, in accordance with the view of revelation in church history outlined above, their existence must be regarded as a revelation of the wrath of God upon the disobedience of the Church. A signal instance in church history demonstrates this view. The corruption of many aspects of the Church's life in the Middle Ages and its distortion of vital elements in the Christian faith[4] made it almost inevitable that a reform movement should arise within it and that the protagonists of reform should find it impossible to remain in unity with those who were entrenched behind a decadent tradition and determined to resist change. On

[3] I venture to refer to an essay entitled 'The Ministry in Scripture and Tradition', *Theology*, April, 1951, in which I have developed this point.
[4] Cf. *Catholicity*, p. 19.

the other hand, the reformers may be said to have precipitated division by their impatience, and, though the burden of responsibility for the schism ought to be laid at the door of the traditionalists, the excesses and distortions, of which both sides were guilty, show that all alike were under sin, and all who were involved in the historical crisis of the Reformation stood alike under the divine judgment revealed therein.

This judgment was manifested partially in a rupture in historical continuity in the life of the reforming Churches, particularly in their ministry, on account of their having seceded from the established Church which had unbroken links with the past and a ministerial succession which, it was claimed, went back to the Apostles. Yet this cannot be regarded as necessarily destroying the validity of the reformed church order in general or the ministry of these Churches in particular. The validity of ministry rests on divine action. If, therefore, the Reformation was, so to speak, the matrix of a divine act in history, the Churches of the Reformation and their ministries, which were the instruments of God's working —the rods of His anger and, at the same time, the harbingers of His salvation through faith,—derive their justification as true Churches and true ministries from the divine commission thus historically given. Further, that blessed *non liquet*, which scholars both of 'Catholic' and Protestant standpoint must needs admit lies upon the New Testament evidence for the Ministry,[5] is surely a divine Word *ex silentio* to the Churches, justifying episcopal and non-episcopal ministries alike; because it proclaims that what cannot be demonstrated from the documents of the Apostolic Church cannot be made the criterion of apostolicity in the Church of succeeding ages.

Thus, in biblical terms, God partially, though by no means wholly, rejected the then existing ministry, because of sin, after the pattern of the rejection of the house of Eli in the Old Testament and the still more tragic rejection of the Jewish church and priesthood in the New. Alongside the old ministry He raised up the ministry of the Churches of the Reformation both to exercise pastoral care amongst those who, as they believed, in the interests of truth had separated from the established Church, and also to stand, so to speak, as fingers of accusation pointed at the deficiencies of the traditional ministry and the doctrine and liturgical

[5] A. M. Farrer in *The Apostolic Ministry*, p. 168.

practice which accompanied it. In so far also as the Reformers represent the rediscovery of the Gospel, as set forth in the New Testament, they bear a commission as witnesses of that Gospel in the face of its misunderstanding equivalent to the apostolic commission to witness to it before Jew and Gentile in the first century.

On the other hand, the equally vigorous survival and extension of the traditional Churches and their ministries are historical facts which should lead us to consider whether they, too, have not preserved some essential characteristics of a true Christian faith and life which have been obscured in many or all of the Churches, which have come into being since the beginning of the sixteenth century. In this case they, too, must be regarded as standing in judgment upon the reformed Churches; so that neither side can claim to be the exclusive possessor of the form of a true Church. It is the express exclusion of this latter assertion in the recent Vatican pronouncements, which makes it impossible to be very hopeful of their consequence as regulating the participation of Roman Catholics in ecumenical discussions.

It should further be emphasised that, while the human obstinacy and pride, which is disclosed in the repeated refusal of long-established Churches to listen to the prophetic voice of reform, inevitably draws down upon the Church as a whole the divine chastisement of schism, God's supreme purpose to save humanity in Christ, in and through the Church which is Christ's body, though it may be frustrated at this particular point, is not thereby finally defeated. A modern historian has argued that there is a sense in which history appears to be pregnant with a purpose above and beyond the immediate and separate purposes of its human participants, and often overriding their decisions.[6] The relevance of this insight to the post-Reformation history of the Church is manifest. The human decisions which led to the Reformation schisms are part of a tragic pattern of divine nemesis: these same schisms would appear to have been used by God to preserve vital truths both of the Gospel of salvation through faith and of the nature of God's operation in and through His Church, which had been obscured by the distortions of the Middle Ages. If the medieval Church had not resisted repeated attempts to reform it, these insights, now regarded as characteristic of Protestantism, might have been preserved within the wider fellowship

---

[6] Herbert Butterfield, *Christianity and History*, p. 109.

of the Great Church and thus have escaped the exaggerations consequent upon separation. But, as it is, they have, by divine providence, been given a markedly vigorous expression in the separate denominations. Indeed, in face of the rigid traditionalism of the hierarchy of the western Church and its ruthless suppression of all supposed heresy, separation may be regarded to have been an unavoidable condition of the freedom of the Spirit.

Yet just as it is God's purpose to unite Jew and Gentile in the New Israel,[7] so too His ultimate plan for the Church in its present divided state cannot be that it should continue in division, but that the new doctrinal insights and the varied heritages of worship and common life gained in independence should be gathered together to the enrichment of the whole in the surpassing unity of the Great Church which is to be.

The same principles may be shown to have been at work in the history of the separation, for instance, of the Methodists from the Anglican communion. Their ministry, too, may be said to have received a divine commission by historical revelation both to stand in accusation of the failure of Anglicans to preach the Gospel both then and often since, and at the same time to show forth in independence the power of that Gospel with a fresh zeal and a new intensity of fellowship. Again, the fact that Methodists, like other Protestants, have gone forth to establish the Church overseas is a sign that God has used even our human failure in fellowship, as embodied in schism, as an instrument to achieve His purpose for mankind. On the other hand, many Methodists to-day would doubtless admit that, if the Church of England was judged at the end of the eighteenth century by means of Methodism for its somnolence, the early Methodists also stand under condemnation for precipitating the separation. They would also recognise that their common life has been greatly impoverished by their continued separation from the Anglican communion, as from the rest of Christendom, and that an inestimable enrichment awaits them when reunion becomes possible.

Thus we must conclude that the survival of these separate denominations, their vigorous proliferation throughout the world, their zeal in evangelism, their devotion in worship, their bearing of the essential marks of Christian faith and life, are all part of the historical revelation that God means to continue His blessings

7 Rom. 9-11.

towards them and to use them as instruments for the effecting of His purpose of salvation. This in itself validates their claim to be Churches; for continuity with the past can never be the only basis for validity. There must be the present call of God to the individual and to the Church. The preservation to the present day of a true witness to the teaching of the Apostles is at least an essential element in the apostolic succession, an element to which, as we have argued, those denominations without the 'historic episcopate' can lay at least equal claim with those which have preserved it.

All this must be regarded as cumulative demonstration that there should be no obstacle to intercommunion between the denominations on the ground that they are not true parts of the Church of Christ, or that they have not a real and divinely appointed ministry. Further, our previous estimate of the present situation in the younger Churches, and the immediate, practical, urgency of intercommunion which it reveals, is in accord with our theological conclusion. Indeed, the very difficulties and stringencies, which have arisen from the attempt by the denominations to evangelise the world in separation, is surely part of God's historical discipline of His people, that He may lead them back to that unity which is according to His will.

The Way to Unity

When we come to consider the question whether intercommunion should precede union, as a presbyter of the Church of South India, the writer can only cite the example of that Church, in which union has in fact been achieved without a previous intermediate state; i.e. one in which full reciprocal intercommunion had been permitted by all the denominations now united.

Those who have experienced union in South India would agree with the Roman, Orthodox and Anglo-Catholic theologians, who assert that the question of intercommunion cannot be considered in isolation from the ministerial order, doctrine and liturgical tradition and, indeed, the whole life of the Churches concerned. But, instead of using this as an argument for delaying negotiations for union until all are united on those points, they would draw a very different conclusion. They would say that, compared with the richness of full union, intercommunion is a poor thing, a mere half measure, likely, like the half measure of 'comity', to produce as many difficulties as it resolves. They would recommend to the Churches, which have already achieved a measure of co-operation and which are sufficiently close to each other in faith and practice to make union possible, to launch out on the same brave adventure as they have undertaken, an adventure which, in spite of its many difficulties and disappointments, they would claim, with thanksgiving to God, had already brought an inestimable renewal of their life and fellowship.

The establishment of united regional Churches, as autonomous provinces of the universal Church in communion with each other, should be an immediate goal wherever possible: intercommunion, though a permissible arrangement to meet present exigencies, should not be regarded even as the next step, wherever the more excellent way is feasible.

It may be objected to this, that outward unity of organisation, which contains within it profound differences of belief and practice, is an inadequate basis for sacramental fellowship. But thus to put first obedience to our Lord's will for His Church that it should be visibly one may well be, from the psychological point of view, to say the least, the only way by which a deeper unity in other matters of vital import may be attained. As long as denominations remain in separation there is a natural tendency, born, perhaps, of the herd instinct and accentuated by selfishness and pride in their corporate manifestation, for members of each confession or denomination to be unduly complacent about its particular heritage and to give such emphasis to its distinctive tenets and practices that these come to resemble flags or badges to be flaunted in the face of all who dissent from them.[8] For instance, there is a widespread tendency in contemporary Anglicanism to stress the apostolic succession and the thin purple line of bishops which safeguards it as the position at which the Church stands or falls. This is often countered by those who adhere to a Presbyterian ministerial order by an equally one-sided denial that

[8] For examples of this in the doctrinal sphere see *Catholicity*, which is the report of a commission composed of Anglo-Catholic scholars, and *The Catholicity of Protestantism*, which is largely a reply to the former by a group of theologians of the English Free Churches.

For the idea underlying this and the following paragraph I am indebted to Bishop Newbigin's article on the Church of South India in *The Student Movement*, May-June, 1950.

the historic episcopate has any basis in the New Testament what-soever or any value for the discipline and order of the Church. Similarly the stricter Baptists exclude from their fellowship even those, baptised in infancy, who have renewed their baptismal vows and publicly professed their faith in confirmation; while the members of Churches which practise infant Baptism are generally unwilling to recognise the strength and cogency of the Baptist position, particularly in face of what has been called 'indiscriminate Baptism'. Again, extempore prayer, on the one hand, and liturgical prayer on the other, have become watchwords and shibboleths to accentuate our divisions.

In contrast with this, it has already been the experience of South India that, once the denominational barriers are down, these often right and important points of confessional emphasis cease to be objects of dissension and become instead elements in the heritage of the uniting confessions which are accepted as contributions to the united whole. Thus former Anglicans need no longer be afraid to use extempore prayer, where fitting, in their services or to introduce congregational elements to the invigoration of their church life. Former Congregationalists, on the other hand, may come to recognise the value of a liturgical order of worship and accept episcopacy, confirmation and other elements in the 'Catholic tradition', not only as enhancing their own heritage, but as bringing them into living fellowship and continuity with the Church of all the ages.

The unity, therefore, in faith and order, which Roman Catholic, Orthodox and Anglo-Catholic rightly stress as requisite for full sacramental fellowship, can hardly be achieved by waiting until the separate confessions have sufficiently progressed in approximation to each other for union to take place. The strengthening of confessional loyalties, which has been one of the marked results of the Ecumenical Movement during its brief history, suggests that this growing together in separation is an unlikely event. Is the World Council of Churches anything but a will-o'-the-wisp, if it is going to lead to nothing more than this?

The word of Christ, 'Whosoever would save his life shall lose it; and whosoever shall lose his life for my sake and the gospel's shall save it', is true for societies and institutions, as well as for individuals. Have not the Churches, in their eagerness to defend their own position in distinction from that of others, rather than lose themselves in a wider allegiance, failed hitherto to grasp this truth? Only in the give and take, the mutual enlightenment and co-operation, of those who have determined to 'break down the middle wall of partition' may the sacramental fellowship, which has thus been won, be made more real by a growing harmony in the common faith and life of Christ's Body.

A further point needs to be added, namely, that the Churches in South India have been most concerned with relations both of union and intercommunion with their immediate neighbours and would find it hard to understand the policy adopted by members of some Churches of seeking to make agreements with Churches, with whom their contact can never be anything other than remote and occasional, while delaying to take steps towards unity with the members of other denominations beside whom they find themselves situated as neighbours, and in a measure rivals, in every town and village.

The Church of South India is, however, not yet united with all the denominations established in its area. As far as those with whom the uniting Churches, or any one of them, had fellowship before union are concerned, the following extracts from a statement approved by the Synod of the C.S.I. may be regarded as authoritative:

'The principle that "The Church of South India desires to be permanently in full communion and fellowship with all the Churches with which its constituent groups have had communion and fellowship" (Constitution II, 15) is absolutely basic and is not subject to reconsideration. It is not conceivable that in any reasonably foreseeable circumstances the Church of South India should break off relationships with those parent Churches with which it now enjoys unrestricted fellowship.'

' "Any minister (of any Church with which the C.S.I. has relations of fellowship) shall be free as a visitor to minister or celebrate the Holy Communion in any Church of the C.S.I. if he is invited to do so" (II, 14). This is not one of the provisions subject to decision at the end of the 30-year period.'[9]

[9] *Documents dealing with the Relations between the Church of South India and the Anglican Communion*, pp. 10 f.

There is, however, a divergence at present within the Church itself in this matter. Former Anglicans, whose consciences forbid their receiving communion from ministers of the united Church not episcopally ordained, would *a fortiori* not be prepared to receive communion in non-episcopal Churches not yet united with them, nor would any former Anglican congregations invite a non-Anglican minister from outside the C.S.I. to celebrate communion. Those congregations, on the other hand, which were accustomed to issue open invitations before union, have clearly no intention of ceasing to do so now. This is an indication of the fact that the process of growing together is not yet complete.

Further, although the mind of the C.S.I. has been generally expressed in the above statement, the details have not yet been worked out. With what Churches were the constituent Churches in communion before union? What attitude is the C.S.I. to take to the Salvation Army and the various faith missions which are at work in the same area, the ecclesiastical orders of which, in the view of any of the constituent Churches, must be regarded as in some measure defective, and which do not observe the principle of 'comity'? These questions will need careful thought and considered decisions. The only reason why the Church of South India has not been able to give full attention to them hitherto is that it has been fully engaged in discovering the implications in discipline and common life of the union which it has been led to inaugurate.

Additional Note

'If the Holy Communion is really the Lord's Supper, then every person who has accepted Christ as his or her Saviour and Lord has the right to come to it wherever the Table is set in His name. A Church can refuse to admit a person to the Lord's Table only on the ground that that person by reason of his or her conduct presumes to approach it unworthily. If only Churches would show as much zeal in exercising their inherent right and inescapable duty as in the effort to maintain traditions of uncertain authenticity and value, this central act of Christian worship would acquire a reality and potency which the Church as a whole has not yet experienced.

'Those Churches that invite all humble and penitent people to join with them in "the Holy Communion of the Body and Blood of our Saviour Christ" do constantly proclaim that the Table they have set is not theirs but the Lord's. Those Churches which place restrictions upon members of Churches other than their own do so for two reasons: viz. that only those ordained to the Christian ministry in a particular manner can make the administration of the Sacrament a valid administration, and that only those who have been admitted to full membership of the Church by a specific procedure can come worthily to the Holy Communion. It is difficult for a large body of Christian believers in all conscience to concede the validity of the first presupposition. Even those who, in order to promote unity, are prepared to accept episcopacy as an essential order of the Church, find it impossible to agree that only episcopal confirmation can make a person fit to come to the Lord's Table. The Book of Common Prayer very rightly states the adequate conditions of fitness. They are true repentance, neighbourly love, and the intention "to lead a new life, following the commandments of God". If the emphasis is laid on the spiritual aspects of this supremely spiritual Sacrament, Churches should have no difficulty in extending an open invitation to all who are in good standing in any of the Churches. Intercommunion would then become the first and most obvious step towards mutual understanding and the drawing together of the divided limbs of the Church Universal. But when a Church transfers the emphasis from the fundamentals of the Christian faith to historical developments, it is driven to the necessity of bringing in a second tradition to support the one which is considered valuable and adopted. The progress (strictly regress) is then from one doubtfully scriptural and spiritual position to another and yet another unscriptural and unspiritual position. Existing cleavages widen and denominations multiply.'

(*Mr. G. Vethanayagam Job, Secretary to the Synod of the Church of South India*)

XI

INTERCOMMUNION:
A PERSONAL OPINION

*

S. L. Greenslade
Church of England
(Great Britain)

Christian disunion is a sin and a scandal, but not one which can be quickly overcome. On the contrary, the immense difficulty of corporate or organic reunion is apparent to all. Some hold that it requires an absolute, and not simply a substantial, agreement in doctrine; a common order seems to be indispensable and—despite the principle that unity is not the same thing as uniformity—a good deal of common ground in worship and in other ecclesiastical practices would probably be necessary; and all this may be complicated by the matter of Church and State.

It is my belief that there are many who, consciously or unconsciously, carry some of these difficulties unnecessarily over into the different problem of intercommunion; they seem unwilling to risk the temporary anomalies without which one cannot get out of an anomalous situation. That they should be so cautious is understandable in the light of the past history of the Church, and I do not suggest that foolhardiness is in itself a mark of the Spirit's guidance. But we have passed the days when reunion could be caricatured as the sacrifice of all distinctive beliefs and practices; the prevalent danger is rather a certain procrastination and passivity, the more insidious because in part based upon the truth that it is God Himself who will give unity to the visible Church in His own time and His own way. Nevertheless, God works through men, who must be awake to His calling and direction. It is generally agreed that we may certainly discern the operation of the Holy Spirit in the aspirations after unity which mark the last two or three generations. If we may not take short cuts, neither may we be for ever timid. This essay is written in the conviction that God is calling us now and urgently to make the venture of intercommunion as a step towards corporate union, in and through which we may learn to see more clearly the way to the final goal. To put the point over-sharply for the moment, while every scheme of reunion must prove its case, the *onus probandi* is now upon those who hold back from fuller inter-communion.

The Church which is the Body of Christ *is* one. This is not only a true theological proposition but also a fact of experience. Over against a secular society, sincere Christians of all communions are increasingly conscious of their unity. And if this is true of the visible Church, it is even more plainly true of the Church Triumphant and of our communion with the saints of all ages and of all 'Churches'. In that communion we who belong to different denominations are already one with Erasmus and Luther, with Laud and Bunyan and Wesley and Newman, and with all the humble folk of East and West who have put their faith in Christ.

It is manifestly wrong that spiritual unity should not be expressed in visible unity, and visible disunity, though it does not destroy the unity of the Spirit, detracts both from its fullness and from its evangelical efficacy in the world. As it is, our division shows itself at the most vital point, namely in our inability to share without hindrance in the very Sacrament of unity, the Holy Communion. If this barrier could be overthrown, the major scandal of disunion would be removed. My position is briefly:

(*a*) It is impossible to allocate the guilt of schism, in which we are all involved, among different communions. Even if a dissident body had plainly been the more guilty party, it is no longer possible to demand that its descendants, once they have built up ecclesiastical traditions of their own, should simply return as penitents to the original fold.

(*b*) There is already enough true unity of faith and practice between many of the Churches at present out of communion with each other to justify immediate intercommunion between them. Their true fellowship in Christ demands expression in the Eucharist.

(*c*) The sin of exclusiveness here is greater than any sin which we might incur or any mistakes we might make by boldness in intercommunion. (I repeat that I would not say this at all confidently of schemes for corporate reunion.)

(*d*) Fellowship in the Holy Communion is a necessary means to 'wholeness'. I dissent entirely from the argument that intercommunion should not be the means, but only the crown of unity. If much of the deepest and most distinctive piety of a Church is expressed in its use of this Sacrament, the various Churches need to share their spiritual riches at this point before they are ripe for full reunion. Those who guard a particular tradition should have faith that what is good in it will prevail. Eucharistic fellowship requires not complete agreement in all points of doctrine and order, but sufficient and substantial agreement in essentials. An Anglican can bear testimony to this principle.

I do not propose, then, positively to advocate intercommunion so much as to examine some of the objections which are commonly urged against it. The term intercommunion is used in a number of ways. I use it here for reciprocal sacramental communion between autonomous Churches, involving the right to participate in the Holy Communion in each other's churches and the possibility, though not necessarily the constant practice, of an interchange of ministries. The extent of the latter might vary as between any two communions pending further advances towards corporate unity. Indeed, a worthwhile measure of intercommunion could be achieved without any more interchange than takes place at present.

(1) The first class of objections to such intercommunion turns upon a particular conception of the unity of the Church which, in its first form, was set out most clearly by Cyprian. The New Testament teaches that the Church is one; this is and must be true of the visible Church, he held, thinking of it as a single, recognisable and concretely historical body, continuous both generally and locally with the Church of the Apostles. It is recognisable outwardly by its governing authorities, the bishops in apostolic succession; separation from them implies separation from the one Church, so that any bodies outside this single institution, though they claim to be Christian, are outside the Church. In other words, schisms as well as heresies are outside the Church. But (he held) the sacraments are gifts of the Lord to His Church, and do not

operate or exist outside it. Schismatic bodies have no sacraments, either valid or efficacious; the Holy Spirit does not dwell or work outside the Church, schisms have no spiritual life and are bound to wither away. *Extra ecclesiam nulla salus.* Intercommunion between the Church and a schismatic body would be both wrong and meaningless.

This is a coherent and intelligible doctrine, and yet it has been almost universally abandoned. Historical facts (for even the Novatianists whom Cyprian was attacking did not wither away for some centuries) and the intuitions of Christian charity were against it. Since it was logical, its error must lie in its premises, either in its definition of what constitutes the Church or in its assumption that the Holy Spirit will not work outside the Church so defined. It presumed to know too much about what Christ can or will do in certain circumstances. My immediate conclusion is that no repudiation of intercommunion should be based upon the Cyprianic position except by those who are prepared to stand by its implications. Most of us, perhaps all, are not; we recognise the spiritual power of those communions which stand outside the apostolic succession of bishops, a recognition which suffices to refute the Cyprianic position *as a whole*. There are sound elements in it to which we shall return.

The second form of this doctrine is the Augustinian modification of Cyprian. Rome had already maintained against Cyprian the validity of schismatic and in some cases of heretical baptism. Augustine, building on Optatus, extended this to Holy Orders. Thus the principle was accepted that non-Catholic sacraments are in certain circumstances valid, Christ being the true minister when the proper (i.e. the Catholic) matter and form are used. Not only does the moral or doctrinal unworthiness of the human minister not affect the validity of the sacrament, but he need not even be a minister of the Church.

It is important to bear in mind how much of Cyprian's teaching Augustine retained. The Catholic Church, the only Church, is still defined in terms of the apostolic succession of office, the lines of bishops in each see, and not by chains of consecrators. Outside this Church the Holy Spirit does not work, at least sacramentally, and the benefits of valid, but non-Catholic, sacraments are only to be enjoyed upon return to the Church. Those who hold the Augustinian position cannot have reciprocal sacramental fellow-

ship with bodies whose sacraments they thus regard as ineffica-
cious, though they may admit members to their own Eucharists
by economy.

I do not know enough of modern Roman or Orthodox
doctrine to say how far this theology is accepted. I rather suppose
that the Orthodox stand nearer to Cyprian, but make a freer use
of the principle of economy, though accepting Roman orders as
valid; while Rome holds in the main to the Augustinian view.
And both of them—on what principle I will not venture to say—
have so far departed from both Cyprian and Augustine as to
recognise a measure of efficacy as well as validity at least in each
other's sacraments. Anglicans, I believe, are very much muddled
(and I do not exclude myself). One commonly hears Anglican
theologians declaring that they do not unchurch the non-episcopal
Churches, that they recognise their ministries to have been
spiritually blessed, that their Eucharists are efficacious—but of
course not valid! Augustine, too, would have denied the validity
of non-episcopal ordinations and so of Eucharists in non-episcopal
bodies, but both he and Cyprian would have denied their efficacy
also. Recognition of the efficacy of non-episcopal Eucharists and
ministries must therefore rest upon premises or arguments
different from those of either Cyprian or Augustine, and these
grounds, despite a professed loyalty to the doctrine of the early
Church, remain obscure.

I believe that those who admit the efficacy of non-episcopal
ministries and sacraments are acting upon a right instinct, which
should be made to yield, or be connected with, explicit theological principles. They are taking a step which was too bold for
Augustine, and having done so, they should advance still further.
Augustine was worried by the vitality of Donatism and came to
believe that some Donatists, at least, must in some sense be
members of the Church. Perhaps he should have said (as would
commonly be said now) that in such cases their Baptism was
efficacious as well as valid. Should he have gone on to consider
whether a corporate body of such persons is, in its collectivity,
part of the Church—in modern language, a church? This is the
crux of the matter. The older view, both in Cyprian and Augustine, considers all schisms to be departures from the Church, and
holds that this one Church is to be recognised empirically by
apostolic succession, that is, by a particular kind of continuity

with the primitive Church of the apostles. The alternative is to say that the one Church, while remaining one fundamentally, can lose its visible unity, breaking up by schism into separated communions whose catholicity and continuity from the apostolic Church have now to be recognised by other empirical tests than the apostolic succession of ministry. Doubtless it will then be much more difficult for fallible men to say when a communion has so far lost catholicity that it cannot be recognised as within the *Una Sancta*, and the apprehension of this increased difficulty has probably played some part in inducing many to stand by the more easily used criterion. But the recognition that this or that communion has spiritual life, and that its ministry and sacraments are in fact Christ's ministry and sacraments and therefore means of grace, is the beginning of a better way. It judges a Church by what it has, not by what it lacks. Even if it is impossible to draw up a specification of catholicity and to know quite where to draw the line of exclusion, it is possible for particular communions on this positive basis to recognise each other as corporately parts of the one Church and thus to consider what is necessary for sacramental fellowship.

(2) A second class of objections rests upon a particular conception of the ministry, closely related, of course, to the first and third classes but allowing to some extent of separate treatment. It is held by many Anglicans who say that they do not unchurch the non-episcopal Churches and who recognise some efficacy in their sacraments, that, nevertheless, non-episcopal ministries are invalid and as such incapable of celebrating the true Catholic Eucharist. Ministers validly ordained priests, namely by episcopal ordination within the apostolic succession, are held to have received the full authority of Christ to act for His whole Church, and therefore they can celebrate the Catholic Eucharist in which the whole Church is united.

To my mind, this begs the question of what is the whole Church. I should say, rather, that in one sense no Eucharist celebrated to-day is fully Catholic, since its catholicity is marred by our disunion; and that in another sense many non-episcopal Eucharists are Catholic, since they are intended to be what the Lord intended and intends them to be. On the one hand, no minister now living has an authority recognised by the whole

Church to act for the whole Church; on the other hand, that ministerial authority conferred by Christ is limited to those in apostolic succession has never been proved, and, short of distinct proof from Scripture, it is an intolerable presumption that men should suppose Christ to be so bound that He cannot raise up true ministers of His sacraments in separate bodies once schism has happened. Here again one must distinguish between what is necessary for reunion and for intercommunion. It may well be that the apostolic succession ought to be preserved and that no communion which has it can unite corporately with another except on that basis. For organic unity we must certainly aim at a state in which Christ confers ministerial authority in and through His Body, the Church, by means of a human authority universally recognised to be acting for the whole Church. But since such a human authority at present exists nowhere, it does not follow that the ministers of the several communions lack adequate authority from the Lord to celebrate as fully Catholic an Eucharist as can be open to us in our divided state. They are presented to Christ by their several communions with prayer that He will accept them as His ministers and enable them so to be; and they are received from Him by their communions as His ministers. If they lack anything, it is because our disunion is preventing Christ from doing all He would do and also preventing the whole Church from acting representatively in every ordination; and this is true of all present ministries. Moreover, the element of faith is not to be eliminated even when ordination takes place within the succession. That Christ responds to the human prayer and action and confers 'orders' is always a matter of faith, not sight.

In relation to intercommunion, then, I believe that where a corporate body of baptised Christians (a phrase to which I must return) has chosen someone to be a minister of the Word and sacraments and has, in virtue of its corporate priesthood and by means of the acknowledged ministerial authority of that body, presented him to Christ with prayer that he may be accepted as Christ's minister to it, such a man is not by defect of ordination barred from celebrating the Catholic Eucharist within the Church, in so far as any Eucharist in a divided Church can be Catholic. There may yet be reasons why he should not minister in my Church, but I need not fear to communicate in his Church *solely* on the ground that a Communion Service of which he is the celebrant is therefore not the Catholic Eucharist. The sacramental worship of such a body of Christians is united with the worship of the saints in heaven—and may I not join in it? If I am to be debarred, it must be as a matter of discipline or as a penalty imposed for the sin of disunion, not as a sheer impossibility, a necessary consequence of a theory of ordination.

But, some will say, in a number of communions the minister is not presented to Christ to be made a priest, and only a priest can celebrate the Catholic Eucharist. This objection turns fundamentally upon a particular conception of the Eucharist rather than of ordination, and will be considered below. For the moment it is enough to say that the New Testament nowhere lays down that a minister need be, or was, explicitly ordained *hiereus*, and that we have no evidence of this requirement in the primitive Church. It cannot be imposed as necessary upon the whole Church.

(3) The third type of objection to intercommunion lies in the varying conceptions of the Eucharist itself which are to be found in the different Churches. The objection generally takes the form of saying that in some communions the Eucharist is not thought of as an act of sacrificial worship, so that those for whom it bears above all this character cannot share in a service of Holy Communion which means something else to most of those taking part; the physical fellowship would give a false impression of a non-existent spiritual unity.

This is a serious difficulty. It may well be that we are not ready for reunion until there is a closer approximation in eucharistic doctrine, until Rome has renounced her errors and until Protestants have learned to understand the Eucharistic Sacrifice. To my mind there is no need to despair here. Some Roman theologians and not a few Anglo-Catholics have restated the doctrine in a form which appears much more compatible with the Protestant and Evangelical apprehension of Christianity, while many Protestants are less frightened of the name and notion of the Eucharistic Sacrifice. Meanwhile, I should myself have to overcome at least as much prejudice against communicating at a Roman Mass as any Anglo-Catholic would against communicating in a Calvinist church. But during this 'meanwhile' I believe that the objections of both should be overcome, and for the following reasons:

(*a*) My willingness to communicate together with other Christians must not depend on an absolutely common interpretation of the rite. Probably no one demands this.

(*b*) Nor must I be deterred because the rite used does not express the fullness of what I believe to be the meaning of the Eucharist. (A plain contradiction of the truth would be a deterrent.)

For (*c*) I must rest upon the more positive principle that this or that Church sincerely intends to celebrate that Sacrament of Holy Communion which the Lord gave to His Church and of which He is the present minister. I may not agree at all points with those with whom I am joining; but our basic intention is the same, much of what we do and think is the same, and the Lord Himself understands that we are all present to do what He wills to be done and to take what He wills to give. Complete mutual understanding would be admirable, but is not a pre-requisite. Moreover, the lack of complete agreement is not due to schism *simpliciter*. It exists within single communions, notably but not only in the Church of England.

(*d*) Intercommunion should be a positive help towards this mutual understanding. That is not likely to be achieved by reading doctrinal treatises on the Eucharist; we shall learn from each other by sharing what each has and does. Those who set great store by sacramental worship or by any particular aspect of the Eucharist should have faith that those who come to know it as guests will want to find it in their own communions.

(4) Another objection which demands sympathetic consideration concerns confirmation. Can a Church which makes episcopal confirmation the condition of communicant status for its own members admit the unconfirmed to its Eucharists? This difficulty needs subdivision.

(*a*) In so far as it means that there can be no indiscriminate admission to Communion, it can be met easily. Intercommunion does not imply a merely open Communion without any fencing of the Table; it is proposed only that those who have communicant status in their own denominations should be admitted to Communion in another.

But (b) it is urged that confirmation (and most who urge this would mean episcopal confirmation) is an essential part of Christian initiation and so a necessary condition of communicant status. It is sometimes added that, since the whole theology of Christian initiation is now under discussion in several denominations, it would be wrong for a Church which has the rule of episcopal confirmation to prejudice the issue by admitting unconfirmed persons to its Communions. But it is not unreasonable to look at the latter point quite the other way round. The existence of so much confusion, even within a single denomination, shows that there is no absolutely certain doctrine on which we must insist. Present reconsideration, which may take a very long time, ought not to be a barrier to intercommunion if that is on other grounds justifiable. No Church would be abandoning its own discipline for its own members, nor relinquishing its belief as to what form Christian initiation should take in a reunited Church. An anomaly, awkward but not sinful, would be accepted in the interim, as a means to fuller agreement. At present the Church of England would not be justified, by its own formulae and history, in insisting upon episcopal confirmation, or any particular kind of admission to communicant status, as an absolute necessity on dogmatic grounds; and discipline may be varied, or exceptions permitted, by the authority which imposes the discipline.

The position which I have sketched is fundamentally simple. It is that at least the most elementary form of intercommunion, freedom to communicate at each other's Eucharists, is both demanded and justified by the measure of common Christianity which already exists between many of the historic Churches, and that the objections commonly urged against it are inadequate to frustrate its inherent propriety. But my position would be naïve rather than simple if no more were said about this common Christianity and these historic Churches or corporate bodies of Christians. It was stated above that the Cyprianic teaching, though untenable *in toto*, contained elements of value. Its strength was the integration of Church, Ministry and Sacraments, while the weakness of Augustine and theories dependent upon him is that they produce the monstrous birth of valid orders and sacraments outside the Church, thus tearing the doctrine of the ministry away from the doctrine of the Church. Cyprian's strong point should be maintained. It is improper to seek grounds for the recognition of ministries and sacraments outside the Church and then to speculate about their validity or efficacy. Neither Cyprian nor Augustine would face the fact that the visible Church *is* divided; we who try to face it and its implications, and are prepared to entertain the possibility that several existing sects are within the Church, must consider the grounds of such a recognition. Granted that the primitive Church was the Church founded by the Lord through the apostles, what kind and degree of continuity with it is requisite in order that a Christian communion to-day may be recognised as part of the Church of Christ? And if it is so recognised, what follows about its ministry and sacraments?

Apostolic succession of ministry is one of several instruments of continuity, among the others being continuity of credal doctrines, the use of Scripture, the preaching of the Word, the practice of the Gospel Sacraments, evangelism and Christian morality. Probably no Church is perfectly 'apostolic', even in theory. It may well be that a reunited Church ought to preserve the historic continuity of apostolic succession; but, given existing divisions, I find it impossible to conclude that bodies which manifest their essential continuity in such other respects as I have mentioned cannot be treated as Churches within the Church, and are debarred only by lack of apostolic succession (in the Catholic sense) from having a true ministry of the Word and sacraments. Christ is not so bound to a single method of ordination. I hold, therefore, that, while no precise blueprint of catholicity can be laid down, no percentage of approximation determined, as prerequisites of intercommunion, it is possible and desirable for existing communions to satisfy themselves empirically that this or that other communion has sufficient continuity and catholicity, sufficient Christian vitality, sufficient power of nurturing the people of God, to be recognised as a constituent part of the visible Church of Christ. If we are to err here, let us err on the side of faith, hope and charity.

Among the conditions of such catholicity, I should myself require an ordered ministry of men 'chosen and called to this work (as Article XXIII says) by men who have publick authority given unto them in the Congregation, to call and send Ministers into the Lord's vineyard', and the acceptance of Baptism and Holy Communion, with the intention to use them as the Lord intends. I could not doubt the possibility that Christ might accept and enable men so ordained as ministers in His Church nor, when such a Church had manifested its vitality over a reasonable period of time, could I doubt that He had in fact raised up a true ministry of His Word and sacraments for that communion. For intercommunion, in the elementary sense so far considered, this would satisfy me.

Interchange of ministries raises a further problem, for there is no doubt that, as things are, an Anglican minister has not been authorised by the Methodist Church to minister in it, and vice versa. Schism within the Church has brought about a situation in which no minister, even one episcopally ordained within the apostolic succession, is recognised as a minister de facto of the whole Church. The problem is to know whether a minister in one communion has in fact been ordained as a minister of the whole Church and needs only open recognition by the several other communions, or whether the fact that the human ordaining agent of a part is not recognised to be acting on behalf of the whole Church causes a defect in orders, schism preventing Christ Himself from conferring the complete authority which He would give if the ordaining agent were so acting. The defect, if any, would apply to all orders; it would not be lack of jurisdiction simply, but of an authority which is part and parcel of the notion of orders.

I have to confess to hesitation between the two views. I incline to the opinion that the Lord of the Church accepts the part as representative of the whole (taking advantage, one might say, of the fundamental unity of the Church). When I look, for example, at the Presbyterian Church of Scotland or the Church of Rome, as well as the Church of England, I am convinced that each, despite its defects, is a constituent part of the Church of Christ. On that basis I am prepared to act on the belief that Christ has overcome the anomalous state of schism and has made, in and through these parts, ministers of the whole Church, whom the several parts need only recognise by some appropriate solemn act, not ordination, when interchange of ministries is agreed upon. That is, the decision as to ministries is taken as a consequence of a decision as to churchhood, not vice versa.

Those who believe that orders can only be conferred by apostolic bishops can presumably make no concession. But if those who admit that Christ makes, ordains, ministers for the several communions, urge nevertheless that we cannot be sure that they are ordained as ministers of the whole Church, and if this hesitation blocks the movement towards fuller intercommunion, then more consideration must be given to the next most promising way, some such procedure as is suggested in the proposals for reunion in Ceylon, whether or not this is to be called supplemental ordination. In this the Churches, confessing that disunion leaves us baffled about possible defects in our orders, ask the Holy Spirit to grant 'such character, grace, gifts and authority as they may now need'. Such a procedure, though more appropriate to a final act of unification (its repetition would raise new problems) might perhaps be permissible as a prelude to intercommunion and exchange of ministries.

What I have tried to state is of course only a personal opinion; it is not one which the Church of England has ever officially endorsed, and I am well aware that very many, especially of the clergy of to-day, would repudiate it. Still, it is based upon much that the Church of England has admitted piecemeal, officially or by its traditional practice.

(a) By its unquestioned recognition of Rome and Orthodoxy as Churches, or parts or embodiments of the Church, as well as itself, it has rejected both the Cyprianic and Augustinian doctrines of unity and schism. Recent publications (e.g. by Bishop Bell and Professor Sykes) have reminded us that the Church of England treated the main Lutheran and Calvinist communions of the Continent during the sixteenth and seventeenth centuries as Churches; and in modern times it has become common to disclaim any intention to 'unchurch the Free Churches' at home.

(b) That intercommunion may precede corporate unity and that it does not demand complete agreement in doctrine or worship, but the essentials of the Christian faith, is made explicit by our terms of intercommunion with the Old Catholics.

(c) Participation of Anglicans in Protestant Eucharists abroad was common in the past (cf. Bell, Sykes). The Church of England has never declared it to be impossible in principle. It is the movement against it which is, in its present strength, a comparative innovation.

(*d*) Free Church ministries have been acknowledged as 'spiritually real' (Lambeth, 1920). A weighty, though not official statement, was that of the Anglican representatives holding discussions with the Free Churches in 1923. 'It seems to us to be in accordance with the Lambeth Appeal to say, as we are prepared to say, that the ministries which we have in view in this memorandum, ministries which imply a sincere intention to preach Christ's Word and administer the Sacraments as Christ has ordained, and to which authority so to do has been solemnly given by the Church concerned, are real ministries of Christ's Word and Sacraments in the Universal Church.'

(*e*) The Report of the Committee on Unity, Lambeth, 1930, discussing South India (p. 127), says: 'We assent to the provision that the acceptance of Confirmation should not be insisted on as a pre-requisite of union.'

With such support, I do not feel disloyal as an Anglican in appealing for faith and courage to accept intercommunion between those communions who, whatever they think of each other's defects, cannot help recognising each other as constituent parts of the Church of Christ. Such intercommunion need imply no sitting loose to one's own convictions and traditions. Further, it must not imply a determination, or even willingness, to remain in schism. It must be a means of growing together, a step towards fuller unity. The more we stress the objective character and efficacy of the Sacrament of Holy Communion, the more faith we should have that it will promote 'the building up of the body of Christ, till we all attain unto the unity of the faith and of the knowledge of the Son of God, unto a full-grown man, unto the measure of the stature of the fullness of Christ'.

XII

A ROOT OF DIFFERENCE
AND OF UNITY

*

A. G. Hebert, S.S.M.
Church of England

(Great Britain)

I

The starting-point of the train of thought which led to the writing
of this essay was a certain bewilderment at the course which
discussions about intercommunion regularly take. There are the
two opposed sides; and those who disagree about any general
adoption of a policy of intercommunion are the same people
who disagree about the question of the ministry, about apostolic
succession and valid orders. In both cases we seem to be at an
impasse. Our Commission, in its Report, has been unable to
recommend an agreed policy about intercommunion; and we are
scarcely beginning to understand one another, as yet, about the
problem of the ministry.

The perplexing thing is that this difference can exist side by side
with a deep and cordial agreement about the fundamentals of the
Christian faith, particularly in the sphere of biblical theology. On
this biblical ground, those who bear the labels of Catholic and
Protestant can meet together in a study which involves the most
intimate issues of faith and devotion, and not find themselves
driven apart at every point by disagreements of principle, such as
would arise if either of them were to engage in such study with
'Liberals' of an older generation: they find that they are thinking
substantially the same thoughts, and standing on common ground.
Yet these same people disagree hopelessly about 'valid orders'.
Why is this? There must be a reason.

In this essay I want to try to find the reason. I am not going to raise, except incidentally, the problem of the ministry; I do not think that it, taken by itself, is the real root of our differences about intercommunion. I believe that the root of the difference lies in our different ways of worship. On the theological side this involves the Eucharistic Sacrifice, or Sacrifice of the Mass, about which fierce controversies have been waged in the past. But the difference does not lie primarily in a doctrine discussed and formulated by theologians; it concerns the ordinary Christian. It lies in the diversity of our liturgical and devotional practice, as shown in the different ways in which Protestants and Catholics respectively are accustomed to worship God on Sunday morning.

In Protestant Christendom, generally speaking, the service finds its climax in the preaching of the Word; praise is given to God, prayer is made, the Scriptures are read, and then through the ministry of the preacher the word read becomes the living Word of God, with power to reach the heart, there to be received with humble faith. Here is seen God's gift of salvation to man. In the Sacrament the same gift of salvation is mediated under another form. In both cases it is a movement from God to man, and man's part is essentially receptive. There is indeed a Godward movement on man's part; but it is of the Spirit, and is in danger of being killed when the attempt is made to formalise it in fixed liturgical rites; it must largely therefore be left to the individual, though it does find spontaneous expression in hymns of praise.

On the Catholic side there is the conception of the assembly of the Church to join in the liturgy; that is, essentially, that the members of Christ may worship God and pray to Him through Christ who is the Head of the Body. He, the Son of God, came down from heaven to redeem us from servitude to sin into the liberty of the City of God; and Christian worship can be seen as typified in Christ ascending into heaven and bearing His people with him, so that the congregation on earth is joining in the prayer which Christ prays. The climax of the service comes in the offering of Christ's own Sacrifice, and the union of His people with Him in Communion, to receive His gift of life and thereby be offered up in Him as a living sacrifice. Here the manward movement is present, for as Christ came down from heaven for our salvation, so in the service there is the gift of His salvation to us. But this is completed in the Godward movement of liturgical prayer, praise and adoration, 'through Jesus Christ our Lord'.

I have been setting out a contrast between the regular and habitual ways of worship of Protestants and Catholics respectively; and I do not see how the fact of the contrast can be denied, whatever qualifications may be needed in detail. It was for this reason that I called this essay 'A Root of Difference'. But then I came to see that I must add the words 'and of Unity'. How is this?

There is no doubt about the 'difference' with regard to the eucharistic sacrifice; for this has been one of the chief storm-centres of controversy. The whole conception of 'the Sacrifice of the Mass' has been violently repudiated from the Protestant side, because it has seemed to involve the notion that we can propitiate God by a sacrifice that we make, and that Christ has, as it were, put Himself into our hands, so that we, by offering the Eucharist, can apply the benefits of His Sacrifice to whatever intention we will. It must be admitted that there has been much in Catholic teaching and practice to justify the protest; and it would be idle to pretend that the ground of offence has ceased.

And yet, now that the dust of the sixteenth-century controversies has cleared away, and a more accurate biblical study has brought a better understanding of the meaning of sacrifice, a doctrine of the eucharistic sacrifice has arisen which is really not a new doctrine, but a return to that which the ancient liturgies of the Church imply, and which appears to be fully 'evangelical', and indeed, as I shall claim later in this essay, is a re-expression in liturgical terms of the truth of Justification by Faith. This doctrine is associated in this country with the name of the late Bishop Hicks,[1] and is represented among Roman Catholic theologians by the work of Masure.[2]

If now it be really true that at this central point of difficulty the difference between Catholics and Protestants has in principle been overcome, and if they can now begin to understand and to trust one another here, as they do already in the field of biblical interpretation, then there is hope that in time, and perhaps quite soon, they will begin to reach a true mutual understanding about the

---

[1] F. C. N. Hicks, *The Fullness of Sacrifice* (Macmillan, 1930). A summary of the argument was made for the Edinburgh Conference of 1937, and is reprinted in the volume issued by the Commission on Ways of Worship.

[2] E. Masure, *Le Sacrifice du Chef* (Beauchesne, Paris, 1932). E. T., *The Christian Sacrifice* (Burns, Oates and Washbourne, 1943).

meaning of priesthood, and valid orders, and apostolic succession. When that has happened, difficulties about intercommunion will disappear and unity will be in sight.

II

We must start with a study of the biblical idea of Sacrifice and of its fulfilment in Christ. I am compelled to state this in the briefest possible way, without giving references; for it is a choice between giving many hundred references, or none at all.

The sacrificial ordinances of the Old Covenant dumbly testified that somehow, through the offering to God of a costly victim, and a victim which must be without blemish, and through death and the offering of blood there was to be a way for sin-stained man back to peace with God at last. The offerer brought his victim (the verb means 'to cause to draw near'), laid his hands upon it, and killed it. The priest then took over the action; he sprinkled, or threw, or poured out the blood, and then burnt all or part of the flesh, and then, in some sacrifices all partook of the sacrificial feast, in some others the priest alone ate of the flesh. Here the order of the ritual reveals a point of great importance, the neglect of which has vitiated the popular notion of sacrifice, has driven theologians into serious error, and has led to false notions of the Christian Atonement: namely, that in the ritual the emphasis lies not on the immolation of the victim, but on the subsequent manipulation of the blood, the burning, the eating. The idea that the death of the victim was the centre of sacrifice is simply false. The animal was killed not in order that its life might be destroyed (for 'the blood is the life'), but that the life offered in death might become available for the holy purposes of the sacrifice.

But the interpretation of Christ's death as sacrificial would be merely illustrative, and we should be able only to say that His death was *like* a sacrifice, and not that it *was* a sacrifice, if it were not for the teaching of the prophets about sacrifice, and their vigorous denunciations of the sacrificial system as they saw it. Briefly, the points are these:

(*a*) They denounce the offering of sacrifice to the Ba'alim (Elijah, Hosea) and the assimilation of the worship of Yahweh to the Canaanite nature-religions, and similarly the flood of super-stitions which came in when Judah was threatened by the militaristic empires. This was apostasy from Yahweh the God of Israel.

(b) They denounce the idea that the favour of the gods, or of Yahweh Himself, can be bought by offering the appropriate sacrifices, without repentance and personal effort to obey His will. His relation to man is personal; He asks of man his loyalty, obedience and love.

(c) They see that at best the offering of a victim other than man himself is inadequate; God does not need to be provided with food. But a sacrificial victim had to be without blemish, and how could sin-stained man make an offering acceptable to God. The true sacrifice, the reality which the sin-offering symbolised, would be 'a broken and a contrite heart'; but had man got that to offer?

(d) In one place only, Isaiah 53, we have the picture of the righteous Servant of Yahweh, suffering shame, unjust accusation, and finally martyrdom, and in all this bearing the sins of the people; and then it is said that all this is the good pleasure of Yahweh, and that He will make the Servant's soul a sacrifice for sin. The best exegetes hold that the poet was thinking of One who was yet to come; One whose unblemished life would be an accepted sacrifice.

It seems to be right to speak of this conception of sacrifice as wholly up to the New Testament level, and as one that our Lord could accept and use as it stood. In the poem of the Servant it was an unrealised hope. In Jesus Christ it was actualised in the flesh, in history. From His prophecies of His passion it can be inferred that He identified Himself with the Servant; in Luke 22. 37 He affirms it explicitly.

In the eucharistic institution He interpreted His death as sacri-ficial; this is clear from the words 'body', 'blood', 'poured out', 'covenant', *anamnesis*. There and elsewhere in the New Testament the fulfilment of the various types of sacrifice is shown. He is the sin-offering, Matt. 26. 28, Rom. 3. 25, Heb. 9. 14, and often; at once the Victim without blemish, being sinless, Heb. 9. 14, etc., in a holy sacrificial death, and the sin-bearer, dying the unholy death of the criminal, Gal. 3. 13, II Cor. 5. 21. He is the burnt offering, 'for an odour of a sweet smell', Eph. 5. 2, in virtue of that whole obedience to God's will for which the prophets looked, Heb. 10. 5-10. He is the peace-offering, bringing the reconciliation with God symbolised in the sacrificial feast, the Sacrifice of the New Covenant foretold by Jeremiah, the Paschal Lamb: I Cor. 5. 7. Furthermore, He is not only the Victim but also the Priest, Heb. 8. 1. Thus in Him is fulfilled not only the typology of the sacrificial ritual, but also the spiritual and moral demand which the prophets made; hence, looking at the whole development of the biblical theology of sacrifice, it is not only that His death is comparable to a sacrifice, but that it is the true and real fulfilment of sacrifice. This is *The Sacrifice*, of which the Old Testament ritual was a type and a shadow.

But we cannot stop here; we have also to think of the worshippers, those for whom the Sacrifice is offered. In the Old Testament they were mainly onlookers at a rite performed on their behalf; they offered animal victims, which represented themselves but were not themselves. The rite was a liturgical action, symbolising an offering of their whole lives which they, because of their sins, were unable fully to make. But in the New Testament the worshippers are themselves offered in sacrifice; and the offering is made not only in liturgy but also in their lives. They are offered up in union with Christ as a reasonable holy and living sacrifice, Rom. 12. 1, and Eph. 5. 1-2. Their Christian life itself consists in union with Christ, buried with Him by Baptism into death and sharing in His risen life. So St. Paul pictures himself as an officiating priest, manipulating the burnt-offering which consists of the souls of his Gentile Christians, Rom. 15. 16; at a time when he expects martyrdom he sees his own life as poured out in Sacrifice, Phil. 2. 17; and he can even speak of his sufferings as completing that which is still to be made up of the sufferings of Christ, Col. 1. 24. So thoroughly is the life of the Church seen to be a life of sacrificial oblation that even the gifts of the Philippians to St. Paul (Phil. 4. 18) are called a burnt-offering, and similarly the praises and charitable works of the Hebrews (Heb. 13.15-16).

Thus in Christ and in His Church the whole meaning of Sacrifice is fulfilled; all the lines are drawn together.

III

'Having therefore, brethren, freedom of access to enter into the Holy Place by the Sacrifice of Jesus, by the new and living way which He has consecrated for us, through the Veil, that is to say, the way of His flesh, and having a great Priest set over the household of God, let us draw near' (Heb. 10. 19-22, free translation).

We must try to grasp what it is that the author is saying to his readers. He is at the conclusion of his great argument, that the Levitical sacrifices were types and shadows, and that the Reality has appeared in the person of Jesus, the Highpriest and the Victim of the Sacrifice which was enacted in time on Calvary, but which now is offered by Him at the heavenly altar. What are we to think that he is saying in these words? Surely it is plain that he is calling on them to join in the Christian liturgy. He calls on them to 'draw near'; it is the old ritual word; they are to join in sacrificial worship with the ascended Christ. Not to immolate Christ over again, for any such notion would seem blasphemous to him (cf. 9. 26), nor to offer some sacrifice additional to His Sacrifice, for that would be to bring back the Levitical multiplication of sacrifices (cf. 7. 23 and 10. 11); but to join as participants in the One Sacrifice which the Lord makes at the heavenly altar. They are on earth; therefore he exhorts them repeatedly to lift up their hearts to Christ, by faith (see e.g. 3. 1, ch. 11; 12. 18-24), to have communion with Him where He is. And were not those Christians accustomed to celebrate the Eucharist every Lord's day?

Let us then start from this point in our consideration of the eucharistic sacrifice in the Church. *First*, since the Lord's own Sacrifice is an action, the Christians who in the Eucharist 'proclaim the Lord's death till He come' (I Cor. 11. 26), will naturally do so by an action. That action is comparable as an action to Jewish and to pagan sacrifices (I Cor. 10. 18-22), and in it the one bread is the efficacious sign whereby their unity in one body is both symbolised and effected (10. 17).

Secondly, the Sacrifice of Christ, in which every Eucharist is a participation, is in itself one, however much it is multiple as regards us men: multiple in being celebrated in very many different places all over the world, and multiple as regards time, because our life is divided into days and weeks and years, and because in the history of the Church one generation succeeds another, and the Christian Eucharist is celebrated by generation after generation 'till He come'. But there is no multiplicity in the Sacrifice itself; it is one, and is therefore the meeting-point of the whole universal Church, those whom we call 'living' on earth, and the faithful departed, and the Saints in heaven. Hence the liturgies think of the presence of the whole Family of Christ around the altar at the Eucharist, and the presence of the Saints with us, or rather our presence with them; for they are more really there than we.

As then in the Eucharist we join in one common worship and prayer with God's whole Family, so in the ordinary prayers of the Church (according to the Catholic conception) we are joining in the common prayer of the whole Body, and with the prayer which Christ Himself makes, of which the pattern is given us in John 17. It is not that the church service is an assembly of people met to make their individual devotions together; it is rather that the individuals come to join in praise, meditation, and supplication, with the whole Body.

Thirdly, let us look at the essential shape of the Liturgy of the Sacrament, after the first part of the service, the Liturgy of the Word, is finished. There is the Offertory, the Consecration, and the Communion (also the Fraction, properly the dividing of the Bread for the Communion, but sometimes interpreted symbolically, of the breaking of the Lord's body, and put in connection with the Consecration); these correspond to the New Testament verbs, He took bread, blessed (or, gave thanks), brake, and gave it to them.

The *Offertory* was in the early Church the action of the people. At Rome they continued for many centuries to bring their bread and wine to church; from this was taken what was needed for the Sacrament. Bread and wine, food and drink, sustain life; to the offerers the bringing of these gifts week by week must have been the symbol of the laying of their whole lives on God's altar, placing them in God's hands. An offertory prayer, in Latin so terse that it defies translation, reads thus: *Propitius Domine quaesumus haec dona sanctifica: et hostiae spiritualis oblatione suscepta, nosmet ipsos tibi perfice munus aeternum: per Dominum. . . .* (Secret for Whit-Monday, Roman Missal.)

Then the *Consecration*. In the eucharistic prayer they saw their own bread and wine used by the celebrant-bishop for the act which the Lord had commanded, to become His body and blood in the re-enactment of His death, resurrection and ascension. Now they were in the heavenly places: *jube haec perferri per manus sancti Angeli tui in conspectu divinae majestatis tuae: ut quotquot ex hac altaris participatione sacrosanctum Filii tui corpus et sanguinem sumpserimus, omni benedictione coelesti et gratia repleamur* (Roman canon). So the imagery of 'Hebrews' reappears. And the Sacrifice of Christ includes in itself the offering to God of all the created life which He has redeemed: 'by whom and with whom in the unity of the Holy Ghost all honour and glory be unto thee, O Father almighty, world without end. Amen.'

In the *Communion* they received back their own bread and wine, not as they had offered it, but as transformed by Him who had taken on Him their nature to redeem it; they received back the substance of their own lives, as transformed by Him who had incorporated them into His body, that they might dwell in Him and He in them. In St. Augustine's words, it was the mystery of themselves that they received, their life as hid with Christ in God. At the end of the Mass, the words *Ite, missa est* are perhaps rightly understood as meaning 'The Church is dismissed', from serving God in His sanctuary to serve Him in His world.

Such was the eucharistic sacrifice, and such it is. It was then, and ought to be to-day, in each place the act of the whole local church met together to present its corporate life to God, and unite it with the one Sacrifice of the Lamb of God; to offer, and be offered, in union with the whole mystical Body of Christ.

IV

The truths of the Christian Faith ought to be labelled as 'highly dangerous', in so far as the Old Adam in us is always liable to misunderstand them and pervert them; and church history, in the past and the present, provides countless instances of this. The right understanding of them demands a humble and sincere heart, ready to be led by the Holy Spirit; and the Church militant on earth is always imperfect, and a ceaseless conflict goes on within it between the Spirit of Truth and the spirits of error. The Old Testament speaks of the Sanctuary as 'dwelling with the children of Israel in the midst of their uncleannesses' (Lev. 16. 16); and the

Christian Church has the Gospel of God, the Scriptures, Creeds, Sacraments, Ministry, and the various monuments of her tradition, to witness against the uncleannesses of men: manifold errors, corruptions, worldliness, and schisms.

All this is true of the pattern of Christian worship of which we have been speaking. It contains a multitude of things liable to misunderstanding and perversion; and this has happened on a disastrous scale, as indeed our present state of confusion testifies. When schisms occur, they come as the result of corruptions and perversions; and at the end of the Middle Ages these existed in abundance.

The supreme disaster in the history of the liturgy was the maiming of the great Sunday Eucharist by the cessation of the Communion of the people. This happened gradually, and it is hard to trace its history; but by the later Middle Ages on nearly all Sundays the celebrant was left to communicate alone. The old Offertory, made by the people, had disappeared long before. Like the Jews under the Old Covenant the people became onlookers at a rite performed by the clergy in the sanctuary.

The Elevation of the Host now became the centre of the rite, and the theology of the Eucharist concentrated not on the Sacrifice but on the Real Presence and Transubstantiation. In St. Thomas' *Summa* there are some twenty *Quaestiones* on the Real Presence, and only one on the Sacrifice.

Difficulties were found, then and later, in the theological explanation; they were rendered insoluble by the mistake of treating the immolation as the central point in sacrifice. Was the Mass only a symbol or acted parable of the death on Calvary? It was assuredly more than this; but it was hard to say how it could be so, unless Christ were somehow 'mystically' re-immolated through the separate consecration of the bread and the wine, or unless each Eucharist were somehow a fresh sacrifice, perhaps through the substance of the bread and wine being annihilated in being transubstantiated, and so 'immolated'. It could even be said that the Sacrifice of Calvary was offered for original sin, and those of the masses for actual sins, though it seems that this was never the official teaching.

As regards practice, there was the monstrous growth of chantry masses, and the payments for them; prayers for the departed dropped to what was in fact a pagan level, and so did the cult of the saints, as it was bound to do when it was divorced from its proper setting in the common worship of the liturgy. The Mass came to be seen not as the common act of the worshipping Church, but primarily the act of the individual priest saying 'his' mass.

It is not surprising that when the Reformers came on the scene, burning to restore to the people the Gospel of God, they acted very drastically, bringing to an end all the obvious abuses. What positive contribution did they make to the reform of the liturgy? They insisted, first, that the Communion of the People was an integral part of the eucharistic action; and second, that the celebration of the Eucharist was the act of the assembled Church, and not the act, primarily, of the individual priest. Everywhere in Protestantism these two positive points have been maintained; the Eucharist is always a Communion Service, and when it is celebrated the whole congregation assembles for it.

But these points were gained at the cost of the idea of the eucharistic sacrifice. There could indeed be a sense—as, I am told, among the early Congregationalists—that the Church, in celebrating the Eucharist, was engaged in a sacrificial action. There was 'the offering of all possible praise to God' for the one Sacrifice of Christ; there was the self-oblation of the people to God's service. Further, Luther had noted the teaching of the Epistle to the Hebrews about the ministry of Christ at the heavenly altar, and had some valuable things to say about it; but he could not fit on to it any positive conception of a sacrificial action in the Eucharist, and he turned rather to the unfruitful interpretation of the Sacrament as our Lord's testamentary bequest. As the ancient Offertory had long since disappeared, it seems that he made the mistake of taking the phrases in the Missal which had in fact referred to the people's offerings of bread and wine, as referring to the masses offered by individual priests. Of the Mass regarded as a sacrifice, he wrote: 'I say that nothing is left.'

Indeed the abuses connected with the eucharistic sacrifice seemed to be irreformable. The difficulty was increased on the theological side by the false identification of Sacrifice with Immolation, which had made it appear that each Mass was a separate sacrifice. Hence it was proclaimed, and in some quarters it is still believed, that the Sacrifice of Christ consisted solely in His death on the cross, so that when He died the whole ordinance of sacrifice was at an end; the Old Testament law of sacrifice was now 'fulfilled', and no further sacrificial action was possible. The Church would only look back to Calvary, and make a thankful commemoration of His death.

Consequently in Protestantism the interpretation of the meaning of the act of Holy Communion has centred in the coming of Christ to the faithful soul in the holy Sacrament, to bring forgiveness of sins—this phrase being understood, especially among Lutherans, in the largest sense, as embracing the whole work of grace and as including the gift of salvation and deliverance, joy and peace. Here the soul meets with her heavenly Bridegroom, Shepherd, Husband, Friend; here the soul receives all the benefits of His passion, and is strengthened for His service with the heavenly Food. Here is indeed one of the classical themes of Christian devotion; the 'Jesus-worship' of this period has brought a permanent addition to the treasures of Christendom. But in its individualism it is narrower than the conception enshrined in the ancient liturgies of the eucharistic thanksgiving and prayer of the whole Body of Christ, the whole fellowship of the redeemed.

The intention of Luther and of the Anglican reformers, and the express desire of Calvin, that the Communion Service should form the climax of each Sunday morning's worship, remained unfulfilled. In the Middle Ages the people had been accustomed to communicate rarely, for the most part once only in the year; and they could not be brought back to frequent Communion by the enactment that if communicants did not present themselves there should be no Eucharist. Thus it came about that throughout Protestant Christendom the regular type of Sunday service has been the non-sacramental service, the Liturgy of the Word.

v

In the last hundred years there has been a slow coming-together of Christendom to recover in various ways the elements of the Tradition which had been lost, and the various traditions have been learning from one another. Of this process the Anglo-Catholic movement in the Church of England has possibly been the most striking instance. In our day the tempo of the process has been accelerated. Liturgical movements have arisen in many parts of Christendom, most notably in the Roman Catholic Church on the continent of Europe, where the renewed study of the liturgy and a sustained effort to bring back the laity to an active participation in it has led to a new and fruitful study of the Scriptures; for the liturgical texts are predominantly Scriptural.

Thus it has come about that on the Catholic side there has been a reassertion and a practical application of the two positive principles upheld by the Reformers, that the Communion of the People is an integral part of the eucharistic action, and that the Eucharist is properly the act of the assembled Christian community; this is seen alike in the French Catholic *messe de communauté*, and in the Anglican Parish Communion. On the theological side, a view of the eucharistic sacrifice, such as has been sketched out in this essay, has gained wide acceptance. It is encouraging to find that the comments of some Protestant friends, both Lutheran and Reformed, have been that such a view represents very much what they themselves intend when they celebrate Holy Communion.

For indeed there is no incongruity, but an essential unity, between the Pauline thesis of Justification by Faith and the idea of the eucharistic sacrifice. I would put it thus. We are justified, brought into the right relation with God, 'by the Grace of God through the redemption that is in Christ Jesus' (Rom. 3. 24), or 'by the blood (the sacrifice) of Christ' (Rom. 5. 9), apprehended by faith. We are not justified in virtue of any meritorious good works of our own, whether moral or religious; nor yet in virtue of faith regarded as *our* faith, as if our religious experience constituted a species of merit on our part and a claim on God's acceptance. For God only is righteous, and His righteousness has been manifested in Jesus Christ (Rom. 3. 21), 'whom God set forth to be a propitiation' (vs. 25). God has saved us; we are not able to save ourselves. Here is the Christian doctrine of salvation; and it is divinely simple. Yet that which is in itself simple is very easily misunderstood and perverted by us, for we are not simple.

The eucharistic sacrifice is in itself simple, with this same sort of simplicity. In concrete language it comes to this: There is someone for whom I ought to pray, and I pray for him. But on what grounds can I expect that God will receive my prayer? In fact, my prayer is weak, halting, and uncertain; indeed, I scarcely know what to ask. But if I prayed better than I do, could I expect that God would receive my prayer on the ground of its devoutness, earnestness and sincerity? But no; I take it to the altar, and offer it at the Eucharist. There I hold up before God Christ's own Sacrifice, Christ's love for that person, Christ's death for his salvation. Then I am bringing to God, not my devout apprehension of the love which Christ has for this person, but that love itself as it objectively exists in the prayer which Christ makes, and as it objectively exists in the Sacrament which He has given us. Does not the objectivity of the Sacrament correspond precisely to the objectivity of His Death and Resurrection, in excluding all claim to personal merit on my part?

But the paradox of the matter is that the upholding at this point of the principle of Justification by Faith, which the Reformers asserted, appears to be bound up with the 'offering' of Christ in the Eucharist, which they vigorously rejected. We saw in our account of the Eucharist of the early Church that there was there a double act of offering: the gifts of bread and wine made by the people, and the presenting before God, or pleading, or offering, of the one Sacrifice of Christ. It is sometimes said, then, that since the Sacrifice of Christ is His own Sacrifice, and He alone offers it, our offering in the Eucharist can consist only in our offering of ourselves to be a 'reasonable, holy and living sacrifice' in virtue of our union with Him in Communion, together with the offering of our praises and thanksgivings for His saving work.

Such a view, however, appears just to miss the essential point. The offering of ourselves is proper to the Offertory; and what can we men bring to God except our insufficiency and our need? We cannot save ourselves; we can be justified only by the Grace of God, through the redemption that is in Christ Jesus; we can be saved only by the Sacrifice of Christ, and the re-creation of our human nature thereby. There is indeed an actual danger in laying stress on the Offertory action, when this emphasis is not balanced by an equal stress on the action of the Consecration and the Communion.[3]

The eucharistic sacrifice is indeed Christ's own Sacrifice, and He is the true Celebrant; the meaning of the Eucharist is that we participate in His sacrifice. Yet there is an action that we do. If we had not assembled, this very morning on which I write, to celebrate the Eucharist, there would have been no Eucharist. We

[3] As in one eucharistic manual which I have seen, drawn up for parochial use.

did assemble, to make our Offertory, to consecrate the Eucharist, and to receive it. The whole was an act of offering, deriving all its significance from the action which our Lord performed on the night of His passion. We took the elements which He commanded, and used His words: with them we offered His Sacrifice, as participants in His Sacrifice at the heavenly altar, and that action was the sign and means of our justification by faith in Him; and in that action we ourselves were offered up to be a living sacrifice.

The truth here is of the sort that can only be expressed by paradoxes and contradictory phrases. We perform an action; it is a sacrificial action, and the sacrifice that we offer is Christ's own Sacrifice; yet in the reality signified by the sign, it is He who here offers His own Sacrifice. The Sacrament is not a human commemoration of His passion, comparable to a passion play; for it is of the nature of a sacrament that the thing signified is present in the sign, and in the Eucharist the action that we perform is the offering of Christ's Sacrifice. For this reason it is really misleading to say that the only offering which we make in the Eucharist is the sacrifice of ourselves; this notion leads back along that false road which makes the eucharistic offering an offering of ours.

One point remains: that the eucharistic offering, being the act of the visible and organised Church, involves a conception of the Christian Ministry that is priestly as well as prophetic and pastoral. There is indeed a priesthood which is common to all the faithful; it is seen actively in operation when the people make their Offertory. But the celebrant who stands at the Lord's Table has the special privilege of acting representatively both in the Name of Christ and on behalf of the congregation. He is indeed precisely on a level with any member of the congregation in making his own personal offering of prayer and praise and self-devotion; but in his action as celebrant he is called upon to act in Christ's Name in doing that which He did at the Last Supper and commanded us to do for His *anamnesis*. The meaning of his priestly office in relation to the one Highpriesthood of Christ is precisely similar to that of the eucharistic act of offering in relation to Christ's one Sacrifice; it is exercised only 'in Christ', and derives all its meaning from His Highpriesthood. But it is and must be a priestly office, since the action is a sacrificial action; and just as in the eucharistic sacrifice we have a sacrificial action which is not a reversion to the Old Testament pattern of sacrifice, but is wholly on a New Testament level, so that we have here a distinctively Christian conception of priesthood.

Such are the terms in which I would set out the pattern of the central act of Christian worship. The problem of the priest in his inner life, and in his ministry among his people, and of the people in their sacramental worship and in the living of their daily lives, is to endeavour to overcome the inherited bad customs and the present sins which hinder the pattern from being realised.

VI

But what has all this to do with intercommunion? Much, every way. The problem of intercommunion is closely bound up with that of reunion; indeed, some of us think that intercommunion is in fact the achievement of reunion, in the measure that it becomes complete and includes intercelebration, while others among us regard it as a valuable help towards reunion.[4] And the question of intercommunion brings us face to face with the problem set by our diverse ways of worship; and it is at that point above all that we need to learn a true mutual sympathy and understanding—'we' being not only those who are deeply engaged in the Ecumenical Movement, but also the rank and file of ministers and laity in the churches.

Our ways of worship are diverse. For some of us the preaching-service, or rather the Liturgy of the Word, is the habitual form of Sunday worship; for others of us Sunday would not be Sunday without the offering of the Eucharist. But we all think of the Eucharist as the highest act of our religion; and just at this point the eucharistic sacrifice has been a centre of controversy. In this essay I have sought to show that on the theological side a real solution of the controversy seems to be opening up. But it is not merely a matter of reaching agreement on an important point of doctrine, but, more fundamentally, of mutual understanding among us about the ways in which we worship God. Nor is it a matter of seeking some compromise between opposed views and

[4] Cf. the Report, pp. 15-43.

proving that we do not really differ so much as we think;[5] rather, we need to recognise the differences, and nevertheless learn to trust one another and to pray together in spite of the differences, in the way that Professor Zander exhorts us and helps us to do.[6] That which unites us across all our differences is the saving action of our Lord and the work of His Grace.

The true reunion is to be the reintegration of the Visible Church of Christ, of the Israel of God whose actual existence is presupposed in the whole Bible. This Church of God has existed on earth since the days of Abraham and Moses; it was reconstituted to be the Church of all nations by our Lord's first Advent, in which the messianic promises were fulfilled, and it exists now on earth as an eschatological fact, looking forward to His second Advent, and meanwhile witnessing on earth to the reality of His Reign. As divine, it is holy, one, indivisible; as human, it is imperfect, but it looks forward to its consummation in the heavenly Jerusalem. As a visible society on earth, it bears in its nature and its structure the pattern of its heavenly calling. It must therefore be intolerant of heresy and error, because it can have no true unity except in the truth of Christ, and in obedience to His authority.

It is necessary to stress this last point, on which orthodox Protestants and Catholics are perfectly in accord; for it is directly opposed to a rival belief, which is the accepted creed of multitudes to-day, resting on the great dogma that 'Religion is a Good Thing', and that the Church exists to promote 'Religion'; reunion would then be a federation or amalgamation of various denominations, with no great regard to differences of doctrine or worship. But such a view of religion is quite alien to the Bible; indeed, a large part of the Bible is occupied with the vigorous assertion that religion, in many of its manifestations, is a very bad thing, and falls under the Lord's imminent judgment.

What, then, do we mean by true orthodoxy? True orthodoxy is to 'think-with-the-Church-and-think-with-the-Scripture';[7] I

---

[5] Cf. the Report, pp. 15-43. I accept what is said in the Report, but I think that the desire not to exaggerate the differences leads some of us in the direction of a false compromise.

[6] See his essay in this volume, pp. 351-360.

[7] The Greek word for 'to think', in this sense, is φρονεῖν, as in Rom. 12.3-5, Phil. 2. 1-5.

mean, that the Church is truly seen for what it is, and knows itself to be what it is, when it prays according to the Scriptures, and the Scriptures are seen in their true context in the life of the believing and worshipping community. True orthodoxy is not the same thing as holding all the correct doctrines; for it is possible to hold these in a heretical and sectarian spirit, thanking God that one is not as other men are. Those who thus 'think with the Church' will be truly ecumenically minded; they will endeavour to pray not only *for* other Christians but *with* them, mentally sharing their prayer with them, rejoicing with them in their faith in Christ the Redeemer. So the Apostle says: 'Bear ye one another's burdens, and so fulfil the law of Christ.' To learn to pray in this way is to know that our fellow-Christians, though separated from us by denominational barriers, really are our brothers in Christ. It is the increase and the deepening of this spirit in the Ecumenical Movement that is leading, slowly but very surely, towards the true reunion which is coming.

Many of us have found that it is a great help to worship with Christians separated from us, especially, but not only, at their Eucharist; and that the prohibition of intercommunion, though it emphasises the pain of division, does not impede this community of prayer. For, as was said above, there is a sense in which the Church is indivisible; someone [8]has said that 'the walls of division do not reach up to heaven'. We will communicate with our fellow Christians wherever the visible and organised Church gives us canonical authority to do so; for Holy Communion is the outward sign and means of the unity of the visible Church. Where there is not such permission we will abstain from the act of Communion, and seek by God's grace to rest on the heavenly reality of which the Sacrament is the appointed sign. But it seems to us that the claim that all the servants of Christ ought to be admitted to Communion, regardless of the fact that the Churches to which they belong are in schism from one another, on the ground that 'the Lord's Table is His and not ours', is to disregard the truth of the Visible Church. For in Scripture the Church is always a visible society; on its human side it is a fact in history, and the Bible is the story of God's saving action in history. And it is this visible

[8] A Russian Orthodox bishop, quoted in one of the prayer leaflets issued by the Abbé Couturier for the Week of Prayer for Christian Unity, 18th-25th January.

Church that is in our day seeking to find the way of its reunion.

Such is the bearing of the argument about the eucharistic sacrifice which I have worked out here. This essay has been written primarily in order to help Protestant Christians to a living sympathy with Catholic Christians; and not only with those whom they meet in the Ecumenical Movement, but also with Roman Catholics, who are at present debarred from taking part in our meetings; yet many of whom are following the course of our meetings with deep interest and steadfast prayer. I have been dealing with a subject in which it seems that the root of our difference has been in principle overcome. I have only touched on the other root of difference which still remains, namely that of the doctrine of priesthood, and valid orders, and apostolic succession; but I believe that here also, possibly in the near future, a way of understanding will be capable of being worked out on similar lines.

The solution of theological difficulties is, however, secondary to the mutual understanding which is to be worked out in the fellowship of prayer. For the Church of God exists in the first place for the worship of God, through Christ, in the Holy Spirit; and the visible reunion of Christians is but one element in the gathering together of the Church of God in every land to become in actuality what according to its vocation it already is. The Unity of Christians is a thing that is to be realised not only in ecumenical gatherings but also in the life of every Christian community: 'Grant that all they that do confess Thy holy Name may agree in the truth of Thy holy word, and live in unity and godly love.'

XIII

ANGLICANISM
AND INTERCOMMUNION[1]

*

Leonard Hodgson

Church of England

(Great Britain)

I

It is well known to all the world that the Anglican Church is a
church which finds great difficulty in the way of practising inter-
communion with more than a very limited number of other
Christian bodies. In his sermon at the opening of the 1937 World
Conference on Faith and Order at Edinburgh, the Archbishop of
York said:

'I speak as a member of one of those Churches which still
maintain barriers against completeness of union at the Table of
the Lord. I believe from my heart that we of that tradition are
trustees for an element of truth concerning the nature of the
Church which requires that exclusiveness as a consequence,
until this element of truth be incorporated with others into a
fuller and worthier conception of the Church than any of us
hold to-day. But I know that our division at this point is the
greatest of all scandals in the face of the world; I know that we
can only consent to it or maintain it without the guilt of unfaithfulness to the unity of the Gospel and of God Himself, if
it is a source to us of spiritual pain, and if we are striving to the
utmost to remove the occasions which now bind us, as we
think, to that perpetuation of disunion.'

[1] This paper was originally published in the American Quarterly *Christendom*
in 1939. To a large extent it was reprinted in a pamphlet on the question of
the Church of South India in 1943. It is included in this volume as an attempt
to dispel the obscurity about theological principles referred to by Canon
Greenslade on p. 226.

I have no doubt in my own mind that this Anglican exclusiveness is due to concern in the matter of orders. The Anglican
Church is not indifferent to questions of faith, but when the
representatives of various Churches assembled at the Lausanne
Conference in 1927 agreed upon the following statement:

> 'Notwithstanding the differences in doctrine among us, we
> are united in a common Christian Faith which is proclaimed in
> the Holy Scriptures and is witnessed to and safeguarded in the
> Ecumenical Creed, commonly called the Nicene, and in the
> Apostles' Creed, which Faith is continuously confirmed in the
> spiritual experience of the Church of Christ (from the Report
> of Section VI),'

this gave what most Anglicans would regard as sufficient agreement in faith to justify intercommunion were there no other
obstacles in the way. Elsewhere in Christendom there may be
bodies which hold that the acceptance of doctrines defined at a
later date than A.D. 381, such, for example, as the doctrine of
trans- or consubstantiation, of justification by faith, or of the
immaculate conception, is necessary for this purpose, but only a
non-representative minority of Anglicans would make any such
demand. The situation with which we are confronted is one in
which there exist many Christian bodies with which the Anglican
Church might be in communion so far as questions of faith are
concerned, were it not that the question of orders stands in the
way. And the particular question which causes the trouble is that
of the apostolic succession.

It is well known that this phrase 'apostolic succession' is patient
of many different meanings. (See the *Report* of the Edinburgh
Conference, Ch. V (vii) A.) The form in which it causes the
difficulty is that in which it holds that the minister of the Holy
Communion must be one who has been ordained to his office by
a bishop who has his place in a succession of episcopal ordinations
(or consecrations) going back to apostolic times. It is believed by
the Anglican Church that it has a ministry authorised to minister
the Sacrament by ordination in this succession. For its own
ministers such authorisation is required by its formularies, and
though there may be (and are) Anglicans who set little store by
this requirement and have scant respect for the theology involved
in it, I have little doubt myself that the Anglican Church as a

whole regards itself as committed to this requirement and is not prepared to forsake it or minimise its importance.

It is here that I feel it necessary to avoid raising false hopes by concealing this fact. It is the fashion in some quarters to disregard this fidelity to the doctrine of apostolic succession as though it were the peculiar hobby of a small group described as 'extreme Anglo-Catholics', whose views can be safely ignored in making plans for the reunion of Christendom. Such an attitude I believe to be profoundly mistaken. Respect for the doctrine of apostolic succession is far more widely diffused among us and deeply ingrained in us than that. It characterises our history, as shown in the lives of such men as Timothy Cutler and Samuel Seabury. I know members of the Church of Ireland who set great store by the fact that when the Vatican decided against the validity of the orders of the Church of England care was taken to say nothing about those of the Church of Ireland, knowing that that Church could claim an independent succession unaffected by the accidents which were alleged to invalidate the English claim. The Lambeth Conference may have no legislative authority, or power to bind the Church, but its pronouncements are undoubtedly evidence of what is commonly believed and held among us, and both in 1920 and 1930 its resolutions on intercommunion are clearly based upon this doctrine which, moreover, is included in the so-called Chicago-Lambeth Quadrilateral. The actual steps taken by the Church of England in recent years towards the restoration of intercommunion with other bodies have all kept in view the satisfaction of what this doctrine requires; witness the agreements made with the Old Catholics, the nature of the discussions with the Eastern Orthodox Church and the Church of Sweden, and the conditions required in the provisional agreements with the Churches of Finland, Latvia and Esthonia.

Among workers for unity there seems to exist in some quarters an optimism which is based upon the assumption that the Anglican Church can easily be persuaded to abandon the doctrine of orders which I have just shown to be implied in the utterances of its responsible leaders and the policy embodied in its official acts. When we try to discover the grounds for this assumption we find ourselves face to face with a problem the seriousness of which often seems to me to be insufficiently grasped. It is the fundamental problem of the difference between the Protestant and

I

Catholic conceptions not only of the Church, but of the nature of Christianity itself. This difference finds expression both in the fields of history and of theology proper. It is commonly held among Protestants that recent researches into the history of Christian origins have invalidated whatever historical basis may hitherto have been claimed for the doctrine of apostolic succession. It is also commonly held that theologically the doctrine implies a magical conception of the operation of divine grace which is inconsistent with the principles of true Christianity. From this it is concluded that, since no one in his senses, when once his eyes are opened, will wish to maintain a doctrine which is historically unjustified and theologically superstitious, it cannot be long before it is abandoned by all except that small group of Anglo-Catholic Anglicans whose eyes are blinded by prejudice. The majority of Anglicans must already be coming to regard it as a *damnosa haereditas*, an encumbrance in their efforts for unity from which they have not yet managed to free themselves and for which they have to apologise.

My own experience of Anglicanism from within convinces me that any such estimate of the temper of my fellow churchmen as a whole is completely mistaken. They do not believe that the holding of this doctrine requires any apology, whether it be considered historically or theologically. The late Canon Streeter or Dr. Newton Flew may have advanced arguments against its historical foundation convincing to themselves; but there are other scholars of equal weight who read the evidence differently, and among Anglicans the arguments of these other scholars are more widely accepted. Theologically it is denied that the doctrine, rightly understood, is either magical or superstitious—and 'rightly understood' does not mean understood in such a manner as to dissolve away the belief that God wills to give His grace through the appointed means of rightly ordained ministers.

I must emphasise this last point because of its importance for the whole reunion movement. From many of the writings of Continental Protestants which I have read I have gained the impression that in their eyes fidelity to the principles of the Reformation (which are held to be the principles of true Christianity) requires the rejection of the whole Catholic conception of Christianity, lock, stock, and barrel. Now the Oxford Movement meant for the Anglican Church the recovery of its Catholic heritage, and a growing conviction, verified in the experience of the last hundred years, that this antithesis is falsely drawn. I say 'in experience' because it is clear that the intellectual problems involved have by no means yet been solved. We have proved that it is possible to live and worship together as sons both of the Reformation and of the historic Catholic Church. But this is regarded by many of our Continental fellow Christians as merely another instance of English indifference to logic, and we must confess that we have not yet solved the intellectual problems provided by the co-existence of Protestantism and Catholicism in one Church. If we had, we should be able to show our Continental brethren how the breach could be healed to their satisfaction as well as to ours. As it is, they suspect that we are only able to maintain our own façade of unity either through sheer intellectual laziness or because neither our Protestantism nor our Catholicism is the genuine article.

But we are realists. When we contemplate Christendom we find it impossible to believe that either Catholicism or Protestantism taken alone expresses the full truth of Christianity. We find it impossible to believe that the unity of Christendom will be achieved through either, so to speak, 'swallowing' the other. We therefore conclude that the alternative to the reconciliation of the two in one Church is an arrangement in which, when Christians are sorted out of their present muddle and have crystallised around one or other of these two poles, the two camps will continue until the day of judgment separated by a gulf which only men as individuals can cross, crossing it as converts or perverts according to the point of view. This seems to us an unsatisfactory picture to contemplate as the goal of the reunion movement, and so we cherish the hope that our apparently illogical makeshift of a Church may turn out to provide more valuable food for thought than appears on the surface.

But if this be our hope, then it is clear that we shall not be likely to respond to any appeals to take steps toward unity which involve abandoning either our Protestant or our Catholic pretensions. We do not regard the Oxford Movement as a regrettable relapse into a discredited Catholicism. We regard it as the recovery of a Catholic heritage which is of value to ourselves at present, and which we hold in trust to share with the rest of Christendom if and when our fellow Christians come to perceive its value and to desire it for themselves. In this connection I may here repeat some words I wrote some years ago, which still seem to me to express a typically Anglican outlook.

'For the Anglican, unity means unity vertically down the ages as well as horizontally across the face of the earth, unity with that little company in the Upper Room at Jerusalem as well as with fellow Christians now alive in America, India and Japan. When an Anglican sets out to baptise a convert, he sets out to baptise him into that fellowship; when the Anglican priest stands before the altar to celebrate the Holy Communion, or a lay-reader holds a mission service for half a dozen souls in some isolated region of Montana or Wyoming, that which is being done is an official act of the whole society functioning in that place. The members of a little gathering of twentieth-century Christians in an out-of-the-way corner of the world are to be assured that they are worshipping in communion with Peter and Andrew, James and John, the rest of that company, and the whole company of "just men made perfect" from that day to this.

'This being his aim, the Anglican asks how that unity can be secured. He notices that in any earthly society unity and continuity from generation to generation seem to depend on two factors interwoven like two strands of a single rope: the outward continuity of organisation and the inward continuity of spirit, faith and practice. He notices, for example, that if a body of trustees are challenged as to their right to continue administering some endowment, they have to make good their position by showing both that they have been appointed constitutionally in accordance with the accepted custom of the trust, and that in their administration they are carrying out the intentions of the founder as he would like them to be carried out were he alive at the time. He concludes that he cannot rightly exercise less care in matters spiritual than is required in matters temporal, that he cannot offer to baptise into the fellowship of the Apostles if he is careless about either strand of the rope which links the Church of to-day to the Church of the Upper Room. (From *Essays in Christian Philosophy*, p. 144.)'

The action taken by the Church of England in its negotiations with the Churches of Finland, Latvia and Esthonia illustrates this attitude, and shows, moreover, that on the side of outward organisation the apostolic succession is regarded as one of those valuable elements in the Catholic tradition which we treasure for ourselves and wish to share with others. It therefore seems clear that the Anglican Church is not at all likely to respond favourably to any suggestions which would require it to treat its apostolic succession as a thing of little value. Any hopes of a united Christendom which is to include Anglicanism must include the hope that the rest of Christendom will welcome the opportunity of sharing in this treasure which has been given to the Anglican Church to be its contribution to the riches of the whole united body.

But see what this means. Our hope must include the hope that a way will have been found to reconcile this belief that the apostolic succession is a treasure with the belief that to regard it as such is apostasy from true Christianity! To refuse to face this fact is to behave like the proverbial ostrich, and my first purpose in writing this paper is to lay bare the unpalatable truth. The reunion movement as a whole, in its world-wide aspect, will not have faced realities until it has opened its eyes to contemplate steadily the problem of reconciling the sons of the Reformation with the heirs of Trent. And it is no good treating the problem of the Anglican position about Orders as anything less than a subdivision of this problem, or thinking that it can be disposed of by itself without raising these wider and deeper issues.

If this be so, it is idle to look for any speedy solution of the problem. The issues involved are so deep and far-reaching that to solve their difficulties will require a resolute and determined intellectual effort. At present it has hardly been begun, and we cannot expect to bring it to a successful conclusion unless we are prepared to persevere in it for no short period of time.

Are we then led to the pessimistic conclusion that for this indefinitely lengthy period the Anglican Church must continue to acquiesce in 'the greatest of all scandals in the face of the world' by maintaining the present barriers against union at the Table of the Lord? This is the question which has now to be faced.

II

For anyone who has had borne in upon him the reality of the present situation—not merely the scandal in the face of the world, but also the inner wounding of the Body of Christ—it is impossible to rest content with things as they are. But when an Anglican advocates the raising of the existing barriers to intercommunion, he is inevitably met by the argument that he is allowing his heart to run away with his head. The maintenance of the barriers, it is urged, is demanded by theological principle, and to think that unity in accordance with the will of God can be built upon neglect of or indifference to theological principle is sentimentality at its worst. Theological principle forbids us to equate episcopal and non-episcopal ministries; theological principle requires us to observe 'the general rule of the Anglican Churches that members of the Anglican Churches should receive the Holy Communion only from ministers of their own Church'; at Lambeth in 1930 the Anglican bishops came dangerously near to compromising with theological principle, as indeed they recognised when they appended to their recommendations the words 'we would point out that the very special circumstances and the very strict regulations specified in this Regulation of themselves show that we are not departing from the rule of our Church that the minister of the Holy Communion should be a priest episcopally ordained.'[1]

It is clear, then, that if any proposal for a relaxation of the present restrictions is to have any chance of acceptance it must satisfy two conditions: (i) it must be based on grounds of theological principle, and (ii) it must not prejudge the central issue between the Protestant and the Catholic conceptions of the Church.

Let us first try to state more precisely what the present situation is. The Lambeth Conference may have no binding authority, but in actual practice few Anglican bishops or clergy feel justified in disregarding its resolutions. Those resolutions, while referring to the 'rule' that the minister of the Holy Communion should be a priest episcopally ordained, allow a diocesan bishop to authorise the admission of baptised communicants of other Christian bodies to Communion at an Anglican service in certain circumstances, and it is the custom to include in these circumstances conferences of Christians gathered together from various denominations for

[1] *Report of the Lambeth Conference*, 1930, Resolution 42. Cf. Resolution 12 (B) of 1920.

the purpose of setting forward the cause of unity. But permission to Anglicans to communicate at non-episcopal services is restricted to 'special areas where the ministrations of an Anglican Church are not available for long periods of time or without travelling great distances'. The result is that at conferences for the promotion of unity Anglican clergy feel themselves able with a clear conscience to invite to an Anglican service baptised communicant members of other bodies who may be present, but cannot approve of the Anglicans present communicating at a non-episcopal service. Thus it often happens that when such a gathering is held on the continent of Europe, the only way in which those present can communicate together is if the celebrant is a visiting Anglican priest, or a priest of the Church of Sweden, or an ex-Anglican priest of the Church of South India, and not a minister of the Church of the country whose hospitality they are enjoying. It is this barrier to 'reciprocity' which pains the heart and makes it ask the head whether theological principle does indeed demand its retention.

Now however firmly an Anglican may believe it to be the will of God for the Church that the Sacrament of Holy Communion should only be celebrated by priests episcopally ordained, and however strong may be his conviction that in the apostolic succession the Anglican Church has entrusted to it a treasure to be faithfully guarded for the ultimate benefit of all Christendom, he cannot regard this inestimable blessing as a thing to boast about or as having been conferred upon his Church in recognition of its superior merit. His Christianity and his common sense combine to make this impossible. His Christianity teaches him that boasting is excluded, and forbids either individual or Church to claim that the gracious gifts of God are given in reward for human merit. What common sense has to say about the matter demands a paragraph to itself.

On an objective and impartial reading of the history of the sixteenth and succeeding centuries it is surely impossible to maintain that either those Churches which have maintained or those which have lost the apostolic succession have done so with a full conscious realisation of all that was involved, or with full control over the course of their own history. There are some Churches, such as the Church of Finland, which have lost it through sheer accident. There are other Churches, notably among the Lutherans, in which it was not lost through any desire or deliberate intention to repudiate it, but because when they were forced to choose between the retention of the episcopate and fidelity to what they believed to be true doctrine, they chose the giving up of the former as the lesser evil. What in this respect was true of certain Lutheran Churches in the sixteenth century was equally true of Methodism in the eighteenth. And even in the case of Churches of the Reformed tradition, and of Independency, it is impossible to maintain that what they repudiated was the episcopal apostolic succession as such. The form in which they were acquainted with it was one which in their eyes had become the source of so much corruption that it seemed necessary to make a new beginning, and the effort to restore the primitive purity of the Church led in the one case to the establishment of a succession through the presbyterate and in the other through the calling by the congregation. When one reflects upon the history of the sixteenth century, and all the tangled skein of motives, political, ecclesiastical, doctrinal, moral and religious through which the Western Church became divided, it is impossible to apportion praise or blame to this or that body for having retained or let slip this or that element in the common heritage of the past. We may be thankful that out of the storm and stress of that age our Anglican ancestors emerged with their episcopal succession unimpaired. But if England had 'gone' presbyterian like Scotland, how many of us who as born Anglicans are staunch episcopalians would not have been equally staunch presbyterians? We may with grateful hearts acknowledge that we are episcopalian by the grace of God, but if we are honest we must acknowledge also that we are episcopalian by the accident of history; and this must surely affect our attitude towards those whose zeal for righteousness and honest desire to find and do God's will led them in those difficult days along other paths.

There can be no theological principle more fundamental than the character of God as made known to us in the biblical revelation. This revelation is given in its fullness in Christ, the incarnate Word.[2] When we look back over the Old Testament with the revelation in Christ as our guide to its interpretation, we see that the whole Bible bids us think of God as demanding of man the

[2] For this, see D. M. Baillie, *God was in Christ* (London: Faber and Faber, 1948).

honest pursuit of what he believes to be right.[3] We are not to think of Him as one who would punish us for accidentally spilling the salt, or sitting down thirteen at a table, or going to sea on a Friday. But if this be so, we cannot think of God as penalising either men or Churches for failing to secure such a thing as the apostolic succession, if what they were doing was honestly seeking to find and do His will as it appeared to them in the circumstances of their time.

This is what we should be doing if we were to refuse to regard the sacraments of non-episcopal bodies as in every way equal to our own on the ground that they are not celebrated by ministers episcopally ordained. For every sacrament is what God makes it, and to regard any sacrament as deficient is to believe that God withholds from it the fulness of the gift which it is intended to convey. When we think of those Churches with which we Anglicans are sufficiently one in faith to invite their members to communicate at our altars, and to believe that we might be united were it not for our differences on the subject of order, we may not allow ourselves to have any doubts about the blessings, sacramental and otherwise, which God gives them equally with ourselves. As we thank God for our own history which has preserved for us the apostolic succession which we long to share with them, we realise that to think or speak depreciatively about their sacraments is a blasphemous contradiction of the most fundamental theological principle known to us.

We would seem, then, to be in a dilemma, drawn in one direction by the theological principle which requires us to regard episcopal ordination as willed by God for the ministers of His sacraments, and in another by the theological principle which requires us to recognise the equality of episcopalian and non-episcopalian sacraments. What are we to do?

I would suggest that we can be faithful to both principles if we distinguish between God's will for His Church in its unity and His will for it in its present divided condition. There is no inconsistency in maintaining both that we hold the apostolic succession in trust to be our contribution to the fulfilment of God's will in the united Church of the future, and also that in this interim period of disorganisation between the disruption of the past and

---

[3] I have argued this more fully in my book, *Towards a Christian Philosophy* (London: Nisbet, 1942), pp. 139 ff.

the reunion of the future, He wills us to recognise the equality of His sacramental activity in episcopal and non-episcopal bodies alike.

Do I then advocate an immediate abolition of all restrictions and barriers to intercommunion? I do not. There is a group of considerations arising out of another approach to the subject which have not yet been mentioned but must now be taken into account. For many Anglicans it is not only the question of the ministry which stands in the way of intercommunion; there is also the conviction that the Sacrament of Holy Communion is a corporate activity of the Church expressing its fellowship. Intercommunion between the members of divided Churches is a self-contradiction, and a pretence of non-existent unity. When a group of Christians drawn from different Churches hold a joint Communion Service, they either arrogate to the group the right to function as a Church, or else they combine a number of acts of individualistic lawlessness into the acting of a lie.

Here there are two strains of thought which need to be disentangled. There is the objection to intercommunion on the ground that it dishonestly conceals the divided state of the Church, and there is the objection to members of an *ad hoc* group participating as individuals in an action which can only have any meaning if it is the action of a Church. These must be considered separately.

The objection that intercommunion conceals the divided state of the Church presents a real difficulty and must be taken seriously. I have argued in the earlier part of this paper that full restoration of the Church's unity must wait upon the discovery of how to reconcile very deep-seated differences of conviction concerning the nature of Christianity itself. If this be true, then there is indeed force in the contention that we should not hide this fact from ourselves by behaving as though it were not so. So long as we are not one united fellowship, we have no right to ignore this tragic fact at the altar. So long as we apathetically tolerate this state of affairs, we ought to be made to feel the pain of it. Here again I find myself still in agreement with what I have written before:

'*Intercommunion is unity;* and the steps towards it are the findings of ways to such agreements on faith and order as make it possible for all without qualm of conscience. To initiate immediate intercommunion as though these preliminary steps were unnecessary is like allowing a deep wound to heal over on the surface when its cure requires it to fill up with healthy tissue from within outwards. The question when the skin may be allowed to grow over the wound is an empirical question to be decided by the doctor in charge of the case, and the nurse who works under him must wait for his word before this step is taken. In the life of the Church the local minister is the nurse, and it is not for him to decide whether the relations between his communion and another are such as to justify intercommunion with them. It may be hard and painful for him to refrain from taking this step, but that is as it should be. Disunity should be painful; but the pain should be welcomed as a spur to drive us on toward its healing, not succumbed to as a temptation to conceal it.[4]

This comparison of the local minister with the nurse who must act under authority leads on to our second point, the objection to the individualism involved in an *ad hoc* group of Christians arranging for a service which is not corporately authorised by their respective Churches. This difficulty also needs to be taken seriously.

Let us again review the existing situation. The bishops of the Anglican communion have agreed that they will not call in question the action of any one of their number who in his own sphere of jurisdiction sanctions under certain circumstances the invitation of baptised communicant members of other Churches to communicate at Anglican altars. Although it is argued by some that this decision of the bishops has no authority, and that a bishop who acts in accordance with it is himself committing an act of individualistic lawlessness (e.g. by Dr. W. H. Dunphy in *Oecumenica*, Vol. IV, No. 4, p. 684 [London, S.P.C.K. January 1938]), this view is not, so far as I can judge, generally accepted by Anglicans. Many, if not most, of us would feel that if what we do is done with the approval of our local bishop and in accordance with a resolution of the episcopate as a whole, it is not an individualistic act of our own, but an authoritatively recognised act of the Church to which we belong. For this reason we do not believe that we would be justified in going beyond the limits for which permission can be given under the Lambeth resolutions.

So far as the circumstances are concerned, the maintenance of

[4] From *Essays in Christian Philosophy*, p. 159.

those limits seems to me for the present to be right. They allow an Anglican 'open' Communion Service in two cases: (a) where there are Christians within reach of Anglican ministration but out of reach of their own, and (b) where there is a gathering of Christians assembled for the purpose of setting forward the cause of unity. The underlying principle is clearly this. Where Churches are continuing to live side by side as separated bodies, this fact should be recognised, and the members of each communicate in the fellowship to which they belong. But where this is impossible, and where there is an assembly for the purpose of working to end the divisions and restore a united fellowship, the 'general rule' can be waived without involving the danger of premature intercommunion concealing the divisions and delaying their cure.

What, therefore, I am arguing for in this paper is recognition of the rightness of *reciprocal* open Communion Services in those circumstances in which Anglican open Communion Services are already sanctioned. We have seen that in 1930 the bishops took a step towards this in respect of circumstance (a), though with considerable hesitation and apparently some misgiving lest their Christian charity should be leading them into disregard of theological principle. They took no step forward in respect of circumstance (b). The arguments I have brought forward seem to me to show that the hesitation and misgivings may be removed and that theological principle not only confirms the action taken but demands its extension to cover circumstance (b). I earnestly hope that in the near future the authorities of the Anglican Church will sanction this extension, so that not as individuals but as loyal representatives of our Church we may in practice recognise the equality of the sacraments of our fellow Christians from whom for the time being we are divided. I believe, as I have shown, that such action could be taken without in any way compromising the principles for which Anglicanism stands; I believe that such action, taken on the grounds I have described, would be preferable to any 'concordats' involving the mutual commissioning of individual ministers by formulae of ambiguous meaning; I believe that it would do more than anything else to convince Christendom as a whole that the Anglican Church is serious in its often expressed desire for unity, and that at the present stage of Christian history it would be the most valuable contribution that it could make to that cause.

XIV

INTERCOMMUNION:
A CONGREGATIONALIST COMMENT

*

John Marsh

Congregational Union of England and Wales

(Great Britain)

The term intercommunion is certainly not Congregationalist in origin, nor does it come naturally or easily to the mind of a Reformed Churchman of that ecclesiastical tradition. This is not only because the word is comparatively quite modern,[1] but also because the basic word 'communion' has been given historically a much wider meaning than as a reference to the Sacrament of the Lord's Supper. The Prayer Books of 1549, 1552 and 1662 suggest that it would have been characteristic for a member of the Church of England to think of the Sacrament of the Lord's Supper when he heard the word 'communion'. But while a Congregationalist would have known that in that service he held communion with his Lord and his Lord with him, and while he would have spoken of the 'communion of saints' of the communion of churches, and of Christians in churches, with Christ, and with God in Christ, he would not easily have used expressions like 'going to' or 'making his' communion, nor referred to the service by the Prayer Book title of 'The Communion'.

For the Congregationalist, Communion is characteristically and

---

[1] The earliest use, according to the *New English Dictionary*, was by Law in his *Considerations on the State of the World with regard to the Theory of Religion* (1761) where it refers to connections between Christianity and heathen religions. Yeowell, in 1839, spoke of the 'Unity and Intercommunion of the various branches of the Church of Christ' meaning inter-relation rather than our modern intercommunion. In the same way Stubbs, in his *Constitutional History*, writes that there was less travel to Europe 'after the Reformation had suspended religious intercommunion'. In none of these instances is the word used in the sense it bears in the title of this book.

historically a word which refers in the first place to the life of the local church. Thus the Savoy Declaration,[2] in its chapter 27 'Of the Communion of Saints', asserts: 'All saints that are united to Jesus Christ their Head, by his Spirit and Faith, although they are not made thereby one person with him, have fellowship in his Graces, Sufferings, Death, Resurrection and Glory: and being united to one another in love, they have communion in each other's gifts and graces, and are obliged to the performance of such duties, publique and private, as do conduce to their mutual good, both in the inward and outward Man.'

'All Saints are bound to maintain an an holy fellowship and communion in the Worship of God, and in performing such other spiritual services as tend to their mutual edification; as also in relieving each other in outward things, according to their several abilities and necessities: which communion, though especially to be exercised by them in the relations wherein they stand, whether in Families or Churches, yet as God offereth opportunity, is to be extended unto all those who in every place call upon the Name of the Lord Jesus.'

The life of a Christian disciple is thus inevitably a life in the Church, sharing in the wholeness of its communion. For the earliest—as for the latest—Congregationalists, to be a Christian is to have one's roots deeply in the life of a local community of Christians, and to share in all the acts by which, in that life, the graces of Christ are mediated to men. 'High Churchmanship' is characteristically essential to Congregationalism, and it consists in continuing and regular attendance upon all the ordinances of the Church, and a constant practice of her duties. The sacrament of the Lord's Supper is indeed a central part of the Church's life, but it is not the whole. Christ enters into and maintains communion with His people in Baptism, in the preaching of the Word, in prayer, in the exercise of Godly discipline, as well as in and through the ordinance of the Lord's Supper. Communion is a much wider term than the name of one sacramental service: it represents a Christian's whole life with God in Christ, as that is part of the life, of the life on earth, of the people of God, the Church.

[2] Published in: Williston Walker: *The Creeds and Platforms of Congregationalism*, 1892, pp. 340-408. Reprinted separately by B. L. Manning and J. S. Whale in August 1939.

But with all that said, we have not yet considered the most characteristic use of the word 'communion' in historic Congregationalism as it appears in the phrase 'the Communion of Churches'. The Savoy Declaration states that: 'As all Churches and all the Members of them are bound to pray continually for the good or prosperity of all the Churches of Christ in all places, and upon all occasions to further it; (Everyone within the bounds of the Places and Callings, in the exercise of their Gifts and Graces). So the Churches themselves (when planted by the providence of God, so as they may have opportunity and advantage for it) ought to hold communion amongst themselves for their peace, increase of love, and mutual edification.'[3] If anything in the thought of these earlier Congregationalists can be called 'intercommunion', this is it; but it is important to note that what is under discussion in this part of the Savoy Declaration is the sharing of individual local churches in the one life of communion with God in Christ that belongs to God's people in this world,[4] in all its forms and manifestations; and not simply the question whether one Church may admit members from other Churches to its celebration of the Sacrament of the Lord's Supper. Communion and union are inextricably interrelated.

This is brought out very clearly in John Owen's chapter, 'Of the Communion of Churches', in his book *The True Nature of a Gospel Church*, published posthumously in 1689, thirty-one years after the Savoy Assembly in which Owen had played an influential part. He says: 'Churches so appointed and established in order as hath been declared ought to hold communion among themselves, or with each other, as unto all the ends of their institution and order, for these are the same in all; yea, and the *general end* of them is in order of nature considered antecedently unto their institution in *particular*. This end is the edification of the body of Christ in general, or the *church catholic*. The promotion hereof is committed jointly and severally unto all *particular churches*. . . . But this communion of churches cannot be duly apprehended

---

[3] Savoy Declaration: 'Of the Institution of Churches, And the Order Appointed in them by Jesus Christ', XXV.

[4] Though the 'power of administration of Ordinances' and the 'execution of any authority in Christ's name' is affirmed to be vested by Christ in particular churches, each church shares in the same universal communion with Christ and acknowledges His one undifferentiated authority.

unless we inquire and determine wherein their union doth consist, for *communion* is an *act of union* that receives both its nature and power from it or by virtue of it; for of what nature soever the union of things distinct in themselves be, of the same is the communion that they have among themselves. . . . I say . . . that the true and only union of all particular churches consists in that which gives form, life, and being unto the church catholic, with the addition of what belongs unto them as they are particular; and this is, that they have all one and the same God and Father, one Lord Jesus Christ, one faith and one doctrine of faith, one hope of their calling, or the promised inheritance, one regeneration, one baptism, one bread and wine, and are united unto God and Christ in one Spirit, through the bond of faith and love. . . .

'Two things concur unto the completing of this union of churches. 1. Their *union* or *relation* unto Christ; 2. That which they have *among themselves*. . . .

'These things being premised, I proceed unto that which is our present inquiry,—namely, wherein the communion of particular churches among themselves doth consist.

'The communion of the churches is *their joint actings in the same gospel duties towards God in Christ, with their mutual actings towards each other with respect unto the end of their institution and being, which is the glory of Christ in the edification of the whole catholic church.*

'As unto the actings of the FIRST sort, the ground of them is faith, and therein is the first act of the communion of churches. And this communion of faith among all the churches is fivefold:

'1. *General, in the belief of the same doctrine of truth.* . . .

'2. This communion in faith respects the church itself as its *material object.* . . .

'3. The communion of the churches consists much in the principal fruit of it, namely, *prayer.* . . .

'4. The unity of faith in all churches effecteth communion among them in *the administration of the same sacraments of baptism and the supper of the Lord.* . . .

'5. They have also by faith communion herein, in that *all churches do profess a subjection unto the authority of Christ in all things,* and an obligation upon them to do and observe all whatsoever he hath commanded. . . .

'SECONDLY. Churches ordained and constituted in the way and manner, and for the ends, declared in our former subject, and, by virtue of their union unto Christ and among themselves, living constantly, in all places of the world, in the actual exercise of that communion which consists in the performance of the same church-duties towards God in Christ, unto their own continuation, increase and edification, have also an especial union among themselves, and a mutual communion thence arising.

'*The bond of this union is love* . . . an especial grace of the Holy Spirit, acting in the church as the principle and bond of its union unto itself. . . .

'Herein consists the union of every church in itself, of all churches among themselves, and so of the whole catholic church, their communion consisting in regular acts and duties proceeding from this love, and required by virtue of it.

'*The outward acts* of communion among churches, proceeding from this love, and the obligation that is on them to promote their mutual edification, may be referred unto the two heads of *advice* and *assistance*.

'Churches have communion unto their mutual edification by advice in synods or councils.'[5]

There follows a section dealing with Synods, to which, rather than to the celebration of the Lord's Supper, the word 'communion' would more easily be applied.

There are two elements in this outline of historical Congregationalism which would still be held by Congregationalists to-day. The first is that the communion of the individual believer with God in Christ depends for its nourishment and growth upon a continued and regular participation in the whole life of a local congregation, church or people of God. For Congregationalists, to be a Christian means to be a church member; but to be a church member means to share in the *whole* of a covenanted way of life by *every means* which the Gospel enjoins. The Christian life, properly understood, belongs to a society, the Church; and an individual can participate in the Christian life, properly speaking, only as a member of that society, the Church. The Pauline teaching about the Church as the body of Christ and us as 'severally members thereof' (I Cor. 12. 27; cf. Rom. 12. 4; Eph. 4. 4, 16)

---

[5] I quote from Rev. John Huxtable's valuable abbreviation of Owen's work, issued in 1947, pp. 119 ff. The italics are Owen's.

is claimed as sufficient warrant for such a view. But the life of the body, if that metaphor be more than a figure of speech, is clearly not that of its individual members, but of its unity as a body, i.e. of Christ. Congregationalists have claimed, with all other Reformed churchmen, that the marks of the life of Christ in His body, as these are set out in Scripture for our guidance, are the faithful preaching of the Word, the proper celebration of the Gospel sacraments and the practice of godly discipline. To be in communion with any particular Church is not simply to share in one part, or several parts, of that life; it is to share in it all, continually and continuously. So when the Savoy Declaration affirms in its last article that Congregational churches may admit unto 'occasional communion' with themselves members of other Churches, though deemed less pure, it is not confining itself to a statement about the Sacrament or Ordinance of the Lord's Supper. To admit members of other Churches to any part of the local church's life is to admit them to 'communion'. Thus our modern discussions which are focused upon one element only in the whole communion-life of God's people, the Church, is in many ways a forced, and certainly a distorted question for Congregationalists. Some consequences of this will be considered below (see p. 275ff).

A second element of historical Congregationalism which modern Congregationalists would reaffirm is that the communion of Churches in the life of the Church Catholic depends for its nourishment and growth upon their 'mutual actings towards each other . . . in the edification of the whole catholic church'. This consists of a sharing of a common doctrine, a recognition of the church as part of the Gospel, a common life of prayer and of attendance upon the Gospel sacraments, and a common subjection to Christ, to obey Him in all things which He lays upon them as Churches. It is indeed no accident that the word 'communion', which in other traditions of churchmanship has been focused upon the Sacrament of the Lord's Supper, should have found its characteristic use among Congregationalists to describe the relations between churches. To the outsider it has often seemed that each local Congregational Church is a law unto itself, and no doubt many manifestations of Congregationalism have supported that judgment. But however emphatically Congregationalists of every generation want to proclaim the integrity of the local community, and its responsibility to Christ alone (inasmuch as all the gifts and authorities of Christ are promised and therefore given to it), they would also want to maintain as emphatically that this is not true of any congregation in isolation, but only in the mutuality of life and responsibility that John Owen so long ago so richly described. Christ is not given to the local church then, in isolation, but only in mutuality with the Church Catholic; and that is why the word 'communion', which in other traditions is used of a part of the Church's life where Christ is really given and therefore present, is not inappropriately used by Congregationalists of the relationships of Churches. And we may add that in this understanding of communion, Congregationalists find their age-long and continuing concern for the true union and unity of the Church of Jesus Christ.

No modern Congregationalist would want to maintain that it has always been given to the churches of his order to witness unequivocally to the 'mutuality' he would thus proclaim. Indeed, in years not long past, a specious 'Independency' did much to undermine the characteristic convictions as well as the true order of Congregationalism. But to-day Congregationalists would want to reaffirm two things: first, the integrity of the local church's relationship to Christ in such a way that it was as plain as ever that no authority of any kind—civil or ecclesiastical—had any jurisdiction over it, but only Christ Himself; and second, the inescapable mutuality of all local churches in the one 'body' of Christ, so that none are in full and real communion with Christ unless they share in that mutuality. Particular churches can no more live unto themselves than can individual Christians; no more than individual Christians have they the right, or, in the end, the spiritual possibility, of *solitary* decision for and obedience to Christ.

But what has all this repetition of denominational emphasis to do with the quite different and highly specific modern question of 'intercommunion'? Much!

In the first place, since Congregationalists share with other Christians[6] the conviction that the Sacrament of the Lord's Supper is but one part of the 'communion' of Churches with one another or of Christians in the Church with their Lord; it follows that there is a sense in which they must testify to the Churches of

[6] See e.g. the Essays by Professor Zander and Dr. P. W. Evans pp. 351-360 and 185-195.

Christendom that the modern problem of 'intercommunion' is not in every respect a central problem, and certainly not the whole of the problem of the 'intercommunion' of Churches. This conviction is widely shared, and the conditions upon which various agreements about intercommunion have been made are evidence therefor.[7] Upon examination the question whether Christians of different Churches can eat bread and drink wine together at the Lord's Table always turns out to be a much wider question, embracing matters of both the faith and the order of the Churches concerned.

Second, for this same reason (that 'communion' for Congregationalists is a term much wider in content than 'the Sacrament of the Lord's Supper') it becomes plain that much will turn in discussions about intercommunion upon what precisely is being asked for and (maybe) promised. The emphasis upon churchmanship, and its necessary exercise in all the privileges and duties of the church-state, would make Congregationalists resist any suggestion which tended to undermine that conception of the fullness and wholeness of a church member's duty. Intercommunion, that is to say, is for Congregationalists possible only against the background of an accepted responsibility to the whole life of a local congregation or church. Sacramental promiscuity must not be encouraged by any advance towards intercommunion: there must be no lessening of the tie to the local church, or to its sacramental life. Any measures which tended to impoverish their 'high-churchmanship' Congregationalists would have to resist with all the spiritual means at their disposal.

So it becomes clear, in the third place, that what is being rightly asked for and discussed under the term 'intercommunion' is primarily a regular and recognised provision for certain pastoral and spiritual emergencies. We may put the matter quite concretely, and ask: 'What is to happen if, say, an Anglican finds himself in a place where there is no church of his communion within reach: is he to be deprived of all communion in the life of God's people, the Church, on earth?' The first thing that needs to be affirmed is that such a Christian is never entirely outside the 'communion' of his Church, or of the Church of Christ here on earth. By his past admission to the 'congregation of Christ's flock', he has been made, and inviolably remains (unless he deny

[7] See the evidence set out in Bell: *Documents on Christian Unity*, Vols. 1-3.

his own status) a member of the Church, sharing, in some degree, in its life. At the very lowest he is part of that Church of Christ for which prayer is made daily; and, as we have seen, such prayer is part of the 'communion' of the church. But even more must be affirmed. Such a member would not be excluded, even by the Church of Rome, from attendance upon the preaching of the Word; and even Rome, with some other Churches, is prepared to admit non-members to the worship of the Mass, though not to the reception of bread and wine. But if any Church is thus willing to let members from other Churches share in the preaching of the Word, it has already admitted such a member to 'communion' with itself; at any rate in that sense of the word which represents its richest meaning as depicting the communion of Christians with their Lord in the Church.

This leads directly to the question which the Commission on Intercommunion has been facing in these past years: why is it that even though Churches are normally willing to admit other Christians to the preaching of the Word, they are very often unwilling to admit them to partake of bread and wine at the ordinance of the Lord's Supper? Let us for a moment return to the imaginary Anglican away from the ministry of the churches of his order. His 'needs' in the sacramental life of the Church will vary somewhat with the tradition of that part of the Anglican tradition from which he comes. He may find it a deprivation not to be able to make his communion daily: he may not experience deprivation until he is forced to miss one weekly celebration on Sunday: he may not himself be aware of his need until Easter Day or Christmas Eve comes round. These empirical facts are all real elements in the situation and need to be taken into consideration in any judgment made to accommodate ecclesiastical laws or customs to such emergencies. The problem for individual Christians will vary greatly. For some, a daily communion is necessary; for some weekly, for some monthly, for some quarterly or even less frequently. But this does not of itself raise any deep issue of principle.

But a fundamental issue is not far away. It is this. In any such given pastoral or spiritual emergency the problem has perforce to be raised locally, but decision about admission to participation in the bread and wine at the Lord's Supper is not, in many Churches, decided locally. To a Congregationalist, of course, a plea for local decision on what must be a strictly local problem is a very natural one. Can it be shown a persuasive one to Christians of other traditions? I think it can. Already the Orthodox Churches have a doctrine of 'economy' which covers such emergency action, and what this article would plead for is the widespread adoption by Christian Churches of such a doctrine of 'economy' as would enable the local priests or presbyters or ministers of those Churches to admit to participation in the Sacrament of the Lord's Supper such communicant members of other Christian Churches as are known to be in real pastoral or spiritual emergency. Have we, in fact, been trying to do the wrong thing in making intercommunion the result of what might be called 'treaty relationships' between Churches? Does not that very process of treaty relationship presuppose that what is being asked for is more than the emergency intercommunion which Congregationalists must affirm is the only valid intercommunion; any other suffers from the defect of lessening the integrity of the individual member in his relationship to his local church.

The objection to this is, of course, that a doctrine of 'economy' to meet pastoral and spiritual emergency not only presupposes the existing disunity and divisions of Christendom, but does nothing to overcome them. That is not quite true. Clearly, divided Churches that were willing to practise a mutual 'economy' towards each other's sacramentally deprived members would be in a very different, and far more positive, relationship from those same Churches not practising a mutual 'economy'. Further, while the practice of mutual economy would not of itself be a move towards reunion, that would, surely, be itself a gain. Is there not something inherently wrong in trying to keep two quite separate issues fused forcibly and artificially into one? The two issues can be put into two concrete questions that Christians ask in quite different circumstances, and with quite different intentions. The first, which we have examined, is 'Why may I not, being away from all possible sacramental ministration of my Church for such a length of time as will be a burden to me, fully share with some other Christian Church in the Sacrament of the Lord's Supper?' The other question, a very different one, not asked by all Christians, but increasingly by very many, is: 'Why may not Christians of the various Churches share together from time to time in observing the Sacrament of the Lord's Supper or Holy Communion?' This volume has provided Christians the world over with many weighty and, let it be confessed, depressing reasons why this latter thing may not be done.

But even here there is a question to be asked. It is widely held that the Eucharist, or Holy Communion, or the Lord's Supper, is the sacrament of unity. But is there not even now a unity that exists even in the midst of all our divisions? I ask this question, not that our differences should be slurred over, or that we should come to any lighthearted or cheap decision to do certain things together. But is not one of the most amazing mysteries of the life of the Church that, in its dreadful and sinful dividing of Christ's body, He has never disowned any of us, but that we all, precisely in our separate and therefore mutilated bodies still bear some marks of His 'communion' with us, both in and outside the Sacrament of the Lord's Supper. Now it seems to a Reformed churchman that in a Church so divided, this deep unity, which is nothing less than Christ Himself as the deep reality of all the Churches' life, is 'gospel' or good news. And being such, it is something which has to be 'proclaimed' or 'preached'. But the Gospel can never be properly presented to men in words only: the 'seals' of the sacraments attach to the Gospel, and it has been one of the chief aims of reformed churchmanship to bring Word and Sacrament properly together. Can we expect to present to men the present deep and true unity of the Church by means of words only? Or ought we not to see that this thing which, in however dim a form, we are beginning to *say* in all our divided Churches must be *done* in them, or by them together, as well? Perhaps it has always been possible, even in the darkest days of division, for theologians to speak of the deep unity of the Church in Christ. Indeed we could not read the New Testament and fail to do so. But now, in this twentieth century, we can talk not merely theoretically about that unity, but we can speak of it out of some partial though not yet full experience. And if we can now begin to 'speak of that which we know' we should surely be nearer to acting upon that unity which the Sacrament of the Lord's Supper most clearly sets forth. Is it possible for a Church simply to 'talk' of her unity with other Christians in Christ: is not 'Word' here, as everywhere, properly joined with 'Sacrament'?

With that question I would not be thought to plead for sacramental promiscuity or lack of seriousness. To the end this article pleads that the proper place of sacramental experience for the individual Christian is in his own local church. But to-day the local church is not an isolated unit, but part of a denomination, probably part of a world communion, and possibly a part of the World Council of Churches. How can we bring all this truth home to our people. By sermons on such themes? By the Word only? Or ought our minds to think of intercommunion as related to union in a new way, neither as a means to corporate union, nor as an effect of achieved corporate unity, but rather as the proper 'shewing forth' (in St. Paul's phrase) to ourselves and to the world of the true, deep and *given* unity of the Church in Jesus Christ her Lord. If Christians work together for the unity of the Church in conferences, the Anglican Church will permit its priests to invite fellow workers of other Churches to participate fully in her form of Holy Communion. Can such imaginative permission be extended to local churches who in penitence, prayer, thought and discussion have worked together, say during the annual Octave of Prayer for Unity, for the union of Christendom?

These are bold and certainly difficult thoughts, but at present our discussions seem to have brought us to a deadlock. Can anything fruitful come of a Congregational comment that perhaps we have been seeing intercommunion and union in a false relationship? and that now we should try to discuss it in two forms: first, as a practice of mutual economy for spiritual and pastoral emergencies; and second, as a practice of setting forth to ourselves and to the world not only a new and potent reminder of our dividedness, but also a new, hopeful and sacramental declaration of our true and deep unity in Jesus Christ our Lord.

XV

INTERCOMMUNION IN THE GERMAN EVANGELICAL CHURCH

★

Wilhelm Niesel

Evangelical Church in Germany (Reformed)

(Germany)

In no country has there been so much contention about the union of Protestantism at the Lord's Table as there has been in Germany. It was here at Marburg that the discussions between Luther and Zwingli took place in 1529. It was here that those militant Lutherans had their home, who attacked and rejected even those doctrines of Calvin about the Eucharist which were consonant with Lutheran aims, so that the Genevan reformer had to take up his pen against them on more than one occasion in concern for the unity of the Church. It was here, too, that the discussions took place in the seventeenth and eighteenth centuries between the Lutheran and the Reformed, discussions which were in principle about the Eucharist, in deed about eucharistic doctrine. If the two parties to those discussions had at that time reached an understanding, then union at the Lord's Table and a state of full intercommunion between the Churches would have been attained.

After Pietism and Rationalism had impoverished orthodoxy in one place and another, a union of Lutheran and Reformed was reached. This came about under strong pressure from the German Princes in connection with the secular celebration of the Reformation in 1817, in a number of provincial Churches, among them the great Prussian Church. This union found its visible expression in a common celebration of the Eucharist. In Berlin, under the leadership of Schleiermacher, the Pastorate arranged a celebration with a common rite; the churches and the court followed suit. But in spite of this union, the local churches, in Prussia and elsewhere, kept to their traditional confessions of faith, in so far as they had not yet expressly acknowledged the common elements in both Reformation confessions of faith. By this accession to Union the local churches were only meant to show, under a common church government, 'the spirit of moderation and gentleness'. It was otherwise in Baden and the Palatinate. In both these provincial Churches the union was so concluded as expressly to formulate an unanimity upon questions about the Eucharist. So it is stated in the deed of union in the Palatinate: 'The points of doctrine previously in dispute are now settled on well based principles, by a judgment in conformity with a clear deliverance of the Gospel. Accordingly the Protestant-Evangelical-Christian Church declares that the Holy Eucharist is a feast of commemoration of Jesus and of the most blessed union with him who was given to death for men, raised from the dead, and taken up to his father and our father, as the saviour of man, who also abides with them always even to the end of the world.' It is understandable that such a formula was not recognised elsewhere as a solution of the problem. The stubborn struggles of the Reformers and their successors would be quite incomprehensible if all that divided them in eucharistic problems could have been charmed away by so easy a gesture!

It was in quite another way that the problem of the Eucharist again became a living issue in Germany when, in 1933, under pressure from the State, the different United and Lutheran Churches, and the two small Reformed Provincial Churches were comprised into one German Evangelical Church, and yet in such a way that each provincial Church retained its independence in liturgy and doctrine. There now broke out a persecution of the true Churches which opposed the invasion of the Churches' life by the State. And during this persecution Eucharists were celebrated from time to time at which members from all the provincial Churches took part, even from the most strictly Lutheran. In this situation of flying from the Gestapo—as we experienced it in a free Synod—to the Lord's Table, differences in eucharistic doctrine did not matter at all. But that was only in such 'emergencies'. If the emergency had not been so great, then the question of intercommunion would have been recognised as a real problem in the Confessional Church. Neither at the great Confessional Synods in which delegates from all the Provincial Churches were united, nor even at the Synod of 1934 in Barmen, which composed the famous 'Declaration', was it possible to have a common celebration of the Eucharist.

Many people regarded this fact as a scandal. And so in the very middle of the worst oppression of the Church by the State there arose the desire to clarify the question of intercommunion. In the largest Union Church, the Prussian, a special session of the Confessional Synod was called for this purpose only. It met in Halle in 1937, and dealt exclusively with the Confessional question, in particular with the question of intercommunion. In this largest provincial Church in Germany—it comprises about half of all German Protestants—there has been intercommunion between Lutheran and Reformed since 1817. But this ecclesiastical union was carried through under the guidance of, and indeed under pressure by, the civil authority. In any case there was at that time no real unity established between Lutherans and Reformed on the questions that divided them. But now that the meaning of Confession had been recognised anew in the Churches' struggle, that past failure was felt to be both difficult and burdensome. Accordingly the Synod of Halle concluded: 'Intercommunion . . . is not justified by the state existing in the Union.' On the basis of I Cor. 10. 16 f. the Synod testified:

'Jesus Christ, our Lord and Saviour, who for our sakes became flesh, and offered himself once for all on the cross for us, and is risen bodily from the dead, is himself the gracious gift of the church's Eucharist which he instituted.'

And then it continued — surprisingly at the wish of the Lutherans:

'The differences that obtain between us in eucharistic doctrine concern the nature and manner of the Lord's communicating of himself in the Eucharist. They are not concerned at all as to whether the Lord himself is the Eucharistic gift.' So the fact of belonging to another Reformed Church constitutes no ground for exclusion from the celebration of the Eucharist. 'Therefore open communions do not stand . . . in contradiction to the scriptural administration of the Holy Communion.'

This decision did not create any new situation in the great united Prussian provincial Church. But what at one time took place partly under State pressure, and partly by putting aside serious problems in a certain temper of enthusiasm, now was thoroughly discussed in complete openness and brotherly concord. All members of Synod, whatever Confession they belonged to, came to the recognition that the same gift was distributed to them in the Eucharist: Jesus Christ Himself, and that this fact was the sole and effective ground for intercommunion, as over against their conception of the Eucharist. Were the representatives of both confessions to think entirely differently about the nature and manner of Christ's presence in the Eucharist, that could be no ground, in face of the gracious gift of this feast, for exclusion from the Lord's Table. That this difference could not be overcome in this Synod, but persisted throughout, remained a burden. But this burden had still to be carried, in face of the one common Lord. Precisely because of this, Lutheran and Reformed joined together in praising at His Table the Lord who had been so merciful to their understanding. It must of course be noted that *some* Lutherans understood the proclaimed intercommunion only in the sense that church members of another confession are admitted to the Eucharist, but not in the sense that ministers of different Confessions could celebrate the Eucharist together.

This decision applied only to the Prussian United Church, though it could have been helpful to all the provincial Churches. Yet it was nevertheless immediately *rejected by the representatives of the strict Lutheran provincial Churches*. The Halle Synod in no sense tried to solve the difficulties confronting them. There was no easing for their conscience, but only new difficulties, since the Synod had declared the differences between the Confessions to be inessential. 'The Lutheran Churches on the other hand testify first and last the truly corporeal presence (the Real Presence) of its Lord in the Sacrament, on the basis of the clear words of holy scripture, and it cannot, without new responsible discussions with the Reformed Church, accept the position that the outstanding differences between the Lutheran and Reformed Churches do not concern the issue that the Lord himself is the gift of the Eucharist.' There the matter rested. Unity with these Provincial Lutheran Churches was not achieved during the church struggle. There was indeed little occasion for it, since different ways were pursued in the conflict with the State, and the two wings of the Confessional Church had as yet only little contact with each other.

In 1945 the situation was otherwise, when we confronted the task of ordering anew the relationships of the different provincial

Churches, out of which, under pressure from the State, one German Evangelical Church had come. In the course of negotiations the following decision was reached at Treysa in 1947: 'Unanimity obtains on this point, that members of Evangelical Churches shall not be excluded from the celebration of the Eucharist just because they belong to another Confession in the Evangelical Church in Germany.' Nothing was said about the grounds for this proposition. The Synod of Halle had done that and maintained that because of the eucharistic gift there should be intercommunion at the Lord's Table. Now the leading Lutherans subscribed to this announced conclusion only indeed in the conviction that, for love's sake, no Reformed church member should be kept from Communion. But this concession was taken back again when a year later the Church Assembly at Eisenach had to conclude a basic order for the Evangelical Church in Germany. Leading representatives of the Lutheran Churches did not see themselves able to affirm that access to the Lord's Table in their Churches was freely open to Reformed and United church members. Only in districts where a Reformed or United member had no church of his own communion within reasonable distance, or where some other spiritual emergency arose, ought the member to be admitted to Communion in a Lutheran church. Although other Lutherans with different judgments gave very strong expression to the view that this did not go far enough, and that there should be a real intercommunion in the German Evangelical Church, the others did not see themselves in a position to pass beyond the prescribed and customary practices of their Churches for admission to Communion. In consequence no regulations on this important point could appear in the basic constitution of the Evangelical Church in Germany, but it could only be stated what practice obtained in the different Provincial Churches. Thus Article 4, 4 reads:

'There is no complete unanimity in the Evangelical Church in Germany on admission to Holy Communion. In many constituent churches members of another recognised confession of the Evangelical Church in Germany are admitted without restriction. In no constituent church is access to the Lord's Table denied to a member of a recognised confession of the Evangelical Church in Germany in cases where pastoral responsibility or church relationship commend it. The integrity of church membership and the application of ecclesiastical discipline remains in every case unaffected.'

What does this development have to teach in regard to inter-communion between Lutheran and Reformed?

(a) Intercommunion is not dependent on church 'constitution'. All the territorial Churches in Germany that attested their decision to come together in the Evangelical Church in Germany have therein provided themselves, within certain limits, with a common ecclesiastical constitution: 'The basic constitution of the Evangelical Church in Germany.' In spite of that the majority of Lutheran territorial Churches admit members of other confessions to Communion only in cases of special pastoral need. 'There is no complete unanimity on the admission to Holy Communion.'

(b) The same thing applies in respect of church government. The Evangelical Church in Germany has one Synod, and for the times when the Synod is not in session, a Council with quite definite prescribed powers. These are not far reaching; but they are available. So, within these limits, there is in the Evangelical Church in Germany one church government, and yet no complete intercommunion.

(c) What divides is, first and last, according to the strict Lutheran, eucharistic doctrine. Were full intercommunion to be observed, that would, in their opinion, come very near to invalidating Lutheran eucharistic doctrine. These Lutherans are convinced 'that the preaching of the Gospel and the celebration of the Sacraments which follow from the Confession of the Reformed Church mean in certain respects an obscuring of the means of grace, and therewith in certain respects a hindrance on the way to salvation.' 'But if at the Last Day even one soul should have been lost because it could not hear the full consolation of the gospel as a result of the invalidating of the doctrines peculiar to the Lutheran confession, then that soul will be required of them who have acquiesced in such an invalidation of specific Lutheran doctrine.' So it was emphasised in the Church Assembly at Eisenach that the exclusion of other Protestants from Lutheran Communion did not constitute an act of ecclesiastical discipline. It was much more an act of pastoral care and indeed of love. Clearly the others against whom such a barrier is erected are meant to be brought to reflection on this matter of the Communion.

(*d*) The other Lutherans are of the persuasion that the conviction which is shared with the Reformed, that Jesus Christ Himself is the gracious gift of the Eucharist, abundantly makes possible intercommunion at the Lord's Table. They let the *Confessio Augustana* simply stand: *De coena Domini docent, quod corpus et sanguis Christi vere adsint et distribuantur vescentibus in coena Domini; et improbant secus docentes,* and give up all claim to demand from the Reformed any assent to the particular Lutheran conception of the manner and mode of this presence of Christ.

(*e*) Why the strict Lutherans are not ready to do this is indicated above. But it is very difficult to make the necessity of this position clear to those who are not theologians. A leading Lutheran openly stated in Eisenach that he was much concerned that he and his friends could not make themselves intelligible to the laymen. In fact this brings to light a great need. For theology ought never to become an esoteric science, above all when it brings practical consequences of such gravity that on the basis of its reading of confessional documents it forbids others access to the Lord's Table. Here the provision of clear and universally intelligible information is a necessity. If this matter is fought for by a group of ministers, and is not a responsibility shared with the churches, something decisive is out of order.

(*f*) But it is not only theological grounds that prevent intercommunion between many Lutherans and Reformed or United churchmen. There is a concern lest there should be a severance from World Lutheranism if intercommunion with other Protestants is entered on in Germany. So it is often pointed out that there must first be an understanding about eucharistic doctrine with the Reformed that is sanctioned by the other Lutheran Churches in the world, before intercommunion can be established in Germany. Here it becomes quite plain what a decisive significance ecumenical conversations can have for the relationships of confessions in many lands. The fact that leading Lutherans took part in the Reformed celebration of Holy Communion on the occasion of the World Council of Churches Assembly in Amsterdam surprised all the German delegates at the time. The implications of that have not yet been worked out in Germany.

(*g*) In the Church Assembly which formulated the constitution at Eisenach, 1948, the Bishop of a Lutheran provincial Church said we were on the way to a common understanding in eucharistic doctrine on the basis of the New Testament. Indeed, from that time a considerable loosening of an immobile front followed. Already at the beginning of this century a theologian could claim that the work of theology had led to the result 'that no one considered the formulation which dogma found in the sixteenth century applicable *simpliciter*'. That is much more emphatically true to-day. So with the consent of the Council of the Evangelical Church in Germany a commission of theologians has been meeting for some time to try to assess the significance of the work on the New Testament in the last few decades for eucharistic doctrine. A first report of this Commission is now printed and the discussion, in which theologians of both confessions shared, goes on. We hope that this work will show whether the contemporary practice of Communion in the Evangelical Church in Germany can be vindicated and must be borne with, because we still learn different things from the testimony of Scripture, or whether in light of the New Testament the situation between Lutheran and Reformed is not really essentially different from what it was in the sixteenth century. So could the tensions of the German situation prove fruitful for the question of intercommunion between the Churches of the *Oekumene*.

(*h*) I am personally of the opinion, on the basis of what we experienced in the Church's struggles, that the issues which still remain between many Lutherans and others recede into the background if the Churches are really aware that they live in the time of the End. In the Churches' struggle the eschatological situation of the Church was at certain points quite clear, and intercommunion at the Lord's Table was given to us. I think not only of that Eucharist which Martin Niemoller celebrated in the Concentration Camp at Dachau for a small congregation gathered from members of very different denominations, but also of that unforgettable celebration in the Reinoldi Church in Dortmund to which I have referred, which took place at a particularly critical moment in the church struggle, in which delegates of the different provincial Churches took part. Perhaps the Lord will have to take us into His school once more, so that we do not merely know theoretically, but perceive, that He is near; and that in spite of all our differences we are all called to His eschatological feast together.

XVI

INTERCOMMUNION AND CHURCH UNITY

*

John W. Sadiq

Church of South India

(India)

The question of intercommunion must not and cannot be treated in isolation. It is deeply involved with the wider question of the function of the Christian ministry, the nature of the Christian Church, nay, with the true meaning of the Christian faith, in fact, with the Christian Gospel itself. The best way of dealing with the subject is to do so in the context of the question of Church Unity which takes account of these and other relevant subjects. In what follows, therefore, some reference to those wider questions will be necessary, though, it is hoped that for the most part attention will be concentrated on the question under consideration.

Before the writer gives his own considered views on inter-communion, it may be useful for him to give at the outset a few observations arising out of the historical and geographical background of the church situation from which he comes.

Long before the church reunion movement in India became an ongoing concern, two guiding principles of Christian action had become fairly effectively operative in most non-Roman Churches and missions, namely, comity and co-operation.

The first meant, in the words of Bishop Lesslie Newbigin, 'that in any one place—town or village—there is normally but one Christian congregation, and upon this congregation rests the responsibility for the evangelisation of the area allotted to it under the principles of comity'.[1] But, again, 'Where there is only one congregation, it is impossible for its members to escape from the solemn recollection that on the day of judgment it is they and

[1] *The Reunion of the Church*, J. E. Lesslie Newbigin, S.C.M., p. 15.

they alone who can be questioned about their neighbours who had never heard the good news.'[2] This pressing consciousness of missionary obligation, with which the Christian Church in India is blessed because of the fact that it is surrounded by a vast sea of the non-Christian world, and by forces, linguistic, communal, religious and sectarian, which make for serious division among people of that vast sub-continent, is a factor of utmost significance.

In this connection two further observations may be made. The lack of intercommunion does not merely weaken the force of Christian witness, but proves a positive stumbling block to the intending recipient of the Gospel. One of the most outstanding examples of this latter situation, though many more could be given, is the one in 1935 when the Depressed class community, under its leader Dr. Ambedkar, had announced its decision to renounce Hinduism and to seek another faith, but refused the offer of the Christian Church because there was no unity in the Church. The words of Dr. Ambedkar to Bishop Azariah were as follows: 'At present we are one community all over India and our strength is in our unity. Can you in the Christian Church offer us any unity comparable to that? Have you one body that we can join as one people?' If it is argued that the main stumbling-block was a lack of unity and not intercommunion, it may be answered to the mind of an average non-Christian, and for that matter to the mind of an average Christian, it is not the lack of organic unity, but the lack of fellowship, possible through interchange of pulpit and common participation in the Lord's Supper, that is a scandal and an offence. Bishop Stephen Neill has reminded us that we can exaggerate the sensitiveness of the non-Christian to the existence of different Christian bodies. But sensitiveness to the lack of fellowship as evidenced by the lack of intercommunion can never be exaggerated or overestimated.

It is not, however, merely with reference to the evangelistic task of the Church, that the tragedy of the situation faces us, but also from the point of view of the life of the Christian community itself. The disillusionment and even apathy which has resulted from the lack of this fellowship in the Church can hardly be estimated. We constantly sing in the Church: 'The Church's one foundation is Jesus Christ the Lord', and yet by our practice we

[2] *Ibid.*, p. 15 n.

flout His express will that we all should be one. It is not too much to say that in youth conferences this disillusionment often becomes evident. For in these conferences more than anywhere else Christian young men and women, belonging to different parts of the country and different church affiliations, meet and experience a fellowship which they had probably never dreamed of. Very often a spontaneous suggestion is made that they should seal their fellowship by an act of common participation in the Holy Communion. And then they are up against the tragic fact of the impossibility of such a participation. It is not surprising that an S.C.M. conference wanted to pass a resolution to the effect that the Church Union should take place in three years.[3] Here is an agonising story from a servant of Christ. Let Paul S. Kadambavanam say it in his own words:

'I will never also forget the sad and the most unpleasant experience I had in my life once. Some ten years ago I had the rare privilege of conducting a big mass meeting on a Sunday morning in a big city in South India. Hundreds of people were present and the whole service was left in my hands. This was followed by the Holy Communion service. As I belonged to another Church I had to leave this church and come away with a sad and heavy heart. In the sermon I spoke of service for our country, and union, fellowship and love for our countrymen, but in the very next minute I found that I could not put them into practice. I had to damp the spirit of God that was moving me and was compelled to disobey "the voice of God". I mean the conscience that was pressing within me. I felt I was kicked out of God's presence for the simple mistake of not being a member of that Church, for which I was not, in any sense, responsible. There I realised that "Church" stands between a sinner and God.'[4]

The same tragic fact may be exemplified in another situation. Take the case of a family with several members all living in an area allotted to a particular Church. By reason of necessity a part of the family has to migrate to another area covered by a different Church. In such a situation the choice is often reduced to either disregarding the church rules, or going without spiritual ministra-

[3] Quoted in *The Indirect Effects of Christian Missions in India*, R. S. Wilson, pp. 81-82 (James Clarke and Co. Ltd.).
[4] *Ibid.*

tions. The third choice of changing church affiliation is not a very happy one, because if they have to return to their original home for any length of time, it might mean a change again. The Church becomes a mockery, and it may be accused of putting asunder those whom God has joined together.

The second guiding principle which has been operative is that of co-operation. It had begun to take shape even in the early stages of mission work in India. Since the establishment of the National Christian Council it has become a widely accepted principle in the non-Roman Christian enterprise in India. It need hardly be said that when Christians, however divided by church affiliations, meet together for prayer, consultation and planning, many prejudices and misunderstandings are shed. When the bodies concerned are driven to discuss the basis and purpose of their existence—and this they must do because of the very surroundings in which they live in a country like India—they cannot but come to the conclusion that whatever hinders the preaching of the Gospel must, if necessary, be sacrificed. In this connection the following section of the findings adopted by the Madras Representative Christian Council—strictly speaking matters of church polity and church unity do not come within the purview of a Christian Council—at its meeting held on 16th-18th August 1933 is of special interest.

'The discussion revealed the belief that in spite of the apparent divisions of the Church in South India, a large measure of unity can even now be said to exist. It was felt that this unity should not express itself in any form of organic union which involves a rigid constitution with uniformity of worship, because such an organisation would be contrary to the genius of India. A very simple form of organisation, allowing for wide diversity of belief and practice and making possible the unity into one body of all who believe in the Lord Jesus Christ commends itself to the Indian mind. Some feel that this unity of all believers should begin with and particularly express itself in common participation in the Lord's Supper.'

This co-operation has helped forward the reunion movement, and India can to-day be humbly proud of the measure of union which has been achieved through the coming into existence of the Church of South India.

After these background statements which the writer has given with his comments, it may be readily seen that he is in favour of intercommunion even at this stage of the divided state of the Church. A briefly reasoned statement of his views may be given in the following few paragraphs.

It is matter of history that in the early Church the basis of exclusion from the Holy Eucharist was either the immaturity, in age or preparation, of the catechumen, or unworthiness due to commission of some sin punishable with such exclusion. No requirement as to the theory about the ministry or the sacraments on the part of the communicants is on record. Confession of faith in our Lord, and the acceptance of this faith through Baptism in the name of the Holy Trinity, with due further preparation, seem to be all that was required. Why, then, do Churches exclude one another on other grounds? Why this departure from the practice of the early Church? It seems to the writer that those who invite 'all those who love the Lord Jesus and are members of any branch of the Christian Church' to participate in the Lord's Supper are certainly in line with the practice of the early Church. The early Church knew the mind of the Master better than we can ever hope to know it.

Secondly, the practice of intercommunion between Churches prior to organic union is not unknown. The case of the Church of England in relation to the Old Catholic Church and the Church of Sweden is a case in point, though other instances may be cited. This meets the argument that intercommunion should result from rather than precede organic union. Moreover it seems superfluous to say that intercommunion should follow organic union, because the very word intercommunion loses its meaning once organic union has been reached.

Thirdly, often special permission is given by a church authority to its people, ministerial and lay, under special circumstances, to give and to receive Holy Communion in churches other than their own. This certainly happens in India. During war conditions this has been witnessed in a more radical way. This means that while the matter of church discipline may be involved, there is nothing *inherently* wrong in intercommunion. In fact, if exceptions are demanded by necessity, then it must be essentially right, for the Divine grace must cover all genuine human needs.

Fourthly, if it is argued that it is dishonest to intercommunicate when there is no real unity, the answer may be given that if the church divisions are not only 'unhappy' but 'sinful', then to pretend that fellowship in a 'mutilated' body is genuine seems even more dishonest.

Fifthly, it is significant that two of the uniting bodies in the South India scheme, namely the South India United Church and the Methodist Church, suggested strongly the practice of intercommunion among the negotiating bodies even before the Union. The resolution of S.I.U.C. at its sixteenth Assembly reads thus:

'Resolved that as a confirmation of the mutual recognition of the Ministers of the Word and Sacraments in the three negotiating Churches, so clearly expressed in different ways in the Basis of Union and in the governing principles of the Church, the General Assembly urges the Joint Committee to take steps to secure the adoption of the practice of intercommunion and intercelebration between the negotiating Churches before union. The Assembly believes that if this is done, one of the chief obstacles to Union would be removed.'

And the resolution of the South India Provincial Synod of the Methodist Church, dated January 1929, reads:

'In our judgment, it will help greatly to increase the spirit of unity between the consulting Churches, and within our own Church to win the mind of our people, if, even before union is consummated, united worship, and especially intercommunion between the consulting Churches, can be made possible. The absence of intercommunion at this time constitutes a most formidable obstacle to union in the minds of many of our people.'

These affirmations further confirm the conviction earlier expressed about the adverse spiritual effects of the absence of intercommunion. Moreover, the fact that both in the scheme of reunion in North India and in the Ceylon scheme the immediate unification of the ministries is envisaged at the inauguration of the union, clearly signifies that intercommunion is not dependent upon any one particular theory of the ministry. We need not therefore be deterred by insistence on complete unanimity in regard to the doctrine of the Christian ministry, which doctrine is one of the causes of division. Here is the voice of a representative group of Indian Christian laymen as far back as 1920:

'That this Conference of Indian Christians consisting of members belonging to the Anglican, Wesleyan, Lutheran, Baptist, Presbyterian, S.I.U.C. denominations, held at Bangalore, is of opinion that the several denominations of the Christian Church are in all essential respects within the one Catholic Church, and that in the interests of true Christian fellowship and for the extension of the Kingdom of Christ in this land, a recognition of the equal status of the denominations within the one Church of Christ, and their ministries as of equal validity, is necessary.

'That such recognition should be given effect to along the following lines:

'(a) Ministers may receive due authorisation to minister fully and freely in the churches of other denominations, it being understood that the above authorisation is not to be regarded as reordination or as repudiation of the present position of their ministers as validly ordained. Ministration would mean preaching (interchange of pulpits) and administration of sacraments.

'(b) All the denominations should recognise fully the members of one another and admit them to the Lord's Table. . . .'

Finally, in the voice of the people and the Churches in India, the Holy Spirit Himself, the writer believes, has been speaking, and the consummation of the Union in South India is a seal and sign that the desire for fellowship through intercommunion is one of the surest steps to that fuller unity which is the will of Christ for His Church. The organic unity of the whole of Christendom is yet a far distant dream; but one step is clear, and that is the way of intercommunion. 'Drink ye all of this' is the clear injunction of the Master. If we take that step then we may hope to see the way clearer to the fulfilment of the agonising prayer of the Lord 'that they all might be one . . . that the world may believe', for as Bishop Newbigin has reminded us, 'the connection between the movement for Christian reunion and the movement for world evangelisation is of the deepest possible character. The two things are the two outward signs of a return to the heart of the Gospel itself.'[5]

[5] *The Reunion of the Church*, Newbigin, p. 19.

XVII

LORD'S SUPPER OR CHURCH'S SUPPER

*

Edmund Schlink

Evangelical Church in Germany (Lutheran)

(Germany)

This question is the expression of the great confusion and desperate need of contemporary Christianity. It contains a multiplicity of problems. If I attempted to deal systematically with them, let alone to answer them, it would require a book rather than the space to which I am limited. I therefore want to confine myself to a chain of thought in the form of a few theses, which I can only prove in part in this context, making quite clear the incomplete character of the following analysis.

The Lord's Supper

The celebration of the Lord's Supper takes place between the meal Jesus shared with His disciples 'in the night in which He was betrayed', and the meal to come in the Kingdom of God, which the returning Lord will enjoy with His own. Both these meals are mentioned by Jesus in the words of institution of the Holy Communion. We share in both at the celebration of the Lord's Supper. As according to the word of Jesus the gift of the Maundy Thursday meal consisted in His body and His blood, so also the body and blood of the Crucified is the gift which the risen Lord grants us in the Lord's Supper. As the gift of the meal in the Kingdom of God will be the joy as it were of a wedding feast, of eternal communion of the resurrected faithful with the returned Lord, so in the Lord's Supper we already share here on earth in that future glory. In the Lord's Supper we are present at the death of Christ and at His return, at His first and second advent.

The Lord's Supper is 'the communion of the body of Christ' (I Cor. 10. 16). Those who partake of the body and blood of Christ are made one body with Him. Through His gift of His body and His blood the risen Lord is building up on earth His body, the Church. As there is *one* Lord, *one* Church, *one* body, fellowship at the Lord's Supper belongs to the essence of the Church. 'Since there is one loaf we who are many are one body, for we all share in that one loaf' (I Cor. 10. 17).

The celebration of the Lord's Supper takes place during the Church's pilgrimage from the first to the second advent. The Church has preserved the Apostles' records of Christ's institution of the Lord's Supper; it prepares the meal in which the crucified and returning Lord gives Himself to us. It calls us to that Supper to which the Lord Himself bids us through its invitation. Thus the Church is not only built up in the Lord's Supper; ever since it was built on the foundation of the Apostles by the pouring out of the Holy Spirit at Pentecost, it has been prior to our celebrations of the Lord's Supper.

The Church rightly excludes from the Lord's Supper those who are not yet or no longer members of the Church, either because they have rejected the baptism whereby the sinner is 'baptised into Christ Jesus' (Rom. 6. 3), 'baptised into one body' (I Cor. 12. 13), thus becoming a member of the Church; or because, having been baptised, they have fallen away from Christ through unbelief or wickedness.

Lord's Supper or Church's Supper?

There is no legitimate 'either-or', for the Lord's Supper is essentially the meal of fellowship of the body of Christ and therefore of the Church. Lord's Supper and Church's Supper are not opposed to each other. This, however, only holds good as long as the Church, remaining the receiver, hands on the tradition of the institution of the Lord's Supper, prepares its celebration and 'proclaims the Lord's death till He come' (I Cor. 11. 26). Faith, in spite of all wrestling and calling, clinging and confessing, is essentially an act of receiving; so with the dispensation of the Lord's Supper through the Church. The Church is the place, the creation and the instrument of the Lord's Supper but never its Lord. For that reason the New Testament calls the Last Supper 'the Lord's Supper', not 'the Church's Supper', and certainly it testifies that the body of Christ is the gift of the Supper as well as the reality of the Church.

The 'either-or' of Lord's Supper or Church's Supper presupposes a certain degeneration. On the one hand, this can consist in seeing in the Lord's Supper solely a gift of Christ to the individual, giving it an individualistic misinterpretation. In that case the nature of the Church as the fellowship of Christ created through the common reception of the body of Christ is disregarded and the gulf between the Church and the world, or rather between Church and pseudo-Church is overlooked. In that case we must ask whether this is still the Lord's Supper. On the other hand, we find degeneration where the Church departs from its function as receiver and server of the Lord's Supper and makes itself lord of the Lord's Supper. This can happen through self-invented doctrines of the Holy Communion, through arbitrary orders for celebration or through an autocratic practice of admission to and exclusion from Holy Communion, etc., in short, through supplementing and distorting the apostolic tradition. Here again we have to ask whether this is still a celebration of the Lord's Supper or whether the Church has not become assimilated to the world's religion. This 'either-or' can only apply to a distorted Lord's Supper and a distorted Church's Supper. Over against this 'either-or' stands the true Lord's Supper, which is the meal of fellowship of the body of Christ and therefore also the meal of the receiving and worshipping Church.

The Ecumenical Encounter

This, however, does not yet settle the question of 'Lord's Supper' or 'Church's Supper'. For Christianity to-day is split into many Churches which deny participation in the Lord's Supper to each other. We cannot denounce all those who celebrate the Lord's Supper apart from the communion of our own Church as not being receivers and members of the body of Christ, neither can we denounce those who desire intercommunion beyond the limits of their own Churches as individualists who misjudge the ecclesiological significance of Holy Communion and therefore distort the Lord's Supper. For the very fact which is shaping the present generation of Christians with an intensity hitherto hardly equalled in church history is this: while we have found brothers in Christ and members of the body of Christ beyond the limits of our own denominations where we had not expected to find them, yet, in spite of the reality of our communion in Christ, it seems impossible to share the Lord's Supper with them. We have heard the voice of the Good Shepherd through such brothers in times of persecution and we have seen suffering in the name of Jesus those whom for many reasons we had not recognised as brothers until then. Moreover at ecumenical conferences we have confessed with them before all the world Christ as the Lord of lords, and the unity of His body, the one Holy Church. We recognise with deep sorrow and with great shame that, in spite of the unity which we believe exists, we are separated by barriers which prevent the members of the various confessions from celebrating the Lord's Supper together: the teaching and order of our own Church may hinder us from inviting others or accepting the invitation of others, or the teaching and order of another Church may make it impossible for us to share in their celebration of the Lord's Supper. Thus brothers may not unite though they have recognised their unity! This situation is the more shattering the more lively is our certainty of the return of our Lord who is coming. Then Jesus Christ the Shepherd will gather His flock to the great Supper in the Kingdom of God and as our judge will question us all at the same time why we on earth have not celebrated one Supper as one flock, why through schisms we have blasphemed the majesty of His name before all the world.

The more certainly we recognise members of the body of Christ in other denominations and the more strongly we are united with them by the love of Christ, the more radically we have to change our modes of questioning about our divisions at the Lord's Supper. Where hitherto we took it for granted that we ourselves had preserved the unity of the body of Christ but that the members of other denominations had departed from it, we now feel ourselves increasingly questioned by God whether it is not we who have profaned or even blasphemed the unity of the body of Christ. Whereas hitherto we had thought that only others had given up the unity of true doctrine and order, we now recognise that we are questioned whether we have not done so ourselves. Anybody who has not yet experienced this shattering reversal of the questioning is still outside the gates of real ecumenical encounter.

Whose soul has not been pierced, as if by lightning, by the parable of the Great Supper (Luke 14. 15-25)? The people who were bidden first refused one after another. They have no need to share the feast of their Lord who is calling them, because they are satisfied, because they are fully occupied and fully contented with their own affairs. Though they know that all they have is a gift from the same Lord who is inviting them, they set these gifts over against the Lord and use them as a pretext for declining His gracious invitation. The parable talks about land, cattle and a wedding. Might not this apply to our own theology, our own form of worship, our own piety, our own history, and even our own celebration of the Lord's Supper which prevents us from following the invitation of the one Lord who gathers the one flock? And when Christ walked on earth, was it not just the pious ones who did not accept His invitation? We all know that the parable is immediately followed by an invitation to the poor, the maimed, the lame and blind in the city, and to the tramps outside the gates. Might not the place of those who in the pomp of doctrine and form of their own services shrink from the call to the one Great Supper, be taken by all the others of whom we think to-day as sinners, despisers of the sacrament, on the fringe of Christianity—all those beggars and tramps who precisely have no reason to be proud of their past? We are warned with the greatest emphasis that none of those who were bidden first will taste of the Great Supper (v. 24). Only the poor, the hungry, the downcast, the longing, the homeless will have a share in it. Have then the Churches forgotten that not they but the Lord Himself sends out invitations to the Lord's Supper?

A Radical Self-questioning

Everyone should question himself how far he or his denomination has made himself lord of the Lord's Supper. The introduction of intercommunion is not a question of generosity or pettiness but a task of fundamental reorientation. We cannot carry out this task by occasionally taking part in ecumenical conversations or services, but it is laid upon us as a problem which must exercise our minds incessantly. Its solution demands not only our readiness for penitence but serious engagement in scholarly meditation. The reasons which stand in the way of intercommunion are very diverse and they must be re-examined one by one:

1. The refusal of intercommunion because of differences in the doctrine of Holy Communion can be a sign that men have taken over the Sacrament themselves. There is undoubtedly such a thing as an excessive dogmatism which is without foundation in the institution of the Lord's Supper. Undoubtedly there are dangerous deviations from the attitude of faith: whereas faith receives the mystery with longing expectancy, doctrine assumes sovereignty over the mystery. Undoubtedly there also exists a wrong conception of doctrinal unity which fails to recognise that the peculiar unity of the New Testament comes out of the diversity of its witnesses and their testimony.

2. The refusal of intercommunion because of differences in the order of the Church's ministry can be an expression of the fact that the ministerial office is no longer thought of as the instrument of God's dealings with men but has acquired a significance on its own account, which hinders the action of the one Lord. It may happen here that, in the place of the ministry which was instituted by God's free act, a caste of people and a man-made legal order have emerged which impede the saving and gathering act of God's mercy.

3. The refusal of intercommunion because of differences in congregational structures can signify that the Church's unity is no longer grounded in the one Lord, who calls its members out of the world, gathers them, illuminates them, endows them. Then the unity of the Church is wrongly conceived as primarily the belonging together of men of like views, like history, or even of the same race or nation. It may be that the sociological, even the combined religious and sociological structure of the denominational Church stands in the way of the divine Shepherd gathering His flock.

4. Similarly, we must question the refusal of intercommunion on the ground of differences in liturgical order and customs of worship (e.g. the use of leavened or unleavened bread).

5. Such questions need to be followed through into the last details of the reasons for refusal of intercommunion. They need to be re-thought in the total context of theology and congregational life of the various denominations. Special attention should be given to the relationship between Word and Sacrament. What does it mean that at ecumenical conferences we can always pray

together and proclaim the word of God to each other, but we cannot celebrate the Lord's Supper together?

In such a thorough self-examination we have to win through to the reality of what is taking place in those celebrations, which means we have to win through anew to the reality of Him who gives Himself to the believer in the Lord's Supper, in spite of the strangeness, the faults and errors which stand between our denominations at the point of the celebration of the Sacrament. At all events, this gift 'passes understanding'.

The goal we should have before us is a diversity of Churches opening themselves to each other, to which intercommunion and mutual recognition of ministries and orders is being progressively granted. The goal cannot be abolition of the denominations; it must be a community of denominations in which each is serving the other with the particular gifts given to it by the Lord in the past and present, and in which each one is breaking through its own limitations and correcting its errors.

XVIII

ESCHATOLOGY
AND THE
EUCHARIST

*

T. F. Torrance
Church of Scotland

(Great Britain)

It is a significant fact that in the last thirty or forty years the difference between the Roman Catholic Church and the Evangelical
Church in their teaching on the Eucharist has been narrowed
down considerably. That is most evident in the abandonment by
many leading Roman Catholic theologians of the Tridentine
explanation of the sacrifice of the Mass in literal terms, and in their
return to a deeper understanding of the sacramental and eschatological significance of the Eucharist. The outstanding event in this
movement was the publication of *Mysterium Fidei* by Maurice de
la Taille after the first world war, and since then other notable
works have appeared moving more or less within the same orbit
of thought.[1] To the Reformed theologian much of this discussion
is still hampered by unreal scholastic distinctions and a too literal
approach to the eucharistic sacrifice, but he cannot but be im-
pressed with two major elements in it: (*a*) the distinct sensitiveness
of Roman theologians to the Protestant criticism of the pre- and
post-Reformation doctrine of the Mass, and the concern of all to
maintain the unique character of the sacrifice on the Cross as an
unrepeatable event; and (*b*) the fresh understanding of biblical
teaching and consequently a rediscovery of the eschatological
nature of the sacraments of Baptism and Eucharist. In spite of this
rapprochement, however, we cannot blind ourselves to the fact that
the difference between the Roman Catholic Church and the

---

[1] Cf. the works of Héris, Masure, Casel, Vonier, Barden, Söhngen, Schmaus.

Evangelical Church is very deep,[2] and much deeper than anything which divides the branches of the Evangelical Church.

In the branches of the Evangelical Church, that is in the Churches of the Reformation, differences have also been narrowed down considerably. To a certain extent the modern liturgical movement has tended to harden those differences through its search for a definitive shape of the liturgy, but on the whole it has served rather to bring the Churches together by taking their differences to a deeper level and testing them by the Prophetic and Apostolic foundation of the Church. Here it has become apparent that difference in practice has carried divergence in belief farther than it actually is. That is a heartening discovery for it indicates that in the Evangelical Church, where we do not have to do with irreformable pronouncements of faith, a fresh understanding of the Apostolic Message may so undermine our differences and correct our several traditions that intercommunion will become a compelling necessity for all who confess 'one Lord, one faith, one baptism, one God and Father of all'. This essay is an attempt from within the Reformed Church to engage in discussion at this stage and if possible to penetrate below the existing principles governing intercommunion to theological foundations in the hope of laying bare the significance of the Eucharist as the divinely given Sacrament of unity, indeed the medicine for our divisions.

I

The Sacraments and Eschatology

We may begin with the word *sacrament*, and note that the New Testament does not speak of sacraments, but rather of Baptism and the Lord's Supper. If we are to penetrate to the biblical foundations, therefore we must avoid thinking about Baptism and the Eucharist as if they had to fulfil some man-made definition of a sacrament from Augustine, for example, or Aquinas or Calvin, helpful as they may be. When we set aside for the moment the centuries of theological discussion and turn to the pages of the New Testament Scriptures, we become aware of the fact that again and again the

---

[2] This difference is made very clear by the new Roman dogma. Instead of the Evangelical *solus Christus* at the right hand of the Father, the Roman Church substitutes *Christus et Maria*.

language it uses about Baptism is interchangeable with that it uses about the Eucharist.[3] Indeed, Baptism and Eucharist are just as parallel, and just as one, as *in Christ* and *Christ in us*. If anything, the emphasis is laid upon Baptism, as in the confession of unity cited above, 'One Lord, one faith, one baptism', where the Eucharist is not mentioned, while whole Epistles such as that to the *Romans* do not mention it either. That would not be understandable were it not for the evident fact that the New Testament regards Baptism and Eucharist as two aspects of the same event, and that it is Baptism rather than the Eucharist which is all-inclusive. Both have to do with incorporation into Christ, but whereas Baptism is all-inclusive and final, the Eucharist is the continual renewal of that incorporation in time. The Eucharist cannot be understood except within the significance of Baptism, although the once-and-for-all significance of Baptism bears upon history only through the Eucharist. We may say, therefore, that strictly speaking there is only one sacrament, and that Baptism and Eucharist belong to this indivisible whole.[4] It is the sacrament of the *Word made flesh*, of the *Christ-event*, which includes the life, teaching, death and resurrection of Jesus Christ. It is the same Word which sacramentally becomes flesh in both Baptism and the Eucharist, and it is in that action of the Word becoming flesh that they have their underlying and indivisible unity. In the action of the Church the relation between Baptism and Eucharist is through the *kerygma*: it is a *kerygmatic relation*.

In the elucidation of this we may recall the meaning of the Christ-event as the Word made flesh. It is the Christian message that in the Incarnation of the Son of God the eternal Word has entered into history, and partakes of the relativity of history, without ceasing to be God, and without at the same time destroying the continuity of ongoing history. In the historical Jesus the eternal Word is made flesh so that He is seen and heard in the flesh in history, and yet because He does not cease to be the eternal Word He cannot be seen or heard except in His eternal

[3] Cf. especially Mk. 10. 38 f.; I Cor. 10; 12. 13.

[4] This is borne out very clearly by the art of the Roman Catacombs—cf. Wladimir Weidlé *The Baptism of Art*. The unity of Baptism and Eucharist has been remarkably conserved by the Orthodox Church. It became also a point of cardinal importance in the Reformation writings of Calvin and Peter Martyr, following Augustine.

recession in God. That is why the Synoptic Gospels speak of the Word as *mysterion*. Jesus can be known historically as part of human flesh, but the real significance of the historical Jesus is not apparent except to faith. The Word has become flesh, and cannot be known by men of flesh and blood except in the flesh, but it is the Father in heaven alone who reveals Him, and not flesh and blood.

That, however, is only part of the significance of the Christ-event. The Word is not only eternal Truth but the act of the Eternal in time. That is why in the Gospels there is the closest relation between the Word and the act in Jesus' preaching. Word and act are inseparable and complementary. The Word of the Kingdom is God's saving intervention among men, and that takes place in the preaching and miracles of Jesus in inseparable unity. We may put the matter thus. Jesus is not one whose action falls short of His Word. Therefore, though the Word of forgiveness is spoken in a parable, that same Word is acted out in Himself on the Cross. There the Word of pardon is enacted in flesh and blood and inserted as a reality into our history and life. It becomes an actual fact, not just a mere idea or a word spoken into the air. That was why on the lips of Jesus the Word was indirectly communicated through the parable because the act is also part of the Word. The Word of God is not mere speech but power of God, Christ crucified, as St. Paul said. It is because the Word is also power or act that it cannot be conveyed in mere speech but has to be conveyed in saving acts, in miraculous signs. The parables were designed not to convey a symbolic meaning which can be read off their face but to confront men with Christ Himself as the Word of God, and the miracles were designed not just to prove the divinity of Christ but to confront men with the mighty power of God already at work among them in Jesus Christ. Both parables and miracles, however, pointed beyond themselves to the crucifixion and resurrection, where in the fullest sense the divine Word and act were one in the person of Jesus Christ.

That happened once and for all, and is absolutely decisive for all men and all time. It was not a once-and-for-all event merely in the sense in which every other historical event happens but once and is unrepeatable, but once and for all in the sense of eternal finality. As such, however, it is not merely a piece of past history, but is an enduring event with critical and decisive significance for all time.[5] Everything else will pass away, but this will not pass away. How does this unique and enduring event bear upon men in time now that Jesus Christ has withdrawn Himself from visible participation in history? It is here that the New Testament speaks about *kerygma*, and also about Baptism and the Lord's Supper.

Kerygma means both the thing preached and the preaching of it in one. It is the proclamation of the Christ-event, but such proclamation that by the Holy Spirit it becomes the actualisation of that event among men. It is such proclamation that in and through it the living Christ continues to do and to teach what He had already begun before and after the crucifixion. *Kerygma* is the Word of the Kingdom that cannot be conveyed in mere speech, but is used by God to intervene Himself in the human situation as He who once and for all has wrought out His final act in the death and resurrection of Jesus Christ, so that through *kerygma* the Church is continually being called out of history to become the very Body of Christ, and by the communion of His Holy Spirit is given to taste the powers of the age to come and to stand already on the side of the resurrection. Accordingly, even after the Lord Jesus was received up into heaven and sat on the right hand of God, the disciples 'went forth and preached everywhere, the Lord working with them, and confirming the Word with signs following'. That is the twofold event of *kerygma*.

This means that *kerygma* is in the fullest sense the sacramental action of the Church through which the mystery of the Kingdom concerning Christ and His Church, hid from the foundation of the world, is now being revealed in history. Just as in the Incarnation the Word was made flesh, so in *kerygma* the same Word continues to be made flesh in the extension of the Church. Thus we read in the Acts of the Apostles of the Word as increasing and multiplying. By that is not meant that Christ the Word grows or increases, but that His living Word acting in and through human witness works creatively among men building upon earth the Church which is concorporate with the all-inclusive Body of Christ. It is within this sacramental and kerygmatic activity of Church and Spirit that Baptism and the Lord's Supper are given their place in the New Testament. As such they may be regarded

[5] Cf. E. Brunner, 'The Christian Understanding of Time', *Scottish Journal of Theology*, p. 411.

as bearing a relation to the *kerygma* of the Church similar to that
which the signs and miracles bore to the *kerygma* of Jesus. Jesus
took care in His preaching never to give a compelling manifestation of Himself, lest by an open display of His majesty and
might He might crush men to the ground, leaving no room for
faith or repentance or decision. In Him the *eschaton* had broken
into the present, but if men had been confronted openly with the
eschaton in the Word and Presence of Jesus they would have been
faced with the final judgment. Jesus deliberately held the Word
and its action apart in order to leave room for repentance and
faith, but at the same time He followed up the Word with a sign
which gave ample evidence of His saving power. The classic
example of that is to be found in the Markan account of the
healing of the paralytic, where for the purpose of leaving room
for faith ('that ye may know that the Son of Man hath power on
earth to forgive sins'), an interval of time was inserted between
the Word of forgiveness and the act of healing. It was precisely
that lapse of time or eschatological reserve between the Word of
the Kingdom and its power that Jesus was concerned to preserve
in His *kerygma*. A similar relation between Word and act is to be
found after the death and resurrection of Jesus, for though it is
as one that they take the field in the *kerygma* of the Church, Jesus
has withdrawn Himself from visible participation in history,
reserving that for the *parousia* or the *eschaton*. Here, however, both
the unity between the Word and action and their eschatological
tension are intensified. The Church is redeemed not in Word only
but also in power, and yet it waits for the redemption of the body.
The new age has already overtaken it and through the Spirit it
stands on the resurrection side of the Cross, and yet it still waits
for the day when the form and fashion of this world will be torn
aside and the new creation will be revealed. The Church lives
between those two moments, between the Cross and the *parousia*,
between the Word of forgiveness and the final act of healing,
between Pentecost and the resurrection of the body. In the mercy
of God the Word of the Gospel and the final deed of God are
partially held apart in eschatological reserve until the *parousia*.
This is the age of grace, the age of *kerygma*, in which the Gospel
is proclaimed to all, in which time and space are given for repentance and decision. But this is the age, too, when by the Holy
Spirit, who inhabits the Church and energises its kerygmatic

ministry, all who believe in Jesus Christ may taste the powers of the age to come through sacramental incorporation into the new creation.

It was said above that the relation between the sacraments and the *kerygma* of the Church is similar to that between the signs and the *kerygma* of Jesus—but there is this supreme difference, that now the death and resurrection of Jesus Christ have taken place and the great act for the redemption of the world has been completed. It is true indeed that the unveiling of the full reality of that act is still to take place, but it is equally true that with the death and resurrection of Jesus Christ the Kingdom of God and with it the new creation have already interpenetrated the age in which we live, so that this is already the fullness of time. The two sacraments of the Word made flesh, Baptism and Eucharist, are essentially *signs* belonging to this fullness of time, and as such are charged with the power of the resurrection. They enshrine in time the great *mystery* concerning Christ in His Church.

We must be clear, however, about the meaning of these two words, *sign* and *mystery*. The sign is to be understood in terms of the miraculous activity of Christ, as *kerygma* is to be understood in terms of Christ the living Word. These may be distinguished from each other in thought, but are actually inseparable. As the virgin birth and the resurrection are miraculous and active signs of the Word made flesh, so Baptism and Eucharist are miraculous and active signs of the Word made flesh in the Church as the Body of Christ. The great difficulty about the word *sign* in traditional theology is the unfortunate fact that *signum* corresponds to *res* and involves a quite unhebraic and unbiblical denotation as static matter or significant thing.[6] Even the expression *effective sign* used by the Reformers is inadequate.[7] Sign is essentially event, the worldly form which the Christ-event assumes in action, the point at which Revelation embodies itself actively in history. Sign is not, however, a complete or final embodiment, as if Revelation completely passes into or is absorbed in history, but such an embodiment in conditions of time as to point beyond itself to an infinite fullness. Before the Cross the miraculous signs were actual

[6] Cf. E. Gaugler, *Das Abendmahl im Neuen Testament*, p. 7 ff.; K. Barth, *Die christliche Lehre nach dem Heidelberger Katechismus*, p. 88 f.

[7] This did enable Calvin, however, to teach a doctrine of *dynamic presence* in the sacraments.

anticipations of the saving act of God in the death and resurrection of Jesus; afterwards they are the miraculous signs charged with the incarnate presence of the crucified and risen Lord which point beyond to a fullness which, as signs, in the conditions of our fallen world, they cannot altogether contain. In other words, the whole significance of the sign is bound up with the fact that the ascension comes in between the resurrection of Jesus Christ and His second advent. *Parousia* means both a presence and a coming. The sacramental signs are charged with the real presence, but it is a presence which is also yet to come, a presence whose full reality is yet to be unveiled and consummated.

That takes us to the significance of the word *mystery*. Here it is the Greek idea which has confused understanding. Like *sign*, *mystery* is essentially event, but event as that which is not yet fully disclosed in conditions of the fallen world. It is the event of Revelation in time in so far as it recedes into the eternal, in so far as the sign bears witness to the fullness beyond. In the New Testament, mystery is spoken of in relation to the *kerygma*, and not directly in relation to Baptism and the Lord's Supper, but its bearing upon the sacraments was inevitable. In its fundamental sense mystery refers to God manifest in the flesh, but as the great sign of that event is the Church of Jesus Christ, the relation of Christ to His Church is also spoken of as mystery. It is in that sense that the word may legitimately be applied to the sacraments. We may put it this way. Through its ministry of *kerygma* the Church is regarded in the New Testament as the great sacramental sign, for it is the visible counterpart of the resurrection-body of Christ. As such the Church can neither be fused with Christ nor separated from Him. As the God-Man Christ was Himself the embodiment in the world of the mystery of the Kingdom, but as the Church is the embodiment of the Spirit of Christ (for 'he that is joined to the Lord is one Spirit'), it is also in its way the embodiment of the same mystery. The sacraments of Baptism and Eucharist are therefore the miraculous and active signs through which that mystery is embodied in the Church on earth, but, be it noted, embodied in such a way that, while they anticipate, they point to an eschatological fullness beyond. The sacraments are given to us because of the ascension and cannot be made to impugn it as if they contained a presence fully identical with that of the *parousia*. Had Christ not withdrawn Himself visibly from the world there would doubtless have been no need for sacraments, not in our sense at any rate. When Christ comes again and the Marriage Supper of the Lamb is consummated, the sacraments will give way to literal reality. Until that day comes the sacraments have to do with the breaking of the Christ-event into time here and now, and with our participation in the new creation.

To understand that more clearly we must recall the nature of the Christ-event, which, while it is once and for all in a final sense, is also an abiding or enduring event that can never pass away. The union of God and Man in the incarnation also involves the union of eternity with time, and though that union is inserted into our history with its limitations and relativities it is a union that is carried through the contradiction of sin and death itself into the resurrection. There we have revealed the new creation in the risen Body of Jesus Christ. But just as the original creation involved the creation of time, so this new creation involves new time, time that is no longer at variance with the eternal through sin, but time that is cleansed and restored to union with the eternal. The Christ-event is absolutely unique and decisive in that through it redemption has been wrought once and for all, nevertheless it is an event that involves this new time, and as such it transcends the limitations and relativities of history as we know it from day to day, and endures for ever. It endures and abides for ever as new time just because it is indissolubly united to the eternal. That is the significance of the session at the right hand of God the Father, but it is also the significance of the continuity of the new creation in the Church, the Body of Christ.

We may say that as God and man are united in the God-Man in such a way that the two natures may not be identified with or separated from each other (we recall here the Chalcedonian formula), so the sacraments involves on another plane, in conditions of this fallen world, a like union between divine action and human action, but here let it be noted that the 'divine' action is the action of *Totus Christus*, of the God-Man, and not of God *simpliciter* apart from the incarnation. There is then in the sacraments a union between the divine action and human action, between the *actio* of Christ Jesus, and the *re-actio* of the Church, and *actio* and *re-actio* can neither be identified with, nor separated from, each other. Just as God and Man in Christ Jesus are united in the *communio consubstantialis* of the Holy Spirit, so here in the sacraments the divine action and the human re-action are united in *communio substantialis* through the same Holy Spirit.

This means that the sacraments do not have to do simply with a union between the present and the future, but with a union between the Church in history and the new creation as an abiding union here and now even in the heart of the world's estrangement. It is because that union is only partially revealed in the sacraments that we must talk about it in terms of mystery, and it is because that union will be fully revealed in the future that we must speak about it in terms of eschatology. The sacraments tell us, however, that the reality of the new creation is temporal fact here and now, even though its reality, veiled since the ascension of the Lord, is yet to be unveiled at the *parousia*. The New Testament emphasis upon the future is not so much the future of the reality but the future of its full manifestation, so that the eschatological tension involved in the sacraments is the tension between the time of a present but hidden reality and the time of the same reality revealed in the *parousia*.

It is because the eschatological relation involves both the relation between the present and the future and the relation between the new creation and the old, here and now, that the one sacramental relation between the Church and Jesus Christ has two particular 'moments': Baptism and the Lord's Supper. Just as the Christ-event had its two supreme 'moments' in the virgin birth and in the death and resurrection of Jesus Christ, although neither 'moment' can be understood except as it involves the other, so here in the sacramental union where the Christ-event breaks into the historical life of the Church incorporating it into Christ as His Body, there are two corresponding 'moments', Baptism and the Lord's Supper, each of which involves the other in a single whole. The doubleness of the eschatological tension is enshrined in both of them, but the emphasis upon the once-and-for-all incorporation into Christ or union with the new creation falls most heavily upon the sacrament of Baptism, while in the sacrament of the Eucharist we have emphasised most the breaking in of the new creation as the enduring event in, and in spite of, the conditions of this sinful and historical world. If at Baptism we think of our having died and risen with Christ so that we are born anew in Him, so that old things are passed away and all things are become new, at Holy Communion we think of that not only as a *datum* once and for all, but also as a *dandum* which must be given anew, day by day, in the conditions of our fallen world. Every time we communicate is eschatological time until we drink it anew in the Kingdom of God. It is just because, in the sign of Baptism, the complete event recedes into the mystery of the Eternal that we are given in the Eucharist continual participation and renewal in that complete event. In both sacraments we are told that the Kingdom of God is amongst us not in Word only with suspended action, not in Spirit only, but in deed and in power, as real act in time, as Word-deed enacted in our flesh and blood and inserted into history. But precisely because it is both, it is at once a complete reality and an eschatologically repeated event until Christ comes.

It is important to remember that both Baptism and Eucharist are sacraments of the Word made flesh. They do not have existence or reality independently of the Word. To make them self-sufficient and independent of the Word would be to take away their sacramental character, for it would deny to them their element of mystery, or infinite recession in the Word that is in the bosom of God and is God. That is why, following St. Augustine, the Reformers insisted that it is the Word which sacramentalises, and apart from the Word sacraments cannot exist. Apart from the Word there is only an empty sign that is nothing but a ceremony. *Kerygma* and sign go together and cannot be sundered. In *kerygma* the *Word* is made flesh. In the sacraments the Word is made *flesh*. Baptism, *Kerygma*, and Eucharist together form a whole, the sacramental life and action of the Church. 'And Jesus came and spake unto them, saying, All power is given unto me in heaven and in earth. Go ye therefore, and teach all nations, baptising them in the name of the Father, and of the Son, and of the Holy Spirit: teaching them to observe all things whatsoever I have commanded you: and lo, I am with you alway, even unto the end of the world.' The emphasis here is upon *kerygma* and Baptism, but in the promise of the real presence *alway* we may surely understand the eucharistic communion.

II

The Eucharist or the Lord's Supper

Before we speak more precisely about the Eucharist we must be more precise about Baptism as the primary eschatological act of the Gospel, whereby we are ingrafted into the wholeness of Christ. The Baptism of John clearly had reference to the liturgical washing at the laver in preparation for the sacrifice of the lamb, a sign which pointed to a fullness in the Spirit that was yet to come. That Baptism had its counterpart doubtless in Jesus' cleansing of the Temple in preparation for His sacrifice as the Lamb of God whereby He was to make atonement for sin, a cleansing which pointed to the sanctification of the Church, cleansed with the washing of water by the Word, a glorious Church not having spot or wrinkle, but holy and without blemish. We cannot, however, speak about the Baptism of the disciples and of Jesus in univocal terms. Theirs was a Baptism of repentance and renewal even though the power of the resurrection was not fully released until Pentecost; Jesus' Baptism was substitutionary and was completed in His Baptism of blood on the cross when He died for all men. In the profoundest sense all men are actually involved in that Baptism of Jesus, and it is that Baptism which turns John's Baptism into Christian Baptism. After the crucifixion and resurrection Baptism has much more than parabolic significance, for now the Word and act are one event, and it is because of that unity that *kerygma* and *Baptism* are always thought of together in the New Testament. The Word in *kerygma* presses into physical enactment, creating the bodily Church—and that happens through Baptism. It is through the *kerygma*, however, that Baptism gains its particularity and is given power as concrete event. A purely substitutionary and objective Baptism would have little reference to the life which we live in history, even though after the crucifixion all history happens within and under the shadow of the Cross and the mighty act of God wrought out there. It is through the *kerygma*, through the ministry of the Church empowered by the Holy Spirit, that the Cross exerts its power over men and history. In the *kerygma* of the Church the living Word, Christ crucified and risen, lays hold of men in their sin and weakness. The Word demands decision and through men's obedience and disobedience it acts selectively upon them, calling the Church into being, a work which will be fully unveiled at the last day when the Word will complete its judgment. But already that Word is event, for through the *kerygma* the death and the resurrection of Jesus Christ break into the present, so that all who believe are given to participate in that death and resurrection and are inserted into the operational sphere of the Christ-event. Baptism is the fulfilment of that as the particular actualisation of the Christ-event, so that through it the Church called out of the world becomes the Church which is the Body of Christ. There is only one Baptism, the Baptism of the Spirit at Pentecost which corresponds to the one Baptism of Christ, and into that each believer is incorporated through water-baptism.

Parallel to the hypostatic union between God and Man in Jesus Christ there is a sacramental union in Baptism between the divine action and the action of the Church, between its manward and its Godward action. Baptism is not in any sense an independent agency whose benefit is conferred *ex opere operato*; rather is it the action of the Church in obedience to the divine ordinance, which God uses to fulfil His holy Will. In other words, the mediation of the divine act is not through the element as such but in its particular use in the action of the Church. Baptism is, on the one hand, then, the breaking in of the Christ-event, so that it is not simply an historical event belonging to the past, but as a once-and-for-all historical event it is also precipitated into the present and is active with saving power here and now in the Church. Baptism indicates that the Church is the sphere and the medium in the world whereby the saving acts of Jesus Christ are at work, invading history and subjecting all things to Christ as King and Lord. Baptism is the outworking in time of the absolutely decisive event of the Cross and resurrection of Christ, and gathers to that event the corresponding life and action of the historical Church. The Church is not therefore merely an historical institution, but is a sacramental magnitude maintained in being upon foundations that are not laid with hands, rooted and grounded in the God-Manhood of Jesus Christ. On the other hand, as in Baptism, the Church binds believers to the *Heilsgeschichte*, pledges them to faith in Jesus Christ who died for them and rose again, and offers them to Him as Saviour and Lord, the Holy Spirit uses this Godward action of the Church as the means whereby He gives believers participation in the Baptism of Christ, inserts them into the Christ-event, incorporates them into His Body, ingrafts them into the New Creation, and makes them to sit in heavenly places. This means that something absolutely decisive is wrought in Baptism. Baptism in the Name of Jesus, in the name of the Holy Trinity, means that Christians are delivered from the power of darkness and translated into the Kingdom of the Son of God. A radical change has taken place which can only be described in terms of a complete change of Lordship. The Christian is no longer under the domination of the law or the elements of this world, but is dead to sin and alive to God through the Lordship of the Spirit, so that old things are passed away and all things are become new. Outwardly Baptism is no doubt incorporation into the earthly Church, initiation into the operational sphere of the salvation-events, and outwardly the Church on earth knows itself to be embroiled in the relativities of history and the sin of mankind, but behind all that and beyond, Baptism has a dimension in depth which is its eschatological *mystery*: 'Ye are dead and your life is hid with Christ in God.' The really significant event in Baptism is a hidden event; it recedes from sight in the ascension of Christ and waits to be revealed fully at the last day.

However, the Lord has not simply left His Church stricken with anguish and awe at the foot of the Cross, or standing looking up into heaven from Galilee. He has provided for the renewal and maintenance of its life and faith—in the Eucharist. Through continual communion in the body and blood of the Saviour, the Church finds that Baptism is given its complement and recurring confirmation. After the Baptism of John, Jesus had called twelve disciples and formed them round Himself into one body, the reconstituted Israel of God. They were pledged to drink His cup and be baptised with His baptism, but the mystery of the King-dom, the New Israel incorporate in the Messianic Saviour, baffled them. They understood indeed that they were called to cast in their lot unreservedly with Jesus and to share His life, but in the crucial moment they found themselves standing not with Jesus but with the crowd of sinners who were crucifying Him and for whom He was dying. They had all forsaken Him and fled.[8] At last the Messiah was left unutterably alone under the judgment of

[8] For this and what immediately follows see Prof. W. Manson, *Scottish Journal of Theology*, 3.1, p. 38 f.

God upon the world's sin. He was their Lord and Master. He was their Representative and their very Life, but in the agony of substitution He was unutterably alone, the Lamb whom God had Himself provided for sacrifice.[9] The disciples could only stand afar off in sin and shame and fear, and broken-hearted that the bonds between Him and them were utterly severed. Then they remembered the Last Supper. That was why He had designed it, for He meant them to remember. And they realised that within that awful separation and in spite of it He had effectuated His oneness with them in a way that nothing could break, for He had given them in the Supper a sacramental counterpart to His atoning death. And then they knew that their baptismal incorporation into one Body with their Lord had come to its stark reality in that sacrificial death and its sacramental counterpart. They understood how in that wonderful Last Supper Jesus 'had definitely consecrated them for inheritance in the Kingdom of God as those who, despite their brokenness so soon to be made visible, formed one body with Himself. He had given their lives a sacramental dependence on His own'.[10] In the Lord's Supper and in the enactment on the Cross the mystery of their baptismal incorporation into Christ, and into the Israel of God, actually became materialised in flesh and blood.

After the resurrection and ascension the disciples understood why, again and again, Jesus had gathered the lost sheep of the House of Israel, the cultically unclean and those debarred from the Temple liturgy of sacrifice, and although it scandalised the priests, He deliberately broke down the barriers erected by the cultus, and enacted in their midst a sign of the Messianic Meal, when many would come from the east and the west, and sit down with Abraham, Isaac and Jacob in the Kingdom of Heaven.[11] That eschatological meal was not an eating and drinking between holy priests and holy people, but the marriage-supper of the Lamb, who because He had come to bear their sin, gathered the poor and the outcast, the weary and the heavy laden, the publicans and sinners, and fed them with the bread of life and gave them living water to drink. The disciple remembered also the parables of the prodigal son and his feasting in the father's house, of the

[9] Cf. Prof. O. Cullmann, *Christ and Time*, p. 107 ff.
[10] W. Manson, *op. cit.*, p. 39.
[11] Cf. Lohmeyer, *Kultus und Evangelium*, p. 36 f., 80 and 90 f.

bridegroom and the wedding-feast, and the final judgment which would discover those who had given or not given food to the hungry and drink to the thirsty, and they understood their bearing upon the Lord's Supper as the great eschatological meal of the Kingdom of God through which that very Kingdom is realised here and now, as far as may be in the conditions of this passing world. The disciples recalled, too, those Galilean meals of fellowship with Jesus, the miraculous feeding of the multitudes by the Great Shepherd of the sheep, and the equally wonderful words He spoke about manna and water, about His flesh and blood, and the life-giving Spirit, and they knew that what had been parable and sign and miracle then had at last materialised in the Easter breaking of bread. They saw in His death and resurrection such fulfilment of the Old Testament oracles as gave their teaching creative reinterpretation and threw a flood of light upon the mystery of the Cross. In that Jesus had died for them and risen again, He had inaugurated a new covenant within which they could sit down together and eat bread and drink wine, assured that they were one with their Lord, given to partake of His sacrifice, to share in the power of His resurrection and to be bound up with Him in the same bundle of life. The ends of the earth had already come upon them, for by this sacramental meal they tasted its powers and were given to stand with Christ on the other side of the judgment, in the new creation. The incredible mystery of Baptism was become a visible reality, and the disciples continued in the breaking of bread to commune with their Lord and to proclaim His death as the power of God unto salvation.

In order to unfold more fully the significance of the Eucharist we must return to the event of the Upper Room. The Apostolic records of that night make it clear that they saw converging in the institution of the Supper both the paschal and covenantal meals of the Old Testament and the messianic meals of the wilderness of Sinai and the hills of Galilee. It was charged through and through with eschatological significance. At the beginning of the meal Jesus must have followed the Jewish custom of passing round a cup of wine in token of thanksgiving to God, but before that was done, a piece of bread and a cup of wine were set aside for the Messiah in case He should suddenly come to His own in the midst of the feast. Then at the end of the meal, fully charged with paschal and covenantal significance, Jesus took the bread and wine set aside for the Messiah, and said, 'This is my body broken for you. This is my blood which is shed for you.' By breaking the bread and giving it to the disciples, by passing round the cup, He associated them with His sacrifice, giving their existence in relation to Himself a new form in the Kingdom of God, indeed constituting them as the Church concorporate with Himself. When the Apostolic Church looked back upon that Last Supper they recalled that Jesus had bidden them do this repeatedly in remembrance of Him, proclaiming thus His death till He should come again to drink it new with them in the Kingdom of God. St. John records, too, that the original Supper was set in the context of our Lord's highpriestly prayer in which He consecrated Himself and interceded for His Church.

There is a great deal here which we must discuss in order to elucidate its theological structure. We may begin by noting the two fundamental moments within which the Eucharist has its place: 'the night on which He was betrayed', and 'till He come', as St. Paul puts them. The Eucharist is therefore at once bound to history, and related to the advent of Christ at the end of history. It reaches into the past, to the death of Christ, and sets it in the present as reality operative here and now in the Church. On the other hand, the Eucharist reaches out beyond the present into the future, and becomes the means whereby the Church in the present is brought under the power of the advent of Christ. The Eucharist thus belongs to the very nature of the Church, rooting and grounding it in the historical Christ and His saving acts, and also bringing to the Church its own ultimate reality from beyond history. By the Eucharist that ultimate reality stands not only at the end of time but impinges creatively upon the Church throughout history, for it is both the *proton* and the *eschaton* of its existence. Through the Eucharist the Church becomes, so to speak, the great arch that spans history, supported by only two pillars, the Cross which stands on this side of time, and the coming of Christ in power which stands at the end of history. From age to age the Church is grounded upon these two supports by the Eucharist, so that its very being is bound up with the essential unity of the two events, the perfected event of the death and resurrection of Christ, and the future event of the *parousia*. It is because the Church receives its being ever anew, through the Eucharist, as the new creation which is yet to be revealed at the *parousia*, that it lives in dynamic tension here and now on the very frontiers of eternity.

Once again, we must return to the thought of the hypostatic union between God and Man in Jesus Christ, in order to understand this eucharistic reality clearly. We must think of that hypostatic union, however, not in the static categories of Patristic thought, but in terms of biblical eschatology, that is, in dynamic categories. As the Captain of our salvation was made perfect through suffering, we must think of that holy union inserted into our flesh and blood at the Virgin Birth of Jesus as carried through our human life and death, through the contradictions of sin and the relativities of history, through the passion and agony of the crucifixion to its transcendent perfection in the resurrection of Jesus from the dead, so that He lives on for ever, our Mediator and Atonement, in whom all things cohere, and in whom all things in heaven and earth will be brought back to the fullness of God. It is by the Eucharist, following upon Baptism, that that union is inserted as an abiding union into the heart of our estrangement from God the Father, and into all the conflicts of history.[12] Here we are given the perfect union between the eternal and the temporal, between the divine and the human, inserted into our flesh and blood, and it is that made flesh in the Eucharist which is the inner core of the Church's reality on earth. This has several implications which we must not pass over because of their bearing upon intercommunion.

(1) The enactment of this abiding union within the world's estrangement increases the tension between the new creation and the fallen world. Just as the union between God and Man became fact and reality for us once and for all through the desperate passion and agony of the crucifixion, so the Church bound to its Lord by this sacramental union can only follow Him by taking up His Cross daily. The world continues in its estrangement from God and its contradiction to Him, but that is surely why the Church is given the Sacrament of the Eucharist in addition to the Sacrament of Baptism. It is taught thereby that while in reconciliation and justification and sanctification the Church is already perfect in Christ Jesus, yet in the broken conditions of time, in the conflicts and divisions of history, so long as it waits for redemption of the purchased possession, it is unable to realise that

[12] Cf. Karl Heim, *Jesus der Weltvollender*.

perfection in its wholeness here and now. The Church must nevertheless reckon that it is dead to the old life and alive in the new, for that is what actually takes place in the Eucharist. That the Church is once and for all justified and perfected in Christ is enshrined in the Sacrament of Baptism, but that its justification and perfection are also prolonged in time is enshrined in the Eucharist. The perfection of the Church's union with Christ Jesus has to be carried through the conditions of time, and how it is straitened until that is accomplished! By means of the Eucharist, so to speak, the agony of Calvary is extended into the ages into which the Church goes out as the suffering servant in the mission of the world's redemption. And so it learns to fill up that which is eschatologically in arrears of the sufferings of Christ as it throws itself into the heart of the world's trouble and acts out there, however costly that may be, the reconciliation of the Cross. The Church can do that only because in the heart of its life and worship there is set the Sacrament of Holy Communion in which it is given association with the sacrifice of Christ, and in which also it is given to share in the triumph of the Saviour: 'Be of good cheer; I have overcome the world.' In the consummation of that triumph the Church will have no need of the Eucharist,[13] but so long as it is still the Church Militant in this world, the Eucharist is both its agony and its supreme joy. Here there is the memory of the travail and agony of Calvary as well as expectation of resurrection and the new world beyond. But it is part of the Church's agony that here in the Eucharist the wholeness of its union in Christ is received only sacramentally in the brokenness of time, and the more that wholeness presses toward its complete unveiling at the *parousia* the more evident does it become that the forms of the Church's existence in this passing world are broken up in order that the abiding reality of the new creation may appear. The Sacrament of the Eucharist then is the form which our sacramental union with Christ takes within the brokenness and the divisions of history, and yet mediates the wholeness of that union as such an abiding reality that the brokenness and the divisions of history, in which the Church inevitably partakes, are revealed to be but the shell of the old life which passes away. The Eucharist is the sacrament which God has given to us as the counterpart of the ascension, for while He holds apart as yet the

[13] Cf. Thomas Aquinas, *Summa Theol.*, 3.61.4.

L

faith and sight of the Church until the *ephiphaneia* or the *apocalypsis*, He also joins them together, so that Christ makes Himself known in spite of the fraction of time. Here, as surely as the Church is given healing for its estrangement from God, it is given also healing for its divisions in history. The Eucharist speaks both of the fraction of the body on earth, evident even on the night of the Last Supper, and the 'conversion' of the Church into the risen Body of Christ.

(2) The perfect union of God and Man which has broken into time in the Virgin Birth, and inserted into history at the Cross, is yet not held a prisoner to the relativities of time, because of the resurrection. It entails a new creation which travels through time and history inasmuch as Jesus Christ lives on. Therefore, although we must communicate again and again in the real presence of this Christ-event through the Sacrament of Holy Communion, we cannot forget the reality of Baptism, that inasmuch as through Baptism the Church is once and for all incorporated into the Body of Christ, it feeds uninterruptedly upon the flesh and blood of Christ through faith (John 6). As such the Church has eternal life abiding in it (John 15). That is the reality which is so often misconstrued in terms of temporal repetition or continuity in the relativities of historical succession. To do so is to fall into the error of 'sacramental occasionalism' and to by-pass the resurrection as the enduring reality in the heart of the Church. It is precisely because the Church lives on in the power of the resurrection that it must refuse to be imprisoned in the wrappings of by-gone history or of human systems and decisions. To give these absolute significance in its tradition means that the Church denies its ultimate reality as that which comes from beyond the relativities of history, and that it fails to realise the profound eschatological element in the Eucharist: that as often as the Church communicates in the body and blood of the crucified Saviour, it receives the judgments of the Cross upon the forms and fashions of this passing world in which the Church on earth, waiting for the redemption of the body, inevitably partakes. The Church cannot participate in the Eucharist, and through it become the real Church, without placing itself under the impact of the *eschaton*. Whenever the Church denies that eschatological element in the Eucharist it becomes but a human Church, for then it denies that the Church transcends itself in the new creation, or rather

is given to transcend its embroilment in the passing forms of this world. We must be quite clear, however, that it is because the Church incorporates through the Word and Sacraments the ever-living continuity of the Christ-event travelling through and under the visible and historical continuities that the latter are disrupted, and will finally break up at the *parousia*.[14] The Church, which through Baptism has been planted into the dying and rising of Jesus and initiated into the new order, must learn to put off the old as often as through the Eucharist it participates in its new being. That is partly why apocalyptic is an inner necessity for faith and the sacramental life of the Church, for apocalypse is the fulfilment of history against itself, and apocalyptic images indicate the contradiction between the form and order of the Kingdom of God and the form and order of all earthly institutions. The very fact that in the Eucharist the Church is confronted with its own ultimate reality breaking into history from beyond history, a reality inexpressible in terms of history alone, reveals to the Church that it is also an earthly institution, but that it cannot perpetuate this historical form and order as essentially divine or as belonging to the *esse* of the Church, without either denying altogether or presumptuously anticipating the ultimate eschatological judgment. Inasmuch as by His ascension Jesus Christ has withdrawn from history His visible face and form, the true face and the true form of the Church remain essentially a *mysterion*. To deny that is to deny the essentially sacramental character of the Church's ministry, and to resolve it into a mere worldly institution.

We must now turn to another aspect of the Lord's Supper

[14] Cf. M. Schmaus, *Aus der Theologie u. Zeit* (ed. by G. Söhngen), p. 78: 'Was in der Eucharistie in der Weise des Mysteriums geschieht, wird im Leiden und im Sterben im Raume der Geschichte mächtig. Der ganze Verlauf der auf Christus folgenden Geschichte wird von ihrem Anfang und von ihrem Ende bestimmt. Am Anfang steht das Kreuz, das Zeichen des schöpferischen Untergangs. Am Ende steht der völlige Zusammenbruch der jetzigen Formen der Schöpfung sowie der neue Himmel und die neue Erde. Anfang und Ende wirken in jede Gegenwart herein. Vom Anfang und vom Ende empfängt jede Gegenwart immerfort Stösse, die ihr kein Leben in ungestörter Ruhe und Sicherheit gestatten. Unsicherheit und Ungeborgenheit gehören wesentlich zu der Welt, die im Zeichen des Kreuzes und im Zeichen des neuen Himmels und der neuen Erde steht. Die jetzigen Weltformen haben keine ewige Verheissung. Es ist vielmehr gesagt, dass sie einmal völlig zusammenbrechen werden.'

which requires elucidation, that concerned in the words: 'do this in remembrance of me', and 'ye proclaim the Lord's death till he come'. These words have received a great deal of discussion in recent literature which it is not possible to go into here. It would seem, however, that memory must be understood as *anamnesis* both before God and before man, and that *proclamation* is *objective proclamation* both before God and before man. These involve each other (cf. Mark 14. 9), though we shall have to discuss first one and then the other. The fundamental fact, however, that helps to clear up many difficulties is that memory and proclamation are here set in a sacramental context and must be interpreted accordingly if they are to elucidate the theology of the Eucharist. We are concerned here, then, with sacramental *memory* which, as Zwingli insisted, is more than 'historical faith'. It was at that Last Supper that Jesus also said: 'The Comforter, who is the Holy Ghost, whom the Father will send in my name, he shall teach you all things, and bring all things to your remembrance, whatsoever I have said unto you.' That helps us to understand. Memory that is sacramental has two sides to it (we recall again the Chalcedonian formula about the two natures of Christ) which cannot be fused or separated. It is at once the action of the historical Church for which Christ died, and the action of the eternal Spirit through whom Christ offered Himself without spot to God. The *anamnesis* is both historical and eternal, and in sacramental *anamnesis* they involve each other. The Church's memory of the historical death and resurrection of Christ in itself is merely memory of the historical past, but through the eternal Spirit by whom Christ offered Himself a sacrifice it becomes such *anamnesis* that the past is made a present reality. The eternal Spirit glorifies Christ, who died and rose again and now sits at the right hand of God, and so shows the Church things to come that He makes the Church to sit together with Christ in heavenly places. The Holy Spirit does not speak of Himself but listens to Christ who ever lives to make intercession for us, and what He hears He *echoes* in the *anamnesis* of the Church. To the Church on earth, then, it is given in its eucharistic worship to *echo* the eternal intercession of Christ. The action of the Church is the *anamnesis* of an act that is once and for all, and enduring before the Face of the Heavenly Father, but it is no more than *anamnesis*, for it is not the act itself. It is the living echo of that act which Christ alone performs as Mediator and Saviour, 'the splintered reflection on earth of Christ's presentation of His sacrifice in heaven'.[15] In the sacramental *anamnesis* the Church is raised by the eternal Spirit to the throne of God, made unto Him a kingdom and a priesthood, saying, 'Amen: Blessing and glory and wisdom and thanksgiving and honour and power and might be unto our God for ever and ever. Amen.' The Eucharist is the *Amen*, the counterpart on earth, to the eternal oblation in heaven, and the eucharistic thanksgiving the counterpoint on earth to the new song, 'Worthy is the Lamb', of the saints in the Church triumphant.

We must go on to add that the *anamnesis* of Christ's atoning death and its eternal power includes eucharistic intercession. How could the sacramental memory of His sacrifice be anything other than prayer, the prayer that has nothing to bring but clings to the Cross of Christ and holds it up before the Father, the prayer that has nothing to offer but pleads the merits of the Saviour's oblation, the prayer that knows not how to pray, but is energised by the eternal Spirit who Himself makes intercession for us with groanings that cannot be uttered? And what can His intercession be but the echoing in the Church of the intercession of the great Highpriest? And so through the *anamnesis* the Church enters into the passion of the Redeemer, and in His name travails in prayer for all mankind. We know not what to pray for as we ought, but the Spirit helps our infirmities, and through the same eternal Spirit by whom Christ offered Himself to God, we may offer our intercessions, on the merits of His sacrifice alone. And where even two or three are thus gathered together in His name, the Lord is in the midst of them. When the veil is lifted, and the mystery of that intercession is revealed, we read: 'An angel came and stood at the altar, having a golden censer; and there was given unto him much incense, that he should offer it with the prayers of all the saints upon the golden altar which was before the throne. And the smoke of the incense, which came with the prayers of the saints, ascended up before God out of the angel's hand.' *Anamnesis* before God. And so the early Church prayed at the Eucharist: 'Remember, Lord, Thy Church' (Did. 10. 5).[16]

When we turn to the eucharistic *proclamation* of the sacrificial

---

[15] Prof. D. M. MacKinnon, *Report of the Sixth Anglo-Catholic Congress*, p. 134. I have borrowed from Prof. MacKinnon his use of the word *echo* in this context.

[16] Cf. J. Jeremias, *The Journal of Theological Studies*, January–April 1949, p. 9.

death of Jesus, we find the same sacramental character that we found in the *anamnesis*. That was already apparent in the *kerygma*, where the missionary preaching of the Church was sacramentally contrapuntal to the continuing work of the risen Lord, but here we have the same *kerygma* as it is intertwined with the continuing being of the Church. Here it is *objective proclamation* in the life and action of the Church on earth, which corresponds sacramentally to the eternal action of the Lamb slain before the foundation of the world and to His eternal destination of the Church as the Bride for the future marriage-supper of the Lamb. It is more than parable; it is the actual *homoioma* of the Christ-event, in which the faith of the Church has to do not only with its objective ground but with its *objective duration*.[17] This eucharistic proclamation enshrines therefore as its eternal *canto firmo* the Self-consecration of the Lamb of God, the Self-presentation of the Mediator before the face of the Father in His intercession for the Church, but that is the *mysterion* which is the dimension in infinite depth behind the action of the Church in the Lord's Supper. The Church's proclamation is not itself identical with that mystery, but it cannot be separated from it. It is sacramentally and analogically derivative from it, but as such it is analogically different. There in heaven is the ascended Lamb Himself ever before the Face of the Father; here on earth is the waiting Church of sinners, with all saints, showing forth His death and pleading His sacrifice —'Lamb of God that takest away the sins of the world, have mercy upon us'—but both are united in the *koinonia* of the eternal Spirit, through whom Christ offered Himself to the Father, and through whom we are given to participate in that oblation made on our behalf. That is the profound mystery of Holy Communion, that the Church is given to participate (*koinonein*) in Christ's substitutionary Self-consecration ('For their sakes I sanctify myself that they also might be sanctified through the truth'), as it communicates in His body and blood, proclaiming His death until He come. 'Till He come', however, reminds us that participation in His substitutionary oblation is essentially eschatological. At last the eucharistic rite, with all its wonderful liturgy, will pass away with the passing form of this world, for it will be displaced by the Marriage-Supper of the Lamb. But in so far as that real presence of Christ in the Eucharist is the real

[17] Cf. Karl Barth, *Die Christliche Lehre nach dem Heidelberger Katechismus*, p. 99.

presence of the *Eschatos*, that future Supper in the Kingdom of God interpenetrates the present action of the Church, so that here and now the Eucharist enshrines an essential displacement of the action of the Church by the action of Christ. It is the Risen Lord Himself who is the true Celebrant at the holy table, and unless that eschatological substitution, the *mirifica commutatio*, as Calvin called it,[18] is recognised, the eucharistic sacrifice becomes but a pagan ceremony. No doubt the Church's *re-actio* to the sacrificial *actio* of Christ itself partakes of sacrificial character, but if *re-actio* is identified with the *actio*, the Sacrament is destroyed, because its derivative sacramental and analogical nature is denied. Just as the once-and-for-all sacrifice of Christ entailed the rending of the veil and the ultimate destruction of the Temple, and the undermining of its liturgical validity, so the consummation of Christ's action in the Marriage-Supper of the Lamb sets aside the eucharistic liturgy in which now we see through a glass darkly, for then we shall see face to face. 'And I saw no temple therein,' said St. John of the New Jerusalem, 'for the Lord God Almighty and the Lamb are the temple of it.' But in so far as that future Marriage-Supper of the Lamb is already present eschatologically in the Eucharist, the liturgical *re-actio* of the Eucharist is displaced by the immediate *actio* of Christ Himself, as the reality which the liturgy had proclaimed. Thus there is a point in the celebration of every Eucharist in which the real presence of the *Eschatos* suspends the liturgical action, and makes it point beyond itself for validity and order. The Son of Man is Lord also of the Eucharist, and He dispenses it as He wills. In such an eschatological economy the sacrifice of the Church can only participate in the Sacrifice of Christ by *mirifica commutatio*, and all order and liturgy have validity and truth only in so far as they leave room for such eschatological substitution. Where that is not so the Lord insists on cleansing His Temple.

That is why the life and being of the Church are intertwined with eucharistic proclamation, for the presence of the living Lord in the Church, which is the very essence of the Church, is not a static presence, but is the living action appropriated by the Church in its continuous action of proclamation.[19] In such proclamation the Church declares that its anchor is cast within the veil, that its

---

[18] *Inst.* 4. 17. 2, 4.
[19] This is brought out with great power in K. Barth's pamphlet, *Die Botschaft von der freien Gnade Gottes*.

being is grounded beyond itself in the ascended Lord, that its real life is a divine gift, and by such proclamation it opens the door in the Church for the income of that ultimate reality from beyond ('If any man open the door I will come in and sup with him and he with me'). And so the proclamation includes the *Maranatha* as an essential element in its liturgical action.

It is clear, therefore, that the bringing of the Eucharist under the rubric of proclamation excludes the idea of its being a sacrifice in itself or in its own right. Not the actual and literal offering of the sacrifice, but an action proclaiming a sacrifice once offered and eternally valid before the Father is what the Eucharist effects. In other words, by such proclamation the Eucharist becomes the sacramental counterpart to the unique sacrifice of Christ, and therefore in its own way, inasmuch as it echoes that, and is derivative from it, a sacramental sacrifice. It is thus that in the Eucharist the Church continually represents to itself and makes efficacious to itself, through the eternal Spirit, the atoning sacrifice of Christ 'through the eternal Spirit', because through the Spirit the proclaiming activity of the living Lord stands behind the Church's proclamation, as His intercession stands behind its *anamnesis*, so that it is really Christ in the Eucharist who represents to the Church and makes effective for the Church His own atoning deed of sacrifice.

The eucharistic proclamation, then, points to the *divine action* as the heart of it all. We may bring our best to the sacrifice, as Abraham brought his beloved Isaac, but at last God Himself provides a sacrifice in the place of Isaac, in His only-begotten and well-beloved Son, for the atoning deed is His and His alone, though it is wrought on our behalf. That is the very heart of proclamation and atonement, and it is from there that the significance of eucharistic sacrifice is determined.[20] This crucial point is too often missed by theologians of the 'Catholic' type, for again and again they are found using 'sacrifice' and 'offering' univocally of God and the Church. That is even true of de la Taille, although he can write nobly of this fact. 'Our sacrifices and that of Christ

---

[20] It is essentially false procedure therefore to interpret the atonement from the point of view of a theology of the Eucharist, which is itself drawn from an idea of sacrifice which has not been given creative reinterpretation in Christ, rather than to interpret the Eucharist from the point of view of a true and N.T. doctrine of atonement.

do not exist as members of one and the same genus, in the strict sense, in which the word sacrifice, used of our sacrifices and of His, would be a univocal term, but they are only in the same order by way of analogy. His sacrifice being the principle, and ours being subordinate to it. . . Just as Christ on earth absolutely and simply offered only one sacrifice, so the duality which exists between His sacrifice and ours must be made such as not to imply any repeated sacrificial offering made by Christ, but such as to subordinate immediately our own sacrificial activity to the offering of the sacrifice made by Christ in the past, which continues for ever by its own efficacy.'[21] What is it then that differentiates Christ's unique sacrifice and puts such a holy distance between it and anything that we may do even in His name? Surely that Christ bore God's judgment upon man's sin, that He did that alone on our behalf, and further, that He wrought out that atonement not as Man but as God–Man, as God in Man.

It belongs to the essence of atonement that Christ bore man's judgment, the judgment of God upon man's sin.[22] In the Cross, God identifies Himself with man just where he is farthest from Him, that is, just where he stands under the divine judgment. Such a deed of atonement whose essence is the bearing of divine judgment cannot be prolonged in a ceremonial cultus. It can only be proclaimed and celebrated. That which distinguishes Christ's atoning sacrifice from the Church's sacrifice is the bearing of judgment. We must distinguish, then, between the propitiatory sacrifice and the eucharistic sacrifice,[23] realising that the heart of Christ's unique sacrifice, the bearing of judgment, cannot be repeated in the latter in any sense. Its value lies mainly in its being a sign pointing to the divine action of atonement, and in its being entirely subordinate to that.

The atonement, however, was more than the bearing of the divine judgment. It was the offering to God of a perfect holiness, a holiness corresponding to that of God Himself, the holiness of perfect obedience. Both in bearing the divine judgment and in offering a perfect obedience, Jesus Christ stood absolutely alone, acting on our behalf. What we could not do, He has done for us.

---

[21] *The Mystery of Faith* (English trans.), Vol. II, p. 24 f.
[22] The following is indebted to an Anglican theologian, the late Dr. F. W. Camfield. Cf. *Scottish Journal of Theology*, I, p. 282 ff.
[23] Cf. John Calvin, *Institutes*, 4.18.12 f.

330 CONTRIBUTIONS TO THE PRESENT DISCUSSIONS

It was a substitutionary atonement. As the sacramental counter-part to that, the eucharistic sacrifice has not to do ultimately with our offering, but with Christ's offering on our behalf, His putting of Himself in our place, and taking upon Himself our judgment. 'All that constituted atonement was wrought in our place and in our stead; wrought verily in *our* place, that is, wrought *for* us and *as our act*.'[24] The eucharistic sacrifice answers to that *as our act*, and involves the acceptance of Him as the One who has taken our place, the acceptance of His Self-offering as our offering to God. But in the nature of the case the eucharistic sacrifice must be entirely analogous in character to the substitutionary act of Christ, and involves its wondrous exchange. It might be called the counter-sacrifice of the Church, but never can it be said to be of the same genus as the unique sacrifice of Christ Himself. By participation in His body and blood He gives us to be associated with His sacrifice, but in such a way, as in the Garden of Geth-semane, that He removes Himself to a holy distance from us. We may indeed watch with Him, but in the awful hour of His agony we know that He dies alone and we are found among those who crucified Him.

What makes Christ's sacrifice absolutely unique is the identity between the Offerer and the Offering and Him to whom the Offering is made. In this connection the Reformers were fond of citing the famous words of the great Augustine: 'Since in a sacrifice four things are considered, viz. to whom it is offered, by whom, what and for whom, the same one true Mediator, reconciling us to God by the sacrifice of peace, remains one with Him to whom He offered, made Himself one with those for whom He offered, is Himself the One who offered, and the one thing which He offered.'[25] It is that identity which sets His sacrifice absolutely apart from anything else, and makes it quite clear that the eucharistic sacrifice is only the *anamnesis* or *proclamation* of that lonely sacrifice, and does not involve any identity between a sacrifice of our own and His.

It is quite certain, however, that such a unique sacrifice invokes from us a corresponding sacrifice of thanksgiving and praise, in which we turn our proclamation of Christ's death upwards to God, and not only plead the merits of Christ's sacrifice alone, but

[24] F. W. Camfield, *op. cit.*, p. 292.
[25] *De Trinitate*, 4.24; cf. Calvin, *Inst.*, 4.18.10.

offer Him all that we have and are. How can we answer His grace except by offering ourselves up in obedience and thanksgiving? We know that we are unworthy, and can only offer Him our unworthiness, that He may make us worthy. But the worthiness which He enjoins 'consists especially in faith, which places all things in Christ, nothing in ourselves, and in love, love which, though imperfect, it may be sufficient to offer to God, that He may increase it since it cannot be fully rendered.'[26] Thus all our sacrifices of praise, prayer and thanksgiving 'depend on the greater sacrifice with which we dedicate ourselves soul, and body, to be a holy temple to the Lord. . . . We do not appear with our gifts in the presence of God without an intercessor. Christ is our Mediator, by whose intervention we offer ourselves and our all to the Father; He is our High Priest, who, having entered into the upper sanctuary, opens up an access for us: He the altar on which we lay our gifts, that whatever we do attempt, we may attempt in Him. He it is who "hath made us kings and priests unto God and His Father" '.[27]

There is a way, however, of speaking too easily about the bringing of our offerings in the Eucharist, about bringing the fruit of our labour as represented by the bread and wine, which savours rather much of the sacrifice of Cain. And then it is said that this offering and sacrifice of ours when laid on God's altar becomes identified with, and identical with, the sacrifice of Christ and we do verily offer Christ to God. Surely this *identity* involves an entire displacement of the centre of gravity, for after all, what the Eucharist proclaims is not our offering but Christ's offering on our behalf, which only in that derivative way becomes our offering. The denial of Christ's substitutionary act at this point for some doctrine of identity would mean an undermining of the atoning work of Christ. It is precisely this doctrine of identity between the bread and wine of the Eucharist with the glorified Body in the heavenly places, identity between the action of the Church on earth as it celebrates the sacrifice of Christ, and the perpetual Self-Offering of Christ Himself before the Face of the Father, which the theology of the Eucharist cannot allow, for that entails its destruction as a sacrament.[28]

[26] Calvin, *Inst.*, 4.17.42.   [27] Calvin, *Inst.*, 4.18.16 f.
[28] Cf. Karl Barth, *Die Christliche Lehre nach dem Heidelberger Katechismus*, p. 104.

Behind all this there is something deeper, an essentially Pelagian doctrine of the atonement, and certainly on a Pelagian view any substitutionary notion is impossible and abhorrent. How can Holy God allow one man to die for another, and judge the innocent man for the guilty? The doctrine of the atonement is impossible unless it is the doctrine of the divine action, of God Himself coming to intervene and to save. God indeed became man and translated divine action into terms of human action. 'Thus the background of the atoning deed is not the Godhead *per se*, but the God-manhood of Christ. But if that be so, then the idea of substitution is inevitable, and is constitutive of the doctrine of Atonement. . . . What we could not accomplish Christ accomplished on our behalf. The infliction and judgment which we could not bear, He bore for us. He took our place and on behalf of us all He made satisfaction for our sins and for the sins of the whole world. It was not the Godhead *qua* Godhead that atoned; it was the God-manhood. And that means, not simply God *in* man, but God *as* man. The manhood was integral and essential and not merely instrumental. And that means in the acutest sense, substitution.'[29]

There are, accordingly, false ways of speaking of the eucharistic sacrifice as that which invests the deed of Christ with its sacrificial nature or validity, or as that which continually presents the sacrifice of Christ to the Father. We have seen the element of truth that lies behind such views, but we must be aware of stating this in such a way as to involve a Pelagian view of the atonement as though it were not altogether a divine act.[30] A great deal of the horror of the Reformers for the doctrine of the Mass was recoil from its faulty soteriology, and its Pelagian notion of Man, even if he were the Man Jesus, appeasing God. Once it is clearly seen, however, that the atonement is God's act, and that He bears in Himself our judgment, that He does in Jesus what we cannot do, then the false doctrine of identity falls to the ground, and a true doctrine of eucharistic sacrifice can be enunciated, and a true doctrine of proclamation in which the Church can share

[29] F. W. Camfield, *op. cit.*, p. 292.

[30] This was evidently in the mind of Prof. D. M. MacKinnon, *op. cit.*, p. 134, when he corrects his own statement: 'We consecrate the death of Christ as a sacrifice, or rather, participate in the act whereby He consecrates His Passion as the recreation of the world in Him.'

in the atoning and victorious action of Christ.[31]

We must now turn to yet another aspect of the Lord's Supper, to the words 'This is my body broken for you. This is my blood shed for you.' There can be little doubt, as Calvin used to say,[32] that 'almost the whole energy of the sacrament consists in these words'. The impartial exegete cannot but conclude that it was upon these verbs that Jesus Himself laid the emphasis, that here it was intended not only that by these elements the crucifixion should evidently be set before our eyes, but that the stress should be laid upon the taking and eating and drinking, that is, in communicating in the body and blood of Christ. It is a sign of serious disorder in the Church's Eucharist when Jesus' own emphasis upon our communicating by eating and drinking His body and blood is overshadowed by a disproportionate emphasis upon the Church's sacrifice. The *Summa Theologica* of St. Thomas Aquinas is surely right when it gives the space for only one *Question* to the idea of sacrifice, and some twenty to communion in the real presence of Christ. Though the Last Supper was in point of historical time prior to the Cross, it was clearly designed, as the emphasis upon *broken* body and shed *blood* made clear, to take place as the meal following the completion of the perfect sacrifice once-and-for-all enacted on the Cross. No elaboration of exegesis upon the Old Testament can alter the fact that the sacrificial meals of the Old Testament did not repeat the act of oblation, but were the means by which the benefits of the sacrifice were conveyed.[33] The corresponding emphasis here in the eucharistic communion is the Church's thankful participation in so great salvation and its unrestrained joy (*agalliasis*) in the real presence of the risen Lord.

We can only look at the Lord's Supper through the eyes of the Apostles who were eye-witnesses of the resurrection, and who recalled that again and again when they were breaking bread the risen Jesus chose suddenly to come into their midst. Those Easter meals gave them their understanding of the rite in the Upper

[31] A crude doctrine of identity can lead to terrible extremes. Cf. W. Nicholls, *The Student World*, 1950, 1: 'The most shocking paradox of the Christian faith is that we must now will this death that we have caused.' That is to turn the eucharistic sacrifice into murder.

[32] *Inst.*, 4.17.3.

[33] Cf. Markus Barth, *Das Abendmahl-Passamahl, Bundesmahl u. Messiasmahl*, p. 25.

Room. Recalling again the union between the deity and humanity of Christ, and the nature of the sacramental union grounded upon that, we must understand the Lord's Supper in similar terms. There is then, on the one hand, the historical enactment of the rite which the Church is commanded to repeat in accordance with our Lord's institution, handed on to us by the Synoptic Gospels and St. Paul. On the other hand there are the resurrection events, such as that recorded by St. Luke of the two disciples at Emmaus to whom Jesus was made known in the breaking of bread, or that recorded in the Fourth Gospel, when 'Jesus came and stood in the midst, and saith unto them, Peace be unto you. And when he had so said, he shewed unto them his hands and his side. Then were the disciples glad when they saw the Lord. Then said Jesus unto them again, Peace be unto you: as my Father hath sent me, so send I you. And when he had said this, he breathed on them, and saith unto them, Receive ye the Holy Ghost: whosesoever sins ye remit, they are remitted unto them; and whosesoever sins ye retain, they are retained.' The Last Supper and those resurrection appearances belong together in one sacramental whole. Though Jesus has withdrawn His visible presence from us, there is such an intervention by the risen Lord as the invisible reality behind each celebration of the Lord's Supper. Jesus Christ is as really present in the Eucharist as He was on that Easter day to His disciples. As surely as in the Eucharist we handle bread and wine, we put our fingers into His wounds and He breathes upon us His peace and forgiveness in answer to the prayer: 'Lamb of God who takest away the sins of the world, grant us thy peace.' The Eucharist then is the sacramental enactment of the real presence of Christ. It is the historical action of the Church in which the historical passion of the Saviour is vividly exhibited before our eyes, but we must go on to say, with Calvin, that 'what the minister figures and attests by outward action, God performs inwardly.'[34]

When we say, however, that the Eucharist is the sacramental enactment of the real presence of Christ, we must make clear that it is the real presence of the God-Man. No doubt it is through the eternal Spirit, through an act issuing from the Godhead, but it is the divine enactment of the Incarnate Presence in the Church. Our Lord was not only the bearer of the divine Word of forgive-

[34] *Inst.*, 4.14.17.

ness, but He enacted that Word in our flesh and blood, the flesh
and blood which He had made His own from the Virgin Mary.
We may go on to say that on the ground of that supreme action,
the mystery of the incarnation and the crucifixion is sacramentally
re-enacted in those who have been baptised into Christ. When
we turn to our Lord's teaching as recorded in the Fourth Gospel,
in His discourse on the bread of life, we find that there is an eating
of the flesh and a drinking of the blood of Christ before eucharistic
participation. But how could it be otherwise inasmuch as the
Word was made flesh, for His words are Spirit and Life? The
union of the baptised with Christ through the Word involves
also a continual feeding upon the flesh and blood of Christ.[35] He
who is sacramentally incorporated into the body of Christ is
already participant in sacramental communion. We must allow
ourselves to be reminded therefore that the Eucharist presupposes
baptismal incorporation, presupposes the Church as the Body of
Christ, and that faith brings to the Eucharist a continuous feeding
upon the body and blood of Christ. What are we then to say of
eucharistic communion? Surely, as Calvin has made so clear in
the Reformed Church, that while we can only eat and drink the
body and blood of Christ through faith, that, by the power of
the eternal Spirit, the Church is given through the Eucharist a
relation in being, beyond its relation to Christ through faith. Calvin
was fond of discussing this matter with reference to the words of
the Epistle to the Ephesians: 'That Christ may dwell in your
hearts by faith, that ye being rooted and grounded in love may
be able to comprehend with all saints what is the breadth, and
length, and depth, and height; and to know the love of Christ,
which passeth knowledge, that ye might be filled with all the
fullness of God' (3. 17 f.). Christ dwells in our hearts by faith,
but His dwelling in our hearts is an ontological relation not
identical with faith, though through faith. So we may say that in
the Eucharist believing and actual communication through the
bread and wine are not one and the same thing.[36] There can be
no doubt that as yet we walk by faith and not by sight, never-

[35] Calvin's *Commentary on John*, 6.35, 53; *Inst.*, 4.17.5. Cf. 4.17.30: 'A perpetual connection with Christ could not exist unless He dwells in us *corporeally*,
independently of the use of the Supper.'

[36] See, for example, *Inst.*, 4.17.5. Cf. W. Niesel, *Calvins Lehre vom Abendmahl*, p. 38.

theless the significance of eucharistic communion lies in the fact that by the act of the eternal Spirit the believing Church is given to step over the eschatological boundary, and to partake of the divine nature. As faith and hope pass away, while love endures as the eternal reality, so here already through the Eucharist a relation in being in the love of God follows from faith and hope.[37]

We must pause to say that there is an infinite mystery here which completely transcends the ability of our minds to grasp, a mystery that is more to be adored than discussed. Wise indeed were the Chalcedonian fathers who formulated the *unio hypostatica* only in negatives, and wise are they who likewise are content to adore the mystery in the Eucharist without explanations of how the *unio sacramentalis* actually takes place. The Reformed Church standing upon the Chalcedonian Christology repudiates both Nestorianism and Eutychianism in its doctrine of the sacramental union, denying that there is either separation or fusion between the elements of bread and wine and the reality of the body and blood of Christ.[38] Just as the humanity of Christ remains true humanity even after the resurrection and ascension and is no docetic phantasm, so the bread and wine remain true bread and wine and are no mere species,[39] though by consecration they are converted into instruments of the real presence.[40] Through the consecrated elements the Church partakes of the very body and blood of Christ, and there is enacted a *true and substantial union*,[41] an ontological union, between Christ and His Church. Christ has become bone of our bone and flesh of our flesh, but in the

[37] Cf. W. Niesel, *op. cit.*, p. 95: 'Die eschatologische Grenze wird durch die Tat des heiligen Geistes überschritten, und aus dem Glauben folgt ein Sein in Christus.' Cf. also W. Eugen, *Das Kommen des Herrn*, Vol. I, p. 38 ff.

[38] This was the position taken up by Zwingli against Luther, by Calvin against both Romanists and extreme Lutherans, and by Peter Martyr in his notable controversy with the Bishop of Winchester at Oxford. It passed into Anglican theology and became a feature of the Caroline divines.

[39] Calvin argued that the doctrine of transubstantiation involved docetic heresy, for it undermined the analogy between the elements and the reality which they figured. 'The analogy between the sign and the thing signified cannot be destroyed without destroying the truth of the sacrament.' *Inst.*, 4.

[40] For a clear statement on the conversion of the elements see the *Sermons on the Sacraments* by Robert Bruce, the Scottish divine (Laidlaw's edition), p. 104.

[41] This was Calvin's usual way of stating the nature of the union.

Eucharist we become bone of His bone and flesh of His flesh. No union, save that of the Persons of the Holy Trinity, could be closer, without passing into absolute identity, than that between Christ and His Church as enacted in the Holy Eucharist.

It is in the Eucharist, then, that the Church really becomes the Church, both as the ontological and eschatological reality and as the extension into history of the visible sacramental fact which is the Church's existence on earth. It is both the impregnation of the Church with its divine mystery, and the manifestation of that mystery within history without its ceasing to be mystery. In no sense can the Church be said to be an extension of the incarnation, though here we have to do with the re-enactment by the Word of its becoming flesh. The Eucharist, therefore, together with Baptism, involves the mystery of the incarnation, the Virgin Birth and the resurrection of Christ. The Virgin Birth and the Resurrection were the miraculous signs through which the divine Word both entered history in Self-revelation, and yet ever remained identical with Himself. Parallel to that, Baptism and the Eucharist are the miraculous signs through which the divine Word enters into the Church it has called out of the world, in Self-impartation, and yet ever remains identical with Himself. Baptism and Eucharist as one Sacrament are analogically related in the Holy Spirit to the Virgin Birth and the Resurrection as the one act of divine Self-revelation. Virgin Birth and Resurrection, however, involved more than Self-revelation; they involved the actual descent of the Son of God into our humanity, and the actual ascent of the Son of God in ascension bearing with Him our humanity. Likewise in the Eucharist there takes place an actual *katabasis* of the living Lord, and an actual *anabasis* in which He bears the Church up with Him to the throne of God—whether 'in the body or out of the body', who can tell? But it is an eschatological anticipation both of the Advent of the Son of Man and the rapture of the Church. The Eucharist involves at its very heart the *sursum corda*, for our union with Christ in history and yet out of history is a reality that utterly transcends all our categories of space and time.

The incomprehensible fact is that God begins eternally with Himself. The Son is begotten, not made. And the ineffable mystery of the Eucharist is that in it God begins with Himself in the continuity of the Church's action in the creaturely world, but independent of it.[42] That has supreme importance for what follows in our next section, for it means that the Church through its ministry can no more exercise its authority over the Eucharist than Joseph could exercise his authority over the Virgin Birth. As Joseph could only stand aside at the miracle of the incarnation, so the ministry of the Church can only stand aside even in the Eucharist where it is ordained to serve. The Church can never manage the Eucharist or exercise any lordship over it unless it wishes to be like the kings of the Gentiles that exercise lordship and authority over them and are called benefactors. At the Last Supper Jesus took pains to make that clear, enacting a vivid parable before the disciples in washing their feet that they might learn to forswear all lordship. The Kingdom appointed to the Church and its ministry at the Eucharist is grounded on the abasement of Christ unto death, and is one of service (*diakonia*). The Church is joined to its Lord at the Eucharist only as a body is joined to its head. The Eucharist means the enactment of the authority of Christ the Head over the Church and over its ministry. *Ecce ancilla Domini*. Inasmuch as the mystery of the Virgin Birth is sacramentally present in the Eucharist, it belongs to the Church in the Eucharist humbly to *receive* (*Take ye, eat ye*) the eternal Word as the ground of the Church's being, and to be entirely subordinate to Him as Word.[43] Further, inasmuch as the mystery of the Resurrection is sacramentally present in the Eucharist, it belongs to the Church in the Eucharist to acknowledge that its outward historical form which partakes of the fashion of this passing world is made the empty tomb out of which the new creation is raised up to enter the Kingdom of God. This means that at every true Eucharist, where there is a sacramental enactment of the mystery of the Virgin Birth and the Resurrection of the Body, there is involved an eschatological suspension of historical continuity and the order and authority which that involves.

[42] See the superb discussion by Karl Barth, *Dogmatik*, I, 2. p. 187 ff., *Das Wunder der Weinacht*, to which I am much indebted.

[43] Cf. Edmund Schlink, *The Student World*, 1950, I, p. 48: 'The Church is the place, the creation and the instrument of the Lord's Supper but never its Lord. On the other hand, we find degeneration where the Church departs from its function as receiver and server of the Lord's Supper and makes itself lord of the Lord's Supper.'

Intercommunion and Order

We must now draw the foregoing discussion to a close by working out its implications in regard to intercommunion. We may begin by recalling an incident which all three Synoptic Gospels record, the objection by the Priests and Scribes to our Lord's cleansing of the Temple (or reformation of the Church), and to His practice of teaching in the Temple against the priestly order. They came to Jesus and asked Him: 'By what authority doest thou these things? And who gave thee this authority to do these things?' Our Lord answered first by reference to Baptism and then by a telling parable which the Priests and Scribes recognised as directed against the priestly and legal mind. Jesus was undoubtedly referring to cleansing before sacrifice, and to the eschatological preaching of John that the axe is laid to the root of the tree. He indicated further that one cannot ask questions about the highest authority, for that is to misconceive it—and it is upon that misconception that all rigid doctrine of orders is based. But may we not allow His words to remind us of something else, that the authority for Reformation and the administration of the Eucharist, even against the priestly and legal notion of validity in the idea of episcopal succession, is derived from Holy Baptism? If Baptism means actual incorporation into the Body of Christ, and already means through the Word a continuous feeding upon the flesh and blood of Christ, as our Lord stated so clearly in the Fourth Gospel, who are we to deny those so baptised renewal of their incorporation in the Body of Christ, provided that they are sincere? Baptism reminds us that Christ dwells in us corporeally, independently of the Supper, for otherwise absolute continuity there could not be. Baptism reminds us that the real continuity of the Body of Christ is not to be sought on the plane of historical relativity but in the continuous act of God, which in the Resurrection is continuous temporal fact. Therefore to refuse the Eucharist to those baptised into Christ Jesus and incorporated into His resurrection-body amounts either to a denial of the transcendent reality of holy Baptism or to attempted schism within the Body of Christ. How can we hold apart the Body of Christ from the Body of Christ? How can we hold apart the once-and-for-all incorporation into that Body and its continual renewal in the Holy Eucharist? Surely a clear and high doctrine of Holy Baptism forbids us to allow any wedge to be driven between Baptism and Eucharist. If Baptism is of the living God, then who can deny those baptised the right to partake of the Eucharist? If Baptism is of men, then we disinherit the masses of common people.

We must turn to another incident, however, to see more clearly into this question of authority—to the encounter between our Lord and the Pharisees over the Sabbath-breaking of the disciples, also recorded by all the Synoptic Gospels. It is the incident in which Jesus declared: 'The sabbath is made for man, and not man for the sabbath; therefore the Son of Man is Lord also of the sabbath.' The context speaks about Jesus' eating and drinking with publicans and sinners, which as we have seen was an enactment of the Messianic meal; then it speaks about the coming and going of the Bridegroom, the new wine of the Kingdom of God which always breaks old bottles when poured into them, and the action of Abiathar who did not refuse to give to outcast David and his hungering friends the holy bread that was reserved by sacred law for priests alone. It is in such a significant context that these words about the authority of the Son of Man are recorded. In the presence of the Son of Man the barriers to intercommunion are thrown down, the new wine of the Kingdom breaks the old bottles, the sacred bread from the altar is distributed to the hungry, and publicans and sinners are freely invited to eat and drink with the Lord. The Son of Man is therefore the Lord of Sabbath and all that it stands for, the Lord of the cult, the Lord of the sacred bread. It is in entire keeping for us in the Christian age to say, following our Lord: 'The Eucharist was made for man, and not man for the Eucharist. Therefore the Son of Man is Lord also of the Eucharist.' That is to say, the Son of Man reserves the right to dispense His own Supper to whom He will, and to distribute the holy bread to the outcasts and the hungry, in spite of all priestly protestations. In the presence of the eschatological Christ, the Son of Man, all barriers to intercommunion are broken down. So it will certainly be when the Bridegroom comes, and the Marriage-supper of the Lamb takes place. But in as much as there is the real presence of the *Eschatos*, of the Son of Man, in the Eucharist, the new wine which we drink in the Kingdom of God breaks down the old vessels and spills over freely to all who hunger and thirst after righteousness. So soon as we realise that the Eucharist is charged with the real presence of the Son of Man, to whom all judgment has been committed, we realise that it is the Lord's Supper (*Kyriakon deipnon*) and not our own (*idion deipnon*) and that we cannot send any Church or any sincere baptised believer away, without sinning against the majesty and grace of the Son of Man.

That does not mean that the Church is prohibited from 'fencing the Table', by excluding from participation in the Eucharist the lapsed who have denied their Baptism or the impenitent and insincere, but it does mean that the Church must exercise its discipline *with the authority of the Son of Man*, and not with the authority of Priests and Scribes and Pharisees. It is by the Word that the Son of Man exercises His authority, and by the Word that He judges and divides between men. 'Lord how wilt thou manifest thyself unto us and not unto the world? Jesus answered and said, If a man love me he will keep my word and my Father will love him, and we will come unto him and make our abode with Him.' 'If any man hear my voice and open the door I will come in and sup with him and he with me.' On the other hand, Jesus says also: 'If any man hear my words and believe not, I judge him not: for I came not to judge the world but to save the world. He that rejecteth me and receiveth not my words, hath one that judgeth him: the words that I have spoken, the same shall judge him in the last day.' It is with just such judgment, said St. Paul, that the discernment of the Lord's Body in the Eucharist is concerned. In other words, the real fencing of the holy Table is lodged in the prophetic ministry through which the holy Majesty and Grace of the Son of Man are brought to bear upon the Church. It is when the Son of Man, Christ crucified and Christ to come, is proclaimed with power in all His saving grace and judgment, that the Table is kept holy and undefiled; and it is then when His Word and authority are glorified that it is indeed the Lord's Table and the Lord's Supper, and not a private supper owned and administered on exclusive principles by the Church. It cannot be said too plainly that whenever the prophetic ministry decays, whenever the Church refuses to give priority to the ministry of the Word over the ministry of Tables, the priestly authority gets out of hand, and inevitably falls under the judgment of the Son of Man.

There is another aspect of this matter to which we must give full recognition, for it is of the utmost importance—the place of order in the Church. 'The spirits of the prophets are subject to the prophets; for God is not the author of confusion but of peace, as in all the Churches of the saints' (I Cor. 14. 32). That means that the Church and its ministry cannot be indifferent to church order. There is a subjection even in the realm of spiritual gifts and *charismata*. On the other hand, St. Paul says quite plainly that 'the Lord is the Spirit, and where the Spirit of the Lord is, there is liberty' (II Cor. 3. 17). There cannot be any absolute fixity of order in the charismatic ministry of the Church. How are we to understand this order in which there is both freedom and control? That was one of the crucial problems facing St. Paul in the Corinthian Church, and the answer he gave is taken straight out of the Eucharist, though it is closely linked with Baptism.[44]

We may fill out St. Paul's thought with other New Testament teaching, and put the matter in the following way. In Baptism the Church is incorporated into the Body of Christ and puts on Christ. That is to say, the Church partakes of the form of Christ's Body. The conformity of the Church to Christ, which is once-and-for-all in Baptism, is not static, but dynamic, for it is bound up with the Church's obedience as it carries out the ordinance of the Lord to proclaim His death till He come. That concerns both missionary *kerygma* and the eucharistic proclamation, though it is above all in the Eucharist where the Church knows Christ in the fellowship of His sufferings and the power of His Resurrection that it becomes conformable unto Him. There the Church is crucified unto the world, and is transformed by the renewing of its mind into the image or form of Jesus Christ. It is in the Eucharist, too, that the Church becomes visible as the Body of Christ in history, for it is there that it becomes a membered Body under the Headship of Christ. 'We being many are one body for we all partake of the one bread.' That membering or ordering of the Church is the new order or the new covenant of the Kingdom, into which the Church is initiated at Baptism, but which now materialises in visible bodily fashion. It is the constitution of the Church in Jesus Christ.

Christ is Prophet, Priest and King. Therefore the Church,

[44] Cf. especially for the following, E. Käsemann, *Evangelische Theologie*, 1948, 9-10; and H. Dobert, *Evangelische Theologie*, 1949, 11.

which in Baptism puts on Christ and in the Eucharist becomes one Body with Him, is given to participate in that *triplex munus*. As His Body the Church manifests the form of that Body as it exercises in obedience to Him a prophetic, priestly and kingly ministry. We have to remember, however, that the Church is only joined to Christ as a body is joined to its head, and its ministry as Body is not the same as the ministry of the Head. To take priesthood, for example, with which we are mostly concerned at this point in our discussion: Christ's Priesthood and the Church's priesthood cannot be spoken of in univocal terms any more than Christ's sacrifice and the eucharistic sacrifice. They are not of the same genus. Once that is understood clearly a great deal of the confusion resulting from the ambiguous use of the word 'priesthood' can be swept away. It should be perfectly clear right away, therefore, that the Church's priesthood cannot be thought of as having in any way control over Christ, any more than the body can control the head.

Two further facts about the ministry of the Church must be noted:

(*a*) The Form of Christ in the Eucharist remains a mystery, and is not to be fully discerned. We see Christ by faith, only through a glass darkly, for He is veiled behind the elements as well as unveiled or revealed through them. That means that the whole question of the Church's order and ministry is bound up with the Self-revelation of Christ, and because of that the Church's order cannot come under its ultimate control. It belongs to the nature of Revelation to take concrete form as human word, human form, human ordinance. Revelation therefore conceals Christ behind word, sacrament, ordinance, as well as reveals Him. A direct reading off of the Church's form and order from the Eucharist is impossible. It belongs to the nature of the Church to bear witness in definite orders to the Form of the Body of Christ and so to manifest that Form in historical conditions, but because that Form is the content of Revelation the Church cannot transcribe it into the conditions of time and history in any perfect or indelible or fixed structure. Every time it partakes of the Eucharist it allows its order or historical structure to be called in question by that which here comes from beyond history and is not expressible in terms of history alone. It is only in such a way that we can think of the order or the orders of the Church.

(b) In this situation it is the function of the Church's ministry to build or edify the Church on earth by Word and Sacrament, so that the form and order of the Church in history may correspond sacramentally to the true form and order that are yet to be revealed. This means that we must think of the priesthood of the Church as having an essentially sacramental character. Through Baptism and the Lord's Supper the Church is formed into a corporate priesthood, a royal priesthood,[45] but that priesthood remains essentially a mystery, and only becomes visible in a historical and membered priesthood which points to a fullness beyond itself. That is why St. Paul speaks of this membered priesthood not in terms of priesthood but in terms of *charismata*. We may distinguish then between the Church's priesthood and *charismata*, by saying that the priesthood is essentially corporate, is a whole, and cannot be broken up into parts. *Charismata* are the gifts of the ascended Lord, and are essentially fragmented. Not all are prophets, not all are Apostles, or teachers or workers of miracles. There are diversities of gifts and administrations and operations, but it is the same Spirit, the same Lord, and the same God who worketh all in all, and behind all this diversity of gifts and members there is one body in Christ. The diverse *charismata* have no value in themselves, but only as they minister together to the edification of the whole body.

The Church in history, then, is related to its ascended Lord by means of these diverse *charismata*, which partake indeed of historical fragmentation and which shall therefore pass away before the ultimate reality which is the oneness of the Church to Christ in love (I Cor. 13),[46] but which here and now are the historical means that God uses to build up the Church on earth. In this situation it is the function of the ministry to edify the Church by Word and Sacrament, that its form and order more and more approximate to and partake of the one Body of Christ. That takes place above all in the Lord's Supper, where the *charismata* are to be regarded as the signs pointing to the new divine order which is ever breaking through the eucharistic participation and being

[45] Cf. I Pet. 2. 5, 9; Rev. 1. 6; Luke 22. 29; I Cor. 11. 25; II Cor. 3. 6. The Church in the New Covenant is appointed at once a Kingdom and a priesthood or a ministry.

[46] Cf. W. Eugen, *Das Kommen des Herrn*, I, p. 38 f., 90 ff.

realised afresh in the Church on earth. That new divine order is only visible in orders that serve it truly and never in orders that obscure it or seek to manage it. It is the function of orders to make room in the Church and to keep that room open for the actual intervention of the ascended Lord in Word and Sacrament.

Here in the Eucharist, therefore, we are given our deepest insight into the meaning of order under the Lordship of Christ, as order which is sacramentally and eschatologically conditioned. The actual ordering of the Church partakes of the form and fashion of this passing world, and as such it can never be identified in its historical structure with the essential form of the Church or be allowed to anticipate the order yet to be fully disclosed in the *eschaton*. It can only point beyond itself. The Church that is truly ordered will possess its orders as if it possessed them not, coveting earnestly the more excellent way which abides for ever, the way of love, when all orders, however necessary and sacramental they are within history, will pass away. Such a Church will watch and pray for its Lord, waiting for His coming, when it will put off the image of the earthly, the compromised ecclesiastical shell that marks its continuing historical existence, and put on the image of the heavenly.

From all this, three conclusions follow which are important for our discussion of intercommunion.

(1) The Eucharist cannot be subordinated to any conception of order. If the Church really becomes the Church in the Eucharist, how can it bring order to the Eucharist if it is there that it receives its order with its true being? It is only because there are repeated celebrations of the Eucharist that the Church can bring order to the Eucharist, but the very repetition of the Eucharist means the relativisation of that prior order and its reordering in the presence of the Church's Lord. As often as we celebrate the Lord's Supper we proclaim His death till He come, we enact His death and His resurrection into the existence of the Church, and so bear about the dying of the Lord Jesus in the body of the Church that the life also of Jesus may be made manifest in that body. Through the Eucharist, therefore, death worketh in the Church and its members and orders. If through the Eucharist the Spirit of Christ is in the Church, then its 'body' is dead, mortified by the death of Christ—that is to say, its 'body' understood as its implication in

the forms of this world. It is only when through the eucharistic enactment the judgment inherent in the death of Christ is allowed to break up the hardened forms of the Church's liturgy, into which eschatology is continually being transmuted, that the Church can truly serve the Lord it worships, and at the same time hold out life to the world.

It is sometimes argued that the Eucharist does not stand alone, but is embedded in the historical continuity or the institutional continuity of the Church, including its structure of faith and order, which is part of the significance of its continual repetition in the action of the Church. Undoubtedly the celebration of the Eucharist is so embedded in the institutional continuity of the Church, but the Eucharist by its very nature, in as much as it enshrines the real presence of the Son of Man, the Lord of the Eucharist, stands above the institutional continuity of the Church and *can never be made relative to it*, for that would make the Church the master of the Son of Man and not His servant.[47] This is the crucial point in ecumenical discussion on intercommunion, for it is here that the ultimate difficulty lies, in the difference between Churches which take biblical eschatology seriously and those who are retrenched in a fixity of orders within which they involve the *Lord's* Supper as though it were their own. As Professor Manson has said so well (in the same article): 'The sacrament is a catholic ordinance for catholic approach. It proclaims (not the Church in the Lord) but the Lord in the Church.' It is one of the extraordinary facts about the ecumenical fellowship that to-day the younger Churches are everywhere feeling the pressure of the coming Kingdom upon them and bear evidence of a truly charismatic ministry—that is nowhere more in evidence than in the Church of South India—but some of the older Churches show, on the contrary, evidence of a marked hardening of their orders, which can only be interpreted as a sign of the last times.

(2) The Eucharist cannot be subordinated to history. The enactment of the eucharistic presence into the flesh and blood of history means that the Church can never be allowed to forget its involvement in history. We do not stand before the Son of Man

---

[47] For a remarkably clear discussion of this fact, to which I am much indebted, see Prof. W. Manson, 'Church and Intercommunion', *Scottish Journal of Theology*, 4 1, p. 4 f.

as we shall do when He comes again, for His suspension of final judgment until the last day gives history its course. The Church stands to-day and all through history where the Lord's Supper takes place, between the Resurrection of Jesus Christ and His Second Advent, that is, in the midst of history. The Revelation, which calls the Church into being and recreates it from age to age, takes place within history, and it is there that the living Lord gives Himself to be known to us, within the actual ongoing historical Church and nowhere else. On the other hand, the eucharistic presence involves the power of the Resurrection, which breaks the fetters of history and tells us that the risen Lord cannot be holden in the fixity of the past. In other words, the Eucharist means the enactment of the real presence of the living Christ to-day, and every day it is celebrated. But if we have to do with the real presence of Christ *to-day*, we dare not bind that to the embodiment of Christ in His Church in the passing forms of another day—that would be to perpetuate a dead Christ and to by-pass the resurrection from the dead. If Christ had not ascended and we had continuous visible contact with Him to-day, that would doubtless mean that the historical events of His birth, ministry in Judaea and Galilee, and death under Pontius Pilate, would be relegated to the incidents of past history and perhaps forgotten, but His ascension tells us that to know Jesus Christ and make contact with Him we must concentrate upon those historical events of His birth, life and death; that is to say, we must concentrate upon the historical foundation of the Church's faith. 'I have delivered unto you that which also I have received. . . . As often as ye do this ye proclaim the Lord's death till He come.' At the same time the withdrawal of Christ by ascension from visible implication in ongoing history, and His promise to come again as the Lord and Judge of History, tells us that all historical existence is made relative to His immediate presence. It is that real presence which breaks into history in the Eucharist, from beyond history, and which cannot be construed in terms of history alone, which cannot be imprisoned in history, either in the history of a particular period such as the Catholic ages or the Reformation, or in the long sweep of church history. The Eucharist therefore cannot be made subordinate to history, for it is creative of history.

Nor can we forget the fact that every time in the Eucharist we eat the broken body and partake of the blood of Christ we are communicating in the death of Christ, partaking of the judgment which that death involved, in order that we might also partake of the power of His resurrection. To participate in the Eucharist and its proclamation of the death of Christ until He come is to involve the Church in the final judgment upon the forms of history in order that its new life may appear. The repeated celebrations of the Eucharist do not mean that the Church is growing old with tradition and ancient glory, for its glory is yet to be revealed in the manifestation of the Son of Man, but it means that the Church is ever growing younger and younger, until at last it arrives at the great day when as a Bride it shall be presented to the Bridegroom for the consummation of its joy in the Marriage-Supper of the Lamb. In as much as the Eucharist is an anticipation of that day, it stands above history, and can never be subordinated to it or made relative to the fixity of its passing forms.

(3) If the Eucharist cannot be subordinated to history or to any particular conception of order, but is the transcendent manifestation of the Son of Man within history until He come in the fullness of His glory, then the Eucharist is above all the divinely given means of unity in the Church. 'We being many are one body for we all partake of the one bread.' That is a fact that can never be made relative to anything outside of it, if it is not to be dwarfed and domesticated into a private rite. The very place of the Eucharist between the two Advents of Christ, in the very midst of history with all its divisions and heartrending failures, means that it is designed to be such a means of unity within diversity that in spite of diversity and division that unity is continually recreated in conditions of time until its full reality is disclosed in the Kingdom to come. We are unable to trace the lineaments of the Kingdom in the fragmented patterns of history so that we can say, lo here is the *Una Sancta*, or, lo there is the *Una Sancta*. But we know that we have been baptised into one Body, and that there is one Lord, one Faith, one Baptism. Supervening upon that we have been given the Holy Eucharist as the sacrament of unity in diversity to tell us that our oneness with the Lord does not depend upon our success or failure in loyalty to Him, but on His Will to be one with us and to make us all one in Him. That belongs to the heart of Christ's highpriestly intercession, and we cannot hold that the Eucharist is in any sense

the counterpart on earth to that (not merely in some pious mystic hope, but in actual enactment of the mystery of our unity in flesh and blood) without believing that it is through participation in the Eucharist that we are meant *more and more* (as Calvin put it) *to coalesce in one body with Him and so with each other*. If the Sacrament only proclaimed that unity in word and did not also serve to enact it, it would not be the Sacrament that the Church holds it to be. Here the corporeal Self-communication of Christ to the Church through the one bread and the one cup, actually enacts in flesh and blood the unity of the one Lord, and constrains us to concrete corporeal obedience in the one Body of the Lord. The refusal of intercommunion entails a failure to discern the Body of the Lord and an unworthy participation in His body and blood. St. Paul told the Corinthians quite explicitly that for groups to meet for communion separately is not to hold the *Lord's* Supper, but to turn it into a private supper, and indeed to create schism in the Church. It is for that cause that so many are weak and sickly in the Church. There can be no doubt, therefore, that Churches ought to sit down together before the presence of the Son of Man, and together eat and drink the judgment of the death of Christ upon their sinful divisions and compromised histories, in order that together they might be given anew the power of the resurrection to rise above the trammels of the past and to realise the very unity of the one Body into which they have been baptised. This means that intercommunion should come early in the approach of the Churches toward full unity in the ecumenical fellowship, for that unity can never be reached so long as the separated Churches refuse to give each other the divine medicine for their healing. The Holy Eucharist cannot be celebrated without the breaking of the bread and the pouring out of the wine. Let it be celebrated, then, within the fraction of the Church, wherever the Church is sincere enough to resist unto blood everything that stands between it and its Lord. Let the Church that gives communion to another remember the words of the Lord: 'In as much as ye have done it unto one of the least of these my brethren, ye have done it unto me.' And let the Church that refuses to give communion to another remember also those other words of the same Lord which will be spoken at the final judgment: 'I was an hungered and ye gave me no meat: I was thirsty and ye gave me no drink.' 'Lord, when saw we thee an hungered or athirst, and did not minister unto thee? Then shall he answer them, In as much as ye did it not unto one of the least of these, ye did it not unto me.' Those are solemn words which have direct bearing upon intercommunion.

It is certain that at the last day all the barriers of liturgy and cult and order that have been erected in history around the Holy Table of the Lord will be torn down, for in that great day, 'The Spirit and the Bride say, Come. And let him that heareth say, Come. And let him that is athirst come. And whosoever will, let him take of the water of life freely.' And St. John adds, if any man shall take away these words from the Book of Prophecy, God shall take away his part out of the Book of Life, and out of the Holy City. We cannot afford to wait until the *eschaton* to hear those words. The Eucharist is given to us here and now as an anticipation within history of the Marriage-supper of the Lamb. In every true Eucharist, therefore, the Church, as the Bride of Christ, will join the Spirit, saying, *Come. Whosoever will, let him take the water of life freely.* Only when that happens can it be an eschatologically valid Eucharist.

XIX

INTERCOMMUNION AND CO-CELEBRATION

★

L. Zander

Orthodox Oecumenical Patriarchate (Exarchate for the Russians in the West)

(France)

The Sacrament of Holy Communion is a sacrament of unity. It is the fullest expression of the unity between God and man, of the unity of men with one another and the unity of this world with the kingdom of the world to come. But unity presupposes concord: concord in thought, that is, unity of faith; concord in life, that is, unity of love. If there is no such concord, the sacrament of unity may prove to be merely a symbol of unity, a sign with no reality behind it, a form without content, a collection of letters that do not spell a word. In speaking of spiritual matters we constantly fall into the sin of verbalism: we deceive ourselves and others. We speak of unity and imagine that the word we have uttered indicates a fact already realised. But in approaching the Sacrament we grow more careful and responsible; for a sacrament is faith *in actu*, a crystallisation, as it were, of the Church's life and thought—dogmas and canons in actualised, embodied, sensible form. Therefore everything to do with sacraments is full of meaning, significant and responsible, and in a sense *irrevocable*.

That is why the problem of intercommunion is both the touchstone of our divisions and the judgment upon them; it is the point at which the differences between us inevitably involve both a profession of objective truth and a struggle between feelings. For the paradox which lies at the basis of ecumenism—'concord of the discordant', 'conflict of loyalties', 'unity without union'—becomes at this point a vital personal conflict. Love for the separated brethren conflicts with loyalty to truth; the longing for unity is defeated by the fact of separation: not by the sin of

351

division, not by the desire to be in the right at any price, but by each one being rooted in the life of his Church, of his confession, opposed and contradictory to others.

At one of the Faith and Order Congresses a Protestant pastor reproached the Orthodox Church for not accepting intercommunion. 'It is a lack of love,' he said, 'I should like to communicate with you, but you prevent me, you refuse communion to me.' At that moment another pastor came up and said to him: 'And I wouldn't communicate with you even if you invited me, for your communion is based upon a false doctrine and is a distortion of Christ's commandment.'

This sharp retort expresses a profound thought: a sacrament presupposes faith; faith, expressed in words, is a dogma; a dogma, explained and expounded, is a theological doctrine. By the very fact of approaching the chalice an Orthodox Christian confesses the faith of the Church, the faith of the fathers, and accepts all that is implied by the Orthodox Eucharist: the idea of the bloodless sacrifice, of the participation of all the saints in it—the living and the departed—and first and foremost of the Mother of God and St. John the Baptist, the faith that the consecrated elements are indeed the Lord's body and blood. For him who accepts all these truths (and many others) and shares the Orthodox faith, participation in the Orthodox Eucharist is natural, legitimate and salutary. But for a man who denies the sacrificial character of the Eucharist, does not revere Our Lady, has lost touch with the saints and believes that the consecrated elements are merely bread and wine, participation in an Orthodox Eucharist would be a falsehood, an outward sign without inner meaning, and, indeed, a betrayal of his own faith and disloyalty to his Church.

As a matter of fact Protestants do not seek to partake of the Orthodox Eucharist, but they resent the fact that the Orthodox will not and cannot receive communion from their chalice. But surely to accept eucharistic gifts from the hands of a minister who has no apostolic ordination is tantamount to renouncing the mystical doctrine of apostolic succession? Partaking of bread and wine instead of Christ's body and blood would mean renouncing the Eucharist which the Orthodox regard as the only true one. The Communion Services of different Protestant denominations have theological implications of their own, just as the Orthodox Eucharist and the Roman Mass. True, they have a general background which is the basis of the pan-Protestant intercommunion (as at Oxford, Oslo and Amsterdam), but in truth Lutherans, Calvinists, Zwinglians, Methodists, Baptists, 'Disciples of Christ' and others interpret the meaning of the Lord's Supper so differently that their joint communion from the same chalice can only be regarded as an expression of 'sacramental pietism': what matters is to be united with Christ, to lift one's spirit to the Lord in prayer, but how this is achieved, what a person thinks and believes about it, is of secondary and purely human importance.

There is no doubt whatever that Protestant Communion Services actually signalise spiritual union with Christ of those who believe in it and long for it. But this *spiritual* communion, even if performed by means of external symbols—by partaking of bread and wine—is in direct contradiction with the words of the Lord: 'Verily, verily, I say unto you: except ye eat the flesh of the Son of man, and drink his blood, ye have no life in you. For my flesh is meat indeed, and my blood is drink indeed. He that eateth my flesh, and drinketh my blood, dwelleth in me, and I in him' (John 6. 53-56). Words of which our Lord Himself has said that 'they are spirit, and they are life' do not admit of misinterpretation. The Orthodox accept them as a revealed truth, as the most important dogma of the Church, and the basis of the eucharistic mystery; any other interpretation of them (such as the theory of impanation, or of the bread and wine being a sign, etc.) is in our view a deviation from the true Eucharist, a distortion of the Gospel commandment and an attempt to adapt the 'hard saying' (John 6. 60) of the Saviour to the demands and frailties of human reason. It is therefore understandable that though we love Protestant piety and give it its due, we cannot take part in Protestant sacraments—not because they have no value for us, but because we have no mystical access to that domain. Abstinence from participation in other Churches' sacraments is due not to contempt, but on the contrary to our responsible and respectful attitude to them. If we regarded them as mere ceremonies having no real power, the question of taking part in them or not would be simply a question of inter-ecclesiastic politeness and ordinary good manners. But we cannot participate in Protestant sacraments precisely because they are *sacraments* of the separated Churches: to take part in them would mean entering into the very heart of

Churches whose doctrine and worship we consider incorrect. This is why participation in another Church's sacraments means in fact joining that Church and is a symbolic renunciation of the truth of one's own Church.

It is said in answer to this that 'the sacrament of the holy Communion is the Table of the Lord and not of men'. What right have men to admit or not to admit anyone to it? How can we put ourselves between Christ and those whom He calls to His Supper? This argument is obviously a mixture of sacramental and eschatological conceptions. We know, of course, that 'many shall come from the east and west, and shall sit down with Abraham and Isaac and Jacob, in the kingdom of heaven, but the children of the kingdom shall be cast out into outer darkness' (Matt. 8. 11-12); but this prophecy about the *final* destiny of man (of every man) does not give us a right to admit to the sacrament of Christian communion pious Mohammedans or pagans, even if they resemble the centurion of the Gospel. And indeed this is not suggested by the Churches that have 'open Communion': they admit to it all Christians without distinction, though some limit it to those who have been baptised and are communicants in their own Church. But this already *is* a limitation, and it is in direct opposition to the idea that Christ Himself calls men to His supper, and they must not interfere with it. But how could this be realised in practice? If, approaching the chalice, I receive it directly from the hands of Christ, what have the minister, the parish, the order of the service, etc., to do with it? Why can I not receive Christ in my own home, in my own family, and perform my own Eucharist quite independently of any ecclesiastical ordinances and the theology and the rules implied by them? But this would be a complete disintegration of the Church as an institution; a clear (and pious) spiritual expression of this is the rejection of all sacramentalism by the Society of Friends. For the best among them *every* partaking of bread and wine, even in the ordinary course of life, is the image of the Last Supper. But this sacramental nihilism is scarcely in keeping with what we know about the Eucharist at the apostolic age and throughout the history of Christianity.

Our Lord Jesus Christ entrusted the Sacrament of Communion to the Church. The Church is the body of Christ, living in human history. But having, like Christ, both a heavenly and an earthly nature, it is subject to all the limitations of time and space. Hence, the Church has not only the mystical reality of the Bride of the Lamb but also the earthly form of a sacramentally canonical organisation. As members of this heavenly and earthly, mystical and canonical body, we live both in the eternity promised to the Church and in the fullness of forms which its earthly historical existence assumes; and the latter presupposes a canonical structure, that is, organisation and therefore limitedness.

Hitherto only the dogmatic impossibility of intercommunion between the separated Churches has been discussed, and of that, it seems to me, there can be no doubt. But there is another, less radical impossibility which may be called canonical. It exists when there are no inner obstacles to intercommunion, and the only thing that prevents it is obedience to our respective Churches, which for some reason do not allow it. This is the case between the Orthodox and the Old Catholics, the Orthodox and the Jacobites, and sometimes between the Orthodox and the Anglicans. The doctrinal differences between these Churches do not concern the basic questions of religion, and their eucharistic theology is the same. Accordingly there are no mystical, no dogmatic and no psychological obstacles to intercommunion. But if, for any reason, the ecclesiastical authorities do not sanction it, the faithful must abstain from it, contrary to their own wishes, and even contrary to their inner conviction; the work of the Church is a common work, and not that of separate individuals, and church discipline compels me to follow a practice which in my own personal conviction may be a historical misunderstanding or even a sign of spiritual stagnation in the life of the Church. This canonical abstention from intercommunion gives rise to quite different feelings than does the dogmatic impossibility. It involves no tragic sense of the inner disruptedness of Christ's body, no sorrow about the perversion of the eucharistic sacrament by other Churches. The impossibility of intercommunion in this case does not touch the mystical depths of life, for it depends entirely upon the historical moment which may change at any time. The feeling of sadness and disappointment at being unable to communicate from the same chalice has to do with ecclesiastical policy rather than with the sacramental sphere. I may be angry and annoyed with my Church's inertness, I may be grieved by the rigidity of its rules, but there is no real difference in my feelings when I am present at an Anglican or a Jacobite liturgy (at which I may not communicate) and when I prayerfully take part in an Orthodox liturgy without being a communicant.

The problem of intercommunion is one of the most 'pessimistic' of ecumenical problems. Apparently there can be no positive solution of it, for if Churches of different denominations enter into intercommunion it means either that they renounce their own faith and accept the faith of the Church whose Communion Service it happens to be, or that they do not take the problems of faith seriously and substitute for the tragedy of Christian dividedness an emotional idyll of fine feelings and of psychological unity.

Does this imply that the question of intercommunion should be given up? Certainly not. The whole of ecumenism, as its history shows, is a paradox, something incomprehensible and unexpected, a spiritual achievement which is given us in experience and only later consciously understood. What then can we say of intercommunion from this 'phenomenological' point of view?

Let us note in the first instance that in speaking of intercommunion as partaking together of the Lord's Supper we greatly narrow the idea of it and artificially give it an exclusively sacramental, ecclesiological sense. In truth the idea of communion, as well as of intercommunion, is purely formal and simply refers to the togetherness of an act or of a relation, without indicating what the act consists in, or to whom or to what the relation refers. Hence both logically and grammatically the term 'intercommunion' needs supplementing: intercommunion *in what* or *of what*? In our usual terminology we tacitly answer that question by interpreting intercommunion solely as *communicatio in sacris*, and that exclusively as communion in the Lord's Supper. But such a narrow use of the term is quite illegitimate. For as soon as we ask the question 'intercommunion *in what*?' we see that the idea of communion and of abstention from it may have very different meanings. The true and complete impossibility of communion is described and determined by St. Paul in I Cor. 10. 21 and II Cor. 6. 14-18. It is sufficient to read these passages to see that the impossibility of intercommunion between Christian Churches is something utterly different from what St. Paul has in mind. For even if Christians of different denominations regard one another's Eucharist as 'irregular', they certainly do not think

of it as 'unrighteousness' and 'darkness', to say nothing of 'the
table of the devils'. If they did, ecumenism itself would mean
connivance with the enemies of Christ and therefore a betrayal
of Christ, for what concord hath Christ with Belial?

Thus, the very fact of ecumenical meeting presupposes the
possibility of communion, and the question is only about the
limits of such communion and not about its legitimacy in principle. What then are those limits? In what may we have communion with other denominations without being disloyal to our
own Church? The answer to this is the Ecumenical Movement
itself, in which the possibility and legitimacy of communal prayer
has never been so much as questioned. And this is so in spite of
the forty-fifth Apostolic rule saying that 'a bishop or a presbyter
or a deacon who has *merely prayed* with a heretic, is to be excommunicated'. But what do we find, in fact? Christians of different
denominations who conscientiously regard one another as heretics
not only pray together but actually lead one another's prayers.
This is done both by representatives of Churches that consider
themselves 'a bridge' between different Christian denominations
and by representatives of the extreme right and extreme left (the
Orthodox and the Quakers). What conclusion, then, are we to
draw from this fact which has already become a tradition?
Leaving aside the theological and canonical problem of such
prayer, we must say that the actual occurrence of it is itself an
important instance of intercommunion—of intercommunion in
prayer, in common profession of faith in Christ, in glorifying
Him together and offering common supplications. The limit of
the forbidden and the impossible, evidently, lies further away: it
concerns only the sacramental sphere which is the expression of
the doctrine, the tradition and the whole life of a particular
Church. Moreover, at ecumenical congresses Communion Services are often held by different denominations. Each Church acts
according to its own rules and customs: some invite to partake
of the communion all 'who *love* the Lord Jesus Christ'; some—
those who are baptised and regularly communicate in their own
Church; others—only those who belong to Churches that are in
intercommunion with them; still others—only those who fully
belong to their particular Church. And yet, the presence at the
Eucharist of Christians of other denominations even as non-
communicants is implied, and often explicitly declared to be

desirable. Not being able to share the chalice, the Churches invite one another to share the prayers and to witness the Communion Service. What is the meaning of this invitation? What point is there in this non-communicating attendance? It would be a mockery of sacred things to suppose that the service is a kind of show and that those who are present are mere spectators. It is obvious that if I am invited to be present at the celebration of a Sacrament and I accept the invitation, I am no longer a 'spiritual alien' but *somehow* take part in the Sacrament. What, then, does my participation consist in? And how are we to reconcile the contradiction of mystical participation and ecclesiological separation? It seems impossible and paradoxical, and yet we know that it is a fact—the most significant and profound experience, both tragic and joyful, that we get through ecumenical communion (this is why such heated arguments centre upon this problem). In order to understand the contradiction, let us recall that a Sacrament is performed through the power of prayer. In the Orthodox liturgy this truth finds expression in the *epiclesis*, that is, in the prayer for the descent of the Holy Spirit for the consecration of the elements. The celebrant says this prayer in the name of the whole Church and of all the congregation, as can be seen from the verb being used in the plural. And this is where we find the bond which unites Christians whatever their ecclesiastical divisions may be. If I am present at the others' Sacrament, may I unite my prayer with the prayer of those who are praying for the Sacrament to take place? It is sufficient to ask this question in order to hear in one's heart the words of the answer: prayer as an inward act of turning towards God, as a groaning of the heart, is absolutely free and cannot be limited by any barriers. 'The clergy celebrate the sacraments and think that sacraments are all-exhaustive,' writes Péguy, 'but in doing so they forget about prayer, and prayer is at least a half of the whole thing. There are sacraments and there is prayer. The clergy deal with sacraments, but to us there is always left the possibility of prayer.' (*Lettres et entretiens*, p. 138.) In this passage sacrament is contrasted with prayer, and this of course is a mistake, for a sacrament itself would be impossible without prayer. But there is sacramental, ecclesiastically formulated prayer, and there is personal, free prayer—direct and simple conversation with God. And this second kind of prayer always lies at the basis of the first. The Psalmist compares prayer with incense. It rises to the sky in vertical columns, but on high they merge into one fragrant cloud. And however high the partitions that divide Christians may be, they do not reach to heaven (according to the wise saying of Metropolitan Platon of Kiev); and there, on high, the prayers that rise out of the depths of our separateness overcome those limitations and merge into one. Thus *communio sanctorum* makes up for the impossibility of *communicatio in sacris*.

The heights are calling to the depths. Roman Catholics are forbidden by their ecclesiastical rules to pray with non-Catholics, even when being present at their sacraments. Several Roman Catholic priests were present one day at the Orthodox liturgy in an emigré church near Paris. Obedient to their discipline they stood like statues: they did not make the sign of the Cross, did not kneel when the Host was brought out. . . . But after the service the senior among them said: 'You must understand us: we could not have behaved differently, but *we were with you in spirit*.' The litany of Whitsunday vespers has a petition 'of those who bend their hearts and their knees before the Lord.' Men can be forbidden 'to bend the knee', but it is impossible to forbid them 'to bend the heart'. Even if I wanted to obey the prohibition, my heart would of itself, apart from my will or reason, bow down before the Holy and my soul pour itself out in 'groanings which cannot be uttered, with which the Spirit itself maketh intercession for us according to the will of God' (Rom. 8. 26-27). And this is the solution of the problem. When present at the celebration of another Church's Sacrament, *each* of us can pray, 'Lord, fulfil their prayer. . . . They have distorted Thy commandment, they serve Thee wrongly, but they love Thee and they glorify Thee. Be with them, descend upon them, unite them to Thyself.' This is how an Orthodox may pray at a Methodist Communion Service, a Protestant at a Catholic Mass, a Quaker at an Orthodox liturgy. But perhaps no words at all are needed. For there are 'unspoken prayers, unuttered words: secret groanings of the soul, good impulses of the heart. The person to whom they belong often knows them not and is unconscious of them; but God—the Judge of that which is secret—hears, accepts and treasures them' (Péguy, *Mystère des Saints Innocents*).

If a sacrament is performed through the power of prayer, and we can prayerfully witness another Church's Sacrament, our presence will be a spiritual co-celebration of it (but only spiritual: this is the tragedy of our dividedness). The conception of co-celebration is wider and more exact than that of intercommunion. The latter, especially when understood as communion at the Lord's Table, has as it were a passive character: we together receive the Holy Gifts. But the idea of co-celebration emphasises our spiritual activity—in praise, in blessing, in thanksgiving, in prayer—one in the mystical depths of the spirit and separate in the ecclesiastically determined sacramental actions.

We shall be told that such spiritual co-celebration is incomplete; it is one-sided, Monophysite in character, it has no outer form or embodiment and therefore signifies nothing and leads nowhere.

Yes, that is true; the idea of such co-celebration is imperfect and incomplete, but it is the only possibility open to us, the only door we can enter—not knowing what awaits us beyond it. And if we do not take advantage of this minimum there is nothing left to us but resignation.

The name which the Orthodox Church gives to sacraments is *Mysteria* (mysteries), thus emphasising the mysterious nature of these meetings between man and God. A great deal in them is evident, known and understandable; but at the basis of them is the mystery of Divine condescension to which there corresponds in the created world the mystery of prayer. We cannot fathom the Mystery. But in our longing for grace, in our prayer for one another, in our coming forward together, we are mysteriously united with God and with each other, anticipating the unity of the world to come, when 'God shall be all in all'.

APPENDICES

A. EXISTING RULES AND CUSTOMS OF THE CHURCHES

*

J. P. Hickinbotham

Church of England

(Great Britain)

The Intercommunion Commission was instructed by its terms of reference to set forth the existing practices of the Churches in regard to intercommunion. The report of the American section of the Commission (booklet 98, published in 1942) contained a series of statements concerning the practice of some of the principal Churches in the United States, by representative members of those Churches. A somewhat similar series, chiefly from members of Churches in the United Kingdom and the British Commonwealth, was collected by Dr. Leonard Hodgson and published in 1944 as booklet 99 in the Faith and Order Series. Since the end of the war, further material has been collected by Prof. J. de Saussure and the present writer, which includes a number of statements from members of the chief European Churches, of the Orthodox Churches, and of some of the 'younger Churches'.

The survey here presented is based on the two published pamphlets and on the additional information received more recently. It cannot claim to be exhaustive, for it has not been possible to make effective contact with all Churches. It cannot claim to be an exact statement, because intercommunion is for the most part governed by custom rather than rule, and the custom is often ill-defined and its application varies from time to time, from place to place, and even from individual to individual. Not only within denominations but even within a single regional Church there are sometimes widely divergent practices existing side by side.

The survey must therefore be taken as not more than a general summary. It in no way commits any of the Churches concerned or their governing authorities. It is, however, in each case except that of the Roman Catholic Church, based directly on statements prepared by theologians belonging to the Church under review, and it is therefore hoped that what is given is a fair general summary of the situation as it exists at present. The correspondents quoted are in each case members of the Church about which they write.

For the sake of brevity, denominational groups are usually described as a whole, with representative illustrations; but in some cases it has not been possible to 'group' Churches in this way, and such Churches are described individually.

The Anglican Churches

There have always been different interpretations within the Church of England of her governing formularies, the Prayer Book, Articles of Religion, and Ordinal, in so far as they concern the Church, Ministry and Sacraments. These differences have been accentuated in the last hundred years. They are now reflected in the Anglican Communion as a whole, which consists of autonomous Churches acknowledging loyalty to the general tradition expressed in the above formularies but not bound by them in detail except in so far as they freely adopt them. This variety of interpretation results in variety of practice about intercommunion both within individual Anglican Churches and as between them.

The principal relevant passages in the formularies are as follows:

'The visible Church of Christ is a congregation of faithful men in the which the pure Word of God is preached and the Sacraments be duly ministered according to Christ's ordinance in all those things that of necessity are requisite to the same.' (Article XIX.)

'It is not lawful for any man to take upon him the office of public preaching or ministering the Sacraments in the congregation before he be lawfully called and sent to execute the same. And those we ought to judge lawfully called and sent which be chosen and called to this work by men who have publick authority given unto them in the congregation, to call and send Ministers into the Lord's vineyard.' (Article XXIII.)

'It is evident unto all men diligently reading Holy Scripture and ancient authors that from the Apostle's time there have been these Orders of Ministers in Christ's Church; Bishops, Priests, and Deacons; which offices were evermore had in such reverend estimation that no man might presume to execute any of them except he were first called, tried, and examined, and known to have such qualities as are requisite for the same; and also by publick prayer, with imposition of hands, were approved and admitted thereunto by lawful authority. And therefore to the intent that these Orders may be continued, and be reverently used and esteemed in the Church of England: No man shall be accounted or taken to be a lawful Bishop, Priest, or Deacon in the Church of England, or suffered to execute any of the said functions, except he be called, tried, examined, and admitted thereunto, according to the Form hereafter following, or hath had formerly Episcopal Consecration or Ordination.' (Preface to the Ordinal.)

'And there shall none be admitted to the Holy Communion, until such time as he be confirmed or be ready and desirous to be confirmed.' (Rubric in the Order of Confirmation.)

Some Anglicans hold that Articles XIX and XXIII mean that the Church is constituted by the Gospel, which is mediated through the preaching of the Word and the administration of the sacraments; and that the essential condition for ministry in the Church is not episcopal ordination as such but orderly commission by recognised Church authority. The Preface to the Ordinal is regarded as stating what is to be done in the Church of England (*viz.* that episcopacy is to be retained owing to its primitive character and historical continuity), but as deliberately refraining from judging the ministries in other Churches. The Confirmation Rubric is regarded likewise as applying to members of the Church of England whom the Prayer Book, as the Church of England's directory of worship for her own members, always has in mind unless it is explicitly stated otherwise. Other Anglicans hold that the Preface to the Ordinal implies that episcopacy is the necessary form of ministry in any true part of the Church of Christ, and that the Articles must be interpreted in the light of this implication. Many Anglicans hold views which lie in between these two interpretations.

On the former view it is possible fully to recognise non-episcopal Churches as true parts of the Church Catholic, their ministries and sacraments as true ministries and sacraments. The lack of episcopal Confirmation thus does not rule out the possibility of intercommunion. The latter view makes intercommunion normally impossible since the status of non-episcopal Churches, their ministries and sacraments, must be regarded as at best doubtful; and the most that can be allowed is that in a divided Christendom exceptional cases may arise which can be dealt with by 'Economy'. While these differences about Order exist, all Anglicans hold that no Church can be recognised which does not hold the essentials of the Faith, nor could there be intercommunion with such a body.

Until the present century the application of the formularies to questions of intercommunion was for the most part left to individuals to determine, and practice varied. There have always been some who have communicated as visitors with the Reformed Churches outside England, and there have always been some who have objected to this custom. There have always been some who have welcomed members of such Churches to communion as visitors, but since the Oxford Movement there have been some who objected to this. In recent times these customs of fellowship have been extended by some to include the English Free Churches and their off-shoots overseas, and there are some who object to this. In recent times there have been some who have followed a similar practice in regard to the Orthodox Churches, so far as the authorities of those Churches have permitted it. But in recent times official regulations have been made by different parts of the Anglican Communion, covering some parts of the field; and there have been pronouncements carrying no legal force but considerable moral influence by advisory bodies such as the Lambeth Conferences. The result has certainly not been uniformity; the regulations vary from one Anglican Church to another; they cover only fractions of the field; the Lambeth resolutions are likewise partial in scope, and they have no binding power. The following is an attempt to summarise a position which has arisen from a varied custom modified by occasional and sometimes contradictory local regulations and by occasional weighty admonitions which lack any sanction in church law.

So far as the Faith and eucharistic doctrine are concerned, most Anglicans are ready to take the requirements of the 'Lambeth Quadrilateral' as a sufficient basis for intercommunion. The Scriptures must be accepted as the ultimate standard of faith; the historic creeds as a sufficient statement of that faith; and the two Sacraments as dominically instituted means of grace. Where Churches accept also the fourth point of the Quadrilateral—the historic episcopate—the chief difficulty in regard to Order also disappears. Thus some Anglican Churches have official agreements for mutual admission of members to Communion with the Old Catholic and Polish National Catholic Churches, and official agreements with the episcopal Lutheran Churches of Finland, Latvia, and Esthonia, and with the Mar Thoma Syrian Church for similar mutual admission of members when the ministrations of their own Churches are not available. In Anglican Churches which are not formally parties to these official agreements there would usually be no objection to the actions sanctioned in them being taken as a matter of unwritten custom. A similar unwritten custom is also widely followed between the Church of Sweden and the Anglican Communion and action to give it formal sanction has been recommended by the Lambeth Conference.

In the case of Churches which do not so clearly accept all four points of the 'Lambeth Quadrilateral' agreement is less easy. Among the episcopal Churches, the attitude of the Roman Catholic Church combines with the serious doctrinal disagreements to prevent any intercommunion. With the Eastern Orthodox Church there are difficulties deriving from that Church's emphasis on tradition as an authority co-ordinate with Scripture and from its insistence on complete dogmatic agreement as a condition of intercommunion. But an unofficial practice whereby individual Anglicans and Orthodox communicate in each other's churches when cut off from the ministrations of their own has become not uncommon, and would probably find little serious objection among Anglicans. A similar practice in regard to some of the separated Eastern Churches is not unknown.

In regard to non-episcopal Churches, the Lambeth Conference of 1920 advised that the general rule should be that Anglicans should only receive Holy Communion from ministers of their own Church or of a Church in communion with it, and the Conference of 1930 assumed this to be the case. But the Lambeth Conferences have also advised that bishops may approve the admission of baptised communicants of other Churches to Holy Communion in Anglican churches when they are out of reach of the ministrations of their own Church or in certain other cases such as at conferences designed to promote Christian unity; and they have further advised that a bishop may approve of an Anglican receiving Communion in a non-episcopal Church when, in certain special areas, he is separated by distance and for a long time from the ministrations of his own Church. It should be noted that these resolutions are advisory, and are directed to cases where the bishop is asked for a ruling. In many cases individuals act on their own responsibility within the liberty allowed by custom and by any local regulations of their Church. The conclusion may be drawn that the general attitude of the episcopate is not unfriendly towards the admission of members of non-episcopal Churches to Communion as occasional visitors when there is a good reason for it; but that a reciprocation of this practice is not generally favoured save in conditions of unusual and extreme urgency.

In some parts of the Anglican Communion this advice has been, in whole or part, incorporated in official rules. For example, in the Lagos diocese mutual admission of members to Communion when cut off from the ministrations of their own Churches is officially sanctioned as between the Anglican and Methodist Churches. But for the most part the matter is still one of custom rather than rule. For example, the former Metropolitan of India, after mentioning the official sanction given by the Church of India, Burma and Ceylon for members of non-episcopal Churches to communicate at Anglican celebrations of Holy Communion at certain interdenominational gatherings, adds: 'Though there is no definite resolution passed by the Episcopal Synod on the subject, it is the general practice of the Church in this Province to admit persons of full standing in other denominations to receive Holy Communion in our Churches in those places where there is no church of their own denomination.'

Similarly in England the bishops have approved, and even gone beyond, the Lambeth resolutions in regard to admission of members of other Churches to Communion, while declaring that the conditions in regard to Anglicans communicating in other churches in the special areas do not apply in the provinces of Canterbury and York. But they have refrained from seeking to translate their resolutions into synodical rules, and the result is that practice continues to vary. Some members of the Church of England consult their bishop about every case that arises, some continue to admit members of non-episcopal Churches whenever they desire occasional communion as visitors, and also continue to communicate themselves as occasional visitors in non-episcopal Churches. Some, again, continue to refuse admission to members of non-episcopal Churches on all occasions and to decline ever themselves to communicate in a non-episcopal church.

In some other Anglican Churches there is similar diversity of custom. In others, again, where churchmanship tends to be more uniform in character, there is more or less uniform custom, which may approximate either to closed Communion or to open Communion or be something in between. The divergence was illustrated at the Holy Communion Service celebrated by the Dutch Reformed Church at the World Council Assembly at Amsterdam, when some Anglican bishops, clergy and laity communicated while others felt compelled to refrain from communicating.

In regard to the Church of South India, which is unique in that it is in process of becoming episcopal, the Church of England has officially ruled that not only former Anglicans but also, at the discretion of the bishop, all other communicants of the Church of South India may be admitted to Communion; and members of the Church of England are free to communicate in the Church of South India. The rules in other Anglican provinces vary considerably in regard to former non-Anglicans, though all agree that former Anglicans may be admitted to Communion.

The Baptist Churches

Correspondents in the Baptist Union of Great Britain and Ireland draw attention to the 'Declaration of Principle' which is the basis of this Union, and which includes the statement: 'That our Lord and Saviour Jesus Christ, God manifest in the flesh, is the sole and absolute authority in all matters pertaining to faith and practice, as revealed in the Holy Scriptures, and that each church has liberty, under the guidance of the Holy Spirit, to interpret and administer His laws.' The word 'church' in this context refers to the local congregation; and this Declaration sums up the conviction of Baptists everywhere that the local church is autonomous in matters of faith and practice. There are two principal views held among Baptists about intercommunion; and in accordance with the liberty described above, the practice varies from one local church to another, though in some areas one practice is the predominant custom.

Some Baptist churches practise 'close Communion'; i.e. they admit only believers who have been baptised by immersion on confession of faith. Other Baptist churches practise 'open' Communion; i.e. they welcome Christians who are outside the Baptist tradition. In this case, we are informed, the invitation is sometimes addressed to 'church members' (i.e. presumably, members of some branch of the Church visible), but more often, it appears, to 'all who love our Lord Jesus Christ'. Some Baptist churches practise not only 'open Communion' but 'open membership'; i.e. they are prepared to admit to membership of the local Baptist church all Christians who give satisfactory evidence of their faith, whether they have received believer's Baptism or not.

'Close Communion' is based on the belief that Baptism by immersion on profession of faith is the means of entrance to the visible Church prescribed in the New Testament, and that it is consequently a necessary condition of communicant status. 'Open Communion' is usually based, to quote one of our correspondents, 'on the exaltation of the Lord's Table above all ecclesiastical differences of judgment and practice'. Behind this may lie the conviction that while other forms of Baptism are defective when viewed by New Testament standards, they cannot be dismissed as not being Baptism at all, and the communities which use them can be recognised as true branches of the Church of Christ. As one correspondent puts it: 'Other churches, while adhering to Believers' Baptism as a condition of church membership, since they believe it to be essential to the maintenance of the Baptist witness to what they regard as a vital element of Christian truth, are yet willing to receive to Communion any genuine members of the Church Universal.' On the other hand, it may rather be based, especially when it is linked with 'open membership', on the belief that the only essential condition of church membership is not Baptism but faith. 'Their contention,' says the same correspondent about those who take this view, 'is that salvation is of faith and not baptism, and that therefore no believer should be excluded from church membership or from the Lord's Table'.

It is difficult to estimate in detail the extent to which these practices are followed relatively to each other. In the Baptist Union of Great Britain and Ireland the churches which follow 'open Communion' are stated by our correspondent to be a majority. In the United States most Northern Baptists practise 'open Communion', but most Southern Baptists invite only 'those of like faith and order', i.e. members of other Baptist churches, to participate.

In regard to Baptists receiving Communion in other Churches, it is not usual for a Baptist church to have explicit rules. 'The individual church member', writes one correspondent, 'is free to take advantage of any opportunity that is presented to him of partaking of Communion in any other Church. Presumably the attitude of each would be determined by his views on 'open' or 'close' Communion.

The Church of the Brethren (U.S.A.)

A correspondent writes: 'That which is known to be the practice of several congregations of the Brethren illustrates the attitude of Brethrenism. In these congregations, friends whose membership is in other denominations attend the Brethren services and work with them. Having won the respect of their Brethren friends, these people have been invited individually to attend the Lovefeast and Communion. When they have felt themselves disposed to avail themselves of this invitation, they have been accepted in this intimate service of the congregation without any objection. Their conversion is not in question. Their manner of life satisfied their Brethren acquaintances that they exhibited a quality of moral living sufficiently high and distinctive to be of Jesus Christ and not of the world—and so Brethren were willing to commune with them—an evidence of Christian friendship. It need not be argued that this is quite a different thing from a broadcast public invitation to everyone to attend the Sacrament.

The Church of South India

This Church has grown from a union of Anglican, Congregationalist, Methodist, and Presbyterian elements. It has formally expressed, in its Constitution, its desire to maintain the relations of fellowship and intercommunion with all the Churches with which its constituent parts had such relations before the union took place. In the 'Interim Reply to the Archbishop of Canterbury' approved by the Synod of the Church in 1950 it is further

stated: ' "The principle that the Church of South India desires
to be permanently in full communion and fellowship with all the
Churches with whom its constituent groups have had communion and fellowship" (Constitution ii, 15) is absolutely basic
and is not subject to reconsideration.' Thus the Church of South
India welcomes to Communion not only members of the
Churches from which its constituent parts derived their existence,
but also members of all the Churches with which those constituent
parts were themselves in communion prior to the union. It likewise permits its own members to communicate in all such
churches, provided that such Churches are willing to receive them.

The Congregational Churches

Admission of members of other Churches to Communion is
the almost universal practice among Congregationalists. The usual
formula of the invitation appears to be 'to all who love our Lord
Jesus Christ' or some similar phrase, though it is sometimes
qualified (as in a memorandum submitted by certain members of
the Congregational Union of England and Wales on the practice
within that Union) by some such addition as 'to whatever part of
His Church they may belong'. Congregationalists are equally
generally held to be free to communicate in churches of other
denominations.

The memorandum referred to above quotes from R. W. Dale's
Manual of Congregational Principles, Book iii, chapter iii, section 5,
in explanation of this practice. 'The Lord's Supper', writes Dale
'is a visible Gospel to the Church. Those who sit at Christ's Table
sit there as His friends to commemorate Him as their Saviour and
Lord, and to receive the great gifts of His love. It belongs to the
very conception of the Sacrament that those who receive it should
be "in Christ" and therefore in the Church.' The memorandum
points out that 'there is a theological question raised by the clause
"in Christ and therefore in the Church" when applied to those
not of our own membership'; and this problem of determining
in practice who are to be reckoned as fulfilling this condition is
solved in the following way. 'The general principle under which
we act is that we have no right to exclude those who are members
of the Body of Christ, and we must exclude those who are not.
Those who are responsibly committed to the common life of
some Christian congregation, which has the ordinances of Word,

Sacraments and Ministry, are reckoned by us "among the faithful to whom the Sacraments may be dispensed according to the tenor of the Covenant of Grace, whereof they are seals".' (John Robinson's Catechism, 1620.)

But not all Congregationalists would lay such stress on 'responsible commitment' to the common life of a Christian congregation as a condition of admission to Communion. The most frequent form of invitation does not explicitly mention it, and some of our correspondents emphasise only the necessity for personal faith which must normally be judged by the individual himself rather than by the Church, whose invitation he accepts. Thus a member of the Congregational Union of Scotland writes: 'Christ Himself is the Host who gives the seals of His redemptive grace to all His disciples who humbly and trustfully respond to His invitation to share in the Feast of the Covenant. Therefore all who profess their faith in and devotion to the Lord Jesus Christ may claim the privileges and blessings of sacramental fellowship. Except on the ground of manifestly unworthy moral character we cannot debar from the Table of the Lord any Christian believer who presents himself. It is for such a communicant to "examine himself and so let him eat of that bread and drink of that cup" (I Cor. 11. 28).'

The Disciples of Christ and the Churches of Christ

'The Disciples of Christ' and 'the Churches of Christ' are the names normally used in the U.S.A. and Great Britain respectively for what is in essence the same type of church body. Those who belong to these Churches follow the Baptist tradition in so far as they stand for the principle of Baptism of believers as the only form of Baptism which is fully in accord with New Testament teaching, while in other matters they have distinctive beliefs and practices of their own.

The Disciples of Christ in the U.S.A. follow the custom of 'open Communion'; i.e. they invite members of other Churches to communicate, even if they follow the practice of infant Baptism. The Churches of Christ in Great Britain and, we are informed by a correspondent, most of those in Australia follow the custom of 'close Communion'; i.e. they admit to communion only persons who have been baptised on profession of faith. There are, however, certain Churches established in Britain from America which follow the American custom.

'Those practising "open communion",' writes a member of the Disciples of Christ in the U.S.A., 'regard Baptism as a necessary prerequisite to reception, but welcome at the Table as fellow-Christians church members who are satisfied that the Baptism they have received is acceptable to the Lord, even though this Baptism does not follow exactly the form exhibited in the New Testament.' The basis of the practice of 'close Communion' is described by a member of the Churches of Christ in Great Britain as follows: 'Baptism is the rite of entrance to the Church, and therefore Baptism is a necessary prerequisite to the celebration of the Lord's Supper. All the baptised, who have not by the discipline of the Church been separated from her fellowship, are therefore welcomed at the Lord's Table. But we contend that Baptism is valid only when administered to penitent believers who are able to confess their faith in Christ as Lord and Saviour. . . . It will be seen that our practice is really that of "close Baptism" rather than of "close Communion".' Followers of both customs would agree with this writer when he says that 'the Lord's Supper is a rite *within* the Church, a corporate rite to be celebrated by the Church as the Body of Christ, and by the Church only'. It is on this principle that all who can be recognised as members of the Church which is the Body of Christ, and only they, are admissible to the Lord's Supper.

No rules are laid down as to reception by members of these Churches of Communion in other Churches; and our correspondent in Great Britain is of opinion that members who are away from the ministrations of their own Church 'frequently receive Communion at Presbyterian and Free Church services, especially Baptist Churches'. Those who hold very strictly to the 'close Communion' view as described above would, it may be presumed, find it difficult to accept an invitation to communicate in a Church which practised infant baptism.

The Evangelical Church in Germany

The Evangelical Church in Germany (E.K.D.) is a combination of the formerly separate Lutheran, Reformed, and United Churches, but each of these retains something of its former distinctness, and full intercommunion between them is not establshed by law. 'The E.K.D.', writes a member of it, 'is an association of independent Churches. Lutheran, Reformed, and United Churches are brought together in it. The United Churches include those which are united in their confession as well as others which are united only in government. In these latter Churches, the local congregations remain within their own confessions, namely Lutheran or Reformed. . . . According to law there is up to the present time no reciprocity in Communion between the various Churches which make up the E.K.D. It is a disputed question whether *according to law* there is reciprocity of Communion among the Prussian churches united in government. Certainly there is no reciprocity between the Lutheran and Reformed Churches; indeed, between the individual Lutheran Churches there is no intercommunion *according to law*.'

The same writer notes that the church struggle in the period of Nazi rule had different effects on the attitude of church members towards intercommunion. 'On the one side, particularly in Hanover and Bavaria, the church struggle was experienced as a re-awakening of the confessional consciousness in its particularity. On the other hand, especially in Prussia, the church struggle was above all experienced in terms of what the Reformation had brought to the Churches in common. So it has come about that the effect of the church struggle in respect of intercommunion has not been entirely uniform. Whereas one party seeks to govern the Communion of the Lord's Supper according to the principle of the Reformed Churches alone, others are inclined to regard this question as out of date.'

Moreover, our correspondent notes that the movements of population since 1945, with millions of refugees settling far from their homes, has made the enforcement of any strict discipline impossible. The Church in Germany is for the most part territorial in basis, and thus the only form of worship available for such settlers is that of the locality to which they have come. Hence 'less than ever before is it possible for the Churches to bring their sacramental life into proper order. . . . In practice there is without exception complete reciprocity in Communion between all German Churches.' It may be presumed that the question of members of the E.K.D. communicating with Churches outside the E.K.D., and of members of such Churches being admitted to Communion in the E.K.D., would be decided by the rules and customs of the particular part of the E.K.D. which was concerned in each case, and that the practice might vary according as that part was Lutheran, Reformed, or United in its tradition.

The Free Evangelical Congregations (Holland)

Members of other Churches who confess Jesus Christ as their God and personal Saviour may be admitted to Communion on application to the Consistory. There is usually no objection to members receiving Communion in other Churches, except that (to quote a correspondent) 'receiving Holy Communion in Churches of a catholic structure as well as participation in the Lord's Supper in community with Modernists are universally rejected'.

The Lutheran Churches

Lutheran Churches vary in their attitude to intercommunion. Some start from the conviction expressed by a Norwegian correspondent who says: 'The practice of the Church of Norway is based on the theological conviction that the Holy Communion is not in the hands of man, not even in the hands of the minister or the Bishop, but in the hands of the Lord. In all places where a Christian Church is celebrating Holy Communion according to the Holy Scripture, the words of institution being read, it is the same Sacrament, irrespective of different views and doctrines.' Others stress rather the need for correct belief about Holy Communion as a condition of worthily partaking of it. 'It is believed', says a member of the United Lutheran Church in the U.S.A., 'that all communicants should be instructed as to the meaning of the Sacrament and this involves pastoral and congregational oversight.'

Thus some Lutheran Churches practise a fairly large degree of intercommunion with other Churches. 'Members of non-Lutheran Churches', writes our Norwegian correspondent, 'will ordinarily be welcomed to partake in the Holy Communion in the Church of Norway. It is presupposed that the members are baptised communicant members of their own Churches. It might also be presupposed that this participation in the Holy Communion is of an occasional rather than a permanent character. No rules are codified in laws concerning the participation of members of the Church of Norway in the Communion of other Churches. No objections will be raised as to the receiving of the

Holy Communion in other Churches on special occasions (e.g. ecumenical conferences) or in places where there is no Lutheran Church.' A Finnish correspondent notes the existence of an agreement with the Church of England, and mentions (as also does our Norwegian correspondent) that members of all other Lutheran Churches are admitted to Communion. The custom of admitting members of other Churches to Communion at special inter-denominational gatherings, and of Lutherans communicating in services according to non-Lutheran rites at such gatherings, also exists in the Church of Finland. (For further information about the agreements between the episcopal Lutheran Churches of Finland and elsewhere with the Anglican Churches see under 'The Anglican Communion'.) The Evangelical Lutheran Church of Holland 'has an open Communion Table', writes a member of that Church. 'Anyone can participate in it who believes that in this act Christ is dealing with him and is presenting Himself together with bread and wine, as a present reality. As only Christ can judge of anybody's faith a preceding disciplinary examination by the Church is out of the question, and least of all can there be a moral censorship.' It is, however, thought advisable for an intending communicant to have a pastoral conversation with the minister before doing so. The Church leaves its members free to decide for themselves about communicating with other Churches. We are informed indirectly that the Lutheran Churches in France and Hungary have a measure of intercommunion with the Reformed Churches in those countries.

On the other hand, other Lutheran Churches allow much less intercommunion. Our correspondent in the United Lutheran Church in the U.S.A. states that 'open Communion is not favoured as a general practice. . . . The generally accepted rule is: "Lutheran pulpits for Lutheran ministers only. Lutheran altars for Lutheran communicants only". Exceptions to this rule belong to the sphere of privileges not of right. The determination of the exception is to be made in consonance of this principle by the conscientious judgment of pastors as the cases arise.' . . . This difference of practice is reproduced in the Churches founded by Lutheran missionary endeavour. A correspondent in India notes that there are ten Lutheran Churches in that country, and says: 'The attitude to intercommunion in these Churches is very much that of the Western Church from which they have been founded and are being supported. Thus the practice in the Missouri Evangelical Lutheran India Mission is very strict and exclusive, corresponding to that of the Missouri Synod in the U.S.A. . . . The least restrictions in the matter of intercommunion are perhaps found in the Arcot Lutheran Church, as the Danish missionaries working there mostly belong to the "Inner Mission" Group in Denmark.'

The Mennonite Churches

The Mennonite Churches accept the principle that local congregations are independent, and decisions about intercommunion would be made by the congregation concerned. Correspondents in the Dutch and German Mennonite Churches write that most congregations freely admit members of other denominations to Communion, even if they practise infant Baptism instead of believers' Baptism to which the Mennonite Churches themselves adhere, and that Mennonites are regarded as free to communicate in other Churches. It is understood that the Mennonite Churches in the U.S.A. follow a similar custom.

The Methodist Churches

The Methodist Churches for the most part welcome members of other Churches to Communion and regard their own members as free to communicate as visitors in other Churches. This is usually a matter of custom rather than of rule. Thus, for example, a correspondent in the Methodist Church in the U.S.A. writes: 'Open Communion (while not official) is general. Those are invited who are seeking to "follow the Lord Jesus Christ in sincerity and truth".' A correspondent in the Methodist Church in England writes: 'Some, following Congregationalist usage, invite "all who love the Lord Jesus Christ in sincerity and truth"; others do not use this formula, which indeed has no authority; but all would welcome the communicant members of other Churches whether they invite them explicitly or not. This is so firmly established by custom as to need no formal authority. The question whether Methodists may rightly take part as occasional visitors in the Communion Services of other Churches is settled similarly. They are free to do so wherever they are welcomed.' The same writer notes that, in addition to individual acts of intercommunion owing to distance from one's own church and similar reasons, Methodists often take part in joint Communion Services arranged on special occasions in a particular locality as an expression of Christian fellowship, and in joint Services held at conferences arranged by the Student Christian Movement and similar bodies. The Methodist Conference of Great Britain resolved in 1939 that 'The Methodist Conference would urge again that nothing would do so much to manifest and deepen the sense of unity in the Spirit in the period before union can be consummated, and actually to hasten the consummation of union, as fellowship between the members of the several Churches at the Table of their Lord.'

Sometimes a similar practice, either in general or with reference to some particular Church, is expressed in formal rules. Thus, for example, the Methodist Church of New Zealand has adopted resolutions which include the following:

'(1) In regard to intercommunion the Methodist Church of New Zealand is truly ecumenical. There are no barriers raised at the Lord's Table, racial, social, or denominational; it is free and open to all who desire it, and it is not asked whether or not they are members of any organised Communion. . . .

'(3) In accord with the above there are no laws, rules, or regulations governing the actions of its members regarding their communicating with other Communions; rather are they enjoined to partake of the Lord's Supper as frequently as possible (*vide* Wesley's Sermon No. 101) even when their own Communion Services are not available but others are.'

The Methodist Church in Ireland has an official agreement with the Presbyterian Church in that country under which there is mutual reception of members to Communion, and arrangements are sanctioned for the holding of the regular Sunday Services jointly in certain places; such Services are to be conducted by a minister of one or other of the two Churches and are to include administration of the Sacraments.

In the past some branches of Methodism had a stricter discipline, and this to some extent survives in some places. The Methodist Church of South Africa, for example, has a rule requiring members of other Churches who desire to communicate to obtain a ticket of admission, renewable quarterly, from the Superintendent or another minister of the circuit. But a correspondent in this Church notes that 'our general practice is governed much more by custom than by this rule. It is the almost universal custom of ministers of the Methodist Church of South Africa to use some such words as these: "All who love Our Lord sincerely, and desire to follow Him more faithfully, though they be not members of this Church, are invited to stay and partake with us of the Sacrament of the Lord's Supper".' A correspondent in the Methodist Church in Italy states the custom of that Church in terms rather less wide than those quoted above. 'L'Eglise Méthodiste d'Italie,' he writes, 'en parfait consentement avec le Méthodisme mondiale, pratique la plus large intercommunion avec toutes les Eglises Chrétiennes qui acceptent la Bible comme unique règle de foi et de vie, et croyent en Jésus Christ, le Fils Unique de Dieu, comme leur Sauveur at Seigneur, sans aucune discrimination nationale, raciale, ou de constitution ecclesiastique. En consequence, dans ses Eglises, elle admet à la Table de la Sainte Cène tout Chrétien Evangelique appartenant aux autres denominations. Elle permet aussi aux membres des Eglises Méthodistes leur participation à la Communion célébrée chez les Eglises Evangeliques.'

The basis of Methodist practice is expressed in Resolutions of the New Zealand Methodist Conference referred to above, as follows: 'We believe that it is unquestionably the Lord's Table, not a denominational one. It is He who invites and His invitation is to all His people, and none have a right to erect barriers preventing their coming thereto.' This statement would probably be in substance acceptable to most Methodists, but some would wish to qualify it by a reference to communicant membership of some part of the visible Church, as a pledge and token of the intending communicant's standing in the Body of Christ which may rightly be demanded as a condition of admission to Communion.

The Old Catholic Churches

The Old Catholic Churches in communion with the see of Utrecht have a formal agreement for intercommunion with the Church of England and most other parts of the Anglican Communion. This agreement, concluded at Bonn in 1931, reads:

'(1) Each Communion recognises the catholicity and independence of the other and maintains its own.

'(2) Each Communion agrees to admit members of the other Communion to participate in the Sacraments.

'(3) Intercommunion does not require from either Communion the acceptance of all doctrinal opinion, sacramental devotion or liturgical practice characteristic of the other, but implies that each believes the other to hold all the essentials of the Christian Faith.'

An Old Catholic correspondent comments: 'By this agreement the conditions are elucidated on which members of other denominations can receive Holy Communion in the Old Catholic Church. It implies that this is only possible for members of the Anglican Church.' He adds that 'A Church is Catholic if it keeps untainted the *depositum fidei* that has been transmitted to the apostles. A Church cannot be called Catholic unless there is a continuity between this Church and the Church of the Apostles. This unity with the Church of the first centuries is manifest in creed, liturgy, and orders. These three elements cannot exist separate from each other; they belong to each other and cannot be severed. The bishop maintains liturgical pureness and at the same time propagates the Faith. Therefore this office is essential for a Catholic Church.' It should be noted that the Agreement is not interpreted by most of the Anglican Churches in an exclusive sense, since they have rules and customs by which members of other Churches beside the Old Catholic, including in some circumstances members of non-episcopal Churches, are admitted to Communion.

It is understood that, on the principles set out above, there is no practice of intercommunion, official or unofficial, between the Old Catholic Churches and non-episcopal Churches. In regard to the Orthodox Churches, however, a correspondent writes: 'Intercommunion with the Orthodox Churches is not generally permitted. It can only take place as a result of a resolution of a General Synod of the Orthodox Churches. The Old Catholic Churches allow Orthodox believers to take part in the Sacraments, provided they have no access to a priest of their own faith.' Another Old Catholic writer regards this practice of admission to Communion in case of emergency as being reciprocal. He couples with the assertion that no official or canonical arrangement has been reached the statement that 'In the meantime a customary law has come into existence. The authorities of both parties approve the custom that members of the Churches in question who have no opportunity to receive the Sacraments in their own Church are admitted to the Sacraments.'

The Orthodox Churches

Only the various autocephalous Orthodox Churches are recognised as being in the full sense parts of the Church of Christ, and therefore there can be no canonical or regular intercommunion between the Orthodox Churches and others.

Some members of the Orthodox Churches uphold this position in its strictness, and regard even occasional unofficial acts of intercommunion as unjustifiable breaches of church order. 'Singular instances of such Communions', writes one Orthodox correspondent, 'cannot be taken into consideration'. 'The Orthodox Church', writes another, 'does not know the practice of "open Communion," while rules exclude the very possibility of it.'

Other Orthodox churchmen, while emphasising the canonical position, not only admit that occasional exceptions to the rule take place but are prepared to justify them in cases of emergency on the principle of Economy. One Orthodox correspondent says: 'There are no regulations allowing Orthodox to take Communion in non-Orthodox Churches, but in cases of emergency when there is no Orthodox priest available, if a member of our own Church on his own initiative takes Communion in another Church, particularly an Anglican Church, he will not afterwards be censured by his own Church. There are no regulations permitting non-Orthodox persons to come to Holy Communion in the Orthodox Church, but if some priest or bishop allows it by Economy because the person is unable to receive the Sacraments in his own Church, then again the action is tolerated by the Church and the priest or bishop who has allowed it will not be censured. The practice therefore depends entirely on the individual circumstances in each case, and it would be possible to cite instances of Communion both being given or refused according to the attitude taken by the local bishop.' Another Orthodox correspondent recalls that at the Lambeth Conference, 1930, the American bishops explained to the Orthodox delegation led by the Patriarch Meletius that Orthodox living in places where there was no Orthodox priest were admitted, where they so desired,

to Communion in the Anglican Church. The Orthodox delegation declared itself unable to give a positive answer about this
practice, because the matter could only be officially dealt with by
the Orthodox Churches together in a Synod or Pro-synod. But
until action was thus taken the practice of the American bishops
might continue unless there were a protest from the local Orthodox bishop. The same writer envisages the possibility of a similar
practice in regard to the Roman Catholic Church, the separated
Eastern Churches, and perhaps the Old Catholic Churches, and
under the following conditions:

'1. The necessity owing to the absence of a priest belonging to
   his own Church.

'2. The same belief in the meaning of the Sacrament of the
   Holy Eucharist.

'3. The administration of the Sacrament by a priest who is
   canonically ordained in his own Church.'

Of the reception of members of other Churches to Communion the same correspondent writes: 'In modern times two of
the Patriarchs of the East, the Patriarch Demetrius of Serbia and
the Patriarch Myron of Roumania have received Anglicans for
Communion to the Holy Altars exceptionally but not of necessity.
The *praxis* was not agreed upon even by Anglicans, but I do not
know any criticism on the part of the Orthodox. Anyhow this
praxis is an exception.'

To sum up. There is no canonical sanction in the Orthodox
Church for any form of intercommunion with members of other
Churches. Some Orthodox adherents regard any acts of intercommunion as being in consequence inadmissible. Others allow
that exceptions to the rule may be (and are) occasionally allowed
by Economy in cases where a member of the Orthodox Church
is out of reach of a priest of his own Church and therefore wishes
to communicate elsewhere, or where a member of some other
Church is similarly out of reach of his own Church's ministrations
and therefore wishes to communicate in one of the Orthodox
Churches. But such cases are exceptional, and permission to follow
this practice cannot be claimed as a right.

The Reformed and Presbyterian Churches

The customary starting-point in the attitude of Churches in the Reformed and Presbyterian tradition is typified by a statement from a correspondent belonging to the Church of Scotland. He writes: 'According to the Westminister Confession, its (i.e. the Church of Scotland's) doctrinal standard, "the visible Church, which is also catholick or universal under the Gospel, consists of all those throughout the world who profess the true religion, together with their children"; and it is added that "to this catholick visible Church Christ has given the ministry, oracles, and ordinances of God" (Westminster Confession, Chapter XXV, paras. ii, iii). Since Holy Communion is the gift of Christ to the catholic visible Church, the Church of Scotland, in order to fulfil Christ's intention, must offer the sacraments to all who belong to the catholic visible Church, i.e. "to all who profess the true religion". But with the distrust of individualism and the emphasis on discipline characteristic of the Reformed Churches, the Church of Scotland interprets the phrase "all who profess the true religion" as signifying all who by public profession of faith are members of any branch of the Catholic Church. The Sacraments thus belong to the Catholic Church; the Catholic Church is known by its profession of the true religion, and by its possession of the ministry, oracles, and ordinances of God; and all who belong to a recognisable branch of this Catholic Church ought to be admissible to Communion in any part of it.'

Usually no attempt is made to define which of the existing Christian bodies come within the visible Catholic Church, and baptised communicant members of any of the existing Churches which are loyal to the substance of the historic Christian faith are normally admitted to Communion when they so desire. A correspondent in the Reformed Church of Holland, for example, writes: 'As early as 16th July 1817 the Synod adopted a resolution that members of other denominations should be admitted to the Lord's Supper in the Dutch Reformed Church "provided that there are no reasons to the contrary (which is left to the judgment of the consistory) and provided that, being of an upright walk, they have given evidence of membership of their Church". (Note 3 and Article 14 of the synodical rules in force for the consistories.) Therefore it is customary that members of other denominations are admitted on their request. (It has never been made sure whether any denomination should be excluded.) . . . As far as I can judge from forty years of practice, no case has occurred that members of other denominations have not been admitted because of their membership of another Church. . . . This Church has no regulations concerning a permission for its own members to participate in the Communion of another Church. We are accustomed to leave the members entirely free on this point.' A member of the Reformed Church in France writes of 'a growing tendency towards open Communion, a Communion opened to all faithful members of any Protestant and non-Roman Church'. A Swiss correspondent writes: 'The Swiss Reformed Churches represent the principle of open Communion, i.e. they permit everybody to partake of the Lord's Supper who has received Baptism and is instructed in the Christian Faith.'

The American and British Presbyterian Churches, and the Churches which owe their origin to them, follow a practice similar to that of the Continental Reformed Churches. A correspondent in the Presbyterian Church in the U.S.A. writes: 'The invitation to communicate which (under a constitutional provision) is invariably extended just prior to the administration of the sacrament, by the officiating clergyman, is in the most generous terms and has been interpreted by our General Assembly to refer to all members of Evangelical Churches who may be present.' A member of the Church of Scotland quotes that Church's Act of Assembly No. vi, 1938, as follows: 'The right of a Kirk-Session to admit to the Lord's Table a member of any Christian Church is expressly affirmed', and notes that 'it is the general custom for the officiating minister to invite any "who are members of any branch of the Catholic or Universal Church" to join with the congregation in partaking of Holy Communion'. He adds that members of the Church of Scotland are regarded as 'free to receive Communion in any Church in which they wish to receive it and which is able to admit them'. This practice is explained on the ground that the Church of Scotland has never defined what existing bodies bear the marks of the true Church; 'hence it is left to the individual conscience, whether of members of the Church of Scotland receiving Communion in other Churches or of members of other Churches receiving Communion in the Church of Scotland, to decide whether these other Churches are "branches of the Catholic visible Church" '.

Membership of some visible denomination is thus generally required of an intending communicant as a guarantee of his membership of the Church Catholic. But in some cases this is less explicitly emphasised. A correspondent in the Presbyterian Church of New Zealand mentions 'the special invitation given at each observance of the Lord's Supper to all those who, though not members of the congregation, in sincerity and truth love the Lord Jesus Christ and are in communion with the Church Universal'. A member of the Presbyterian Church of England writes: 'In actual practice some of our ministers, I believe, give an invitation to "all who love the Lord Jesus Christ", but strictly speaking the invitation should be confined to those who are full communicant members of some branch or other of the Church', and his criticism of the wider form of invitation is supported by his quotation from the Presbyterian Service Book of 1948 which reads: 'The Communion Table, being the Table of our Lord, is open to all who are in full communion with His Church Universal in any of its branches. It is therefore fitting that an invitation be given to any such who may be present to unite with the Congregation in the Celebration of the Lord's Supper.'

The Remonstrant Brotherhood (Holland)

A correspondent informs us that in this Church open Communion is extended not only to members of other Christian Churches but to all people who desire to live in communion with Christ. There is no objection to members communicating in other Churches.

The Roman Catholic Church

The Roman Catholic Church holds that it alone is the true Church of Christ on earth, and that to be outside the Roman Catholic fold is either never to have entered the true Church or to have become schismatic from it. Hence Roman Catholics are forbidden to receive Communion in other Churches, nor are members of other Churches allowed to receive Communion in the Roman Catholic Church. The so-called Uniat Churches are integral parts of the Roman Catholic Church, and any regulations concerning the use of their sacramental ministrations by other Roman Catholics or the reception of Communion by their members in other parts of the Roman Catholic Church belong to the sphere of internal church discipline rather than to that of intercommunion between different Churches.

The Salvation Army

The Salvation Army does not as such use a Service of Holy Communion. It does not forbid its members to participate in the Holy Communion Services of other denominations, and this, according to a correspondent, is from time to time done by some members, chiefly as an act of fellowship.

The Separated Eastern Churches

The available information about the rules and customs of these Churches is unfortunately far from complete. It would appear that some of these Churches are in close fellowship with each other; for example, according to the Report of the Committee on Unity of the Lambeth Conference, 1948, the Syrian Orthodox Church is in communion with the Armenian and Coptic Churches (Lambeth Report, Part II, p. 71). But in other cases the Churches which we are discussing have no relationship of intercommunion even with each other; and for the most part their custom has been one approximating to 'close Communion' vis-à-vis Churches of other traditions.

There are, however, some partial exceptions to this attitude of 'close Communion'. Thus, for example, a member of the Mar Thoma Syrian Church refers to the reformation in that Church about a hundred years ago which led to the separation between it and the Jacobite Syrian Church, and writes: 'Interest in missionary activities has brought the Mar Thoma Syrian Church into close connection with the Western Churches engaged in evangelistic work in India, especially with the Church of India, Burma, and Ceylon, whose early missionaries were in part responsible for sowing the seeds of reformation in the Syrian Church. In 1937 a measure of limited intercommunion has been established with the Church of India, Burma, and Ceylon.' The same correspondent adds that 'though in the past the practice has been on the line of close Communion, ever since the Reformation this practice has not been strictly followed. With the permission of bishops, members of other Churches are admitted to Holy Communion, insisting only that all such persons must be baptised persons. . . .

N

Occasionally students going abroad to places where there are no Churches of the Anglican Communion have been known to receive Communion from other Churches'. But our correspondent emphasises that 'the above statements are only interpretations of tendencies rather than declarations of policy'. The Archbishop of the Armenians in England stated in the Faith and Order Pamphlet 99 that 'Any Christian can receive Communion in the Armenian Apostolic Church, provided he belongs to a Christian Church, and in the locality or vicinity there is no priest or church to which he belongs. Any Armenian can receive Communion in any Christian Church, provided there is no Armenian church or priest in the locality or vicinity. These rules are consecrated by long practice and there are no printed authoritative regulations. The theological justification of these rules consists in the admirable spirit of tolerance of our Saviour, specially between Christian brethren.' It has, however, been questioned whether this individual interpretation of the practice of the Armenian Church would be generally acceptable to other authorities in that Church.

The Society of Friends

The Society does not, as such, observe the Holy Communion as a Service, but (writes a correspondent) 'we commonly regard our Meeting for Worship as being in its intention and its experienced effect comparable to the Holy Communion'. The Meeting for Worship is open to members of other Churches. Some Friends occasionally receive Communion in other Churches and value the liberty to do so. But (writes our correspondent) 'if any Friend felt the need of an habitual participation the Monthly Meeting might well doubt whether his place was with us.'

The United Church of Canada

This Church, which has grown out of a union of Congregationalist, Methodist and Presbyterian elements, has a rule under which all are invited to Communion 'who, having come to years of discretion, have made credible profession of faith in and obedience to the Lord Jesus'. This implies membership of some branch of the visible Church in which such profession has been made; and, writes a correspondent, 'Baptism is assumed as a prior Sacrament'. A rather wider form of invitation is, according to our correspondent, sometimes given. Members are, it is understood, free to communicate in other Churches at their discretion.

The Waldensian Church

A correspondent writes: 'L'Eglise Vaudoise permet l'intercommunion avec toutes les Eglises de type réformé même celles qui admettent la consubstantiation comme l'Eglise Luthérienne. On ne voit pas comment on pourrait admettre l'intercommunion avec les Eglises qui affirment la transsubstantiation, par le fait que les éléments deviennent un objet de culte pour elles, contrairement à Jean 4. 24 et Jean 6. 63.'

NOTE.—For recent important conversations on intercommunion between Churches in Great Britain, see the two booklets *Church Relations in England* and *Relations between the Church of England and the Church of Scotland.*—EDITORS.

B. THE REVIVAL OF THE AGAPE[1]

A POSSIBLE ECUMENICAL WAY OF WORSHIP?

*

G. I. F. Thomson

Church of England

(Great Britain)

The suggestion has been made that the Agape, the simple fellowship meal of the early Christian Church, may yet prove to be the point at which the divided churches of Christendom may meet in a common act of worship and fellowship. No one can seriously doubt that the time has come for some outward token of the spiritual unity within which all Christian people are apprehended. Most people will agree that the true focus of our meeting is in the Holy Communion, which is the true sacrament of unity, and that this is the point to which all our labours should be bending—the Supper of the Lord, the Eucharist, the Divine Liturgy, the Holy Communion. There can be little serious argument about this as the object in view. But that day seems still far distant for 'the tables are fenced', and each Church has its own rules and regulations as to admission to Holy Communion. The theological debate on this subject continues, and must continue, and the answer will be made clear in God's good time. Thorny points remain to be resolved on questions touching the doctrines of sacrifice, intention, and validity, and meanwhile the 'great new fact of our time', the ecumenical movement of the twentieth century, cries out for an expression of that inner unity to which it is giving birth.

Is the Agape at least a temporary answer to this dilemma? It is quite simply a fellowship meal, its roots lie in the New Testament, it has about it something of the content of some of the New Testament 'feedings' and is therefore recognisably sure-based in the pattern of the Gospel story. Whether there is a reminder of the bigger feedings on the mountain side, or of the simple

[1] See the statement about this paper in the Editorial Preface, p. 10.

Emmaus supper, or even of the early morning post-resurrection breakfast 'beside the Syrian sea', our Lord is central to the event, and we follow His example of sharing what is provided. Therein is fellowship, and fellowship is part of love, and love is of the nature of God. The spiritual sequence is clear and self-evident. Bread broken: fellowship shared: the Divine Presence realised. The biblical basis of the Agape is therefore one of its strongest claims upon our attention at this particular point in the history of the Christian Church, and especially at this stage of the development of the reunion movement. Has it a place in our meeting together as Christians?

But the Agape has another and almost equally strong claim upon our attention. It is part of the tradition of the Christian Church. The early Fathers, Greek and Latin, write about it, and for several centuries it was part and parcel of the regular worshipping life of the Church in various parts of the world. We have reason to believe that the Agape was still a frequent practice and custom at least as far as the age of Chrysostom and Augustine. It seems pretty clear that the Agape existed for a good many generations side by side with what we all now know as the Holy Communion, but the Agape was sufficiently distinctive a thing in itself for it to be a subject in the writings of the early Fathers, notably in Tertullian, Clement of Alexandria, and Hippolytus. The Agape is therefore rooted in history. It is a part of the Christian tradition, and a part of the universal inheritance of the Christian Church, from the days of its early unity.

There is an important value in these two characteristics inherent in the Agape. The biblical and the traditional are so blended and harmonised that they have a powerful appeal both to the pre-Reformation and post-Reformation traditions within the Church of God on earth. Together they indicate and provide a place where it is possible for the great eastern Churches and the newer western Churches to find a common ground of Scripture and history pin-pointed in fellowship and crystallised in worship. Furthermore, the Agape means that there is no need to hunt around for some new means of expressing what needs to be expressed, no need to concoct or invent some means of expression, for it is already available and provided for in the Agape. It has already been 'given' in the Gospel and in the early practice of the Church, with that degree of hallowedness that comes from both.

Can we afford to neglect what is available, or refuse to consider what may be divinely provided? Nor has the Agape ever died out of the Christian Church. It has always remained a feature of some of the eastern Churches, usually in the simple practice of distributing blessed bread, and is still to be seen in many traditions. The Roman Catholic Church has it in the custom of 'pain béni', which custom is said to have spread of late years in some parts of western Europe. The Agape has therefore a continuous history from the earliest times.

The Agape was revived in England in 1949. It took place as a service of worship in which Anglicans and Methodists joined. The Agape is no part whatever of the normal worship of Anglicans, and was something entirely 'new' in that sense. On the Methodist side, however, there still lingers a little of the tradition and memory of the 'love-feast' which John Wesley discovered from the Moravians. The idea of an Agape therefore came as a great opportunity to a country parish in the county of Norfolk and worked its way acceptably into the minds of those responsible for the congregations in the parish until the vision of holding an Agape became a realised fact. The greatest possible care was taken in preparing for this occasion. The Anglican Rector, to whom the idea came while reading the Bible, first consulted several eminent specialists in subjects relating to the Agape, a professional theologian, an historian, a distinguished liturgiologist, and certain books of reference. There seemed to be no academic reason to hinder the experiment. Everything depended upon the reaction of the people and the permission of authority. The idea was put before the Anglican church council, the local parish body, and proved acceptable. The Bishop of the diocese was approached, enquired carefully of the object in view, and readily gave his approval. An invitation to join in an Agape was extended by the Rector on behalf of his congregation to the local Methodist minister on behalf of his congregation. In a sense, then, the Anglicans were the hosts and the Methodists were the guests, though the service was arranged in such a way that both traditions had an active part in the service, and it was in every sense of the word 'united'. It was made abundantly clear from the start that the Agape was in no way to be confused with the Holy Communion, and this was reiterated in the sermons of preparation. It was also agreed mutually that the condition of attendance was to be Baptism, and a real faith in Jesus Christ as God and Saviour. Before the service was drawn up the Greek Orthodox Archbishop Germanos of Thyateira was consulted, in view of the fact that the Agape remains a part of the Orthodox tradition, and several important suggestions which the Archbishop made were duly incorporated into the service. Another Anglican bishop was also consulted who gave the Agape idea his every encouragement and interested support. It is perhaps well to mention that both the Anglican bishops were among the most experienced and respected of all Anglican bishops, both were trained historians, and each had been a distinguished dean of a college, one at Oxford and one at Cambridge. The Agape took place, therefore, with the backing of authority and the weight of expert advice behind it, though the initiative and impetus came entirely from the parish itself. On the Methodist side, superior advice was also sought and was forthcoming and welcoming.

The Agape was revived in Holy Week, 1949, in the parish of Hilgay, Norfolk, and the order of service was as follows:

Hymn: 'The Church's one foundation'
Versicles and responses
Psalm 145
Lesson: John 17—read by the Methodist Minister
Hymn: 'There is a green hill'
Sermon: by the Rector
Hymn: 'When I survey the wondrous Cross'

Nicene Creed

Agape: (a) Prayers and blessing of the bread
      (b) Breaking of the bread
      (c) Lord's prayer. Other prayers
      (d) Distribution
Hymn: 'Jesus shall reign'
The Blessing.

A copy of the order of service was available for each member of the congregation, and it was clearly stated at the top of the service sheet that the service incorporated 'a fellowship meal, following the ancient and historical Christian practice and tradition'. The versicles and responses were the familiar sequence (to

Anglicans and some others), 'O Lord, open thou our lips' to the words 'The Lord's Name be praised'. Psalm 145 was included on the advice of the Greek Metropolitan, as it is part of the Eastern rite. The Nicene Creed was also chosen to provide a link with the Orthodox Church.

A table was set in the front of the church so that all could see, and on this a tablecloth. The bread was a large, rather flat, loaf made up of a great number of small scone-like pieces of bread, all baked together and very easily broken apart for distribution. At the end of the hymn after the sermon the congregation remained standing. During the last verse of the hymn two laymen had come forward to assist the clergy. They were respectively an Anglican churchwarden and a Methodist local preacher, one a headmaster and the other a farmer. As soon as the hymn had finished the Creed was said by the whole congregation while standing. They remained standing for the prayers that followed and for the breaking of the bread. Then came the Lord's prayer, with the powerful effect of being a grace before a meal. Then the congregation sat and the laymen distributed the broken bread to the people in two silver salvers row by row. The breaking of the bread was done by the Anglican Rector and Methodist Minister together and each had given a piece to the other. A short voluntary on the organ was played until all had partaken, then followed the remaining prayers.

It had been explained to the congregation that in 'blessing' we praise God. In offering the bread we only present what indeed is His gift to us already, and therefore there was no mystical change in the bread itself. Two Orthodox prayers were used: 'Blessed be God, who is merciful, and who nourisheth us from our youth up, who is the author of all sustenance. Fill our hearts with joyfulness, that in thy bountiful providence we may serve thee in every good work, through Jesus Christ our Lord, to whom with thee and the Holy Ghost be all glory and power, honour and worship both now and for evermore. Amen'; and 'Glory be to thee, O Lord; Glory be to thee, O King, because thou hast given us food for our delight. Fill us also with the Holy Spirit that we may be acceptable unto thee, and not be ashamed when thou comest to render to everyman according to his works, through Jesus Christ . . .' Also a prayer from Didache IX: 'We thank thee, our Father, for the life and knowledge which thou didst make known to us through Jesus, thy servant. Glory be to thee for ever. As this bread that is broken was scattered in many places (upon the mountains) and gathered together became one, so let thy Church be gathered together from the ends of the earth into thy kingdom: for thine is the glory and the power through Jesus Christ our Lord.' The familiar Anglican first collect for Good Friday was also used, with its note of unity: 'Almighty God, we beseech thee graciously to behold this thy family, for which our Lord Jesus Christ was contented to be betrayed, and given up into the hands of wicked men, and to suffer death upon the cross, who now liveth and reigneth with thee and the Holy Ghost, ever one God, world without end. Amen'; and a brief extempore prayer was said, largely for the purpose of including an element of the Reformed and Free Church tradition.

Nothing was said or done that might have led to any confusion with the Holy Communion. No use was made of the altar, or communion vessels, or words of service. On this occasion only bread was used, and neither water nor wine were introduced.

It is arguable that the Agape was made more liturgical than it need be, and that the historic and early Agape was more informal. This may be so, and there is no reason why any fixed form should become a universal pattern. But it is desirable that there should be sufficient in the service that is known and acceptable to form a familiar basis. Psalm 145, the Creed, and the breaking of bread with prayer are perhaps a reasonable minimum, allowing each tradition to add its own hymns, choice of lessons, and supporting prayers.

In Holy Week, 1951, the Agape was carried a step further. The Methodists reciprocated the original invitation by inviting the Anglicans in the parish of Hilgay to partake with them in a love-feast, the Methodist form of the Agape. The love-feast has a continuous and honoured place in Methodism, and was once integral with its fellowship life. One of its distinctive features was the practice of giving testimonies to personal and religious experience, and a due place for this was provided in the Methodist order of service at Hilgay. The 1949 order of service was revised, and the 1951 order was a definite improvement. It was as follows:

Hymn: 'O Lord of heaven and earth and sea'
Psalm 145, said responsively: led by the Anglican Rector
Prayers: being twelve petitions from the Anglican Litany,
  and the Lord's prayer
Hymn: 'Jesus, we look to Thee'
Lesson: Luke 24. 13-35
Hymn: 'Let us join ('tis God commands)'[1]
Sermon: by the Methodist Minister
Hymn: 'Come and let us sweetly join'
Agape: prayers, breaking of bread, and distribution
Opportunity for testimony, and extempore prayer
Hymn: 'Christ from whom all blessings flow'
The Blessing.

In greater detail the Agape proceeded thus:
The Rector and Minister descended from the pulpit platform
and gathered round the table set at the head of the congregation,
in company with the stewards. All standing, the order of service
continued.

Prayers for the breaking of bread (adapted from the Didache):

'Thou, Almighty Master, didst create all things for Thy name's
sake, and didst give food and drink unto men for enjoyment, that
they might render thanks to Thee; but didst bestow upon us
spiritual food and drink and eternal life through Thy Son.'

Response: 'Thine is the glory for ever and ever.'

'We give Thee thanks, O our Father, for the life and knowledge
which Thou didst make known unto us through Thy Son Jesus.'

Response: 'Thine is the glory for ever and ever.'

'As this broken bread was scattered upon the mountains, and
being gathered together became one, so may Thy Church be
gathered together from the ends of the earth into Thy kingdom.'

Response: 'Thine is the glory and the power through Jesus
Christ for ever and ever.'

'The Lord cometh!'

Response: 'Amen.'

(As the bread is broken): 'Blessed art Thou, O Lord, God of
the Universe, Who dost bring forth bread from the earth.' (In all

[1] Written by Charles Wesley especially for the lovefeast.

probability the very prayer or grace said by our Lord Himself, in accordance with Jewish custom.)

The bread was then handed round the church by the stewards, the token meal which the congregation naturally ate seated.

(As the cup is taken): 'Our Lord Jesus Christ said: Whosoever drinketh of the water that I shall give him shall never thirst.'

'Blessed be God, Who is merciful, and Who nourisheth us from our youth up, Who is the Author of all sustenance. Fill our hearts with joyfulness, that in Thy bountiful providence we may serve Thee in every good work, through Jesus Christ our Lord, to Whom with Thee and the Holy Ghost be all glory and power, honour and worship, both now and for evermore.'

An actual Methodist love-feast cup,[1] almost certainly made in 1838, the centenary year of Methodism, with two handles, capable of holding about two pints of water, and with the words 'Love-feast' written back and front, and with a picture of John Wesley himself on one side, was given specially for the occasion by a person in Yorkshire, and was used for the service in the Methodist chapel at Ten Mile Bank in the parish of Hilgay. It was decided that only the Minister and Rector, and two stewards, should sip of the cup on this first revived occasion, as the representatives of the whole body assembled.

Four short testimonies followed, simple, direct, and full of grace and power. One spoke of the influence of prayer, another of the vision of unity, and two of the joy of discipleship.

The service closed with one extempore prayer, offering the fellowship meal to the glory of God and the healing of division, followed by the hymn and Blessing.

Only those attended who were frequent or regular worshippers at churches in the parish, and they did so as a genuine expression of their fellowship together within the greater meaning of 'the Church'. Even with five hymns, a sermon, distribution of bread, and testimony, the service lasted less than an hour and a half, and had about it a sense of devotion, reality, purpose and completeness. It fulfilled the principle of reciprocal invitation without which the first Agape was in one sense an incomplete experiment.

In the particular parish in England in which the Agape was

[1] In the Methodist love-feast the custom was to pass around a loving-cup, usually containing water.

revived, it ought to be said that the Agape was only possible because the Anglican Rector and Methodist Minister were on the friendliest terms and because the relationship of their people to one another had been drawn closer and closer by their harmony of mind and purpose. In like manner, and all over the world, there are members of different traditions whose sense of division has been eclipsed by a consciousness of Oneness in Christ, and who look forward to a day of shared worship and genuine fellowship in worship. Surely the day can come when, beginning perhaps in regional areas, Orthodox and Armenians and Copts can meet together in an Agape, while in some other part Presbyterians and Methodists and Baptists and in yet another sphere Lutherans and Anglicans and Old Catholics can be doing the same, until the interchange of worship has woven such a texture of new-found grace and good will that the barriers of division have sunk deep into the ground, and God has given us a new vision of the meaning of the unity He means.

The Agape has already been described as 'an easing of our tensions' (*Ecumenical Review*, Summer, 1949, No. 4); as 'a spiritually helpful manifestation of Christian fellowship' (paper by Dr. E. C. Dewick in the *Modern Churchman*, March 1950); and as 'a mode of interdenominational worship, other than "intercommunion"' (p. 51 in *How Stands Reunion* by the Bishop of Lichfield). But in this account it is described as simply a fellowship meal, deriving from the New Testament, a part of the practice of the early Church, with a continuing history, still a proved means of grace, and perhaps a place where divided Christendom can meet in worship until the way opens up in some more perfect way.

One point deserves emphasis. The Agape has been the means of bringing together episcopal and non-episcopal congregations. It may fairly be said, therefore, that a form of worship that can bring into common worship two traditions that represent the 'catholic' approach and the 'protestant' viewpoint, using these terms in their widest and historical context, is germane to the situation and potent with hopefulness. It may yet be discovered, as it was of old, that 'He became known of them in the breaking of bread'.

INDEX

*